Societal Impact on Aging Series

Series Editor

K. Warner Schaie, PhD
Evan Pugh Professor of Human Development and Psychology
College of Health and Human Development
The Pennsylvania State University
University Park, PA

2005   **Historical Influences on Lives and Aging**
K. Warner Schaie and Glen H. Elder, Jr., Editors

2004   **Religious Influences on Health and Well-Being in the Elderly**
K. Warner Schaie, Neal Krause, and Alan Booth, Editors

2003   **Impact of Technology on Successful Aging**
Neil Charness and K. Warner Schaie, Editors

2002   **Personal Control in Social and Life Course Contexts**
Steven H. Zarit, Leonard I. Pearlin, and K. Warner Schaie, Editors

2002   **Effective Health Behavior in Older Adults**
K. Warner Schaie, Howard Leventhal, and Sherry L. Willis, Editors

2000   **The Evolution of the Aging Self: The Societal Impact on the Aging Process**
K. Warner Schaie and Jon Hendricks, Editors

2000   **Mobility and Transportation in the Elderly**
K .Warner Schaie and Martin Pietrucha, Editors

1997   **Impact of Work on Older Adults**
K. Warner Schaie and Carmi Schooler, Editors

1997   **Societal Mechanisms for Maintaining Competence in Old Age**
Sherry L. Willis, K. Warner Schaie, and Mark Hayward, Editors

1996   **Older Adults' Decision-Making and the Law**
Michael Smyer, K. Warner Schaie, and Marshall B. Kapp, Editors

1995   **Adult Intergenerational Relations: Effects of Societal Change**
Vern L. Bengtson, K. Warner Schaie, and Linda K. Burton, Editors

1993   **Societal Impact on Aging: Historical Perspectives**
K. Warner Schaie and W. Andrew Achenbaum

K. Warner Schaie, Ph.D., the Evan Pugh Professor of Human Development and Psychology, is regarded as one of the foremost scholars in the field of adult development and aging. Dr. Schaie holds a doctorate in psychology from the University of Washington. Since 1956, he has directed the Seattle Longitudinal Study, a major study of intellectual performance in several thousand older adults. He has found that most adults maintain their mental abilities well into their 60s, disproving scientists' earlier beliefs that intelligence peaks in adolescence and then steadily declines. He has also made substantial contributions to research methodology in adult development and aging. His landmark paper, "A General Model for the Study of Developmental Problems," has been widely cited. Schaie is a past president and council representative of the American Psychological Association's Division 20, and in 1992 received that Division's Distinguished Scientific Contributions award. He also received the Kleemeier award, 1987, for distinguished research contributions from the Gerontological Society of America; Method to Extend Research in Time (MERIT) award from the National Institute on Aging, 1989; an honorary Dr. phil. degree from Friedrich-Schiller University, Jena, Germany, 1997; the Mensa Education and Research Foundation Lifetime Achievement Award, 2000; and an honorary Sc.D. degree from West Virginia University. He is the author or editor of 46 books and has contributed over 250 articles and chapters to the research literature.

Dr. Schaie's research interests focus on cognitive and personality development from young adulthood to old age; influences of health on behavior, and studies of multi-generational adult families.

Glen H. Elder, Jr., Ph.D., Howard Odum Distinguished Professor of Sociology at the University of North Carolina at Chapel Hill, has been involved in the development of life course studies as a field of inquiry. He has investigated the Great Depression in the lives of Americans, the impact of military and wartime experiences in the life course and health of U.S. veterans, and the effects of rural change and dislocation on the intergenerational dynamics of aging. Using Add Health data, he is currently investigating sources of resilient and vulnerable pathways to the adult years. He directs the Carolina Population Center's training program on aging and population and co-directs the Carolina Consortium on Human Development at UNC-CH.

Historical Influences on Lives & Aging

K. Warner Schaie, PhD
Glen Elder, PhD
Editors

  Springer Publishing Company

Societal Impact on Aging Series

Springer Publishing Company, Inc.
11 West 42nd Street
New York, NY 10036-8002

Acquisitions Editor : Helvi Gold
Production Editor: Janice Stangel
Cover Design by Joanne Honigman

05 06 07 08 09/5 4 3 2 1

Library of Congress Cataloging-in-Publication Data

Historical influences on lives and aging / [edited by] K. Warner Schaie, Glen Elder.
    p. ; cm. -- (Societal impact on aging series)
    Includes bibliographical references and index.
    ISBN 0-8261-2405-4 (hardcopy)
    1. Life cycle, Human—Social aspects.   2. Life change events.   3. Social change—Psychological aspects.   4. Emigration and immigration—Psychological aspects.   5. Developmental psychology.   6. Social psychology.
[DNLM: 1. Aging—psychology.   2. Adaptation, Psychological.   3. Life Change Events.]   I. Schaie, K. Warner (Klaus Warner), 1928-   II. Elder, Glen H.   III. Series: Societal impact on aging.

HQ795.95.I I57 2005
305.2'09—dc22   2005009935

Printed in the United States of America by IBT.

Contents

Contributors

Carolyn Aldwin, Ph.D.
Chair, Department of Human
  Development & Family
  Sciences
Oregon State University
Corvallis, OR

Johannes M. Bos, Ph.D.
Berkeley Policy Associates,
Oakland, CA

Gordon F. De Jong, Ph.D.
The Pennsylvania State
  University
Demography Population
  Research Institute and
  Department of Sociology
University Park, PA

Greg J. Duncan, Ph.D.
Northwestern University
Institute for Policy Research
Evanston, IL

Andrew J. Fuligni, Ph.D.
University of California, Los
  Angeles
Departments of Psychiatry &
  Psychology
Center for Culture and Health
  Neuropsychiatric Institute
Los Angeles, CA

V. Lee Hamilton, Ph.D.
Duke University
Durham, NC

Mark D. Hayward, Ph.D.
The Pennsylvania State University
Social Science Research Institute
University Park, PA

Aletha C. Huston, Ph.D.
University of Texas at Austin
Human Development & Family
  Sciences
Austin, TX

Jacquelyn B. James, Ph.D.
Harvard University
Henry M. Murray Research Center
Radcliffe Institute for Advanced
  Study
Cambridge, MA

Jessica Y. Y. Kwong, Ph.D.
Chinese University of Hong Kong
Shatin, New Territories
HONG KONG SAR

John H. Laub, Ph.D.
University of Maryland
Department of Criminology and
  Criminal Justice
College Park, MD

Michael R. Levenson, Ph.D.
University of California at Davis
Department of Human &
  Community Development
Davis, CA

Rashmita S. Mistry, Ph.D.
Department of Education
University of California at Los
  Angeles
Los Angeles, CA

Victor Nee, Ph.D.
Cornell University
Center for the Study of Economy
  and Society
Ithaca, NY

Martin Pinquart, Ph.D.
Friedrich-Schiller Universität-Jena
Department of Developmental
  Psychology
Am Steiger, Jena
Germany

Matthias Reitzle, Ph.D.
Friedrich-Schiller Universität-Jena
Department of Developmental
  Psychology
Am Steiger, Jena
Germany

David E. Rohall, Ph.D.
Western Illinois University
Department of Sociology &
  Anthropology
Macomb, IL

Rubén G. Rumbaut, Ph.D.
University of California at Irvine
Department of Sociology
Irvine, CA

Robert J. Sampson, Ph.D.
Harvard University
Sociology Department
Cambridge, MA

David R. Segal, Ph.D.
University of Maryland
Center for Research on Military
  Organization
College Park, MD

Mi-Suk Shim, Ph.D.
University of Texas at Austin
Human Development and Family
  Sciences
Austin, TX

Rainer K. Silbereisen, Ph.D.
Friedrich-Schiller Universität-Jena
Department of Developmental
  Psychology
Am Steiger, Jena
Germany

Regina Smyth, Ph.D.
The Pennsylvania State University
Political Science Department
University Park, PA

Mikk Titma, Ph.D.
Stanford University
Department of Sociology
Stanford, CA

Nancy B. Tuma, Ph.D.
Stanford University
Department of Sociology
Stanford, CA

Maris A. Vinovskis, Ph.D.
University of Michigan
Department of History
Ann Arbor, MI

Preface

This is the 17th volume in a series on the broad topic of "Societal Impact on Aging." The first five volumes of this series were published by Erlbaum Associates under the series title of "Social Structure and Aging." The present volume is the 11th published under the Springer Publishing Company imprint. It is the edited proceedings of a conference held at the Pennsylvania State University, October 13–14, 2003.

The series of Penn State Gerontology Center conferences originated from the deliberations of a subcommittee of the Committee on Life Course Perspectives of the Social Science Research Council chaired by Matilda White Riley in the early 1980s. That subcommittee was charged with developing an agenda and mechanisms that would serve to encourage communication between scientists who study societal structures that might affect the aging of individuals and those scientists who are concerned with the possible effects of contextual influences on individual aging. The committee proposed a series of conferences that would systematically explore the interfaces between social structures and behavior, and in particular identify mechanisms through which society influences adult development. When the first editor was named director of the Penn State Gerontology Center, he was able to implement this conference program as one of the center's major activities.

The previous 16 volumes in this series have dealt with the societal impact on aging in psychological processes (Schaie & Schooler, 1989); age structuring in comparative perspective (Kertzer & Schaie, 1989); self–directedness and efficacy over the life span (Rodin, Schooler, & Schaie, 1990); aging, health behaviors, and health outcomes (Schaie, House, & Blazer, 1992); caregiving in families (Zarit, Pearlin, & Schaie, 1993); aging in historical perspective (Schaie & Achenbaum, 1993); adult intergenerational relations (Bengtson, Schaie, & Burton, 1995); older adults' decision making and the law (Smyer, Schaie, & Kapp, 1996); the impact of social structures on decision making in the elderly (Willis, Schaie, & Hayward, 1997); the

impact of the workplace on aging (Schaie & Schooler, 1998); mobility and transportation in the elderly (Schaie & Pietrucha, 2000); the
evolution of the aging self (Schaie & Hendricks, 2000); societal impact on health behavior in the elderly (Schaie, Leventhal, & Willis,
2002); mastery and control in the elderly (Zarit, Pearlin, & Schaie,
2003); impact of technology on the elderly (Charness & Schaie,
2003); and with religious influences on health and well-being in the
elderly (Schaie, Krause, & Booth, 2004).

The strategy for each of these volumes has been to commission six
reviews on three major topics by established subject–matter specialists
who have credibility in aging research. We then invited one or two formal discussants for each chapter—usually one drawn from the writer's
discipline and one from a neighboring discipline. This format seems to
provide a suitable antidote against the perpetuation of parochial or-
thodoxies as well as to make certain that questions are raised with respect to the validity of iconoclastic departures in new directions.

To focus each conference, the organizers chose three aspects of
the conference topic that are of broad interest to gerontologists. Social
and behavioral scientists with a demonstrated track record are then selected and asked to interact with those interested in theory building
within a multidisciplinary context.

The present volume focuses on historical influences on lives and
aging. Recent dramatic events, such as the September 11, 2001, incident, have focused our attention on the different manner in which individuals of different ages and population cohorts will be thereby affected. Historical events can be of dramatic impact but have brief
duration or may be location specific. Other historical events, such as
the Great Depression, World War II, and the Korean and Vietnam wars
were of much longer duration and directly affected broader sectors of
the American population. Changes in political systems, such as the dis-
solution of the Soviet Union or the reunification of Germany, represent international examples of historical events that may differentially
shape lives. All these events have had both immediate as well as
long–range effects that differentially influenced the life course of individuals depending upon the age at which they were first experienced.
In addition, social class membership and ethnic identity have also led
to differential experiences and consequences stemming from historical events.

Some literature is beginning to emerge that reflects long–range
consequences of the Great Depression as well as individual behaviors
and behavioral choices that were influenced by individuals' experiences during that period. Some data are also beginning to appear on

the consequences of other historically influenced experience such as military careers, experiences during the civil rights movement, or as a consequence of societal transitions such as the political changes in the former Soviet Union.

This volume gives equal emphasis to the refinement of theoretical issues and to assembling current empirical knowledge. Its far–reaching goal is to gain a better understanding of the immediate and long–range effects of historical events. An immediate aim is to explore three pivotal concerns that have the potential to influence future research. The first involves bringing historical contexts to the study of aging within an intergenerational context. The second focuses on the transitions between and within societies that affect lives and the course of aging. Finally, possible mechanisms are considered that account for the impact of historical events on individual behavior.

The first topic in this volume brings some historical context to the study of lives and aging. In chapter 1, Maris Vinovskis traces historical changes affecting the life course from colonial times to the past century. It also explores the impact of changes in child rearing and educational practice upon the individual life course. In chapter 2, Rubén Rumbaut focuses on a particular American phenomenon, the role of immigration, and distinguishes between the characteristics of different waves of immigrants. It then considers the differential integration of immigrants depending on the life stage during which they immigrated.

The second topic concerns the impact of historical transitions between and within societies. In Chapter 3, Titma and Tuma explore the impact of the collapse of the Soviet Union upon men's lives, as well as the differential impact in member states of the USSR with differential levels of industrial, educational, and commercial levels of development. One of the discussions of this chapter draws comparisons with the impact of the reunification of Germany. In Chapter 4, Rohall and colleagues consider the more specific impact of one of the consequences of the collapse of the Soviet Union; namely the downsizing of the Russian army. This chapter considers how the individuals' life stage impacted their obtaining re–employment and thus reintegration into a changed society.

The third topic concerns possible linking mechanisms. In chapter 5, Laub and Sampson consider how coming of age in wartime affected young people during World War II and the Korean War. The major mechanism discussed here is the role of educational opportunities offered by the GI bill and the associated upward social mobility facilitated by education that would not otherwise have been available to many. In chapter 6, Huston and colleagues consider explicit interventions in the lives of disadvantaged people in peace time and discuss their impact and possible mechanisms on children and adults.

We are grateful for the financial support of the conference that led to this volume, provided by conference grant AG 09787 from the National Institute on Aging, and by additional support from the vice president for research and dean of the Graduate School of the Pennsylvania State University. We are also grateful to Judy Hall and Lindsey Estright for handling the conference logistics, to Jenifer Hoffman for coordinating the manuscript preparation, and to Jenifer Hoffman and Susan Hofer for help in preparing the indexes.

K. WARNER SCHAIE
September, 2004

REFERENCES

Bengtson, V. L., Schaie, K. W., & Burton, L. (Eds.). (1995). *Adult intergenerational relations: Effects of societal changes.* New York: Springer Publishing Co.

Charness, N., & Schaie, K. W. (Eds.). (2003). *Impact of technology on the aging individual.* New York: Springer.

Kertzer, D., & Schaie, K. W. (Eds.). (1989).*Age structuring in comparative perspective.* Hillsdale, NJ: Erlbaum.

Rodin, J., Schooler, C., & Schaie, K. W. (Eds.). (1990). *Self–directedness and efficacy: Causes and effects throughout the life course.* Hillsdale, NJ: Erlbaum.

Schaie, K. W., & Achenbaum, W. A. (Eds.) (1993). *Societal impact on aging: Historical perspectives.* New York: Springer.

Schaie, K. W., & Hendricks, J. (Eds.). (2000). *Evolution of the Aging Self: Societal impacts.* New York: Springer.

Schaie, K. W., House, J., & Blazer, D. (Eds.). (1992). *Aging, health behaviors, and health outcomes.* Hillsdale, NJ: Erlbaum.

Schaie, K. W., Krause, N., & Booth, A. (Eds.). (2004). *Religious ,influences on health and wellbeing in the elderly.* New York: Springer.

Schaie, K. W., Leventhal, H., & Willis, S. L. (Eds.). (2002). *Societal impacts on ,health behaviors in the elderly.* New York: Springer.

Schaie, K. W., & Pietrucha, M. (Eds.). (2000). *Mobility and transportation in the elderly.* New York: Springer.

Schaie, K. W., & Schooler, C. E. (Eds.). (1989). *Social structure and aging: Psychological processes.* Hillsdale, NJ: Erlbaum.

Schaie, K. W., & Schooler, C. E. (Eds.). (1998). Impact of the work place ,on older persons. New York: Springer.

Smyer, M., Schaie, K. W., & Kapp, M. B. (Eds.). (1996). *Older adults decision–making and the law.* New York: Springer.

Willis, S. L., Schaie, K. W., & Hayward, M. (Eds.). (1997). *Impact of social structures on decision making in the elderly.* New York: Springer.

Zarit, S. H., Pearlin, L., & Schaie, K. W. (Eds.). (1993). *Social structure and caregiving: Family and cross–national perspectives.* Hillsdale, NJ: Erlbaum.

Zarit, S. H., Pearlin, L., & Schaie, K. W. (Eds.). (2003). *Mastery and control in the elderly,* New York: Springer.

CHAPTER 1

Historical Changes and the American Life Course

Maris A. Vinovskis

T he life course of individuals is influenced by the historical contexts in which they live. Sometimes larger changes in the society
where people reside are so pervasive that they alter the opportunities and incentives available to many of them. The nature and impact
of those changes can vary considerably, but they remind us that our
lives are closely intertwined with the ever-changing environment we inhabit.

To analyze and illustrate how historical changes have affected
Americans in the past, this chapter will consider three issues: first, an
examination of the variations and shifts in family life in early America;
second, an analysis of the changing perceptions of young children
from colonial America to the present; and finally, a consideration of
the impact of the Civil War on the lives of 19th-century Americans.

I. FAMILY LIFE IN EARLY AMERICA

Family life was a central goal for most English settlers to the New
World, but there were considerable regional differences in their likelihood of marrying and raising their children. Most immigrants to the
South came as individuals rather than as members of a family. The
large excess of male to female immigrants (about 6 to 1 initially) to the
Chesapeake in the 17th and early 18th centuries made it difficult to
create families; three quarters of the immigrants were servants. More-

over, many of the single women came as indentured servants and could not marry until their mid-20s—thereby limiting their ability to marry earlier and have larger families (Horn, 1994; Kulikoff, 1986; Main, 1982; Rutman & Rutman, 1984).

The high 17th-century adult mortality rates in the South meant that many children were likely to lose at least one parent. It also led to a smaller proportion of aged members in the society as few adults survived into old age. Given the initial scarcity of kin in the Chesapeake, parents could not rely upon grandparents or other relatives to care for their orphaned children. As a result, new institutions and practices evolved to handle the problem of orphaned children. Virginia and Maryland, for example, created special orphan courts to protect the financial interests of children who had lost their parents. And parents selected godparents who were likely to provide assistance to those children if the parents died (Horn, 1994; Kulikoff, 1986; Rutman & Rutman, 1984).

In New England, on the other hand, Puritans usually migrated as entire families and often came with other community members from England. Very few servants came and those that did often had their way paid by the family with which they emigrated. Therefore, it was easier for Puritans to maintain family life in the New World than their Southern counterparts. Death rates in New England were relatively low compared with the South, especially in rural areas. Life expectancy of adults in rural New England meant that the presence of elderly was more commonplace. In addition, household disruptions due to the premature death of a parent were less likely; the longer life expectancy also increased the probability that grandparents or other relatives would be available to care for orphaned children. Moreover, Puritan baptismal practices dispensed with the role of godparents and placed responsibility for upbringing the child on the parents (Anderson, 1991; Cressy, 1987; Demos, 1970; Greven, 1970; Lockridge, 1970; Main, 2001; Vinovskis, 1981).

During the late 17th and early 18th centuries, Chesapeake death rates dropped; and the relative contribution of immigration to the White population growth decreased as fewer settlers arrived from abroad and more local families had children who survived into adulthood. Moreover, Southern kinship ties and networks expanded and thereby provided additional sources of assistance for orphaned children. As a result, the nature and extent of family life in the Chesapeake gradually came to resemble more closely the situation in New England (Brown, 1996; Horn, 1994; Kulikoff, 1986; Main, 1982; Rutman & Rutman, 1984).

Interestingly, family life for African slaves perhaps became somewhat easier to achieve in the South than in the North. With the decrease in Southern death rates, it became more profitable to purchase slaves than import short-term indentured servants. As the number of slaves in 18th-century Maryland and Virginia grew, for example, the ability of African slaves to create families and have children improved—though the long-term stability of those slave families was always threatened by the sale and removal of either parent or of any of their offspring (Berlin, 1998; Jordan, 1977; Morgan, 1998; Sobel, 1987).

Slaves were also present in colonial New England, but they were fewer in number than in the South. As a result, it was often more difficult for slaves to find suitable mates and create their own families than in the South—though the lower New England death rates contributed to somewhat longer unions than in the South where death rates were still higher (Cottrol, 1982; Melish, 1998).

At the same time that it became demographically easier to start and maintain a family in the New World, parents also played a larger role in the upbringing of their own children. The medieval Western family did not have a sharp division among the role of parents, servants, or neighbors in the socialization and oversight of children (Aries, 1962; Stone, 1977). In the 17th-century English colonies, neighbors as well as the local community were expected to help monitor and ensure proper behavior of children and adults in other households (Norton, 1996). But gradually in the eighteenth century there was a growing sense of privacy within the household (Flaherty, 1972). Neighborhood interference in household activities was reduced; and the church and community became less likely to intervene if parents did not bring up their family as expected. In the early 19th century the idea that home was sacrosanct from outside interference increased, but communal intervention in family affairs did not disappear entirely—especially if the families were poor and might become an economic burden to the local town (Shammas, 2002; Turner, 1980).

Considerable debate has ensued over how much parents loved and cared for their children in the past. Some historians of European families have argued that parents in the 16th and 17th centuries paid little attention and provided scant affection for their young children (Aries, 1962; De Mause, 1974; Hunt, 1970; Stone, 1977). Some historians (Shorter, 1975) even postulate that this indifference to children continued among ordinary Western Europeans into the 18th and 19th centuries. They point to the evidence of parents abandoning their children, sending infants to wet nurses, or even practicing infanticide (Badinter, 1981; Sussman, 1977).

Other scholars disagree and point to the economic desperation of French mothers who could not afford to nurse their own children (Boswell, 1988; Sussman, 1977). Moreover, Pollack (1983) has uncovered considerable evidence of parental affection and attention to their offspring in Western Europe in large part based on a study of more than 400 diaries and autobiographies in Britain and North America. Other historians have found similar results (Houlbrooke, 1984; MacFarlane, 1970; Wrightson, 1982).

The practice of infanticide and child abandonment was not prevalent in England and America (Hoffer & Hull, 1981; Stone, 1977; Thompson, 1986). Yet a few scholars argue that American parents also were reluctant to become too attached to infants lest those children die suddenly (Saum, 1974). Most analysts (Demos, 1970; Graham, 2000; Main, 2001; Moran & Vinovskis, 1992; Morgan, 1966) have challenged this interpretation and point to the numerous instances where colonial parents loved their children and grieved even if they died in infancy. Rather than being actually detached or indifferent to their offspring, Puritan parents were advised by their religion to stoically accept the loss of their children as God's will—something which many of them failed to do either publically or privately.

Although there is growing agreement that colonial parents loved their children, there is less consensus on the division of labor in the care of young children. Many scholars simply assume that the mother had always had the primary responsibility for the care and socialization of the young child (Main, 2001). Certainly, mothers provided for most of the child's physical needs. But Puritans felt that the head of the household, usually the father, had the responsibility for catechizing the children and servants. The father's primacy in educating the child was reinforced by the fact that he was often more literate than his spouse (Moran & Vinovskis, 1992).

The father's role in catechizing children and servants continued in early New England. But the Puritans faced a difficult challenge when most second-generation fathers stopped joining the church and thereby were no longer ideally suited for religiously instructing others. Although mothers might have substituted for fathers in fulfilling this duty, the Puritan leaders and the community were reluctant to yield too much religious responsibilities to women—especially in light of the unorthodox and extraordinary religious activities of Ann Hutchinson during the Antinomian Crisis in the mid-1630s. Hutchinson was a dissenter who began holding gatherings of women in her home to discuss the weekly church sermons, and she challenged the Puritan idea that parishioners could not communicate directly with God (Dunn, 1980; Hall, 1968).

New England communities explored a variety of alternatives to the nonchurch member fathers instructing children in households. Some towns tried to hire a second minister to assist in instructing households while other communities employed male teachers to address this need. The high costs of hiring either a second minister or a town school teacher, however, made these solutions usually impractical—especially in rural areas (Moran & Vinovskis, 1992). Parents often turned to local private dame schools to teach their young children the alphabet and reading (Axtell, 1974; Graham, 2000; Moran & Vinovskis, 2001; Murphy, 1960).

Gradually, Puritan society reconciled itself to relying upon pious mothers who continued to join the church in larger numbers than their husbands. The increasing literacy of colonial New England women reinforced their suitability for catechizing and instructing young children in the home (Lockridge, 1974; Moran & Vinovskis, 2001). Indeed, over time Puritan ministers praised women for their piety and portrayed them as the natural caretakers of young children (Malsheimer, 1973; Ulrich, 1980).

One might imagine that gradually the father's role in the Puritan family diminished as mothers took over more of the socialization of young children. There is an extensive literature on growing importance of mothers in the late 18th and early 19th centuries (Bloch, 1978; Kerber, 1980; Lewis, 1987; Norton, 1980). The growing absence of the father from the household affairs seems to have been reinforced by the increasing separation of work and home in the early 19th century (Cott, 1977).

Yet more recent studies of the role of the father in antebellum America suggests that they continued to play an important and active part in the raising of children at home. The importance of a father's role in the household was emphasized by Protestant writers in the 1830s and 1840s. Evidence from antebellum diaries and letters suggests that fathers devoted considerable time and effort to their families and children (Frank, 1997; Vinovskis & Frank, 1997).

The continued active involvement of fathers and mothers in the upbringing of their children meant that parents throughout their life course devoted considerable energy to their children. It also led to further closer interactions between parents and children and may have contributed to the particular willingness of daughters to care for their widowed elderly mothers.

II. CHANGING PERCEPTIONS OF YOUNG CHILDREN

Considerable variations abound in how children have been perceived and handled in the past. According to some scholars (Aries, 1962; Elias, 1978), the concept of childhood was missing in medieval and early modern Europe; instead, children were viewed and treated basically as "miniature adults." More recent scholarship, however, has challenged the notion that childhood in the Middle Ages was seen only as miniature adults (Hanawalt, 1986; Kroll, 1977; Schultz, 1995; Shahar, 1990). Looking at actual parent-child relationships rather than just ideas about childhood, these historians have seen parents as more involved and caring about their children (Cunningham, 1995; Pollack, 1983).

The idea that children in colonial America were miniature adults was first raised more than 70 years ago. As Fleming noted: "Children were regarded simply as miniature adults" (1933, p. 60). But little attention was paid to this interpretation by other scholars. This portrayal of American children became more popular among historians (Calvert, 1992; Demos, 1970, 1996; Modell & Goodman, 1990; Trattner, 1989; Zuckerman, 1970) in the 1970s and 1980s. At the same time, other scholars (Axtell, 1974; Beales, 1975; Graham, 2000; Kaestle & Vinovskis, 1980; Moran & Vinovskis, 1992; Stannard, 1975, 1977) questioned that interpretation. They pointed to the various ways in which colonial Americans differentiated between children and adults such as creating of special catechism books and furniture for children.

If colonial America didn't view children as miniature adults, the populace saw them as more intellectually and emotionally capable than many Americans see young children today. For example, children were able to learn to read at an early age. This view of childhood was so prevalent that John Locke (1964) simply noted in passing that "when he can talk, 'tis time he should begin to learn to read" (pp. 186–187). Early reading was encouraged by Puritans who felt that everyone should be able to read the Bible—including young children who were apt to die at early ages (Moran & Vinovskis, 1992; Slater, 1977; Stannard, 1975, 1977).

In 18th-century Europe early childhood education was advocated by Johann Pestalozzi, the Swiss educator who developed infant schools. Robert Owen, a British reformer familiar with Pestalozzi's ideas, built an infant school at New Lanark, Scotland, in 1816 to provide early training for disadvantaged children and allow their mothers to work outside the home (Silber, 1960).

American common schools were widely available in New England in the early 19th century and some youngsters enrolled in them at early ages. Drawing upon the ideas about infant schools imported from Great Britain, reformers throughout the United States developed these institutions in the 1820s and 1830s—though there was considerable disagreement on whether 2- and 3-year-olds in these infant schools should be taught to read (Beatty, 1995; Jenkins, 1978; May & Vinovskis, 1977). The popularity of infant schools and early childhood education were so widespread that an estimated 40% of all 3-year-olds in Massachusetts in 1840 were attending school (Kaestle & Vinovskis, 1980).

The widespread popularity of infant schools was undermined by the medical community in 1830s. Amariah Brigham (1833), a specialist on brain development and mental illness, warned parents that excessive and premature intellectual development of children would stunt normal brain growth and might lead to their insanity as teens or young adults.

The middle-class female reformers who had advocated and financed early childhood education for disadvantaged children gradually abandoned their support of infant schools and now renounced early intellectual activity. Although many working-class parents continued to favor infant schools, the withdrawal of financial aid by the reformers forced most infant schools to disband. As a result, early school attendance was discouraged and by 1860 there were almost no 3- or 4-year-olds in Massachusetts schools (May & Vinovskis, 1977; Kaestle & Vinovskis, 1980).

When kindergartens were imported into the United States in the mid-19th century, they encouraged organized play rather than early literacy training. Moreover, kindergartens were intended for children ages 5 to 7 rather than for 2- to 5-year-olds as had been the case in the infant schools. And former infant school teachers who now worked in kindergartens did not acknowledge their previous experiences with early childhood education lest the public and policymakers mistakenly confuse the activities of the two initiatives (Beatty, 1995; Winterer, 1992).

Early education in nursery schools and day care facilities did not receive much attention or support in the United States during the early decades of the 20th century. There was a temporary expansion of day care facilities during World War II in order to allow mothers to work in war-related industries; but the additional federal funding for these day care services ended at the conclusion of World War II (Getis & Vinovskis, 1992; Steinfels, 1973).

Early childhood education was rediscovered in the late 1950s and early 1960s as child developmentalists and others sought ways to help disadvantaged young children. Preschool education received a major boost in the Kennedy and Johnson administrations as policymakers drafted programs to combat juvenile delinquency and poverty. While much of the justification for these preschool programs was based upon raising the IQ of these "culturally deprived" children, the actual implementation and operation of Head Start after the mid-1960s focused more on the provision of comprehensive medical, social, and nutritional services than providing education services and fostering literacy readiness (Vinovskis, 2005; Zigler & Muenchow, 1992; Zigler & Valentine, 1979).

The ongoing battles over the need, control, and type of services for Head Start have continued for the past four decades. Interestingly, George W. Bush and many of his GOP colleagues in the 105th Congress are now stressing the need for early literacy training in Head Start and other preschool programs as part of the administration's larger "No Child Left Behind" education initiative. Opponents of the increased emphasis on literacy training and more state experimentation with Head Start claim that the existing programs are already a proven success and should not be fundamentally changed (Nawrotzki, Smith, & Vinovskis, 2004).

Thus, we are rediscovering early childhood education more than 180 years after importing infant schools. Moreover, there is a concerted effort today among some experts and policymakers to emphasize early literacy training—just as many of the original infant schools had urged earlier. One concern among some policymakers, however, is that the growing attention paid to early childhood education may be occurring at the expense of retraining older adults who do not have sufficient skills to compete in our growing global economy.

III. IMPACT OF THE AMERICAN CIVIL WAR ON THE LIFE COURSE

Few conflicts have received as much scholarly and public attention as the Civil War. Yet surprising little effort has been made to assess the impact of the conflict on the lives of 19th-century Americans. Fortunately, scholars (Cashin, 2002a; Clinton & Silber, 1992; Jimerson, 1988; O'-Connor, 1997; Paludan, 1988; Vinovskis, 1990) are now beginning to undertake studies of the impact of the Civil War on the participants.

One useful perspective on the impact of a war is to estimate the military and civilian casualties. Compared with some other military conflicts, the number of direct civilian deaths probably was relatively modest, though undoubtedly some in the South died due to disruptions in their food supply and the increased spread of diseases as armies traveled across the countryside. One estimate puts Civil War civilian deaths at about 50,000 (McPherson, 1988).

In terms of military casualties, the Civil War was by far the most deadly conflict in our history. The best estimate is that about 618,000 Union and Confederate soldiers died—more than 50% greater than American servicemen who perished in World War II. Indeed, before the Vietnam conflict, the number of deaths in the Civil War almost equaled the total number killed in all other U.S. wars (Goldin, 1980; Vinovskis, 1990).

Another perspective on the Civil War losses is provided by calculating the number of military deaths per 10,000 population. During the Civil War, about 182 individuals per 10,000 population died; the comparable figure for the next highest-ranked war, the American Revolution, was only 118. While the United States suffered heavy casualties during World War II, the much larger population base in the 1940s meant that the number of deaths per 10,000 population was only 30 (about one sixth of the Civil War ratio). The Vietnam War, which caused such emotional and political anguish in the 1960s and 1970s, resulted in only 3 military deaths per 10,000 population (Vinovskis, 1990).

Since the North and South were very unequal in population and resources, the demographic impact of the Civil War was quite different in the two regions. The North, with its larger population base, was able to assemble much larger armies than the South; but the Union also sustained greater absolute military losses. About 360,000 Union men died compared with 260,000 Confederates (Goldin, 1980). Among the Union deaths, an estimated 36,000 African American soldiers died in the Civil War (Berlin, Reidy, & Rowlands, 1982).

Although Northern military casualties were nearly 40% greater than Southern losses, the relative impact on the South was greater because of the smaller population base of the Confederacy. Looking at both the North and South, approximately 8% of the estimated population of White males aged 13 to 43 in 1860 (the broad age-group most likely to participate) died. But while only 6% of Northern White males in that age group died, 18% of their Southern counterparts perished. In other words, young white men in the South were almost three times as likely to die as in the North (Vinovskis, 1990).

Civil War deaths were higher than in more recent wars because over half of the deaths were due to diseases rather than combat wounds. Moreover, the poor medical care available at that time meant that once a soldier was wounded in the Civil War, he was much more likely to die (Adams, 1952; Cunningham, 1958; Steiner, 1968).

In addition to war deaths, the Civil War resulted in large numbers of desertions on both sides. It is estimated that at least 200,000 Union soldiers deserted (80,000 of whom were caught and returned); and at least 104,000 Confederate soldiers deserted (21,000 of whom were caught and returned) (McPherson, 1982). War-weariness and concern about the welfare of their families at home persuaded nearly 1 of 10 Union soldiers and 1 of 8 Confederate soldiers to desert (Lonn, 1928; Cashin, 2002b). If we hypothetically assume that soldiers who died had not previously deserted, approximately 12% of Union soldiers and 16% of surviving Confederate soldiers deserted.

Large numbers of Americans fought in the Civil War, including many African Americans. But up to now it has not been possible to ascertain the different experiences of various subgroups of the population because we do not have detailed information at the community level who fought in the Civil War and what happened to those that did participate. During the past decade, however, a few community studies (Kemp, 1990; Rorabaugh, 1986) of the Civil War are providing valuable information on differential rates of enlistment in the conflict.

One interesting Northern community to examine is Newburyport, Massachusetts—a city that historians and other scholars have analyzed in the past (Thernstrom, 1964; Warner, 1963). Although no city is representative or typical of the North as a whole, Newburyport provides a useful setting for analysis because of the availability of its excellent military and social records. In 1860, Newburyport was a small maritime community of 13,000 inhabitants with an ethnically diverse population (almost entirely White, but about one fifth foreign-born).

Compared with Northerners in general, Newburyport men were more likely to enroll in the army or navy. Most of those who enlisted were in their 20s and 30s (age was the best predictor of whether someone enlisted). There is considerable controversy over the participation rate of foreign-born men in the Union forces. Many scholars claim that foreign-born soldiers predominated in Northern units, but more recent work suggests that foreign-born men were about equally likely to enlist (Lonn, 1951; Rorabaugh, 1986). In Newburyport, foreign-born were less likely to enroll than native-born, but second-generation Americans were more likely to enlist than children of native-born parents. Ethnicity was the second best predictor of participation in the Civil War (Vinovskis, 1990).

Many contemporaries portrayed the Civil War as a "poor man's fight" since the well-to-do could afford to hire substitutes or pay commutation fees to avoid the draft. Yet the Newburyport investigation reveals that the sons of fathers employed at high-status white-collar or skilled jobs joined at much higher rates than sons of unskilled workers. Sons from wealthier households enlisted at about the same rate as those from families with less wealth. During the early phases of the war when patriotism was high, the sons of the more wealthy families were more likely to enlist; as the war continued and casualty lists grew, participants were more likely to come from the lower classes. Therefore, although there were disparities in the rates of enrollment in Newburyport by occupation and wealth, those differences were not large enough to justify describing the war as a "poor man's" fight in that community (Vinovskis, 1990).

Of the Newburyport servicemen studied, 13% died of wounds or disease (less than the 17% of white Union soldiers who died). Fewer died in Newburyport because those who served in the Navy were less likely to die. Approximately 1 of 6 Newburyport soldiers and sailors were wounded, but survived. Altogether, about 3 of 10 of the town's servicemen were either wounded or killed during the Civil War.

Only 2% of those in the military were identified as deserted; probably a higher portion had deserted, but the records on desertion are incomplete (Cashin, 2002b). And about 1 of every 5 servicemen was discharged due to a disability. Thus, at least 42% of those who fought in the Civil War from Newburyport were killed, wounded, deserted, or discharged as disabled (Vinovskis, 1990).

Newburyport soldiers' and sailors' chances of being killed or wounded during the Civil War depended in part on their age and socioeconomic status. Younger solders were somewhat more likely to die or be wounded—perhaps because they entered the armed forces in the later period of the war when casualties were higher. Foreign-born and second-generation servicemen were more likely to die or to be wounded—maybe because they were more susceptible to diseases than their more affluent, native-born counterparts. And soldiers and sailors from disadvantaged backgrounds were more likely to die or to be wounded (Vinovskis, 1990). Again, was the health of Newburyport's lower-status citizens generally poorer at enlistment, leaving them more susceptible to disease? Or were they assigned to units and tasks that were particularly dangerous?

Considerable regional, state, and community variations dictated how the war was experienced. And the impact of the Civil War did not end at General Robert E. Lee's surrender at Appomattox Courthouse in April 1965. In the South, for example, military casualties had been larger than in the North; and the civilian population suffered more in the Confederacy as opposing armies crisscrossed the South. In addition, the disruptions following the war also were much greater in the South due to such factors as the massive physical destruction during the war, the ending of the slave system, and Northern reconstruction of the South (Ash, 1987; Carter, 1985; Lowe, 1991; Ransom & Sutch, 1977; Studley, 1969).

Although Northerners also suffered heavily during the Civil War, they were better able to recover and prosper than their Southern counterparts. For example, the Civil War pension benefits for Union veterans and their widows were generous. The number of Union veterans or their dependents receiving a federal pension immediately after the Civil War was rather small but then grew rapidly after the passage of the Pension Act of 1890. The Act now provided assistance for Union veterans who were disabled from any cause whatsoever—in essence it became a general assistance program for veterans as they became incapacitated due to normal illnesses associated with aging (Glasson, 1900; Weber, 1923; Weber & Schmeckebier, 1934).

Although two thirds of all Union veterans by 1895 received a pension, only a small percentage of the White adult American population received a Civil War pension—about 4% of the population in 1900. Yet if we take into account the age distribution of the veterans, the impact of the pensions on certain age-cohorts become larger. Almost one third of all White males aged 55 to 59 and one fifth of those aged 60 tp 64 were receiving a federal pension in 1900. There were over a million pension recipients (including a few veterans of the Spanish-American War) in 1902. The last Union veteran survived until 1956; and in 1986, more than 120 years after the end of the Civil War, there were still 78 Union widows and children receiving pensions (the last Civil War widow died in 2002) (Vinovskis, 1990).

The size of the Union pensions was substantial and grew rapidly after the Civil War. In 1900 the average annual pension was $139— at a time when the average annual earnings of all employees was $375 (Vinovskis, 1990). Moreover, there are some preliminary indications that Union widows who received pensions may have been better able to care for their children (Holmes, 1990; Holmes & Vinovskis, 1992).

And the Union pension program was a surprisingly large part of the federal budget. By 1893 Civil War pensions rose to $165 million and accounted for more than 40% of the total federal budget (veterans' pensions today are only about 3% of the federal budget) (Vinovskis, 1990).

The tracing of the some of the impacts of the Civil War Union pension programs illustrates the need to look at the long-term consequences of wars. If we were also to trace the diverse emotional, political, and socioeconomic impacts of that conflict on American society and the Civil War survivors, we might better appreciate and understand what a major influence that event had on the life course of 19th-century Americans.

IV. CONCLUSION

There are considerable variations in the life course over time and across different cultures. Though some general characteristics of Homo sapiens seem to have evolved over time, our species has the ability to adapt to different settings and cope with many unexpected events.

From the beginning of European colonization of North America, broad demographic and socioeconomic factors affected the ability of the immigrants to start and maintain family life—with considerable regional differences between New England and the South. Moreover, decreases in White immigration to the South as well as reductions in mortality in that region allowed more people to create their own families. The increase in slave trade severed kinship ties and disrupted family life in Africa; however, it also made it possible, under the adverse conditions of the American slave system, to re-create family life in the New World.

Culture as well as demographic and socio-economic factors influenced the lives of early Americans. The settlers brought with them not only the idea of the importance of family, but cultural templates for how it should be organized—particularly in areas like New England where strong Puritan religious influences persisted. When adverse demographic and socio-economic conditions in the South made normal family life difficult, the settlers looked to alternative institutions such as orphan courts and godparents to assist them.

A lively debate continues over whether colonial Americans recognized childhood and loved their youngsters, but the evidence increasingly seems to support the idea that early American children were seen as distinct and that they were usually cherished by their parents. Yet adult perceptions of the nature of those children changed over time. Youngsters in colonial New England were expected to read the Bible at an early age and to be catechized by their fathers. Over time, the father's role in early childhood education diminished while that of their mothers became more important—in part as a reaction to the growing reluctance of males to join the Puritan church. At the same time, the enhancement of the mother's role in socializing the young contributed to the expectation that women needed more education.

The widespread adoption of the idea of European infant schools by early-19th-century Americans reinforced the belief that young children could learn their alphabet as well as elements of reading at early ages. Precocious learning, however, was soon challenged by the emerging scientific notion that early childhood education might lead to insanity. The gradual diffusion of this medical opinion doomed the infant schools and for more than a century led to a general reluctance to encourage early intellectual activities.

Early childhood education was rediscovered in the 1950s and early 1960s as part of the effort to help disadvantaged youngsters increase their IQs. The particular circumstances of early education planning in the Kennedy and Johnson administrations led in a stress on the medical, nutritional, and social aspects of Head Start programs, and a deemphasis of their education components. Nearly 40 years later, the George W. Bush administration is trying to reverse that approach by insisting on early literacy training in Head Start programs. Thus, in the second half of the 20th century public policy is playing an important role in how many young children are perceived and treated in early childhood programs such as Head Start.

The American Civil War provides yet another illustration of how a short-term, devastating military conflict affects the lives of many participants; furthermore, it demonstrates the widespread and long-term repercussions of such an event. Federal pensions for Union soldiers and their dependents, for example, had a lasting impact on the life course of the survivors well into the early 20th century. Preferential treatment for Union veterans and their widows created differential opportunities and challenges for the Civil War survivors that lasted well beyond the end of the military hostilities.

While this analysis can only hint at the complex interactions between historical changes and the American life course, perhaps it will stimulate additional scholarship to explore such relationships. Our own painful experiences with the aftermath of the September 11 terrorist attack on New York City makes us even more aware of the need to study the multifaceted interactions between historical changes and the life course of individuals.

REFERENCES

Adams, G. W. (1952). *Doctors in blue: The medical history of the Union army in the Civil War.* New York: H. Schuman.

Anderson, V. D. (1991). *New England's generation: The great migration and the formation of society and culture in the seventeenth century.* Cambridge: Cambridge University Press.

Aries, P. (1962). *Centuries of childhood: A social history of family life* (R. Baldick, Trans.). New York: Vintage.

Ash, S. V. (1987). *Middle Tennessee society transformed, 1860–1870: War and peace in the upper South.* Baton Rouge: Louisiana State University Press.

Axtell, J. (1974). *The school upon a hill: Education and society in colonial New England.* New Haven, CT: Yale University Press.

Badinter, E. (1981). *Motherly love: Myth and reality.* New York: Macmillan.

Beales, R. W., Jr. (1975). In search of the historical child: Miniature adulthood and youth in colonial New England. *American Quarterly, 27,* 379–398.

Beatty, B. (1995). *Preschool education in America: The culture of young children from the colonial era to the present.* New Haven, CT: Yale University Press.

Berlin, I. (1998). *Many thousands gone: The first two centuries of slavery in North America.* Cambridge, MA: Harvard University Press.

Berlin, I., Reidy, J. P., & Rowlands, L. A. (Eds.). (1982). *The black military experience.* Cambridge: Cambridge University Press.

Bloch, R. H. (1978). American feminine ideals in transition: The rise of the moral mother, 1785–1815. *Feminist Studies, 4,* 101–126.

Boswell, J. (1988). *The kindness of strangers: The abandonment of children in Western Europe from late antiquity to the Renaissance.* New York: Pantheon Books.

Brigham, A. (1833). *Remarks on the influence of mental cultivation and mental excitement upon health* (2nd ed.). Boston: Marsh, Capen, & Lyon.

Brown, K. M. (1996). *Good wives, nasty wenches, and anxious patriarchs: Gender, race, and power in colonial Virginia.* Chapel Hill: University of North Carolina Press.

Calvert, K. (1992). *Children in the house: The material culture of early childhood, 1600–1900.* Boston: Northeastern University Press.

Carter, D. T. (1985). *When the war was over: The failure of self-reconstruction in the South, 1865–1867.* Baton Rouge, LA: Louisiana State University Press.

Cashin, J. E. (Ed.). (2002a). *The war was you and me: Civilians in the American Civil War.* Princeton, NJ: Princeton University Press.

Cashin, J. E. (2002b). Deserters, civilians, and draft resistance in the North. In J. E. Cashin (Ed.), *The war was you and me: Civilians in the American Civil War* (pp. 262–285). Princeton, NJ: Princeton University Press.

Clinton, C., & Silber, N. (Eds.). (1992). *Divided houses: Gender and the Civil War.* New York: Oxford University Press.

Cott, N. F. (1977). *The bonds of womanhood: "Women's sphere" in New England, 1780–1835.* New Haven, CT: Yale University Press.

Cottrol, R. J. (1982). *The Afro-Yankees: Providence's black community in the antebellum era.* Westport, CT: Greenwood Press.

Cressy, D. (1987). *Coming over: Migration and communication Between England and New England in the seventeenth century.* Cambridge: Cambridge University Press.

Cunningham, H. H. (1958). *Doctors in gray: The Confederate medical service.* Baton Rouge: Louisiana State University Press.

Cunningham, H. (1995). *Children and childhood in western society since 1500.* London: Longman.

De Mause, L. (Ed.). (1974). *The history of childhood.* New York: Harper & Row.

Demos, J. (1970). *A little commonwealth: Family life in Plymouth Colony.* New York: Oxford University Press.

Demos, J. (1996). *Past, present, and personal: The family and the life course in American History.* New York: Oxford University Press.

Dunn, M. M. (1980). Saints and sisters: Congregational and Quaker Women in the early colonial period. In J. W. James (Ed.), *Women in American religion* (pp. 27–46). Philadelphia: University of Pennsylvania Press.

Elias, N. (1978). *The history of manners: The civilizing process* (Vol. 1). (E. Jephcott, Trans.). New York: Urizen Books.

Flaherty, D. H. (1972). *Privacy in colonial New England.* Charlottesville: University of Virginia Press.

Fleming, S. (1933). *Children and Puritanism: The place of children in the life and thought of New England churches, 1620–1847.* New Haven, CT: Yale University Press.

Frank, S. M. 1997. *Life with Father: Parenthood and masculinity in the nineteenth-century North.* Baltimore: Johns Hopkins Press.

Getis, V. L., & Vinovskis, M. A. (1992). History of child care in the United States to 1950. In M. E. Lamb, K. J. Sternberg, C.-P. Hwang, & A. G. Broberg (Eds.), *Child care in context: Cross-Cultural perspectives* (pp. 185–206). Hillsdale, NJ: Lawrence Erlbaum.

Glasson, W. H. (1900). *History of military pension legislation in the United States.* New York: Columbia University Press.

Goldin, C. D. (1980). War. In G. Porter (Ed.), Encyclopedia of American economic history: Studies of the principal movements and ideas (Vol. 3) (pp. 935–957). New York: Scribner.

Graham, J. S. (2000). *Puritan family life: The diary of Samuel Sewall.* Boston: Northeastern University Press.

Greven, P. J., Jr. (1970). *Four generations: Population, land, and family in colonial Andover, Massachusetts.* Ithaca, NY: Cornell University Press.

Hall, D. D. (Ed.). (1968). *The antinomian controversy, 1636–1638: A documentary history.* Middletown, CT: Wesleyan University Press.

Hanawalt, B. A. (1986). *The ties that bound: Peasant families in medieval England.* New York: Oxford University Press.

Hoffer, P. C., & Hull, N. E. H. (1981). *Murdering mothers: Infanticide in England and New England, 1558–1803.* New York: New York University Press.

Holmes, A. E. (1990). "Such is the price we pay": American widows and the Civil War pension system. In M. A. Vinovskis, (Ed.), *Toward a social history of the American Civil War: Exploratory essays* (pp. 171–195). Cambridge: Cambridge University Press.

Holmes, A. E., & Vinovskis, M. A. (1992). Impact of the Civil War on American widowhood. In A. Lawson, & D. Rhode (Eds.), *The changing American family: Sociological and demographic perspectives* (pp. 23–45). New Haven, CT: Yale University Press.

Horn, J. (1994). *Adapting to a new world: English society in the seventeenth-century Chesapeake.* Chapel Hill: University of North Carolina Press.

Houlbrooke, R. A. (1984). *The English family, 1450–1700.* London: Longman.

Hunt, D. (1970). *Parents and children in history: The psychology of family life in early modern France.* New York: Basic Books.

Jenkins, J. W. (1978). *The infant schools and the development of public primary schools in selected cities before the Civil War.* Unpublished doctoral dissertation, University of Wisconsin.

Jimerson, R. C. (1988). *The private Civil War: Popular thought during the sectional conflict.* Baton Rouge: Louisiana State University Press.

Jordan, W. D. (1977). *White over black: American attitudes toward the Negro, 1550–1812.* New York: W.W. Norton.

Kaestle, C. F., & Vinovskis, M. A. (1980). *Education and social change in nineteenth-century Massachusetts.* Cambridge: Cambridge University Press.

Kemp, T. R. (1990). Community and war: The Civil War experience of two New Hampshire towns. In M. A. Vinovskis (Ed.), *Toward a social history of the American Civil War* (pp. 31–77). Cambridge: Cambridge University Press.

Kerber, L. K. (1980). *Women of the republic: Intellect and ideology in revolutionary America.* Chapel Hill, NC: University of North Carolina Press.

Kroll, J. (1977). The concept of childhood in the Middle Ages. *Journal of the History of the Behavioral Sciences, 13,* 384–393.

Kulikoff, A. (1986). *Tobacco and slaves: The development of southern cultures in the Chesapeake, 1680–1800.* Chapel Hill: University of North Carolina Press.

Lewis, J. (1987). The republican wife: Virtue and seduction in the early republic. *William and Mary Quarterly, 44,* 689–721.

Locke, J. (1964). In F.W. Garforth (Ed.), *Some thoughts concerning education.* Woodbury, NY: Barron.

Lockridge, K. A. (1970). *A New England town: The first hundred years: Dedham, Massachusetts, 1636–1736.* New York: Norton.

Lockridge, K. A. (1974). *Literacy in colonial New England: An inquiry into the social context of literacy in the early modern west.* New York: Norton.

Lonn, E. (1928). *Desertion during the Civil War.* New York: Century.

Lonn, E. (1951). *Foreigners in the Union army and navy.* Baton Rouge: Louisiana State University Press.

Lowe, R. G. (1991). *Republicans and reconstruction in Virginia, 1856–1870.* Charlottesville, VA: University Press of Virginia.

MacFarlane, A. (1970). *The family life of Ralph Josselin, a seventeenth-century clergy-man: An essay in historical anthropology*. New York: Norton.

Main, G. L. (1982). *Tobacco colony: Life in early Maryland, 1650–1720*. Princeton, NJ: Princeton University Press.

Main, G. L. (2001). *Peoples of a spacious land: Families and culture in colonial New England*. Cambridge, MA: Harvard University Press.

Malsheimer, L. M. (1973). *New England funeral sermons and changing attitudes toward women, 1672–1792*. Unpublished dissertation, University of Minnesota.

May, D., & Vinovskis, M. A. (1977). A ray of millennial light: Early education and social reform in the infant school movement in massachusetts, 1826–1840. In T. K. Hareven (Ed.), *Family and kin in American urban communities, 1800–1940* (pp. 62–99). New York: Watts.

McPherson, J. M. (1982). *Ordeal by fire*. New York: Alfred Knopf.

McPherson, J. M. (1988). *Battle cry of freedom: The Civil War era*. New York: Oxford University Press.

Melish, J. P. (1998). *Disowning slavery: Gradual emancipation and "race" in New England, 1780–1860*. Ithaca, NY: Cornell University Press.

Modell, J., & Goodman, M. (1990). Historical perspectives. In S. S. Feldman & G. R. Elliott (Eds.), *At the threshold: The developing adolescent* (pp. 93–122). Cambridge, MA: Harvard University Press.

Moran, G. F., & Vinovskis, M.A. (1992). *Religion, family, and the life course: Explorations in the social history of early America*. Ann Arbor: University of Michigan Press.

Moran, G. F., & Vinovskis, M. A. (2001). Literacy and education in eighteenth-century North America. In M. V. Kennedy & W. G. Shade (Eds.), *The world turned upside-down: The state of eighteenth-century American studies at the beginning of the twenty-first century* (pp. 186–223). Bethlehem, PA: Lehigh University Press.

Morgan, E. S. (1966). *The Puritan family: Religion and domestic relations in seventeenth-century New England*. New York: Harper & Row.

Morgan, P. D. (1998). *Slave counterpoint: Black culture in the eighteenth-century Chesapeake and low country*. Chapel Hill: University of North Carolina Press.

Murphy, G. J. (1960). *Massachusetts Bay Colony: The Role of government in education*. Unpublished doctoral dissertation, Radcliffe College.

Nawrotzki, K. D., Smith, A. M., & Vinovskis, M. A. (2004). Social science research and early childhood education: A historical analysis of developments in Head Start, kindergartens, and day care. In H. Cravens (Ed.), *The social sciences go to Washington; The politics of knowledge in the postmodern age* (pp. 155–180). New Brunswick, NJ: Rutgers University Press.

Norton, M. B. (1980). *Liberty's daughters: The revolutionary experience of American women, 1750–1800*. Boston: Little, Brown.

Norton, M. B. (1996). *Gendered power and the forming of American society*. New York: Alfred Knopf.

O'Connor, T. H. (1997). *Civil War Boston: Home front and battlefield.* Boston: Northeastern University Press.

Paludan, P. S. (1988). *"A people's contest": The Union and the Civil War, 1861–1865.* New York: Harper & Row.

Pollack, L. (1983). *Forgotten children: Parent–child relations from 1500 to 1900.* Cambridge: Cambridge University Press.

Ransom, R. L., & Sutch, R. (1977). *One kind of freedom: The economic consequences of emancipation.* Cambridge: Cambridge University Press.

Rorabaugh, W. J. (1986). Who fought for the North in the Civil War? Concord, Massachusetts, enlistments. *Journal of American History, 73,* 695–701.

Rutman, D. B., & Rutman, A. H. (1984). *A place in time: Middlesex County, Virginia, 1650–1750.* New York: Norton.

Saum, L. O. (1974). Death in the popular mind of pre-Civil War America. *American Quarterly, 26,* 477–495.

Schultz, J. A. (1995). *The knowledge of childhood in the German Middle Ages, 1100–1350.* Philadelphia: University of Pennsylvania Press.

Shahar, S. (1990). *Childhood in the Middle Ages.* London: Routledge.

Shammas, C. (2002). *A history of household government in America.* Charlottesville: University of Virginia Press.

Shorter, E. (1975). *The making of the modern family.* New York: Basic Books.

Silber, K. (1960). *Pestalozzi: The man and his works.* London: Routledge & Kegan Paul.

Slater, P. G. (1977). *Children in the New England mind: In death and in life.* Hamden, CT: Archon Books.

Sobel, M. (1987). *The world they made together: Black and white values in eighteenth-century Virginia.* Princeton, NJ:: Princeton University Press.

Stannard, D. E. (1975). Death and the Puritan child. In D. E. Standard (Ed.), *Death in America* (pp. 9–29). Philadelphia: University of Pennsylvania Press.

Stannard, D. E. (1977). *The Puritan way of death: A study of religion, culture, and social change.* New York: Oxford University Press.

Steiner, P. E. (1968). *Disease in the Civil War: Natural biological warfare in 1861–1865.* Springfield, IL: Charles C Thomas.

Steinfels, M. O. (1973). *Who's minding the children? The history and politics of day care in America.* New York: Simon & Schuster.

Stone, L. (1977). *The family, sex, and marriage in England, 1500–1800.* New York: Harper & Row.

Studley, E. (1969). *Losing the peace: Georgia Republicans and Reconstruction, 1865–1871.* Baton Rouge: Louisiana State University Press.

Sussman, G. D. (1977). Parisian infants and Norman wet nurses in the early nineteenth century: A statistical study. *Journal of Interdisciplinary History, 7,* 637–654.

Thernstrom, S. (1964). *Poverty and progress: Social mobility in a nineteenth-century city.* Cambridge, MA: Harvard University Press.

Thompson, R. (1986). *Sex in Middlesex: Popular mores in a Massachusetts county, 1649–1699.* Amherst, MA: University of Massachusetts Press.

Trattner, W. I. (1989). *From poor law to welfare state: A history of social welfare in America* (4th ed.). New York: Free Press.

Turner, J. (1980). *Reckoning with the beast: Animals, pain, and humanity in the Victorian mind.* Baltimore: Johns Hopkins University Press.

Ulrich, L. T. (1980). Vertuous women found: New England ministerial literature. In J. W. James (Ed.), *Women in American religion* (pp. 67–87). Philadelphia: University of Pennsylvania Press.

Vinovskis, M. A. (1981). *Fertility in Massachusetts from the Revolution to the Civil War.* New York: Academic Press.

Vinovskis, M. A. (1990). Have social historians lost the Civil War? Some preliminary demographic speculations. In M. A. Vinovskis (Ed.), *Toward a social history of the American Civil War: Exploratory essays* (pp. 1–30). Cambridge: Cambridge University Press.

Vinovskis, M. A. (2005). *The birth of Head Start: Preschool education policies in the Kennedy and Johnson administrations.* Chicago: University of Chicago Press.

Vinovskis, M. A., & Frank, S. M. (1997). Parenting in American society: A historical overview of the colonial period through the 19th century. In T. Arendell (Ed.), *Contemporary parenting: Challenges and issues* (pp. 45–67). Thousand Oaks, CA: Sage Publications.

Warner, W. L. (Ed.). (1963). *Yankee city* (abridged ed.). New Haven, CT: Yale University Press.

Weber, G. A. (1923). *The Bureau of Pensions: Its history, activities, and organization.* Baltimore: Johns Hopkins Press.

Weber, G. A., & Schmeckebier, L. F. (1934). *The Veterans' Administration: Its history, activities, and organization.* Washington, DC: Brookings Institution.

Winterer, C. (1992). Avoiding a "hothouse system of education": Kindergartens and the problem of insanity, 1860–1890. *History of Education Quarterly, 32,* 289–314.

Wrightson, K. (1982). *English society, 1580–1680.* London: Hutchinson.

Zigler, E., & Muenchow, S. (1992). *Head Start: The inside story of America's most successful educational experiment.* New York: Basic Books.

Zigler, E., & Valentine, J. (Eds.). (1979). *Project Head Start: A legacy of the War on Poverty.* New York: Free Press.

Zuckerman, M. (1970). *Peaceable kingdoms: New England towns in the eighteenth-century.* New York: Alfred A. Knopf.

Commentary

This American Life: A Discussion of the Role of History in Developmental Outcomes

Jacquelyn B. James

Vinovskis's discussion of the role of history in developmental outcomes is truly a tour de force. The historical influences on the American life course mapped in the paper span at least three centuries and cover three disparate topic areas of interest to social scientists that seek to link individual development with social change. Most importantly, he suggests historical and contextual variables with potential to add new life to the work of researchers in developmental science.

First among these is an overview of the conditions of family formation for early settlers in the New World, both for White and African American, and how they differed for the northern and southern regions of the country. Interestingly, these differences were apparent from the outset of our development as a young nation and of course, long before the Civil War. Region is another of those contextual variables that still gets short shrift in developmental research although several authors in this volume suggest models for correcting this oversight. There remain today wide regional differences, in not only perceptions and customs, but in opportunities and resources, and in peoples. As Vinovskis points out, very different ethnic groups settled different areas of this vast country. The role of family, and who did what for whom, differed among these groups, and in many ways still does. For these and a host of other reasons, Vinovskis's overview recommends a more intensive focus on region in studying patterns of development. This is especially true in terms of the early lives of African Americans, too long neglected by all of social science. As Vinovskis says, there were, among other things, important differences in the ways that African American lives were shaped depending on whether they were northern or southern slaves.

Vinovskis's discussion also traverses the patterns of family roles delineating who was responsible for what as parents, and how these roles changed over time. The author asserts, for example, that mothers were not always seen as the "natural" caretakers of children, that fathers' involvement in the family gradually diminished in a new economy, and that the medieval Western family did not have a sharp division among the roles of parents, servants, or even neighbors in the socialization and oversight of children. These are important historical trends to consider, especially given our concern today with how these matters get worked out in families as we continue to face changing roles of men and women in families and in the workplace.

Vinovskis also described changing perceptions of children and their capabilities, changes and pendulum swings, as he points out, that continue to this day. Here we are reminded of the importance of a "defining belief" in facilitating or limiting development. How we think about children, their capabilities, and their needs determines what we consider worthy of study, the kinds of questions we ask, and the interpretations we make. These concerns then influence how we treat children, what services we provide, and who provides them.

Vinovskis reports how early education in nursery schools and day care facilities was scant in the United States until World War II, when, in an unprecedented move, the government provided money for day care services so that mothers could replace men in the factories. But then, just as quickly, the funding was withdrawn at the end of the war, never to be resumed in the same way. As we listen to presidential hopefuls tick off their list of important spending priorities, it seems that few mention the need for supplementing day care costs even though history and social science research—from the Early Head Start Study (Raikes, Kisker, Paulsell, & Love, 2000), the Baltimore Schools Study (Entwisle & Alexander, 1999), and the Perry Preschool Intervention (Schweinhart, 2003) projects—show that inattention to our children, especially the neediest among them brings serious repercussions both for the developing individual and the society at large.

Vinovskis also points quite directly to the role of the church in the developing individual, another area that until recently, was all but ignored in social science research, and again, historically an important institution in the lives of African Americans. Social scientists are too seldom interested in the role of religion in human development (for worthy exceptions, please see Dillon, Wink, & Fay, 2003; George, Ellison, & Larson, 2002; and Modell, 1999). In the world we currently inhabit, we do not have to look far to see the importance of institutional church and religious sects on the lives of developing young people, especially a group of young Middle Eastern men in Afghanistan and Saudi Arabia. These influences are powerful in the United States as well, and they continue into later life. We need to heed the historical influence of religion in our study of development and how individuals age.

As mentioned previously, Vinovskis details the impact of the Civil War on the lives of those involved—who fought, who died, and what happened to change lives during and after the war. We see most prominently the impact of region on developmental outcomes. We would do well to learn more about how family roles were affected by the war; Faust (1996), for example, has documented how the lives of the Confederate soldiers' wives were changed irrevocably as they were left to run the farms while their husbands did battle. As we heard, many of these husbands died in the conflict, leaving the wives with unanticipated lifestyles in their later years. It goes without saying of course, that here again is a time of rich African American history that dramatically changed lives in that community, both during and after the conflict— changes about which we still have a lot to learn.

In sum, Vinovskis indeed provides insight to various instantiations of ways that aging and a succession of different cohorts are in continuing interplay with changes in society and its structure. Riley (1998) calls this the "cohort principle." Because society changes, people born at different times grow older in different ways, have different opportunities for and constraints upon their development.

Vinovskis also illustrates the "intersecting lives" principle (Riley, 1998) in that each person's life is intertwined with the lives of others— influencing and being influenced by social relationships. Vinovskis reports how the Church influences individuals, government services influence opportunities for women to work, and the types of schools influence what learning is made available to children, and at what ages. Indeed, we heard of children influencing parents by revealing the extent of their capabilities that might go beyond common perceptions. Indeed Vinovskis crosses a great expanse to show how life courses are shaped by forces external to the individual person, how historical conditions, the good or bad fortunes of national citizenship or institutional arrangements "built the tracks on which individual trajectories are bound to follow" (Mayer, 2001).

Among the colleagues represented here, it is doubtful that we will get much argument about the importance of such concepts and historical trends for our work in understanding how we age. Unfortunately, however, it seems to be easier to marvel at the data presented here than it is to empirically test the extent of these influences on lives today. Indeed, the actual practice of linking historical and social change to individual lives has, by all accounts, lagged behind conceptual advances. There are several reasons for this, but I will focus on two.

The first has to do with the particular kinds of data we need for the kinds of questions suggested by Vinovskis. We know we need longitudinal studies and cohort-sequential designs with the potential for comparative study of cohort subgroups for these kinds of questions. These are all, as Anne Colby (1998) has said, "resource intensive methods." We know that acquiring such data is difficult and expensive. Indeed, one fine example of collecting data prospectively with the knowledge of an impending cohort-defining event is the farm study done by Glen Elder, Rand Conger, and their colleagues tin Iowa (Elder & Conger, 2000).

For our part, there are probably too many cohort-defining events that we cannot anticipate, and the costs of conducting such research are too high for most of us to rely on this method. We do not, however, have to wait such a long time for the data we need. They are already available to us in archives—at the Roper Center, at Inter-university Consortium for Social and Political Research at the University of Michigan, and other archival settings. Of course, such data are also available at the Murray Research Center, at Harvard University, where my colleagues and I have collected over 70 longitudinal data sets (among 270 data sets in general), many of which can be followed up by new investigators, all of which can be used for new research. (See table 1.1 for a list of data sets focusing on midlife and aging.) Many of these data sets contain both qualitative and numerical data and variables of interest that have been suggested by Vinovskis.

In addition to the classic longitudinal studies that the Murray Center has acquired over the past 26 years, we have also built a one-of-a-kind archive of data on the experiences of racial and ethnic minorities in the United States. [See, for example, Giele, *Life Patterns Study* (Giele, 1998; Giele & Pischner, 1994); Johnson's *African American Oldest Old* (Johnson, 1995, 1999); and Wilson's *Three Generations of African-American Families* (Tolson & Wilson, 1990; Wilson, 1984)]. So, the problem

**TABLE 1.1   Studies of Midlife and Aging at the
Murray Research Center**

The Murray Center has a wide selection of studies of maturing lives that include valuable information about career and social responsibility and psychological well-being in midlife, and familial relations within an intergenerational context. Many studies address coping and adaptation in old age and emergent developmental concerns with spiritual reflection, mortality, loss, and bereavement. Holdings draw on diverse methodologies such as follow-up, longitudinal, qualitative, and multiple measure approaches. Equally diverse are the broad array of disciplinary perspectives, which facilitate new interdisclipinary insights about midlife and aging.

Mid-Life
   Baruch, Grace K., & Barnett, Rosalind C., Women in the Middle Years
   Colby, Anne, Social Responsibility at Midlife
   Osherson, Samuel, Patterns of Midlife Career Development Project

Intergenerational Relations
   Bengtson, Vern L., Longitudinal Study of Generations and Mental Health
   Institute of Human Development, Intergenerational Studies
   Rogler, Lloyd H., Intergenerational Study of Puerto Rican Families in New
      York City
   Wilson, Melvin N., Study of Three Generation African-American Families

Aging
   Atchley, Robert, Ohio Longitudinal Study
   Busse, Ewald, Second Duke Longitudinal Study
   Douglas, William, Ministers' Wives
   Johnson, Colleen L., Longitudinal Study of African-American Oldest Old
   Murray Research Center & Schlesinger Library, Coping and Adaptation in
      Older Black Women
   Shulik, Richard N., Faith Development, Moral Development, and Old Age
   Traupmann-Pillemer, Jane, McBeath Institute Aging Women Project

Loss and Bereavement
   Lopata, Helena, Widowhood in an American City
   Southwest Institute for Research on Women, Coping and Health Among
Older Urban Widows
   Weiss, Robert, Going It Alone
   Weiss, Robert S., & Parkes, C. Murray, Harvard Bereavement Study

(Radcliffe) Alumnae
   Brett, Belle, Radcliffe Class of 1969
   Giele, J. Life Patterns Study

(continued)

TABLE 1.1 *(continued)*

Horner, Matina Souretis, Radcliffe College Centennial Survey
Radcliffe College Class of 1943, Radcliffe Class of 1943 Oral History Project
Radcliffe College Class of 1947, Life Patterns Survey

Follow-up Studies
Connolly, John, Follow-up of the Kelly Longitudinal Study
McClelland, David C., Follow-up of Patterns of Child Rearing Subjects
McClelland, David C. & Franz, Carol, Life Patterns Project: 1987–1988
    Follow-up of Patterns of Child Rearing
Roberto, Karen, Friendships of Older Women: Changes Over Time

Life Course
Fiske, Marjorie Lowenthal, Thurnher, Majda; & Chiriboga, David,
    Longitudinal Study of Transitions in Four Stages of Life
Terman, Louis M., Sears, Robert, Cronbach, Lee, & Sears, Pauline, Terman
    Life Cycle Study of Children with High Ability
Heath, Douglas H., Study of Adult Development
Vaillant, George E., McArthur, Charles, & Bock, Arlie, Grant Study of Adult
    Development
Lachman, Margie, & James, Jackie, Health and Personal Styles

Immigrants
Coser, Rose, World of Our Mothers Study of Jewish and Italian Immigrant
    Women
Hurh, Won Moo, & Kim, Kwang Chung, Sociological Study of Korean
    Immigrants' Mental Health
Ybarra, Lea, California Valley Oral History Project

of locating data, while still difficult and dependent on the availability of existing data that contains the variables of interest, or that can be recast in ways to suit a new investigator's quest, is not insurmountable.

The next problem we face and another reason for the lack of advances in illuminating the impact of historical trends on human development (especially true for psychologists), is the sparseness of good conceptual models for this kind of work. It is clear that we do need more models; and the creative among us need to be working actively to develop them. However, a good case can be made that we have too seldom used the models we have.

One such model, proposed by Stewart and Healy (1989), can be

seen in a now classic article published in *American Psychologist.* Building
on the work of a number of sociological, psychological, and political
theorists (especially the work of Elder, 1974; Douvan, 1983; and Kulka,
1982), Stewart and Healy suggest that there are connections between
broad periods of development in the individual's life course and the
impact of major social and historical events.

> According to this model, if you want to make a prediction about the
> kind of impact a social event will have on a particular person, you
> need to know two things: (a) what was the backdrop against which
> this event occurred? That is, did this event mark a drastic discontinu-
> ity in the flow of events, or was it continuous with prior events? If
> events are discontinuous with a previous period in an individual's
> life, they are likely to have a bigger impact. (b) What was the age of
> the person at the time? If a person encounters and event that makes
> a drastic discontinuity (war, change in economic conditions, etc.)
> during the period of identity formation, then that event is much
> more likely to be represented in the person's personal identity, and
> that person is much more likely to feel particularly strongly tied to
> age-peers or members of her or his generation." (Stewart, 2003,
> p. 4).

In the *American Psychologist* paper, Stewart and Healy (1989) use
five data sets (including data collected over the past 40 years and birth
cohorts ranging from World War I to the baby boom generation) to
show the ways that such social experiences have "consequences for individuals' *world views,* when they are experienced in childhood, for
their *identities* when they are experienced in late adolescence and the
transition to adulthood, and are more likely to influence *behaviors*
when they are experienced in mature adulthood" (Stewart & Healy,
1989, pp. 39-40). They argue that psychologists (and others) can see
the impact of these kinds of events most clearly when comparing people with different childhoods—that is, people from different generations—rather than by talking to that particular person about the war or
other defining moments.

Recently, Stewart (2003) extended these analyses to show the ways
that generational differences between those who came of age (became
young adults) during the 1950s, when compared with those who came
of age in the 1960s, differed in midlife in ways that overrode race and
gender differences. In fact, women and men, both White and African
American, from a range of social classes, who came of age in the 1950s
revealed strikingly similar values, values that were remarkably different
from the later 1960s generation.

To illustrate the use of the Stewart and Healy (1989) model, and the use of data that already exists in a data archive, for understanding historical influences on lives and aging, I turn now to an example from my own work conducted with my colleague Janet Malley, a study of three different generations of mothers. While easily available and accessible, the story of this study is not as simple as it sounds. We did not go to the Murray Center website and find a study of three generations, although as indicated in Table 1.1, there are such data available.

Instead, we found a classic study of mothers conducted by Sears, Maccoby, and Levin (1957). It made a major splash at the time and is still cited today. It began as a study of child-rearing practices that seemed more like a sample of one generation, mothers of the 1950s, than a multi-cohort study.

Researchers interviewed 379 mothers, both middle and working class, regarding their beliefs about child rearing. Many of the findings from that study about how best to rear children are still holding up with research on today's generations of children [see also the work of Diana Baumrind (1971) and her construction of "authoritative parenting," which bears remarkable similarity to the "responsible child training orientation" in *Patterns of Child Rearing* (Sears, Maccoby, & Levin, 1957)]. Moreover, this study has continued to make contributions to the field. The children in this study, now in their late 50s, have been followed up every 10 years or so throughout their lives. Most recently, just prior to his death, McClelland and his colleagues produced several publications in major journals showing the effects of child-rearing practices on outcomes for the midlife children during their 30s and 40s (Franz, McClelland, & Weinberger, 1991; Koestner, Franz, & Weinberger, 1990; McClelland & Franz, 1992).

Given the importance of these mothers and their roles in the lives of their children, it is interesting that after 1951, no one recontacted the mothers. So, in 1996, Janet Malley and I, deciding that it was not too late to get the mothers' perspectives, petitioned the committee who oversees this study for permission to follow-up the mothers. This capability is one huge and unique value of using Murray Center data; many of the data sets allow for follow-up studies under the right conditions. We remain grateful for this opportunity afforded us by the center.

Of the 154 mothers located 45 years after the first interview, 50 were deceased, 9 were too ill to participate, and 17 declined, leaving 78 mothers (82%) from the original study willing and healthy enough to participate.

The data have yielded interesting results in a variety of areas. We have for example predicted Erik Erikson's concept of ego integrity and its relation to mental health (James & Zarrett, in press); we have told new stories about the mothers' experiences on the home front during World War II (Malley, 1999), and most recently, we have presented results about the mothers own mental health in relation to their assessments of their sons' or daughters' successes and failures (James, 2003). After reading the Vinovskis discussion regarding the multiple ways that gender roles are perceived and enacted, I wondered whether these data could be used to make better sense of these mothers' experiences in those domains.

The children in the study were all age 5 when the study began, but the mothers' ages spanned several "generations," ranging from 70 to 91, even though all of them were mothers of the baby boom generation. Was the timing of important historical events on the mothers' attitudes and behaviors related to work and family roles? As our starting point, and based on the model, we wondered what the defining historical events of their "coming of age," were (Malley & James, 1999).

Indeed these mothers appear to represent three unique experiences of social history based on the timing of their young adulthood: women who came of age during World War II; women who entered young adulthood during the Depression; and women who became young adults in the period between World War I and the Depression. These different sociohistorical climates are reflected in their adult attitudes about women's roles as well as their individual employment histories.

Mothers from the older cohort were more likely to endorse a traditional perspective on women's roles than were younger cohorts (Table 1.2). They were more likely than the younger mothers to have

TABLE 1.2 Mothers' 1996 Level of Traditionality in Their Views Concerning Women's Roles by Cohort

Cohort	Mothers' Level of Traditionality		
	Nontraditional	Mixed	Traditional
Younger cohort ($N = 19$)	55%	16%	26%
Middle cohort ($N = 23$)	44%	20%	36%
Older cohort ($N = 25$)	16%	44%	40%

$^2(4) = 9.97, p \leq .05$

TABLE 1.3   Mothers' Work History by Cohort

	Mothers' Work History		
Cohort	No Paid Emplyment After Children Born (*N* = 22)	No Paid While Children Young (*N* = 33)	Paid Employment While Children Young (*N* = 22)
Younger cohort (*N* = 21)	24%	33%	43%
Middle cohort (*N* = 28)	18%	68%	14%
Older cohort (*N* = 28)	43%	25%	32%

$\chi^2(4)=13.53, p \leq .01$

permanently terminated employment when the first child was born (Table 1.3). The younger mothers were more likely to have had their children sooner than the older mothers (table 1.4), and to have worked while these children were young.

In addition to finding that historical context mattered for these mothers' later development, we found that individual differences in early childhood experiences also had impact in later life (Fig. 1.1). Specifically, childhood hardships were related to the mothers' lower level of satisfaction with the mother role in 1951 when they were relatively new mothers. This was then related to feelings of regret about giving up paid employment in 1951. These feelings had important implications for the later adult development, expressed as lower generativity, Erikson's concept of having a concern with guiding the next generation (as measured by the Loyola Generativity Scale, McAdams & de St. Aubin, 1992). These analyses seem to provide further empirical

TABLE 1.4   Mothers' Age at First Child's Birth by Cohort

Cohort	Mothers' Mean Age in Years at First Child's Birth
Younger cohort (*N* = 20)	22
Middle cohort (*N* = 28)	25
Older cohort (*N* = 26)	29

$F = (2,71) \ p \leq .001$

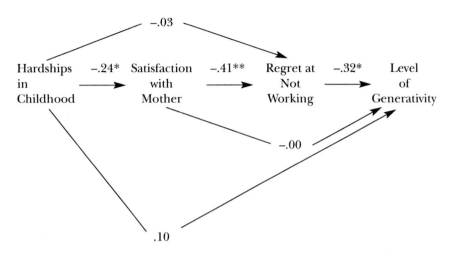

FIGURE 1.1 Sequence of correlational relationships among hardships in early childhood attitudes, in early adulthood and level of generativity in later adulthood.

support for the model proposed by Stewart and Healy (1989) for understanding the link between social change and personality development.

As would be predicted by the model, the oldest cohort of mothers reflect traditional family values and individual identities that do not accommodate combining work and family roles. They were less likely than the younger cohort to experience paid employment after their children were born. Similarly, they delayed childbearing, presumably because they felt they couldn't do both. Correspondingly, they were more likely to endorse traditional views about women's work and family roles on the Attitudes Toward Women Scale (Mason & Bumpass, 1975). In contrast, the youngest cohort of mothers experienced the influx of women into the work world during World War II in their young adulthood, incorporating the notion that women could do both in their own identities. As adults they had their first child at a younger age and were more likely to combine work and family roles when their children were young than the older cohorts. They also endorsed nontraditional views about women combining work and family roles. The middle cohort's early sociohistorical environment was similar to that of the older cohort and their attitudes tend to reflect a more traditional perspective than that of the younger cohort (although less traditional than the older cohort). However, as Stewart and Healy (1989) suggest, the timing of World War II had implications for their development, as well, allowing them to take on a worker identity, but in the context of more traditional family values. It is not surprising, then, that while these mothers did maintain a high level of paid employment in adulthood, they delayed their reentrance into the workforce until after their children had reached late adolescence.

Although these results suggest that the early historical context has general implications for later adulthood, individual differences in early childhood experiences were also found to influence the individual's life course. Specifically, experiences of hardships (death of a family member, poverty, emotional and physical abuse) were related to the mothers' lower level of satisfaction with the mother role in 1951 when they were relatively new mothers. Presumably, serious traumas in their early family lives made the role of mother a more difficult one for these women to take on in early adulthood. Concomitantly, in 1951 a lower level of satisfaction with this role was related to feelings of regret about giving up paid employment. These feelings of regret had important implications for their later adult development; these mothers expressed significantly lower level of generativity in 1996 when they were in late adulthood.

We see these results as highlighting the importance of considering both broad social events and unique individual experience for better understanding their long term consequences for adult development. We also see them as providing further support for the Stewart and Healy model and for the value of using existing data to do so, even with a small sample such as this one.

In closing, Vinovskis argues persuasively that variations in the life course over time and across different cultures have serious implication for current day research in human development. In doing so, he has suggested several contextual variables we need to add to our growing lists of research on this American life; two in particular include the role of religion and region of the country. I have argued that models for conducting such research and data for doing so are both being underused. In short, we have seen that history matters. And generation matters. We have only just begun to learn just how much.

REFERENCES

Baumrind, D. (1971). Current patterns of parental authority. *Developmental Psychology Monograph, Part 2, 4*(1), 1–103.

Colby, A. (1998). Crafting life course studies. In J. Giele & G. Elder (Eds.),

Methods of life course research: Qualitative and quantitative approaches. Thousand Oaks, CA: Sage.

Dillon, M., Wink, P., & Fay, K. (2003). Is spirituality detrimental to generativity? *Journal for the Scientific Study of Religion, 42,* 427–442.

Douvan, E. (1983). Family roles in a twenty-year perspective. In M. Horner, C. C. Nadelson, & M. Notman (Eds.), *The challenge of change: Perspectives on family, work, and education* (pp. 199–217). New York: Plenum.

Elder, G. (1974). *Children of the great depression.* Chicago: University of Chicago Press.

Elder, G., & Conger, D. (2000). *Children of the land.* Chicago: University of Chicago Press.

Entwisle, D. R. & Alexander, K. L. (1999). Early schooling and social stratification. In R. Pianta & M. Cox (Eds.), *The transition to kindergarten.* Baltimore, MD: Brookes Publishing.

Faust, D.G. (1996). *Mothers of invention: Women of the slaveholding South in the American civil war.* Chapel Hill: University of North Carolina Press.

Franz, C., McClelland, D., & Weinberger, J. (1991). Childhood antecedents of conventional social accomplishment in midlife adults: A 36-year prospective study. *Journal of Personality and Social Psychology, 60,* 586–595.

George, L. K., Ellison, C. G., & Larson, D. B. (2002). Explaining the relationships between religious involvement and health. *Psychological Inquiry, 13,* 190–200.

Giele, J. Z. (1998). Innovation in the life course. In J. Z. Giele & G. H. Elder, Jr. (Eds.) *Methods of life course research: Qualitative and quantitative approaches* (pp. 231–263). Thousand Oaks, CA: Sage.

Giele, J. Z. & Pischner, R. (1994). The emergence of multiple role patterns among women: A comparison of Germany and the United States. *Vierteljahrshefte Zur Wirtschaftsforschung (Applied Economics Quarterly), 1–2,* 97–103.

James, J. B. (2003, April). Lives in motion: Older mothers evaluate their midlife children. Paper presented at a meeting for the Society for Research in Child Development biennial meeting, Tampa, FL.

James, J. B., & Zarrett, N. (in press). Ego integrity in the lives of older women: 1951–1996. *Journal of Adult Development.*

Johnson, C. L. (1995). Cultural Diversity in the Late-Life Family. In R. Blieszner and V. Bedford (Eds), *Handbook of Aging and the Family* (pp. 307–331). Westport,CT: Greenwood Press.

Johnson, C. L. (1999). Family Life of Older Black Men. *Journal of Aging Studies, 13*(2), pp. 145–160.

Koestner, R., Franz, C., & Weinberger, J. (1990). The family origins of empathic concern: a 26-year longitudinal study. *Journal of Personality and Social Psychology, 58,* 709–717.

Kulka, R. A. (1982). Monitoring social change via survey replication: Prospects and pitfalls from a replication survey of social roles and mental health. *Journal of Social Issues, 38,* 17–38.

Malley, J. E. (1999). Life on the home front: Housewives' experiences of World War II. In M. Romero & A. Stewart (Eds.), *Women's untold stories: Breaking silence, talking back, voicing Complexity* (pp. 53–70). New York: Routledge.

Malley, J. E. & James, J. B. (1999, August). Changes in Gender Role Identity: 1951–1996. Poster presented at the annual meeting of the American Psychological Association, Chicago.

Mason, K. O., & Bumpass, L. I. (1975). U.S. women's sex-role ideology, 1970. *American Journal of Sociology, 80,* 122–1219.

Mayer, K. U. (2001, October). The sociology of the life course and life-span psychology: Diverging or converging pathways. Paper presented at a meeting for the Society for the Study of Human Development biennial meeting, Ann Arbor, MI.-

McAdams, D. P., & de St. Abin, E. (1992). The theory of generativity and its assessment through self-report: Behavioral acts and narrative themes in autobiography. *Journal of Social and Personality Psychology, 62,* 1003–1015.

McClelland, D. C., & Franz, C.E. (1992). Motivational and other sources of work accomplishments in mid-life: A longitudinal study. *Journal of Personality, 60,* 679–707.

Modell, J. (1999, October). Is god a context that matters for children's development? Paper presented at a meeting for the Society for the Study of Human Development first biennial meeting, Boston.

Raikes, H., Kisker, E., Paulsell, D., & Love, J. (2000) Early Head Start National Research and Evaluation Project: Meeting the child care needs of families. *Head Start Bulletin, 69,* 7–10.

Riley, M. W. (1998). A life course approach: Autobiographical notes. In J. Giele & G. Elder (Eds.). *Methods of life course research: Qualitative and quantitative approaches.* Thousand Oaks, CA: Sage Publications.

Schweinhart, L. J. (2003, April). Benefits, costs and explanation of the High/Scope Perry preschool program. Paper presented at the Society for Research in Child Development Biennial meeting, Tampa, FL.

Sears, R., Maccoby, E., & Levin, H. (1957). *Patterns of child rearing.* Stanford, CA: Stanford University Press.

Stewart, A J. (2003). The 2002 Carolyn Sherif award address: Gender, race, and generation in a Midwest high school: Using ethnographically informed methods in psychology. *Psychology of Women Quarterly, 27,* 1–11.

Stewart, A. J., & Healy, J. (1989). Linking individual development and social change. *American Psychologist, 44,* 30–42.

Tolson, T. F. J., & Wilson, M. N. (1990). The impact of two- and three-generational Black family structure on perceived family climate. *Child Development, 61,* 416–428.

Wilson, M. N. (1984). Mothers' and grandmothers' perceptions of parental behavior in three-generational Black families. *Child Development, 55,* 1333–1339.

Commentary

What Happened to America's Elderly Population?

Mark D. Hayward

In present day social science, the life course of individuals refers to the organization of social roles over a lifetime. Life course analysis addresses the causes and consequences of individual change and emphasizes the intersection between life course changes and biological, psychological, and social institutional forces (Elder, 1994). Life course changes refer to transitions in major roles such as student, parent, spouse, and worker. Professor Vinovskis refines and extends these ideas by considering how key aspects of the American life course have changed over the course of several centuries. How does family life in colonial America compare to today—and what was the range of diversity in family life early in our country's history? How has the concept of childhood changed since colonial times? How did the American Civil War affect the health and retirement patterns of a substantial portion of American men?

Using the historical lens, Vinovskis articulates three arguments about the life course:

- The life course shows considerable variation over historical time—and across place.
- The life course is highly plastic, allowing relatively rapid adaptation along a spectrum of social and physical environmental conditions.
- There is little evidence for the idea that the life course is "socially

evolutionary"—at least in the span of time represented by modern history.

In this brief commentary, I provide additional evidence on these points, focusing on the later stages of the life course. As I demonstrate below, the malleability of the life course extends throughout the life course into old age. Like family life and childhood, the character and quality of the life course for older persons has changed in dramatic ways in recent history. I introduce a theoretical framework, *technophysio evolution,* developed by Robert Fogel and Dora Costa (Fogel & Costa 1997) as a means to understand the long-term historical changes in the life course experiences of the American older population.

ADDITIONAL EVIDENCE IN SUPPORT OF VINOVSKIS'S ARGUMENTS

Historical Changes in Retirement among America's Elders

Much of the modern economics and sociology literature on the trend toward early retirement in America emphasizes changes that have occurred since World War II. In part, this reflects a presumption about the consequences of the creation of the Social Security pension system in the 1930s and its subsequent expansion in terms of population coverage and benefit levels.

In fact, however, the trend toward early retirement following World War II is part of a long-term historical trend that began in the latter part of the 19th century. As Costa shows (1998) (see figure 1.2), the United States experienced a relatively constant and high rate of older men's labor force participation in the latter part of the 19th century until 1890, at which point declines occurred for over a century, with only temporary plateaus. This trend was hardly unique to the United States. Data shown in figure 1.2 for Great Britain, Germany, and France document a similar pattern of historical declines in older men's labor force participation. The international trends reinforce Vinovskis's premise that the life course is highly plastic. Clearly, this is the case for retirement where dramatic changes occurred in a very short historical period.

What are the forces that led to these long term declines in older men's labor force activity? At the outset, it is important to note that the similarity in the long-term trend across countries suggests that the explanation is not due to rise of modern pension systems since these are

FIGURE 1.2 Labor-force participation rates of men age 65 and over, 1850–1990, United States, Britain, France, and Germany. Source: Costa, The American Economic Review, 5, 1998.

largely country-specific. Based on data for the United States, Costa (1998) provides evidence that the decline prior to 1930 was largely fueled by rising secular income. After 1950, however, American workers' retirement behavior appears much less sensitive to rising incomes—despite significant expansions in Social Security private pension benefits. The reasons are multi-factorial in nature. In the latter part of the 20th century, income may have reached a "satisfysing" threshold (i.e., basic consumption needs were being met). This allowed other factors to come into play. For example, the establishment of the Social Security system and its age eligibility criteria for pension access contributed to the development of normative expectations about retirement—increasingly, individuals expected to retire around age 65. At the same time, retirement became an increasingly attractive life course stage due to the growth of non-work related productive and leisure activities.

What does the near future hold as national policy debates swirl around the consequences of the baby boom retirement for the Social Security pension system? Most likely, if incomes continue to rise due to economic growth and leisure remains relatively inexpensive, a significant and long-term reversal in the retirement trend is unlikely.

Historical Changes in the Burden of Disease Among Older Americans

Another example of the plasticity of the life course is the historical change in the burden of disease that occurred among older Americans in the 20th century. Take the case of older men's difficulty in walking shown in table 1.5 (Costa, 2000). The probability of difficulty walking for persons with a range of chronic conditions declined 18 to 54% between 1910 and 1990, depending on the age group and condition in question. Based on the 1910 and 1990 end points, Costa reported that the pace of decline was about .3 to .7% per annum. Note that Costa's estimate is less than the 1% figure estimated by Manton and his colleagues (Manton, Corder, & Stallard, 1997) for the 1982 to 1994 period, pointing to possible acceleration in the decline in this aspect of disease burden in the latter part of the 20th century.

TECHNOPHYSIO EVOLUTION AND CHANGES IN THE LIFE COURSE OF OLDER PERSONS

Robert Fogel and Dora Costa (Fogel & Costa, 1997) have offered a theoretical framework that has utility for understanding long-term historical changes in the life course experiences of the older population. The framework is called technophysiologic evolution. The framework is based on the idea that technological improvements are linked to physiological improvements. This relationship has led to a form of human evolution during the past 300 years—a period of dense technological development—that is biological but not genetic and which is rapid, culturally transmitted and not necessarily stable—attributes similar to Vinovskis's arguments about the sources of plasticity in the life course. The core premise is this framework is that human beings have gained unprecedented control over their environment. This has led to substantial changes in average body size, longevity, and improvement in robustness and capacity of vital organ systems. This point is evident in the historical changes that have occurred in body mass. Figure 1.3 (Fogel & Costa, 1997), shows all age groups have experienced substantial gains in body mass since the American Civil War. These increases in body mass point to decreased susceptibility over the long term to infectious as well as chronic diseases.

The theoretical framework advanced by Fogel and Costa (1997) has significant implications for understanding the life course that warrant serious research. For example, their framework points to the importance of investigating long-term improvement in longevity and the linkages between improvements in life expectancy and long-term de-

TABLE 1.5 **Probability of Difficulty in Walking (Predicted from Probit) for Men with Specific Chronic Diseases, Union Army Sample, 1910, and 1988–1994 National Health and Nutrition Examination Survey**

	All Men	Joint Problem	Respiratory Problem	Murmur	Arrhythmia	None of the Previous Conditions
Age 60						
1910	0.182	0.223	0.121	0.117	0.100	0.085
1988–1994	0.084	0.128	0.073	0.051	0.047	0.040
Age 65						
1910	0.209	0.256	0.143	0.139	0.120	0.103
1988–1994	0.132	0.194	0.119	0.086	0.081	0.070
Age 70						
1910	0.239	0.291	0.169	0.164	0.143	0.124
1988–1994	0.196	0.277	0.183	0.137	0.130	0.114

Source: Costa, *Demography*, 2000.
Notes: The probabilities are predicted from probits of the difficulty of walking on joint problems, decreased breath or adventitious sounds, murmurs, and arrhythmias. The 1910 probit also includes controls for whether a veteran was injured in the war and whether he was discharged for disability. The probabilities are evaluated with the values of these variables set equal to 0. Note that men with "none of the previous conditions" still might have other chronic conditions.

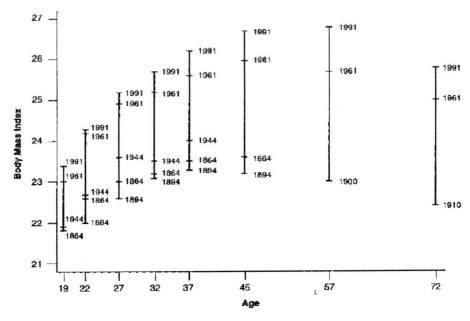

Source: Fogel and Costa, *Demography,* 1997.
Note: The age groups, which are centered at the marks, are ages 18–19, 20–24, 25–29, 30–34, 35–39, 40–49, 50–64, and 65–79. For some years BMI is not available for a specific age group.

FIGURE 1.3   Mean body mass index by age group and year, 1863–1991.

clines in the burden of disease. Their framework also suggests that over the course of time, health should be less and less a factor in explaining historical changes in retirement, family structure, and family living arrangements.

Much of the value of the technophysio evolutionary framework lies in its emphasis on long-term rather than short-term changes. Trends in life course experiences such as morbidity, mortality, and retirement need not move steadily in one direction, since underlying technological changes are neither uniform nor similar in the timing and magnitude of effects. Moreover, it may be difficult to infer long-term trends from short-term change. The technophysiologic evolutionary framework sensitizes researchers to long-term changes in a population's life course—changes brought on technological change and increased control over the environment.

TECHNOPHYSIO EVOLUTION AND
MARIS VINOVSKIS'S KEY POINTS

Vinovskis's historical evidence on the nature of change in the early family life course is bolstered by evidence about historical changes in the life course experiences of the older population. Like children and their parents, older persons have experienced considerable variation in the life course over the course of the previous century. I have provided evidence about changes in the health and retirement experiences of older persons, but similar changes in older person's family roles have also been documented (Watkins, Menken, & Bongaarts, 1987). Clearly, the life course is highly plastic, allowing relatively rapid adaptation along a spectrum of social and physical environmental conditions.

Vinovski also argues that that the life course is not "socially evolutionary"—at least in the span of time represented by modern history. His example of the adoption of European infant schools in the early 19th century, followed by a general reluctance to encourage early schooling, which was then followed by a rediscovery of early childhood education is telling. I suggest a more cautious approach, however, to this general idea of evolutionary change. Morbidity and mortality improvements in the life course can been seen as evolutionary in the sense they reflect humans' increased control over their environmental surroundings. As yet, there is little evidence that the pace of technical change—and control over the environment is abating, suggesting that we should expect continued improvements in the health of populations. As noted by Vinovskis and Fogel and Costa, technological change need not be uniform nor shared across nations. A case in point is the increase in political, economic, and social chaos in a number of the former Soviet Republics—a situation that has produced reversals in population health.

Social scientists often observe life course changes over a short span of time—a decade, sometimes two decades and only occasionally three decades. Such as been the time frame for discussions of the question of whether the declines in old age mortality are signaling a decline in the burden of disease in the population. Historian Maris Vinovskis and economic historians Robert Fogel and Dora Costa remind us that these time frames may be inappropriate for the questions being asked. Significant life course changes often occur over many decades, challenging empirical assessment but mandating close scrutiny of the "...complex interactions between historical changes and the American life course" (Vinovskis, In press).

REFERENCES

Costa, D. L. (1998). The evolution of retirement: Summary of a research project. *The American Economic Review, 88*(2), 232–236.

Costa, D. L. (2000). Understanding the twentieth century decline in chronic conditions among older men." *Demography, 37,* 53–72.

Elder, G. H. J. (1994). Time, human agency, and social change: Perspectives on the life course. *Social Psychology Quarterly, 57,* 4–15.

Fogel, R. W.and Costa, D. L. (1997). A theory of technophysio evolution, with some implications for forecasting population, health care costs, and pension costs." *Demography 34*(1), 49–66.

Manton, K. G.,Corder, L., and Stallard, E. (1977). Chronic disability trends in elderly United States populations: 1982–1994. *Proceedings of the National Academy of Sciences of the USA, 94*(6):2593–2598.

Vinovskis, M. A. (In press). Historical changes and the American life course.In K.W. Schaie and G.H. Elder, Jr. (Eds.),

Watkins, S. C., Menken, J. A., and Bongaarts, J. (1987). Demographic foundations of family change. *American Sociological Review, 52*(3),346.

CHAPTER 2

Immigration, Incorporation, and Generational Cohorts in Historical Contexts

Rubén G. Rumbaut

> *The past is never dead. It is not even past.*
> —William Faulkner

T his chapter aims to contribute to our understanding of historical influences on lives and aging, and of generational influences in the incorporation of immigrants in the United States. The first part addresses the importance of spelling out historical contexts (influences) for understanding virtually any aspect of the study of immigration and incorporation. By not doing so, we may be left with an elegant but ahistorical positivism. The second section specifies the size and composition—and definition—of what is loosely referred to as the immigrant first and second "generations" in the United States, outlines a typology of distinctive generational cohorts (based on differences in nativity and age at arrival), and analyzes their patterns of acculturation as well as educational and occupational attainment. In particular, I consider the utility and validity of "lumping" versus "splitting" such generational cohorts in the study of the adaptation of foreign-born immigrant children and the native-born children of immigrants. These distinctions bear directly on the connections between changing historical times in lives and aging, and—in a field where the study of intergenerational relations has been accurately criticized as "strikingly ahistorical" (Elder, 1978)—underscore the importance of

situating and understanding generational processes in specific historical contexts.

IMMIGRATION, INCORPORATION,
AND HISTORICAL CONTEXTS

Consider immigration itself. The 2000 census reported a foreign-born
population of about 32 million persons in the United States—a his-
toric high—of whom more than 12 million had come in the 1990s
alone, another 10 million in the 1980s, and over 5 million in the 1970s.
What explains this mass migration to the United States over the past
few decades? Changes in U.S. immigration laws—in particular the
amendments passed in 1965, which abolished the racist national-ori-
gins quota system and changed the preference system to give greater
priority to family reunification over occupational skills—have often
been singled out as the principal reason for the "new immigration"
and the change in the national origins of its composition. But the
causal effects of the 1965 Act have been exaggerated and misinter-
preted by this simplistic claim, especially so with regard to Latin American immigration and the large-scale entry of Cold War refugees, to say
nothing of illegal immigration.

It bears emphasizing that until this law was passed, Western Hemi-
sphere immigration (notably that from Mexico) had been unre-
stricted, largely at the behest of American agribusiness; and in fact, as
Zolberg (1995) has pointed out, the legislative history of the 1965 Act
"indicates very clearly that the objective was to deter the growth of
black and brown immigration" (p. 55) from Latin America and the
Caribbean, while increasing that from southern and eastern Europe.
For that matter, the 1965 law had nothing to do with determining, say,
the huge Cuban exile flows of the early 1960s, or the even larger Indochinese refugee flows that would follow later in the aftermath of the
Vietnam War. What is more, the most important consequences of the
1965 Act, notably the removal of barriers to immigrants from Asian
and African countries, were largely unintended. The law does matter,
of course: it influences migration decisions and constitutes a key context of reception shaping the incorporation of newcomers, especially
their right to full membership and future citizenship, and provides a
source of political capital unavailable to residents without legal status.
For example, the right of an immigrant to become a U.S. citizen
through naturalization was legally restricted on racial grounds until
1952. The first federal naturalization law of 1790 gave that right only to

"free white persons," and a revised law in 1870 extended it to persons of African descent or nativity, including Arabs and Hindus. In addition, the original native inhabitants of the continent—doubly misnomered "American Indians"—were presumed to be "loyal to their tribes" and not granted U.S. citizenship until 1924. Most Asian immigrants were excluded from access to American citizenship until the McCarran-Walter Act of 1952. Asian Indians had been able to be naturalized on the grounds that they were Caucasians until the U.S. Supreme Court, in a 1923 case, decided that they would no longer be considered White persons. The Chinese were removed from the classes of "aliens ineligible for citizenship" upon the repeal of the [1882] Chinese Exclusion Act in 1943, when China and the U.S. were World War II allies (see Aleinikoff & Rumbaut, 1998; Ueda 1981). But "the law" as such cannot control historical forces or determine the size or source of migration flows.

To be sure, many possible factors—economic, political, cultural, demographic—help explain contemporary immigration to the United States, but none can do so adequately outside of its concrete historical context. Geographical proximity is one consideration: after all, half of all recent legal immigration (and most unauthorized immigration) originates in nearby Caribbean Basin countries, with Mexico accounting for the lion's share. But 5 of the top 10 sending countries are in Asia, half a world away (the Philippines has ranked second only to Mexico over the past 30 years), and next-door neighbor Canada is not among them. Cheap airplane travel has greatly reduced distances, but Europeans are no longer coming as they did by the millions a century ago when ocean travel was far more difficult. Undocumented immigrants from Mexico surpass from any other country, but some 100,000 Irish immigrants settled illegally (by overstaying their visas) in Boston and New York during the 1980s. And a shorter distance does not explain why Salvadorans and Colombians are coming, but not Costa Ricans or Venezuelans; nor why until fairly recently Jamaicans went to the British metropole and Surinamese to the Netherlands instead of the United States (when Suriname achieved independence from the Netherlands in 1975, the new government could not halt the emigration of skilled Surinamese, most of them Hindus, to the Dutch metropole).

International migrations are rooted in historical relationships established between the sending and receiving countries—especially those rooted in colonialism, war and military occupation, labor recruitment and economic interaction—through which migration footholds are formed and "chain" migration processes are catalyzed. Kinship networks expand, remittances (in the 10s of billions of dollars annually, second only to oil sales worldwide) sent by immigrants to their families abroad link communities across national borders, and all of this turns migration into a social process of vast transformative significance, both for countries of origin and of destination, and one sustained by factors that are largely beyond the realm of government action or the economic impulses that originally generated it. Granted, migration pressures as a result of global inequality can only mount in a world that is more and more a place with a declining proportion of rich people and a growing proportion of poor people. Today, the biggest such development rift is located along the 2,000-mile U.S.–Mexico border, and indeed the longest, largest, and most continuous labor migration anywhere in the world is that from Mexico to the United States. But even in this paradigmatic instance the story is not simply reducible to a function of employer demand and labor supply.

Though today's immigrants come from more than 150 countries, some regions and nations send many more than others, despite the equitable numerical quotas provided to each country by U.S. law since 1965. In fact, only about a dozen countries account for the majority of all immigration to the United States. One pattern, a continuation of trends already under way in the 1950s, is clear: immigration from the more developed countries has declined over time, while that from less developed countries has accelerated. However, among the less developed countries, the major sources of legal and illegal immigration are centered on the Caribbean Basin—in the immediate periphery of the United States—and a handful of Asian nations also characterized by significant historical ties to the United States

Immigrants from Mexico and the Philippines alone account for a third of the total. These two countries share the deepest structural linkages with the United States, dating to the Mexican and Spanish-American Wars in the last century, and a long history of dependency relationships, external intervention and (in the Philippines) direct colonization, as well as decades of active agricultural labor recruitment by the United States—of Mexicans to the Southwest, Filipinos to plantations in Hawaii and California—that preceded the establishment of family networks and chain migrations. The extensive U.S. military presence in the Philippines has also fueled immigration through unique arrangements granting U.S. citizenship to Filipinos who served in the armed forces during World War II, through recruitment of Filipinos into the U.S. Navy, and through marriages with U.S. citizens stationed there. Tellingly, in their analysis of spouse-immigrant flows, Jasso and Rosenzweig (1990) found that the most powerful determinant of the number of immigrants admitted as wives of U.S. citizens was the presence of a U.S. military base in the country of origin. Geopolitical factors thus shape the marriage market in immigrant visas, a vivid example of the connection between macro and micro social structures in concrete historical contexts.

American foreign policy in the post–World War II era, especially the doctrine and practice of global communist containment, is itself a key factor in explaining several of the other sizable migrations from different world regions. They effectively helped to create the conditions that generated the flows in the first place (cf. Zolberg, Suhrke, & Aguayo, 1989). During the Cold War this included direct U.S. involvement in "hot" wars in Korea, Vietnam, Laos, Cambodia, and Central America, and interventions in Guatemala, Iran, Cuba, the Dominican Republic, and elsewhere—all of whom, not coincidentally, are among the leading source countries of contemporary immigrants and refugees. Among the most numerous recent European arrivals have been (former) Soviet Jews and Poles, admitted mainly as political refugees, like other groups from communist countries—ironically, in increasing numbers after the end of the Cold War in 1989 and f the demise of the Soviet Union in 1991. Emigration connections forged by U.S. intervention and foreign policies were also a common denominator in the exodus of the Chinese after the 1949 revolution (and subsequently in the issuance of immigrant visas under separate quotas for applicants from Taiwan and Hong Kong, and most recently to tens of thousands of Chinese students in the United States after the events of Tiananmen Square in 1989), and Iranians after the 1978 revolution. By the late 1990s immigrants from the four communist countries figuring most prominently in American foreign policy—Cuba, Vietnam, China, and the (former) Soviet Union—accounted for nearly one sixth of the total U.S. foreign-born population (exceeded only by Mexico and the Philippines). In short, contemporary immigration to the United States and the creation and consolidation of social networks that serve as bridges of passage to America have taken place within this larger historical context and cannot be adequately understood outside of it, nor reduced to a cost-benefit economic calculus of individual migrants or to the immigration laws of particular states.

The size and source of new immigrant communities in the United States today are thus directly, if variously, related to the history of American military, political, economic and—pervasively—cultural involvement in the major sending countries, and to the linkages that are formed in the process which (often unintentionally) open a surprising variety of legal and illegal migration pathways. Ironically, immigration to the United States can be understood as a dialectical consequence of the expansion of the nation to its post–World War II position of global hegemony, reflecting ineluctably the U.S. role in the world. As the United States has become more deeply involved in the world, the world has become more deeply involved in America—indeed, in diverse ways, it has come to America. What goes around comes around.

Or consider that most familiar of realities: the family. Immigrant family formations are shaped within historically specific contexts of migration and reception (Rumbaut 1997b). For example, the Cuban migration of the past four decades saw both an exodus of intact families as well as of some 15,000 unaccompanied "Peter Pan" children who were sent without their parents during the first waves of 1959 to 1962; the tens of thousands who came annually during the 1965–1973 "freedom flights" brought a disproportionate number of elderly (the Castro government did not allow young people of military age to leave), with a result today that there soon were more three-generation Cuban households in Miami with resident grandparents than almost any other ethnic group in the country, a fact that played a significant role in their family economic "success story"; and the *Marielitos* of 1980 and the thousands of *balseros* in the 1990s disproportionately involved young men, single or separated from their families left behind in Cuba (see García, 1996; Grenier & Pérez, 2003; Rumbaut & Rumbaut, 1976). There is thus no single "Cuban family type" in the United States, but rather family outcomes that have shaped and been shaped by immigrants' reactions to specific contexts and contingencies.

Similar statements can be made about all other immigrant families, past and present. For instance, Wong (1995) and others have noted how exclusionary policies and vastly disparate sex ratios among Chinese immigrants through the early 20th century formed bizarre family structures referred to variously as "split household" and "mutilated family," which later evolved transitional forms (especially after the 1943 repeal of the Chinese Exclusion Act began to make family reunification possible) and, in the wake of large-scale post-1965 immigration waves, bimodal family types ("dual worker," "ghetto" or "downtown" vs. "uptown" and "semi-extended" families). Koreans, Filipinos, and Asian Indians also were marked early on by disparate male ratios, and in California as a result many of the latter married Mexican wives (see Leonard, 1992). Japanese family formation reflected a far more balanced population sex ratio than other Asian groups (in part because the "Gentlemen's Agreement" of 1908 between the two governments allowed wives and children to enter, including "picture brides" (when marriage matches were arranged through an exchange of photographs between *Issei* immigrant men who could not afford to return to Japan to meet prospective brides), but also confronted the generation-defining experience of internment during World War II (Glenn, 1986; Hing, 1993).

War orphans by the thousands were adopted during and after the Korean War by U.S. servicemen stationed there, and by the 1970s and 1980s over 3,000 Korean children annually were adopted by U.S. citizens and admitted to the United States, accounting for 60% of all foreign-born children adopted by in the United States (Min, 1995). By the mid-1990s, over 100,000 Amerasians (children of Vietnamese mothers and American fathers who served in Vietnam during the war) and their immediate relatives had been resettled in the United States under a special law enacted in 1987. Vietnamese and Cambodian families and their sex ratios today reflect fundamentally different contexts of exit and processes of family fission and fusion in the course of flight, resettlement from refugee camps to third countries, and later reunification through "secondary" migrations to join family members elsewhere (Hein, 1995; Rumbaut, 1995). These are but illustrative pieces of complex histories that are irreducible to a single form or cultural ethos. Origins shape destinies.

Or consider historical influences on processes of immigrant acculturation and assimilation: The United States has been aptly described as a "language graveyard," underscoring the rapidity with which immigrant languages are lost and with which the switch to monolingual English takes place—typically within three generations, from the immigrant grandparent to the thoroughly Americanized grandchild (see Portes & Rumbaut, 1996, 2001). But the process can be accelerated in particular circumstances, as was the lot of the German language in the United States during World War I—or it can be sustained bilingually in others, particularly in "institutionally complete" communities where it is taught in the schools and valued in the labor market. Assimilation, in turn, can be seen as a nonviolent, uncoerced, more or less unconscious form of *ethnic cleansing*, a fading into what Alba (1985) called "the twilight of ethnicity," and what Znaniecki much earlier had termed "the euthanasia of memories," referring to the way in which ancestral identities were dissolved in the American melting pot (see Nahirny & Fishman, 1965; Rumbaut, 2005). But in intergroup relations, assimilation and oppression don't mix, regardless of the degree of acculturation. On the contrary, assimilation breeds under conditions of intimacy and mutual acceptance, as indexed by the warmth of the welcome and ultimately by intermarriage and the adoption of American self-identities. Thus in *Italian or American?*, a study of second-generation Italian immigrants written when the United States was at war with Italy, Child (1943) saw the likelihood of their assimilation versus ethnic retentiveness as a function of inclusionary versus exclusionary contexts of reception and terms of membership. He compared two main modes of reaction—the "*rebel*" (who was assimilated into the American milieu) and the "*in-group*" type (who retained an Italian ethnicity)—arguing that:

> If during the present period [World War II], the general American population encourages people of Italian origin to regard themselves as Americans and really offers them the full rewards of membership in American society, the rebel reaction should be by far the most frequent, and adoption of American culture traits should therefore proceed at a tremendous rate. [But] if during this period of war, the non-Italian members of the population uniformly suspect Italian-Americans of treasonable activity and do not offer them the full rewards of membership in American society . . . the in-group reaction will be very frequent and a revival of Italian culture will therefore appear." (pp. 196–197)

By contrast, under a regime of ethnoracial oppression—of segregation, stigmatization, discrimination, and the indignities of what might be called random acts of daily dissing—the process boomerangs: not into the euthanasia of memories, but into what Czeslaw Milosz has called "the memory of wounds" (1980); not into the twilight but into the high noon of what we have called "reactive ethnicity" (Portes & Rumbaut, 1996, 2001); not into thinned but thickened intergroup boundaries and identities, and what W. E. B. DuBois a century ago (1903) called a "double consciousness" and a "merging" that is not the zero-sum game implied in "melting":

> It is a peculiar sensation, this double-consciousness, this sense of always looking at one's self through the eyes of others, of measuring one's soul by the tape of a world that looks on in amused contempt and pity. One ever feels his two-ness—an American, a Negro; two souls, two thoughts, two unreconciled strivings; two warring ideals in one dark body, whose dogged strength alone keeps it from being torn asunder. The history of the American Negro is the history of this strife—this longing to merge his double self into a better and truer self. In this merging he wishes neither of the older selves to be lost. . . . He simply wishes to make it possible for a man to be both a Negro and an American, without being cursed and spit upon by his fellows, without having the doors of Opportunity closed roughly in his face." (pp. 3–4)

For all its appeal as a nationally inclusive (if ahistorical) metaphor, the "melting pot" does not square with the exclusionary side of the country's history and its effects on the collective memory of those who must locate themselves in a narrative of wounds: from *Dred Scott* to *Plessy v. Ferguson* to the era of lynchings and Jim Crow, from the Trail of Tears to Wounded Knee, from the Mexican War to the Spanish-American War, from the Chinese Exclusion Act to the Japanese internment, or the fact that until 1952 immigrants were excluded from naturalization (and others until 1965 from entry altogether) on the basis of "race." It took a bloody civil war in one century, and a civil rights revolution in the next, to end slavery and the legal underpinnings of racial exclusion, but not their bitter legacy. What's past *is* prologue.

IMMIGRATION, INCORPORATION, AND GENERATION

The study of the long-term consequences of international migration for receiving countries has focused increasingly on the incorporation of the immigrants' children (Boyd, 1998; Caplan, Choy, & Whitmore, 1991; Cropley, 1983; Gans, 1992; Hernández, 1999; Levitt & Waters, 2002; Perlmann & Waldinger, 1997; Portes, 1996; Portes & Rumbaut, 2001; Portes & Zhou, 1993; Rumbaut & Cornelius, 1995; Rumbaut & Ima, 1988; Suárez-Orozco & Suárez-Orozco, 2002; Zhou, 1997; Zhou and Bankston, 1998). The "new second generation" is rapidly growing and diversifying through continued immigration, natural increase, and intermarriage, complicating its contours and making it increasingly important, for theoretical as well as programmatic and policy reasons, to clarify who and what is encompassed by that term and to measure its size and composition. Also problematic is the definition, depiction, and measurement of the immigrant "first generation," a large segment of which is composed of persons who migrated as children and who are often regarded as members of the "second" generation.

Many theoretical questions can be and have been raised about the incorporation of children of immigrants vis-à-vis that of their parents: about their "coming of age" in the United States, their modes of acculturation and ethnic identity (and ethnic group) formation; their patterns of language use and mother-tongue shift; and their social, residential, reproductive, marital, educational, occupational, economic, civic, and political trajectories into adulthood. As with issues of language and national loyalties, questions abound regarding what extent any "transnational" attachments of their parents are sustained in the generation of their children, particularly those born in receiving countries such as the United States, who lack the memories and the metaphorical "birth connection" of their emigrant parents. All of these are open empirical questions, but each of them presupposes a clear operational definition of what is meant by "second generation," vis-à-vis the "first generation," and even of something as basic as the ethnicity of second-generation persons. Although there is a consensus about the import of intergenerational analysis for the study of the long-term impact of immigration—indeed, as Kertzer (1983) put it, "generational processes . . . are at the heart of the social metabolism" (p. 143)—there is no such consensus on the meaning and measurement of "generations" (cf. Oropesa & Landale, 1997).

These seemingly simple and straightforward matters become complex and elusive on closer inspection. To begin with, the term "generation" brings with it a variety of meanings. In a kinship context, it refers to a stage in a natural succession comprising those who are of the same genealogical remove from an ancestor (e.g., the generations of the parents, children, and grandchildren). It is also used as a synonym for "cohort," a term preferred by demographers to refer to a set of people born at about the same time (Ryder, 1965; Kertzer, 1983; Riley, 1987). In his seminal essay on "The Problem of Generations," Karl Mannheim ([1928] 1996) distinguished between individuals of the same age group, which he termed a "generational location," and a "generation as an actuality," contemporaries (typically compatriots as well) who are exposed to and defined by the effects of a powerful historical stimulus (especially during the years of the transition to adulthood when "personal experimentation with life begins") and develop a shared consciousness about it—an idea later echoed in Erik Erikson's (1964) concept of identity formation within a common "psycho-historical actuality." Mannheim noted, moreover, that members of a generation may react differently to the common historical stimulus, forming different "generational units" within the same actual generation.

Immigrant families and communities themselves are often acutely conscious of the generational status of their members and of generational differences between them—perhaps none more so than the Japanese in the United States, who have specific terms for the first four generations since the initial migrations of the late 19th and early 20th centuries (Issei, Nisei, Sansei, Yonsei), and another term (Nikkei) to describe all four generations of people of Japanese ancestry. How recent Japanese immigrants fit into this closed generational scheme is another matter altogether, since the scheme posits an original migration (a first generation), in terms of which all subsequent U.S.-born generations are genealogically defined and counted. But the imagery is suggestive: international migration is a powerful and transformative force, producing profound social changes not only in the sending and receiving societies, but above all among the immigrants themselves and their descendants. These effects may begin to fade over time and generation, the greater the remove from the original migrations and the conditions that produced them. But how to grasp and measure that "remove"—including the evolution over time and place of the ethnic self-identities of the referent populations—in widely different and rapidly changing circumstances and often in a context of continuing immigration, is problematic.

An example may be instructive. We raised th complexity of some of these issues in the Children of Immigrants Longitudinal Study (CILS) as soon as we set about to analyze the first wave of survey data collected in 1992 (Portes & Rumbaut, 2001; Rumbaut & Portes, 2001). The CILS sample consisted of 5,262 respondents on both coasts of the United States, most born in 1977 or 1978, representing 77 different nationalities. Half were foreign-born youths who had immigrated to the United States before age 12 (the "1.5 generation"), and half were U.S.-born children of at least one immigrant parent (technically the "second generation"). Among the foreign-born youth, the sample was also evenly split by age at arrival: about half had lived in the United States for 10 years or more (that is, they were of preschool age at arrival), whereas the other half had lived in the United States 9 years or less (that is, they had reached elementary school age in their native country but arrived in the United States before reaching adolescence and secondary schooling). Time in the United States for these immigrant children was thus not solely a measure of length of exposure to American life, but also an indicator of different developmental stages and contexts at the time of immigration. In theory, as will be elaborated below, it may make a great deal of difference to processes of socialization, acculturation, and reference-group identification whether children of immigrants are born in the United States or arrive during their preschool years or have already reached primary or secondary school age in the country of origin.

The determination of ethnicity for CILS respondents was mostly straightforward and unambiguous among foreign-born youths and those whose parents were co-nationals (born in the same foreign country), except for ethnic minorities (such as the Hmong from Laos, the ethnic Chinese from Vietnam) or in cases involving unique historical circumstances (such as Cambodian children who were born in refugee camps in Thailand), where country of birth could not serve as a proxy for ethnicity (on "internal ethnicity," see Bozorgmehr, 1997). But in a fourth of the cases in the CILS sample, the parents were born in different countries, and in over half of those cases—accounting for 13% of the overall sample—one of the parents was U.S.-born (a "2.5" generation, inasmuch as it is situated between the "second" generation of foreign parentage and the "third" generation of native parentage). In the case of the latter, ethnicity was assigned on the basis of the national origin of the foreign-born parent, whether it was the father or the mother (for evidence supporting this assignment rule, see Oropesa & Landale, 1997; Waters, 1990). In the case of the former—in mixed marriages wherein the parents were born in different foreign countries—the nationality of the mother took precedence in the assignment of ethnicity, reflecting both the mother's more influential role in the children's socialization and the fact that fathers were absent in 30% of the homes in the sample (Rumbaut, 1994).

Of course, what is a methodological problem to the researcher is a central psychosocial issue to an adolescent in arriving at a meaningful ethnic self-definition (cf. Erikson, 1968). Over time, as those adolescents come of age, marry (or intermarry), and have children of their own, issues of ethnic identity and the determination of ethnicity in comparative research studies can be confidently predicted to become more complicated still, and their measurement and analysis methodologically more challenging.

Conceptualizing the First and Second Generations

Differences in nativity (of self and parents) and age at arrival, which are criteria used to distinguish between generational cohorts, are known to affect significantly the modes of acculturation of adults and children in immigrant families, especially with regard to language and ethnic identity, educational attainment and patterns of social mobility, outlooks and frames of reference, and even their propensity to sustain transnational attachments over time (Portes & Rumbaut, 2001; Rumbaut, 1994, 1998a, 2003). To carry out such analyses—and setting aside only for the time being the problem of the determination and evolution of "ethnicity" in given historical contexts—the measurement of "first" and "second generations" requires at a minimum data sources that contain information on the country of birth of the respondent; and, if foreign-born, the age and date of arrival; and, if native-born, the country of birth of the mother and father. Those data, by and large, have come from the decennial national censuses. Spurred by the mass migration of the 1840s to the United States, the 1850 census was the first to collect data on the nativity of the population; beginning with the 1870 census, a question on parental nativity was added and collected in each decennial U.S. census until 1970 (see Gibson & Lennon, 1999).

However, study of the "second generation" and of the intergenerational mobility of immigrant-origin groups in the United States was severely undercut after 1970 when the U.S. Census Bureau dropped the question on parental nativity from the "long-form" questionnaire of its decennial census, the largest and most reliable nationally representative data source for the analysis of the myriad of immigrant groups. As a result, ironically, just at the very moment when a new era of mass migration made the collection of such data indispensable in the United States, the last three censuses (1980, 1990, 2000) have permitted only an examination of the foreign-born population by country of birth and date of arrival, but not of their U.S.-born children. The only exception in this regard has been the innovative use of the Public Use Microdata Samples (PUMS) of the decennial census to construct child files for all children under 18 residing in households with at least one foreign-born parent, and then concatenating information on the parents and household to each record (Jensen & Chitose, 1994; Oropesa & Landale, 1997). However, those efforts are limited only to those children still residing with their (foreign-born) parents, and cannot consider any second-generation persons 18 and older.

Fortunately, in 1994 the questions on paternal and maternal nativity were incorporated in the annual (March) supplement of the Current Population Surveys (CPS) conducted by the Census Bureau for the Bureau of Labor Statistics. The CPS has since become the main national-level data set in the United States permitting more refined intergenerational analyses (from the first to the second and third-and-beyond generations)—but the sample size for a given year, while substantial, is not large enough to provide reliable information on smaller immigrant populations, or for comparative analyses by national origin and by generational cohorts defined by age-at-arrival and parental nativity. This limitation can be addressed to some extent by merging annual demographic data files for several consecutive years to generate sufficient sample sizes for analytical purposes. This is the methodological strategy that I pursue below.

Aside from the problem of relevant data sources and data needs, the measurement of the size and composition of the first and second generations—which together comprise the country's "immigrant-stock" or foreign-parentage population—depends on what is meant by these terms, which have not been uniformly defined in the literature or operationalized in research studies. When referring to the *first gener-*

ation, immigration scholars in the United States commonly have in mind persons born and socialized in another country who immigrate as *adults.* Similarly, the *second generation* technically refers to the U.S.-born and U.S.-socialized children of foreign-born parents, although under this rubric immigration scholars also often if imprecisely lump together foreign-born persons who immigrated as *children,* as well as U.S.-born persons with one U.S.-born parent and one foreign-born parent, treating them together as the de facto second generation. Indeed, the expression "second-generation immigrants" is a commonplace in the literature—although it is technically an oxymoron, inasmuch as persons born in the United States cannot also be "immigrants" to the United States Still, none of these conventional usages accurately captures the experience of youths who fall in the interstices between these groupings nor, among those born abroad, takes into account their different ages and life stages at the time of immigration.

That there are fundamental differences in the pace and mode of adaptation between persons who immigrate as adults and those who do so as children is a well-established observation—indeed, it is the stuff of a rich popular literature and culture—and wider still are the differences in adaptive outcomes among native-born children of foreign-born parents (cf. Berrol, 1995; Child, 1943; Ebaugh & Chafetz, 2000; Nahirny & Fishman [1965] 1996; Piore, 1979). By 1914, Robert Park could write convincingly that "In America it has become proverbial that a Pole, Lithuanian, or Norwegian cannot be distinguished, in the second generation, from an American born of native parents" (in Park & Burgess, 1924 [1921], pp. 757–758). Thomas and Znaniecki, writing a century ago in *The Polish Peasant in Europe and America,* referred in passing to the "half-second" generation to describe foreign-born youths coming of age in the United States in contrast to "second-generation" native-born youths (1958 [1918–20], p. 1776). Warner and Srole, in *The Social Systems of American Ethnic Groups* (1945), distinguished the foreign-born—whom they called the "parental" or "P" generation—from the U.S.-born generations—the first of which (the offspring of the immigrants) was dubbed the "filial first" or "F1" generation, the second (the grandchildren of the immigrants) was dubbed F2, and so on. They divided the immigrant generation, in turn, into those who entered the United States after the age of 18 (labeled the P1 generation) and those who entered at age 18 or younger (the P2 generation). Both the P2 and the half-second concepts are akin to the terms "one-and-a-half" or "1.5 generation," which I coined in studies of Cuban and then Southeast Asian youths and applied particularly to those who had immigrated after reaching school age but before reaching adolescence (Rumbaut, 1991; Rumbaut & Ima, 1988; Rumbaut & Rumbaut, 1976; cf. Pérez Firmat, 1994).

Those segments of the foreign-born first generation consisting of persons who immigrated as adults or as children can be further refined into distinct types, depending on their ages and life stages at migration. Unique historical circumstances notwithstanding (such as the case of war-torn refugees), among those who immigrate as adults their general orientation and processes of adjustment and incorporation can be expected to vary significantly depending on whether they immigrated during *early, middle,* or *older adulthood.* For example, unlike the youngest of these (ages 18–24) who are more likely to be making their transitions to adulthood, young adults aged 25 to 34 generally migrate after having completed their educations, at the beginning of their work careers, and in their peak childbearing and family-formation years—but both bring a future-oriented outlook to their new arrangements. By contrast, mid-adulthood immigrants (aged 35–54) come with years of prior work experience, by and large have already had their children, and indeed are often motivated to migrate by the search for opportunities for their children; they are unlikely to shed their native language, customs, and identities in the process of their accommodation to the new society. Older adults (55 and older), who are relatively rare in immigrant (and even refugee) flows, are already near or at the end of their work careers and tend to be followers of children; they lack the plasticity of young migrants and are least likely to learn the new language or acculturate other than superficially to their new environment. Each of these types comprise persons who immigrate as adults, but their modes of economic, social, cultural, and psychological adaptation are likely to follow divergent paths.

Similarly, those immigrants who arrive as children can be further refined into three distinct groups, depending on whether their migration occurred during *early childhood* (ages 0–5), *middle childhood* (6–12), or *adolescence* (in their teens). Foreign-born adolescents and preschool immigrant children are at starkly different life stages at the point of migration, begin their adaptation processes in very different social contexts, and can be classified accordingly. Specifically, I have distinguished between (a) pre-school children (ages 0–5 at arrival), who retain virtually no memory of their country of birth, were too young to go learn to read or write in the parental language in the home country and are largely socialized here, whose experience and adaptive outcomes are most similar to the U.S.-born second generation—whom I have labeled the *"1.75" generation*; (b) pre-adolescent primary-school-age children (ages 6–12), who arrive having learned to read and write in the mother tongue at schools abroad, but whose education is largely completed here—the classic *"1.5" generation*; and (c) adolescents (ages 13–17 at arrival), who may or may not come with their families of origin and who either attend secondary schools after arrival or in the older ages may go directly into the workforce—a *"1.25" generation* whose experiences and adaptive outcomes are hypothesized to be closer to the first generation of immigrant adults than to the native-born second generation (Rumbaut, 1997a).

In a rigorous empirical test of this classification, which they referred to as "decimal" generations, Oropesa and Landale (1997) found significant differences between each of these generational cohorts, and strong cohort effects on language outcomes (being bilingual, or English or Spanish monolingual) in multivariate analyses of native-born and foreign-born second-generation children of Latin American origin—suggesting that these are distinctive populations and that it is inappropriate to combine them, at least when the focus of the analysis is on language or on phenomena affected by language competencies.

While more precise distinctions based on age and life stage at arrival are not only possible but theoretically important for the analysis of modes of acculturation among immigrant parents and their children (Portes & Rumbaut, 1996, 2001), the aim here is more limited. For purposes of estimating and depicting the size and composition of the immigrant-stock population of the United States, I distinguish initially by nativity between the "first" (foreign-born) and "second" (native-born of foreign parentage) generations, and contrast them to the "third-and-beyond" generations of native parentage. A demographic profile of the immigrant-origin population is then presented, broken down by detailed national origins. Next, I break down the foreign-born first generation (by applying the above age-based typology to both adults and children at different life stages at arrival in the United States) and the native-born second generation (by distinguishing between persons born in the United States of two foreign-born parents vs. persons born in the United States of one foreign-born parent and one U.S.-born parent), and estimate the size of these generational cohorts by national origin. Restricting the analysis to young adults 25 to 39 years old, the educational and occupational attainments of these generational cohorts are then compared for the larger national-origin groups. The data are drawn from an analysis of merged CPS annual demographic files for the 5 years from 1998 to 2002, yielding an overall sample of about 740,000 cases. A final section will address generational differences in language acculturation with pertinent data available not from the CPS but from the decennial census.

Measuring the First and Second Generations

Based on the 1998–2002 CPS merged data files, table 2.1 provides a simple tabulation of the first, second, and third-plus generations, classified solely by nativity, broken down by self-reported "race" and Hispanic origin. The table shows the weighted estimates for these populations (the merged data files contain a sample of approximately 750,000 cases), which apply to the civilian non-institutionalized resident population of the 50 states and the District of Columbia. The first-generation estimate *includes* nearly 2 million persons who were born in a foreign country but who had one parent who was a U.S. citizen. The Census Bureau classifies such persons as part of the "native-born population" and *excludes* them from the "foreign-born population," even though many are in fact recent U.S. arrivals. Most of them come from Mexico, Canada, Germany, Great Britain, Japan, Korea and the Philippines (countries from which immigration via marriages with U.S. citizens is common). Given the focus on immigrant generations, American Indians and Alaska Natives are not included in table 2.1. Included under first generation are island-born Puerto Ricans, who are U.S. citizens at birth; and under second generation are mainland-born Puerto Ricans of island-born parents. These figures do not include the 3.8 million who resided in Puerto Rico, or the population of other U.S. territories.

For an estimated national population of nearly 275 million, the CPS estimated a first generation of some 32 million, a second generation of about 29 million, and a third-and-beyond generation of 211 million. Thus, over 60 million people, or 22% of the total U.S. population, were of foreign birth or parentage around the year 2000—including 70% of the Mexican-origin population, 95% of the Cubans, Central and South Americans, and 90% of the Asians, reflecting the relative recency of their migrations. By contrast, only about one in ten of "non-Hispanic Whites" and "non-Hispanic Blacks" were of immigrant origin. Short of examining the specific national origins of the foreign born (to which we will turn next), this is the most detailed picture of the American ethnoracial mosaic, such as it is—consisting of one-size-fits-all pan-ethnic categories ("White," "Black," "Asian") that conceal far more than they reveal about the extraordinary ethnic diversity subsumed under those labels.

Moreover, as a methodological caveat, it is worth noting that the

Table 2.1   The Population of the United States, 1998–2002, by Immigrant Generation and Self-Reported Race and Hispanic Origin*

Race and Hispanic Origin	Generation in the United States**				% Foreign Parentage (1st & 2nd Generation)
	First	Second	Third+	Total	
Hispanic:	14,559,468	10,337,124	8,416,598	33,313,190	75
Mexican	8,457,887	7,016,435	6,503,121	21,977,443	70
Puerto Rican***	1,229,780	1,144,343	671,745	3,045,868	78
Cuban	905,626	338,565	74,763	1,318,954	94
Central–South American	3,295,509	1,296,310	218,938	4,810,757	95
Other Spanish	670,666	541,471	948,031	2,160,168	56
Non-Hispanic	17,513,047	18,540,381	202,892,992	238,946,420	15
White, non-Hispanic	8,341,444	14,339,679	170,899,381	193,580,504	12
Black, non-Hispanic	2,156,234	1,290,433	30,924,468	34,371,135	10
Asian, non-Hispanic	7,015,369	2,910,269	1,069,143	10,994,781	90
Total Population	32,072,515	28,877,505	211,309,590	272,259,610	22

Source: Merged Current Population Survey (CPS) annual demographic files, 1998–2002. Data are weighted CPS estimates.

*Based on self-reported responses to CPS questions on "race" and "Hispanic origin." American Indians and Alaska Natives are not included in this table.

**Immigrant generations are defined as follows: First = foreign-born; Second = U.S.-born of foreign-born parents; Third-and-beyond = U.S.-born of U.S.-born parents.

***Persons born in Puerto Rico are U.S. citizens; "first" generation here refers to island-born persons; "second" generation refers to mainland-born persons with island-born parents.

data on race and Hispanic origin are subjective self-reports chosen from a list of ethnoracial categories specified by the survey and may be susceptible to changes in self-definition over time, place, and historical circumstance. Consider, for example, the findings of an exploratory analysis of merged 1996–1997 CPS data (Rumbaut, 1998b), which focused on Cubans, Mexicans, and Puerto Ricans—the only distinctive Hispanic groups for which the CPS permits a self-report of ethnic identity (the remaining are lumped under Central/South Americans or Other Spanish). Against that *subjective* measure of ethnicity, I contrasted an alternative, *objective* measure based on the country of birth of respondents and of their mother and father. By using both approaches to "define" who is Cuban, the data yielded a weighted 1997 "subjective" estimate of about 1.2 million Cubans in the United States (based on the self-report of respondents who said they were Cuban), in contrast to an "objective" estimate of 1.6 million Cubans (based on the data on nativity—i.e., if either the respondent or one or both of the parents were born in Cuba, they were classified as of Cuban origin). I referred to that difference as "the case of the 400,000 missing Cubans," pointing out that subjective self-reports may miss large numbers of people who, as a result of intermarriage and assimilation, especially by the third generation, may stop identifying ethnically as such and fade into the "twilight of ethnicity"—or "fade to White," as far as what the CPS data on ethnic and racial identity can measure, much as Afro-Caribbean groups (Haitians, Jamaicans and other West Indians) have been observed to begin to "fade to Black" by the second generation (see Alba, 1990; Kasinitz, Battle, & Miyares, 2001; Waters, 1999). The "missing Cubans" tended to be U.S.-born, to live outside of the dense Miami enclave, more likely to be children of mixed marriages, and did not self-report as "Cuban" to the CPS question on Hispanic origin. For the Cuban sample, that was a large discrepancy (a 25% difference between the subjective and the objective measures of ethnicity). But for Mexicans and Puerto Ricans, the comparisons between subjective and objective definitions yielded only small single-digit discrepancies in size estimates, suggesting that those groups are more likely to maintain "thick" ethnic identities over time and generation in the United States. Naive intergenerational studies relying on self-report measures of ethnicity may thus underestimate the generational slippage and the erosion of ethnicity that may occur among differentially advantaged or disadvantaged groups by the third generation.

Table 2.2 focuses on the first and second generations only, but replaces the race and Hispanic origin classification for the specific countries of birth of the respondents (or, for the U.S.-born second genera-

Table 2.2   The Immigrant First and Second Generations of the United States,1998–2002, by Region and National Origin

Region and National Origin	First Generation (Foreign-born)			Second Generation (U.S.-born)			Total (1st + 2nd)	
	Weighted Estimate	Median Age	Sex % (male)	Weighted Estimate	Median Age	Sex % (male)	Weighted Estimate	% Foreign-Born
Latin America and Caribbean	15,006,700	35	52	10,422,919	12	50	25,429,619	59
Mexico	8,255,639	32	55	7,051,133	12	50	15,306,772	54
Cuba	928,831	52	49	436,143	17	48	1,364,974	68
Dominican Republic	669,359	37	40	446,122	10	51	1,115,481	60
El Salvador*	753,236	33	52	228,993	8	51	982,229	77
Guatemala	386,802	32	56	176,677	7	51	563,479	69
Other Central America	784,891	35	47	439,145	11	50	1,224,036	64
Colombia	486,272	39	46	236,848	12	47	723,120	67
Ecuador, Peru	552,521	37	50	263,477	10	51	815,998	68
Other South America	607,923	36	50	263,011	13	53	870,934	70
Haiti	472,444	38	51	241,569	11	48	714,013	66
Jamaica	441,896	40	47	250,275	13	51	692,171	64
Other West Indies	666,886	39	47	389,526	13	47	1,056,412	63
Asia and Middle East	8,015,700	38	48	3,884,143	13	50	11,899,843	67
Philippines	1,401,792	41	43	819,497	13	50	2,221,289	63
China	921,941	42	48	410,999	20	50	1,332,940	69
Hong Kong, Taiwan	510,773	37	47	195,997	13	48	706,770	72
Vietnam	894,880	37	51	306,718	8	57	1,201,598	74
Laos, Cambodia	259,436	36	46	213,762	10	48	473,198	55
India	991,647	35	55	332,436	11	51	1,324,083	75
Korea	764,097	38	41	274,146	12	50	1,038,243	74

Japan	428,232	37	44	335,253	35	48	763,485	56
Other S.E. Asia	821,489	34	49	368,338	7	50	1,189,827	69
Iran	286,976	43	55	125,722	12	51	412,698	70
Israel	91,448	36	56	68,570	16	44	160,018	57
Arab Middle East**	642,989	37	57	432,705	16	51	1,075,694	60
Europe and Canada	6,199,879	45	47	11,839,018	57	48	18,038,897	34
Canada	928,037	45	47	1,698,139	48	50	2,626,176	35
Great Britain	755,340	43	48	1,136,724	46	49	1,892,064	40
Ireland	174,020	54	47	613,326	60	46	787,346	22
Germany	1,125,007	40	42	1,537,435	40	49	2,662,442	42
NW Europe	582,790	46	46	1,384,288	63	46	1,967,078	30
Italy	481,498	58	53	2,146,489	66	48	2,627,987	18
Poland	424,106	46	46	1,034,512	71	45	1,458,618	29
Russia, Former USSR	809,073	39	47	883,402	70	47	1,692,475	48
SE Europe	920,008	47	50	1,404,703	51	47	2,324,711	40
Sub-Saharan Africa	536,755	34	55	200,166	10	50	736,921	73
All Others	880,258	35	53	644,116	18	49	1,524,374	58
Total Immigrant Origin	30,639,292	37	50	26,990,362	23	49	57,629,654	53
Puerto Rico***	1,243,848	43	47	1,319,611	22	48	2,563,459	49
Other U.S. Islanders***	212,266	36	51	179,639	19	44	391,905	54

Source: Merged Current Population Survey (CPS) annual demographic files, 1998–2002. Data are weighted CPS estimates.

*The CPS estimate for the Salvadoran population has been adjusted based on data from the 2000 census.

**Includes North African Arab countries.

***Persons born in Puerto Rico or other U.S. island territories (Guam, American Samoa, U.S. Virgin Islands), or whose parents were born there, have birthright citizenship.

tion, of their parents). The result yields a vastly different panorama, revealing the extraordinary diversity of national origins that comprises the so-called immigrant-stock population of the United States. In table 2.2, "native-born" Puerto Ricans and other U.S. islanders, as defined by the Census Bureau, are listed separately at the bottom of the table and not included with the immigrant-origin totals, to separate these different citizenship categories (although island-born vs. mainland born first and second generations are reported for them as well). Again the table provides weighted estimates for each group. Each of the groups listed have sample sizes at least in the thousands (the data for the first- and second-generation Mexicans are based on a sample size of over 50,000 cases), with only two of those listed (the Iranians and Israelis) limited to sample sizes in the hundreds, still large enough for reliable estimates. In addition, the table provides data on sex and age for each group, as well as the proportion of each group that is foreign-born.

The data presented in table 2.2 allow for an approximate rank ordering by size and median age of the largest national-origin groups within the first and second generations. As the data show, the Mexican-origin population clearly dwarfs all others in both the first and second generations. The first generation of Mexican immigrants totaled over 8.2 million persons—about 7 million more than the next sizable immigrant groups (the Filipinos, Chinese, Cubans, and Vietnamese)—and with a median age of 32 years they were one of the youngest immigrant populations in the United States as well. The Mexican-American second generation added another 7 million persons—over three times larger than the next largest second-generation group (the "old second generation" of Italian Americans, estimated at 2.1 million); but with a median age of 12 years the Mexican-American second generation was much younger than Italian Americans of foreign parentage (whose median age was 48, mostly the children of Italian immigrants who had come to the United States in the early 20th century). Both through immigration and natural increase, the Mexican-origin population of the United States is growing more rapidly than virtually any other group, and is as such of central interest for the study of immigrant intergenerational mobility.

More than three out of every four immigrants in the United States today come from Latin America and the Caribbean and Asia, with Mexico alone accounting for more than one fourth of the total. While only one fifth of the 31 million comprising the immigrant first generation hailed from Europe or Canada, nearly half of the 27 million comprising the second generation did so. Indeed, the Italian as well as the Canadian, German, British, Polish, and Russian second generations are larger than any other except for the Mexican—but their median ages are much older, reflecting the fact that they consist largely of the surviving offspring of immigrants who had come to the United States before World War II. The age data reveal sharp differences between the "old" and the "new" second generation. As table 2.2 shows, the median age of the combined European and Canadian second generations was 48 years, compared with a much younger average of 12 or 13 years for the U.S.-born offspring of Latin American, Caribbean, and Asian-origin immigrants. For the latter groups, the median age of the generation of their children is still very young—in fact, they mostly consist *of* children, with median ages ranging from 7 to 17 years for almost all the groups, the principal exception being the Japanese second generation with a median age of 35 years—a telling marker that reflects the recency of the immigration of the rest of the first-generation groups from Latin America and Asia.

Distinguishing Generational Cohorts

A more precise rendering of the generational composition of the *foreign-born* population (the "first" generation) is presented in table 2.3; a breakdown of the *native-born* population of immigrant parentage (the "second" generation) follows in table 2.4. Table 2.3 uses age at arrival (constructed from other variables in the CPS) to define and distinguish the foreign-born cohorts from one another; table 2.4 considers whether one or both parents were foreign-born.

Table 2.3 estimates the size and proportion of *foreign-born* persons who arrived in the United States as adults or children, broken down by our proposed typology of "seven ages" or life stages: early childhood (the "1.75" cohort who arrived as preschool children, ages 0–5); middle childhood (the "1.5" generation, ages 6–12); adolescence (the "1.25" cohort, ages 13–17); adult transition (ages 18–24); early adulthood (ages 25–34); middle adulthood (ages 35–54); and late adulthood (ages 55 and older). Of the approximately 30 million foreign-born (excluding Puerto Ricans and other U.S. islanders), an estimated 18 million (60%) arrived as adults and another 12 million (40%) as children under 18. Indeed, international migration is the province of the young: among the "1.0" adult cohorts, most came between the ages of 18 and 34 (44% of all immigrants), with the largest groups composed of immigrants 18 to 24 years old (about 6.9 million) and 25 to 34 years old (6.3 million). Very few (13%) immigrated in mid-adulthood (ages 35–54), and fewer still (3%) in late adulthood.

Remarkable generational-cohort variances by national origin sug-

Table 2.3 The "Immigrant First Generation" of the United States Population, 1998–2002, by Age/Life Stage at Arrival and National Origin

First Generation (foreign-born) by Age/Life Stage at Arrival

Region and National origin	Total N	Age 0–5 Early Childhood N	%	Age 6–12 Middle Childhood N	%	Age 13–17 Adolescence N	%	Age 18–24 Adult Transition N	%	Age 25–34 Early Adulthood N	%	Age 35–54 Middle Adulthood N	%	Age 55 and older Late Adulthood N	%
Latin America and Caribbean	14,845,274	1,976,265	13	1,887,070	13	2,413,614	16	3,729,898	25	2,863,994	19	1,679,849	11	294,534	2
Mexico	8,158,207	1,214,113	15	1,040,642	13	1,561,137	19	2,251,647	28	1,342,177	16	650,450	8	98,041	1
Cuba	910,189	105,862	12	102,673	11	76,281	8	98,982	11	217,109	24	244,343	27	64,939	7
Dominican Republic	663,278	82,119	12	101,308	15	93,027	14	133,232	20	136,970	21	97,743	15	18,879	3
El Salvador	753,236	59,498	8	86,418	11	131,684	17	248,828	33	146,186	19	66,242	9	14,380	2
Guatemala	385,372	39,271	10	49,485	13	69,563	18	105,058	27	73,261	19	46,804	12	1,930	1
Other Central America	768,606	117,999	15	93,498	12	93,033	12	189,628	25	184,182	24	78,215	10	12,051	2
Colombia	485,661	56,592	12	51,858	11	49,580	10	107,215	22	122,430	25	81,138	17	16,448	3
Ecuador, Peru	551,605	58,599	11	67,432	12	71,546	13	133,712	24	127,782	23	76,208	14	16,326	3
Other South America	601,742	82,135	14	69,138	11	59,797	10	124,257	21	164,892	27	89,847	15	11,676	2
Haiti	471,715	44,666	9	68,897	15	52,802	11	104,151	22	112,267	24	75,695	16	13,237	3
Jamaica	437,835	34,389	8	69,093	16	62,973	14	84,906	19	99,863	23	78,779	18	7,832	2
Other West Indies	657,828	80,622	12	86,628	13	92,191	14	148,282	23	136,875	21	94,385	14	18,845	3
Asia and Middle East	7,941,695	1,105,156	14	778,366	10	736,020	9	1,824,985	23	1,943,557	24	1,181,246	15	372,365	5
Philippines	1,384,723	189,994	14	136,648	10	116,643	8	298,039	22	345,733	25	212,919	15	84,747	6
China	891,402	76,750	9	73,618	8	67,970	8	170,695	19	253,867	28	162,804	18	85,698	10
Hong Kong, Taiwan	510,294	66,649	13	73,981	14	60,870	12	124,622	24	106,973	21	63,634	12	13,565	3
Vietnam	894,879	100,289	11	119,319	13	107,707	12	178,784	20	158,607	18	181,217	20	48,956	5

Origin															
Laos, Cambodia	259,436	34,684	13	35,790	14	38,754	15	57,957	22	49,580	19	33,714	13	8,957	3
India	989,481	85,988	9	57,585	6	56,345	6	342,715	35	273,926	28	127,976	13	44,946	5
Korea	762,645	168,368	22	64,688	8	55,170	7	131,765	17	201,026	26	114,226	15	27,402	4
Japan	422,058	129,473	31	24,650	6	24,636	6	79,974	19	107,028	25	50,134	12	6,163	1
Other SE Asia	819,742	118,944	15	84,266	10	88,631	11	205,206	25	199,385	24	101,970	12	21,340	3
Iran	286,306	21,336	7	31,142	11	44,458	16	57,447	20	69,337	24	43,793	15	18,793	7
Israel	90,677	22,253	25	11,794	13	10,289	11	22,882	25	21,064	23	2,395	3	0	0
Arab Middle East	630,052	90,428	14	64,885	10	64,547	10	154,899	25	157,031	25	86,464	14	11,798	2
Europe and Canada	5,500,303	1,367,132	25	596,576	11	448,436	8	981,809	18	1,183,116	22	765,428	14	157,806	3
Canada	775,014	209,516	27	96,033	12	69,428	9	137,757	18	155,390	20	96,918	13	9,972	1
Great Britain	666,672	173,840	26	65,973	10	51,335	8	118,548	18	163,846	25	83,828	13	9,302	1
Ireland	142,043	15,910	11	6,254	4	13,885	10	48,076	34	36,593	26	20,707	15	618	0
Germany	1,035,447	529,452	51	104,879	10	59,360	6	134,875	13	142,529	14	58,415	6	5,937	1
NW Europe	500,258	106,115	21	52,840	11	34,192	7	110,074	22	124,361	25	67,485	13	5,191	1
Italy	369,528	76,743	21	41,012	11	40,276	11	79,320	21	78,350	21	45,935	12	7,892	2
Poland	385,306	29,742	8	43,663	11	35,893	9	85,915	22	98,152	25	82,309	21	9,632	2
Russia, USSR	763,398	102,185	13	85,173	11	57,973	8	93,422	12	165,713	22	170,616	22	88,316	12
SE Europe	862,637	123,629	14	100,749	12	86,094	10	173,822	20	218,182	25	139,215	16	20,946	2
Sub-Saharan Africa	536,020	55,956	10	60,826	11	59,809	11	130,640	24	155,601	29	65,793	12	7,395	1
All Others	861,837	127,403	15	94,612	11	107,478	12	207,369	24	203,153	24	100,175	12	21,647	3
Total Immigrant Origin	29,685,129	4,631,912	16	3,417,450	12	3,765,357	13	6,874,701	23	6,349,421	21	3,792,491	13	853,797	3
Puerto Rico	1,155,060	290,737	25	178,584	15	169,440	15	242,623	21	146,896	13	103,069	9	23,711	2
Other U.S. Islanders	204,768	65,282	32	25,870	13	25,175	12	41,119	20	29,412	14	13,968	7	3,942	2

Source: Merged Current Population Survey (CPS) annual demographic files, 1998–2002. Data are weighted estimates.

**Table 2.4   The "Immigrant Second Generation" of the
United States Population, 1998–2002, by Parental Nativity and
National Origin**

Region and National Origin	TotalN	Second Generation (U.S.-born)			
		Both parents foreign-born (2.0)		One parent foreign-born, one parent U.S.-born (2.5)	
		N	%	N	%
Latin America					
and Caribbean	10,422,920	7,070,172	68	3,352,748	32
Mexico	7,051,133	4,821,870	68	2,229,263	32
Cuba	436,143	264,630	61	171,513	39
Dominican Republic	446,122	338,236	76	107,886	24
El Salvador	228,993	155,715	68	73,278	32
Guatemala	176,677	134,998	76	41,679	24
Other Central America	439,145	275,147	63	163,998	37
Colombia	236,849	164,804	70	72,045	30
Ecuador, Peru	263,477	171,816	65	91,661	35
Other South America	263,011	138,393	53	124,618	47
Haiti	241,569	206,686	86	34,883	14
Jamaica	250,275	152,247	61	98,028	39
Other West Indies	389,526	245,630	63	143,896	37
Asia and Middle East	3,884,141	2,660,039	68	1,224,102	32
Philippines	819,497	495,087	60	324,410	40
China	410,999	312,272	76	98,727	24
Hong Kong, Taiwan	195,997	146,617	75	49,380	25
Vietnam	306,717	263,885	86	42,832	14
Laos, Cambodia	213,762	186,206	87	27,556	13
India	332,436	289,268	87	43,168	13
Korea	274,146	174,327	64	99,819	36
Japan	335,253	139,169	42	196,084	58
Other SE Asia	368,338	243,923	66	124,415	34
Iran	125,721	83,395	66	42,326	34
Israel	68,570	39,879	58	28,691	42
Arab Middle East	432,705	286,011	66	146,694	34
Europe and Canada	11,839,017	5,106,917	43	6,732,100	57
Canada	1,698,139	374,031	22	1,324,108	78
Great Britain	1,136,724	266,046	23	870,678	77
Ireland	613,326	311,847	51	301,479	49

(continued)

Table 2.4 *(continued)*

Region and National Origin	TotalN	Second Generation (U.S.-born)			
		Both parents foreign-born (2.0)		One parent foreign-born, one parent U.S.-born (2.5)	
		N	%	N	%
Germany	1,537,435	378,747	25	1,158,688	75
NW Europe	1,384,288	539,508	39	844,780	61
Italy	2,146,489	1,224,123	57	922,366	43
Poland	1,034,512	677,662	66	356,850	34
Russia, USSR	883,402	541,983	61	341,419	39
SE Europe	1,404,702	792,970	56	611,732	44
Sub-Saharan Africa	200,166	121,070	60	79,096	40
All Others	644,115	338,859	53	305,256	47
Total Immigrant Origin	26,990,359	15,297,057	57	11,693,302	43
Puerto Rico	1,319,611	858,799	65	460812	35
Other U.S. Islanders	179,640	81,913	46	97,727	54

Source: Merged Current Population Survey (CPS) annual demographic files, 1998–2002.

gest both differences in migration histories as well as potentially significant implications for social and economic adaptation outcomes. For example, Mexico, El Salvador, and Guatemala—the sending countries with the highest proportion of undocumented immigrants in the United States —had the highest proportions of immigrants who arrived in their teens and early twenties, with the age cohorts 13 to 17 and 18 to 24 age accounting for nearly half of their immigrant totals. More than a third (35%) of those born in India, however, came to the United States between the ages of 18 and 24 alone, a reflection of the large number of young Indian immigrants who have arrived in the United States with college degrees and preferred job skills, and possibly of others who entered with H1B work visas or as international students (and who may subsequently gain permanent residence). In contrast, persons who came from Cuba, China, and the former Soviet

Union (all communist countries) were far more likely than other nationalities to have arrived in middle and late adulthood (with over a
third of the Cuban and Soviet/Russian totals coming in the 35 to 54
and 55-and-older arrival cohorts). Children under 6 years old predominated among those born in Germany, Japan, South Korea, Canada,
and Great Britain (countries with large numbers of international marriages to U.S. citizens, and of child adoptions in the case of South
Korea).

Table 2.4 focuses on the approximately 27 million *native-born* persons of foreign parentage who form the second generation, and distinguishes between two groups: a "2.0" generation of persons who were
born in the United States of two foreign-born parents, and the "2.5" cohort of persons who were born in the United States of one foreign-
born parent and one U.S.-born parent (approximating a more accul-
turated and intermarried population situated between the second and
third generations). These data show that a high proportion (43%) of
the second generation belongs to the 2.5 cohort, with one U.S.-born
parent. But as would be expected, considering the relative recency of
migration of different nationalities, regional origin reflects very sharp
differences, with 68% of the Latin American and Asian-origin second
generation having two foreign-born parents, in contrast to only 43% of
those of European and Canadian parentage.

Theoretically, we may hypothesize that these generational cohorts
differ significantly with regard to a variety of adaptation outcomes,
among which I have previously pointed to social mobility, language,
and acculturation. But that is an open empirical question—the answer
to which requires research that breaks down the first and second generations by nativity (of self and parents) and age at arrival into 1.25,
1.5, 1.75, 2.0, and 2.5 generational segments, rather than lumping
them together into a de facto second generation. If there are no significant differences between these cohorts, and if they add little or nothing to our understanding of adaptive trajectories in the "second generation" broadly conceived, then it would make practical as well as
theoretical sense to aggregate them. A similar logic would apply to the
life-stage distinctions made among immigrants who arrive as adults. It
is to that question I address the remainder of this study.

Educational and Occupational Attainment
across Generational Cohorts

Tables 2.5 and 2.6 focus on patterns of educational and occupational
attainment across these generational cohorts, for all young adults 25 to

39—ages at which formal education can be expected to have been completed, and which effectively control for age within each generational cohort (the mean age is 32 for each of the cohorts). Table 2.5 presents a pair of polar indicators of educational attainment—the percent of college graduates, and the percent of those who did not graduate from high school—for the largest national-origin groups in the data set, ranked by college graduation rates. The last column of table 2.5 provides a single indicator for the national origin groups as a whole—the *ratio* of college graduates to high school dropouts. The patterns are very revealing, both by region and nationality, and by generation. By region, a huge gulf is evident between the patterns for the "1.0" generation of immigrants who arrived as adults (18 and older) from Asia, Europe, and Africa, on the one hand—with college graduation rates above 50%, and high school dropout rates in the single digits—and for those from Latin America and the Caribbean as a whole—with only 10% of 25- to 39-year-olds having college diplomas, and over 50% without high school diplomas, virtually the reverse of the pattern for the first three regions. For immigrants from Latin America and the Caribbean as a whole, the ratio of college graduates to high school dropouts is 0.3, in sharp contrast to the ratios for immigrants from Africa (10.5), Europe and Canada (8.6), and Asia and the Middle East (7.6).

In most cases, these levels of education may be presumed to have been brought over from the home country—having arrived in the United States as adults, it is likely that they completed their education abroad—unlike the situation for those who arrived as children or who were born in the United States, who presumably completed their education here. These data, especially when they are examined by country of origin for the 1.0 cohorts who migrated as adults, reveal extremely sharp differences in human capital from the top groups (the Indians and Chinese, Russian Jews, Koreans) to the bottom (the Mexicans, Salvadorans, and Guatemalans), with patterns of attainment that are virtually the polar opposite of each other. Indeed, as table 2.5 shows, a wide gap exists between the *lowest* ranked 1.0 group in the *upper tier* of immigrant nationalities—the Filipinos, 50% of whom were college graduates, and only 6% failed to complete high school—and the *highest* ranked 1.0 groups in the *lower tier* of nationalities—the Jamaicans and the Cubans, with identical proportions of 18% with college degrees and 18% without a high school diploma. The rates for immigrant groups listed in the upper tier of table 2.5 are well above national norms, while those for immigrant groups in the lower tier are well below the national average. That is, among all 25- to 39-year olds-in the

Table 2.5 College Graduates and High School Dropouts among Immigrant-Origin Groups in the United States, 1998–2002, by Generation and National Origin: Persons 25–39 Years Old, Ranked by College Graduation Rates

| | First Generation (Foreign-born) Cohorts* | | | | | | | | Second Generation (US-born)* | | | | | | College Graduate to H.S. Dropout Ratio |
| | 1.0* | | 1.25* | | 1.5* | | 1.75* | | 2.0* | | 2.5* | | Total | | |
Grad	% College Grad	% Not HS Grad	% College Grad	% Not HS Grad	% College Grad	% Not HS Grad	% College Grad	% Not HS Grad	% College Grad	% Not HS Grad	% College Grad	% Not HS Grad	% College Grad	% Not HS Grad	
Region:															
Asia and Middle East	56	9	41	10	51	4	45	2	65	3	50	4	53	7	7.6
Europe and Canada:	53	6	41	8	37	8	37	8	46	4	39	4	43	5	8.6
Africa	39	4	46	6	60	3	46	0	44	0	48	0	42	4	10.5
Latin America and Caribbean:	10	52	6	55	14	34	18	23	23	15	21	14	13	42	0.3
National Origin															
India	81	4	64	3	72	3	85	2	82	4	70	0	79	3	26.3
Chinese (incl. Taiwan)	63	9	53	11	69	0	63	0	79	3	68	0	65	6	10.8
Russia, USSR	58	4	63	6	70	15	40	13	56	4	56	1	58	5	11.6
Korea	53	2	45	0	62	1	56	1	94	0	49	8	55	2	27.5
Middle East**	51	8	64	4	48	2	41	7	54	5	70	10	53	7	7.6
Other SE Asia	51	12	38	15	41	6	34	1	72	4	51	3	48	9	5.3
Great Britain	55	6	31	16	33	12	42	5	43	4	37	6	43	6	7.2
Other Europe	47	7	41	6	21	12	30	14	48	5	42	2	43	6	7.2

Other South America	41	12	44	10	36	6	40	7	51	2	60	7	43	10	4.3
Canada	58	4	36	19	52	3	43	11	31	5	36	5	42	6	7.0
Italy	53	12	35	9	32	2	31	5	44	2	39	3	41	3	13.7
Germany	55	1	37	0	52	0	36	4	52	2	37	7	41	4	10.3
Philippines	50	6	26	6	40	2	34	4	42	2	17	5	41	5	8.2
Jamaica	18	18	30	7	43	7	39	3	51	8	25	2	31	10	3.1
Cuba	18	18	12	20	23	10	29	5	44	6	40	1	29	10	2.9
West Indies	23	13	15	21	27	8	39	6	41	4	44	1	27	11	2.5
Colombia	28	14	8	20	23	8	29	3	35	6	16	4	26	12	2.2
Ecuador, Peru	23	22	18	15	33	17	26	20	38	4	29	4	25	18	1.4
Vietnam	14	28	21	18	42	11	33	0	83	0	40	11	23	20	1.2
Haiti	16	32	11	28	22	12	48	0	48	0	49	0	21	23	0.9
Other Central America	12	47	13	31	26	23	28	11	31	11	35	4	18	34	0.5
Dominican Republic	12	42	9	38	7	23	19	27	25	9	27	8	14	32	0.4
El Salvador, Guatemala	4	64	5	52	9	36	13	23	23	10	21	12	7	50	0.1
Mexico	5	65	3	67	6	47	9	33	12	20	15	19	6	53	0.1
Total Immigrant Origin	29	32	17	41	28	22	32	12	37	9	35	7	29	25	1.2
Other U.S. Islanders	16	32	16	23	21	13	39	2	15	11	24	1	22	15	1.5
Puerto Rico	21	29	16	30	14	29	10	28	12	22	17	22	14	25	0.6

Source: Merged Current Population Survey (CPS) annual demographic files, 1998–2002.

*Generational cohorts defined as follows: 1.0 = Foreign-born (F.B.), 18 years or older at U.S. arrival; 1.25 = F.B., 13-17 at U.S. arrival; 1.5 = F.B., 6–12 at U.S. arrival; 1.75 = F.B, 0–5 at U.S. arrival; 2.0 = U.S.-born, both parents born in foreign country; 2.5 = U.S.-born, one parent F.B., one parent U.S.-born.

** Includes Arab Middle East, Iran, and Israel.

Table 2.6. Upper White-Collar and Lower Blue-Collar Immigrant-Origin Workers in the United States, 1998–2002, by Generation and National Origin: Persons 25–39 Years Old, Ranked by Proportions in Upper White-Collar Occupations*

| | First Generation (Foreign-born) | | | | | | | | Second Generation (US-born) | | | | Total | | Upper White to Lower Blue Ratio |
| | 1.0* | | 1.25* | | 1.5* | | 1.75* | | 2.0* | | 2.5* | | | | |
Grad	% Upper White	% Lower Blue	% Upper White	% Lower Blue	% Upper White	% Lower Blue	% Upper White	% Lower Blue	% Upper White	% Lower Blue	% Upper White	% Lower Blue	% Upper White	% Lower Blue	
Region:															
Europe and Canada:	38	8	40	10	29	10	34	7	39	7	36	8	37	8	4.6
Asia and Middle East:	32	10	34	11	39	7	37	7	50	4	39	7	35	9	3.9
Africa	23	13	51	7	45	7	46	3	33	0	55	3	30	10	3.0
Latin America and Caribbean:	6	28	7	30	15	21	19	16	25	13	23	14	11	24	0.5
National Origin															
India	51	4	39	1	52	1	66	0	59	4	34	18	51	4	12.8
Chinese (incl. Taiwan)	39	6	42	1	46	4	61	0	64	2	45	4	45	4	11.3
Canada	51	5	28	14	36	8	37	8	44	7	39	7	42	7	6.0
Great Britain	48	4	43	16	22	17	44	7	37	10	35	9	39	8	4.9
Middle East***	29	9	51	1	41	3	35	13	45	6	50	0	37	7	5.3
Germany	40	4	43	5	30	4	35	5	45	5	33	8	36	6	6.0
Italy	39	5	47	0	35	3	31	7	38	6	35	5	36	6	6.0
Russia, USSR	31	8	41	8	56	5	42	6	41	4	44	12	35	8	4.4
Other Europe	34	10	40	10	23	13	24	9	36	7	38	7	34	9	3.8

Origin															
Philippines	29	14	25	16	38	5	41	5	39	5	33	9	32	11	2.9
Korea	22	7	45	5	41	3	24	7	36	0	33	13	29	6	4.8
Other SE Asia	26	10	28	22	27	16	28	10	44	4	38	9	28	12	2.3
Other South America	20	13	29	8	34	5	47	5	41	6	43	7	27	10	2.7
West Indies	20	9	20	15	25	3	46	16	44	7	35	18	27	10	2.7
Jamaica	19	10	20	10	38	11	41	36	40	1	29	22	27	11	2.5
Cuba	6	31	9	15	26	6	29	4	37	6	38	9	23	14	1.6
Colombia	15	14	7	26	26	10	12	5	42	9	42	14	20	14	1.4
Vietnam	11	23	23	17	36	10	29	5	53	0	35	0	20	17	1.2
Haiti	10	14	11	12	23	15	52	11	41	11	49	0	18	13	1.4
Ecuador, Peru	10	24	19	24	27	8	17	13	32	9	36	9	16	20	0.8
Other Central America	7	20	9	15	32	19	26	9	26	14	37	8	14	17	0.8
Dominican Republic	6	23	10	29	11	15	21	8	27	6	28	9	12	19	0.6
El Salvador, Guatemala	4	32	7	27	11	15	12	23	32	11	16	16	8	26	0.3
Mexico	3	32	5	36	8	28	12	19	17	17	19	15	7	29	0.2
Total Immigrant Origin	18	19	16	24	24	15	29	10	34	9	33	9	23	16	1.4
Other US Islanders	14	16	19	14	25	1	25	14	24	17	32	18	22	15	1.5
Puerto Rico	13	13	14	17	10	13	11	18	15	11	20	10	14	14	1.0

Source: Merged Current Population Survey (CPS) annual demographic files (March), 1998 through 2002.

*Upper White-Collar = professionals, executives, and managers; Lower Blue-Collar = operators, fabricators, and laborers.

**Generational cohorts defined as follows: 1.0 = Foreign-born (F.B.), 18 years or older at U.S. arrival; 1.25 = F.B., 13–17 at U.S. arrival; 1.5 = F.B., 6–12 at U.S. arrival; 1.75 = F.B., 0–5 at U.S. arrival; 2.0 = U.S.-born, both parents born in foreign country; 2.5 = U.S.-born, one parent F.B., one parent U.S.-born.

*** Includes Arab Middle East, Iran, and Israel.

United States, 28% were college graduates and 8% were high school dropouts (as estimated from the same merged 1998–2002 CPS data set). The rates for non-Hispanic Whites of native parentage (third-generation-plus) were 32 and 7%, respectively.

Table 2.5 details how those initial advantages or disadvantages of the 1.0 generation of different immigrant nationalities play out across the generational groupings. One pattern that stands out is the seemingly fairly rapid advancement of the most disadvantaged groups from the 1.0 to the 1.5 and subsequent generational cohorts. Mexicans, for example (with the largest sample size by far in this data set), start out at the 1.0 cohort with only 5% college graduation rates and 65% having less than a high school diploma. By the 1.5 generation, those figures improve to 6 and 47 (a tiny increase in college graduation rates, but a nearly 20 point reduction in dropout rates), then to 9 and 33 (in the 1.75 generation), 12 and 20 (in the 2.0), and 15 and 19 (among the 2.5ers). Thus, by the second generation (2.0 and 2.5), Mexican young adults in their late 20s and 30s had nearly tripled their college graduation rates, and cut by more than a third the proportion of high school dropouts, relative to their 1.0 co-ethnics. They were still lagging behind their Asian and European counterparts by wide margins, to be sure, but had made substantial progress in the course of a generation. By contrast, the children of the highly educated immigrant nationalities listed in table 2.5 tend to maintain the level of attainment of their parents from the 1.0 to the native-born second generation (although small sample sizes in some cells for some groups—yielding the 0's seen in some cells for dropout rates—call for caution in interpreting those results). The top achiever by far—and the most highly educated ethnic group in the United States—is the population of Indian origin: 81% of young adults in the 1.0 generation have college degrees whereas only 4% lacked a high school diploma; in the 2.0 generation, the commensurate figures were virtually identical: 82 and 4%, respectively.

Other patterns in table 2.5 are worth examining, but perhaps most notable is the finding across most of the national origin groups (with but a few exceptions) that those who arrived in the United States in their teen years (13–17)—the 1.25 cohort—do worse or no better than their 1.0 compatriots. Even among the Indians, a notable slippage is seen among the 1.25ers, whose college graduation rates of 64%—although still well above the national average—represent a drop of nearly 20 points from the 1.0, 1.75, and 2.0 averages. In general, the 1.25 cohort comes across as a distinctive and seemingly vulnerable one, all the more when compared with the patterns of their younger-at-arrival 1.5 and 1.75 compatriots. This evidence, added to other findings reviewed below, suggests that 1.25ers may undergo a comparatively more problematic adaptation, which should be taken into account in studies of the incorporation of the new second generation.

Table 2.6 sketches a similar picture, but switches the focus now to patterns of occupational attainment among employed young adults 25 to 39, again broken down by region and national-origin groups, and across by generational cohorts. (Data on labor force participation and unemployment rates were examined separately but are not shown here; by and large they point to similar levels of labor force participation for most groups and generational cohorts at these ages.) Specifically, table 2.6 presents a pair of polar indicators of occupational attainment—the percent employed in upper white-collar occupations (professionals, executives, and managers), and the percent working in lower blue-collar jobs (operators, fabricators, and laborers)—for the largest national origin groups in the data set, ranked by their proportion in upper white-collar professions. The last column of table 2.6 provides a single indicator for the national origin groups as a whole—the *ratio* of upper white-collar to lower blue-collar occupations.

The patterns and rankings are similar but not identical to those seen for education in the previous table. By region, for instance, the Europeans and Canadians now rank slightly ahead of Asians. By national origin, the Indians and Chinese remain at the top, with approximately half of them employed in the top occupations, although in the 1.0 generation (of recent immigrants 25- to 39-years-old) the Canadians, British, Germans, Italians, and Russians follow closely and exhibit occupational profiles well above national norms. (As a standard of comparison, for native-parentage non-Hispanic whites in this age group in the U.S., the proportions employed in the top and bottom occupational categories were 29 and 12%, respectively.) Bunched in the middle and matching national norms, with upper white-collar employment above 25% and lower blue-collar employment hovering around 10%, were groups originating from the Philippines, Korea, the Anglophone West Indies, and other Asian and South American countries. By contrast, about a third (32%) of all Mexicans, Salvadorans and Guatemalans in the 1.0 generation labored in the lowest rungs of the occupational ladder, with only a very small proportion enjoying employment in top occupations (3 or 4%)—a pattern characteristic of labor migrants that was, perhaps surprisingly, matched only by 1.0-generation Cubans, with 6% in top occupations and 31% concentrated in lower-blue-collar jobs.

That last datum illustrates and underscores again a larger analytical and methodological point in this sort of comparative cross-generational study, even when age at arrival and current age are controlled for; namely, the need to place the data in the larger historical context of particular migration flows and forms of reception. For example, in the Cuban case (as implied earlier), the 1.0 generation in their late 20s and 30s is made up preponderantly of those who came in the chaotic Mariel boatlift of 1980, and to a lesser extent the *balseros* of the early 1990s. In contrast, the Cuban 2.0 generation in these age groups, who are preponderantly the children of more advantaged and better-received Cubans who came to the United States in the early 1960s, shows an occupational profile that is the exact opposite of their 1.0 counterparts: 37% are employed in top professions, whereas only 6% are at the bottom of the occupational structure. It is not the passage of time and "generation" alone that explains this about-face in socioeconomic trajectories, but fundamental differences between these cohorts in their social class backgrounds, migration histories, and historical contexts of exit and reception. The data in tables 2.5 and 2.6 do not present controls for such varying historical circumstances, but they need of course to be contextualized in any definitive interpretation of intergenerational difference and social mobility.

Linguistic Acculturation across Generational Cohorts

For immigrants who come to the United States from non-English-speaking countries, learning to speak the new language is a basic step to enable them to participate in the life of the larger community, get an education, find a job, obtain access to health or social services, and apply for citizenship. Instrumentally, language is often cited as the principal initial barrier confronting recent immigrants, from the least educated peasants to the most educated professionals. But language assimilation is expected of immigrants not only for instrumental reasons but for symbolic ones as well, since language also lies at the core of national identities and ethnic solidarities (Portes & Rumbaut, 1996, 2001). Because the CPS does not collect data on language, I rely on data from the 2000 census (5% Public Use Microdata Sample) to examine patterns of linguistic acculturation among the generational cohorts composing the foreign-born population.

Table 2.7 presents cross-sectional census data on English language proficiency among all first-generation immigrants ages 5 or older from non-English-speaking countries, by age/life stage at arrival in the United States (i.e., early and middle childhood and adolescence for those younger than 18 at arrival, and early, middle, and late adulthood

Table 2.7   Language Acculturation among First-Generation Immigrants from non-English Speaking Countries, by Age/Life Stage at Arrival and Years in the United States, 2000*

	First Generation (foreign-born) by Age/Life Stage at Arrival					
English Proficiency and English Monolingualism	Age 0–5 Early Childhood	Age 6–12 Middle Childhood	Age 13–17 Adolescence	Age 18–34 Early Adulthood	Age 35–54 Middle Adulthood	Age 55+ Late Adulthood
Speaks English not well or at all	11.2	14.4	33.6	37.3	53.9	73.5
Speaks English very well	68.9	61.4	37.2	34.1	21.6	12.7
Speaks English only	37.4	14.8	9.1	8.6	7.0	6.7
By time of arrival in the U.S.						
Speaks English not well or at all						
Arrived after 1980	13.5	16.8	38.1	41.4	54.6	73.8
Arrived before 1980	6.9	9.1	21.2	26.6	51.8	71.0
Speaks English very well						
Arrived after 1980	62.8	56.6	33.2	31.2	21.2	12.5
Arrived before 1980	80.6	72.1	48.2	41.8	22.9	14.3
Speaks English only						
Arrived after 1980	25.4	9.7	7.1	6.9	6.3	6.5
Arrived before 1980	52.0	24.5	14.1	12.8	9.4	9.2

Source: 5% PUMS, 2000 U.S. Census.

*Excluded from this table are immigrants from English-speaking countries, 88% of whom speak English only regardless of age at arrival in the United States. Those countries include: The United Kingdom, Ireland, Canada, Bermuda, Jamaica and the anglophone West Indies, Guyana, Australia, and New Zealand.

for those 18 and older at arrival). Excluded from this analysis are immigrants from English-speaking countries, 88% of whom speak English only, regardless of their age at arrival in the United States. (These countries include the United Kingdom, Ireland, Canada, Bermuda, Jamaica and the anglophone West Indies, Guyana, Australia, and New Zealand.) The table focuses on three (self-reported) language measures: the proportion who speak English "not well or at all" versus those who speak English "very well" (among persons who report speaking a language other than English at home), and the proportion who speak English only.

Without exception, sharp linear differences thrive in each of the language measures in the generational progression from those who arrived in early childhood (ages 5 or younger) through those who arrived in late adulthood (ages 55 or older), although the differences are not equivalent between the cohorts. Thus, among persons who use a language other than English at home, only 11.2% of early-childhood immigrants spoke English "not well or at all," as did 14.4% of those who came in middle childhood (ages 6–12); that figure jumps to 33.6% among those who came as adolescents (ages 13–17), and 37.3% of those who came in early adulthood (ages 18–34); more than half (53.9%) of those who came in mid-adulthood (ages 35–54) did not speak English well or at all, along with nearly three fourths (73.5%) of those who were 55 or older at arrival. The proportions who speak English "very well" are reversed, ranging from over two thirds (68.9%) of early-childhood immigrants to only 12.7% of late-adulthood immigrants. (Subtracting from 100% the sum of those two indicators yields the proportion who reported speaking English "well.") Indeed, the data suggest that already among the foreign-born from non-English-speaking countries, a process of language extinction is under way, with over a third (37%) of those who came in early childhood speaking English only, and 15% of those who came in middle childhood; the English-only proportions for the other cohorts fall below 10%.

To illustrate the influece of time in the United States on language competencies, the bottom panel of table 2.7 shows the outcomes for immigrants who arrived in the United States before 1980 and those who came after 1980. The pronounced linear differences between generational cohorts persist, and indeed they are clearly stronger than time in the United States, especially at the poles. For example, among those who arrived in the United States after 1980 and spoke English "not well or at all," the generational progression moves from 13.5% of those who came in early childhood to 73.8% of those who arrived in late adulthood; the corresponding figures for longer-established immigrants who arrived in the U.S. before 1980 range from only 6.9% of the early-childhood cohort to 71% of the late-adulthood cohort. The greatest improvement in this measure exists among those who immigrated in their teens or early adulthood. When the measure is the ability to speak English "very well," the increases are largest over time in the United States for the youngest arrival cohorts and minuscule for the oldest arrival cohorts, as table 2.7 demonstrates. Finally, the shift to English-only is especially pronounced for those who arrived before their teen years and who have been in the United States for more than two decades. For example, in the middle-childhood cohort, only 9.7% of those who arrived after 1980 spoke English only, but the proportion jumped to 24.5% among those who arrived in the U.S. before 1980; the corresponding figures for the early-childhood cohort are 25.4 and 52% for those who arrived in the U.S. after and before 1980, respectively. Breaking down the foreign-born first generation into distinct generational cohorts thus clarifies the process of language acquisition and makes plain the importance of accounting for age and life stage at arrival in that central aspect of the process of immigrant incorporation.

CONCLUSION

I have argued in the forgoing that distinguishing among distinctive generational cohorts defined by age at arrival and nativity (of self and parents) makes the definition of "immigrant second generation" theoretically and empirically more precise, and thus avoids semantic confusion. Life stages and generational cohorts matter in processes of adaptation and social mobility; they are not epiphenomena. Current evidence tends to support both the value and the validity of these calibrations—as well as the need for greater consensus in the conceptualization and operationalization of second generation. Intergenerational analyses of such multiple outcomes as explored here on a preliminary basis, however, need to take into account multiple other possible determinants, and situate and interpret the data within larger social and historical contexts. Not all second generations are "new," for example, as are the Vietnamese or the Cambodians in the United States; others are only the latest second generation in a much longer history of sustained migration, as is the case of the Mexicans in the United States (cf.

López & Stanton-Salazar, 2001). "First waves" and later waves of migrants from the same sending country (such as the 1975 first wave of Vietnamese refugees vs. subsequent flows) may differ fundamentally in their class origins, ethnic composition, motives for migration, and reception in the United States—that is, there are different "vintages" in migration flows, not just "waves," need to be taken specifically into account in studies of intergenerational mobility, to avoid confounding period and cohort effects.

At the same time, I have also pointed to a variety of methodological and definitional problems with such measures as age at arrival (e.g., there may not be a single date of arrival but multiple entries), nativity (e.g., definitions of "foreign-born" and "native-born" in U.S. official statistics have varied historically and are based on assignments of citizenship status, while immigrant status is not asked in the CPS or the decennial census; international migration statistics differ in the meanings of common terms and measures), and the determination and allocation of ethnicity for children of mixed marriages, where the ethnic and national origin of the mother and father differs. The continued reliance on one-size-fits-all racial categories in the United States (an "ethnoracial pentagon" of White, Black, Asian, Hispanic/Latino, and American Indian/Alaska Native categories), in lieu of more refined classifications by national origin and ethnicity, is particularly pernicious to an understanding of the history, diversity, and complexity of the new immigration, and to the study of processes of acculturation, assimilation, and social mobility—indeed, to theory building and policymaking. All of these considerations, in turn, underscore the need for better data and better measures that can help address those specific problems in comparative research.

Among urgent data needs, perhaps none is more important for the study of intergenerational mobility than the restoration of the parental nativity question in the decennial U.S. census—and in the recently implemented American Community Survey (ACS). The ACS is intended to replace the long-form questionnaire of the decennial census and, if funding is secured (although that is not certain at this writing), to collect long-form-type data annually between decennial censuses. As stated previously, the data on parental nativity in the annual CPS yields much valuable information for the study of the "new second generation," but the CPS is hampered by small sample sizes when the available data are broken down by national origin and generational cohort—let alone by other basic demographic variables, such as age and sex. These variables reduce cell sizes to the point where it becomes impossible to carry out reliable analyses, even when merging multiple years of the CPS (as done here). In addition, data on English language use and ability (which is included in the census long-form) are not collected by the CPS, but should—all the more since the CPS remains at present the principal source of national-level information on second-generation populations.

The need for such data, from the national to the local level, remains critical both for social science and for public policy. However, in the United States at present, dark clouds are looming on the data horizon, for a variety of political, practical, and budgetary reasons. Current plans call for dropping the long-form questionnaire (the one which asks questions about nativity, citizenship, year of entry, and language, among many other items) from the 2010 census, but there is no assurance that the U.S. Congress will fund its intended replacement, the ACS—a scenario that could precipitate a "data crisis" for the study of international migration and its consequences in the United States (see Grieco, 2003). Even if basic funding is ensured, the need to add critical items to the ACS questionnaire, and to the CPS and other relevant surveys, remains to be negotiated. Thus, clarifying and specifying our own definitions and methodological approaches in the study of the newest first and second (and soon to become third) generations has practical as well as theoretical value. It would not only help the field of immigration studies and expand our knowledge of a phenomenon of both national and international importance that is transforming both sending and receiving societies, but also make a compelling case for averting a potential data crisis and boost the likelihood that urgent data needs are met.

Nonetheless, no amount of methodological refinement, even if basic data needs are met, will lift the study of international migration and its transformational consequences beyond an elegant but ahistorical positivism unless it is guided by what Elder (1978) long ago characterized, in distilling the chief contribution of Thomas and Znaniecki's *The Polish Peasant* (1958) as "a processual view of group and individual experience in changing and historically specific times, but one that does not lose sight of the larger context and its structural trends" (p. S17). In addition to pointing to the significance of age-bounded generational cohorts in the study of immigration and adaptation processes, I have also sought to underscore the importance of taking historical influences into account, by placing the objects of study in their larger sociohistorical contexts. It is such contexts, after all, that determine what meaning the data will have. The past, as William Faulkner saw long ago, is never dead. It is not even past.

REFERENCES

Alba, R. D. (1985). *Italian Americans: Into the twilight of ethnicity.* Englewood Cliffs, NJ: Prentice-Hall.

Alba, R. D. (1990). *Ethnic identity: The transformation of White America.* New Haven: Yale University Press.

Aleinikoff, T. A., & Rumbaut, R. G. (1998). Terms of belonging: Are models of membership self-fulfilling prophecies? *Georgetown Immigration Law Journal, 13*(1), 1–24.

Berrol, S. C. (1995). *Growing up American: Immigrant children in America, then and now.* New York: Twayne Publishers.

Boyd, M. (1998). Triumphant transitions: Socioeconomic achievement of the second generation in Canada. *International Migration Review, 32*(4, Winter), 853–876.

Bozorgmehr, M. (1997). Internal ethnicity: Iranians in Los Angeles. *Sociological Perspectives, 40*(3), 387–408. Special issue on "Immigration and Incorporation," R. G. Rumbaut & C. F. Hohm, eds.

Caplan, N., Choy, M. H., & Whitmore, J. K. (1991). *Children of the Boat People: A study of educational success.* Ann Arbor: University of Michigan Press.

Child, I. L. (1943). *Italian or American? The second generation in conflict.* New Haven, CT: Yale University Press.

Cropley, A. J. (1983). *The education of immigrant children: A social-psychological introduction.* London: Croom Helm.

DuBois, W. E. B. (1989 [1903]). *The souls of Black folk.* New York: Bantam.

Ebaugh, H. R., & Chafetz, J. S. (2000). *Religion and the new immigrants: Continuities and adaptations in immigrant congregations.* Walnut Creek, CA: AltaMira Press.

Elder, G. H., Jr. (1978). Approaches to social change and the family. *American Journal of Sociology, 84,* S1–S38.

Erikson, E. H. (1964). Psychological reality and historical actuality. In E. H. Erikson (Ed.), *Insight and responsibility* (pp. 161–215). New York: W. W. Norton.

Erikson, E. H. (1968). *Identity: Youth and crisis.* New York: W. W. Norton.

Gans, H. J. (1992). Second generation decline: Scenarios for the economic and ethnic futures of the post-1965 America immigrants. *Ethnic and Racial Studies, 15* (April), 173–192.

García, M. C. (1996). *Havana USA: Cuban exiles and Cuban Americans in South Florida, 1959–1994.* Berkeley: University of California Press.

Gibson, C. J., & Lennon, E. (1999). Historical census statistics on the foreign-born population of the United States: 1850–1990. *Population Division Working Paper No. 29.* Washington, DC: U.S. Bureau of the Census. Online at http://www.census.gov/population/www/documentation/twps0029/twps0029.html#data

Glenn, E. N. (1986). *Issei, Nisei, war bride: Three generations of Japanese women in domestic service.* Philadelphia: Temple University Press.

Grenier, G. J., & Pérez, L. (2003). *The legacy of exile: Cubans in the United States.* Boston: Allyn and Bacon.

Grieco, E. M. (2003). Census 2010 and the foreign born: Averting the data crisis. *MPI Policy Brief, 1* (February). Washington, DC: Migration Policy Institute. Online at http://www.migrationpolicy.org/pubs/MPIPolicyBrief-Census.pdf

Hein, J. (1995). *From Vietnam, Laos, and Cambodia: A refugee experience in the United States.* New York: Twayne Publishers.

Hernández, D. J. (1999). *Children of immigrants: Health, adjustment, and public assistance.* Washington, DC: National Academy of Sciences Press.

Hing, B. O. (1993). *Making and remaking Asian America through immigration policy, 1850–1990.* Stanford, CA: Stanford University Press.

Jasso, G., & Rosenzweig, M. R. (1990). *The new chosen People: Immigrants in the United States.* New York: Russell Sage Foundation.

Jensen, L., & Chitose, Y. (1994). Today's second generation: Evidence from the 1990 U.S. Census. *International Migration Review, 28*(4, Winter), 714–735.

Kasinitz, P., Battle, J., & Miyares, I. (2001). Fade to black? The children of West Indian immigrants in South Florida. In R. G. Rumbaut & A. Portes (Eds.), *Ethnicities: Children of immigrants in America* (pp. 267–300). Berkeley and New York: University of California Press and Russell Sage Foundation.

Kertzer, D. I. (1983). Generation as a sociological problem. *Annual Review of Sociology, 9,* 125–149.

Leonard, K. (1992). *Ethnic choices: California's Punjabi-Mexican-Americans, 1910–1980.* Philadelphia: Temple University Press.

Levitt, P., & Waters, M. C. (Eds.). (2002). *The changing face of home: The transnational lives of the second generation.* New York: Russell Sage Foundation.

López, D. E., & Stanton-Salazar, R. D. (2001). Mexican Americans: A second generation at risk. In R.G. Rumbaut & A. Portes (Eds.), *Ethnicities: Children of immigrants in America* (pp. 57–90). Berkeley and New York: University of California Press and Russell Sage Foundation.

Mannheim, K. (1996 [1928]). The problem of generations. In W. Sollars (Ed.), *Theories of ethnicity: A classical reader* (pp. 109–155). New York: Oxford University Press.

Milosz, C. (1994 [1980]). Nobel lecture. In S. Allén (Ed.), *Nobel Lectures, Literature: 1968–1980.* Singapore: World Scientific Publishing, Inc.

Min, P. G. (1995). Korean Americans. In P. G. Min (Ed.), *Asian Americans: Contemporary trends and issues* (pp. 199–231). Thousand Oaks, CA: Sage.

Nahirny, V. C., & Fishman, J. A. (1996 [1965]). American immigrant groups: Ethnic identification and the problem of generations. In W. Sollars (Ed.), *Theories of Ethnicity: A Classical Reader* (pp. 266–281). New York: New York University Press.

Oropesa, R. S., & Landale, N. S. (1997). In search of the new second generation: Alternative strategies for identifying second generation children and understanding their acquisition of English. *Sociological Perspectives,* *40*(3), 427–455. Special issue on "Immigration and Incorporation," R. G. Rumbaut & C. F. Hohm, eds.

Park, R. E., & Burgess, E. W. (1924 [1921]). *Introduction to the science of sociology.* Chicago: University of Chicago Press.

Pérez Firmat, G. (1994). *Life on the hyphen: The Cuban-American way.* Austin: University of Texas Press.

Perlmann, J., & Waldinger, R. (1997). Second generation decline? Children of immigrants, past and present—A reconsideration. *International Migration Review, 31*(Winter), 893–922.

Piore, M. J. (1979). *Birds of passage: Migrant labor and industrial societies.* Cambridge: Cambridge University Press.

Portes, A. (Ed.). (1996). *The new second generation.* New York: Russell Sage Foundation.

Portes, A., & Rumbaut, R. G. (1996). >I>Immigrant America: A portrait (2nd ed.). Berkeley: University of California Press.

Portes, A., & Rumbaut, R. G. (2001). *Legacies: The story of the immigrant second generation.* Berkeley and New York: University of California Press and Russell Sage Foundation.

Portes, A., & Zhou, M. (1993). The new second generation: Segmented assimilation and its bariants. *Annals of the American Academy of Political and Social Sciences, 530*(November), 74–96.

Riley, M. W. (1987). The significance of age in sociology. *American Sociological Review, 52,* 1–14.

Rumbaut, R. G. (1991). The agony of exile: A study of the migration and adaptation of Indochinese refugee adults and children. In J. Frederick L. Ahearn & J. Athey (Eds.), *Refugee children: Theory, research, and practice* (pp. 53–91). Baltimore: Johns Hopkins University Press.

Rumbaut, R. G. (1994). The crucible within: Ethnic identity, self-esteem, and segmented assimilation among children of immigrants. *International Migration Review, 28*(4, Winter), 748–794.

Rumbaut, R. G. (1995). Vietnamese, Laotian, and Cambodian Americans. In P. G. Min (Ed.), *Asian Americans: Contemporary trends and issues* (pp. 232–270). Thousand Oaks, CA: Sage.

Rumbaut, R. G. (1997a). Assimilation and its discontents: Between rhetoric and reality. *International Migration Review, 31*(4, Winter), 923–960.

Rumbaut, R. G. (1997b). Ties that bind: Immigration and immigrant families in the United States. In A. Booth & A. C. Crouter, & N. S. Landale (Eds.), *Immigration and the family: Research and policy on U.S. immigrants* (pp. 3–46). Mahwah, NJ: Lawrence Erlbaum.

Rumbaut, R. G. (1998a). Coming of age in immigrant America. *Research perspectives on migration, 1*(6), 1–14. Online at: http://www.migrationpolicy.org/files/RPMVol11-No16.pdf

Rumbaut, R. G. (1998b). *Growing up American in Cuban Miami: Ambition, language, and identity in the "1.5" and second generations.* Paper presented at the XXI International Congress of the Latin American Studies Association, Chicago.

Rumbaut, R. G. (2003). *Legacies: The story of the immigrant second generation in early adulthood.* The Sorokin Lecture, presented at the 74th annual meeting of the Pacific Sociological Association, Pasadena.

Rumbaut, R. G. (2004 [1976]). The one-and-half generation: Crisis, commitment, identity. In P. I. Rose (Ed.), *The dispossessed: An anatomy of Exile.* University of Massachusetts Press.

Rumbaut, R. G. (2005). The melting and the pot: Assimilation and variety in American life. In P. Kivisto (Ed.), *Incorporating diversity: Rethinking assimilation in a multicultural age.* Boulder, CO: Paradigm Publishers.

Rumbaut, R. G., & Cornelius, W. A. (Eds.). (1995). *California's immigrant children: Theory, research, and implications for educational policy.* La Jolla, CA: Center for U.S.–Mexican Studies, University of California, San Diego.

Rumbaut, R. G., & Ima, K. (1988). *The adaptation of outheast Asian refugee youth: A comparative study.* Washington, DC: U.S. Office of Refugee Resettlement.

Rumbaut, R. G., & Portes, A. (Eds.). (2001). *Ethnicities: Children of immigrants in America.* Berkeley and New York: University of California Press and Russell Sage Foundation.

Rumbaut, R. D., & Rumbaut, R. G. (1976). The family in exile: Cuban expatriates in the United States. *American Journal of Psychiatry 133*(4), 395–399.

Ryder, N. B. (1965). The cohort as a concept in the study of social change. *American Sociological Review, 30,* 843–861.

Suárez-Orozco, C., & Suárez-Orozco, M. M. (2002). *Children of immigration.* Cambridge, MA: Harvard University Press.

Thomas, W. I., & Znaniecki, F. (1958 [1918–1920]). *The Polish peasant in Europe and America.* New York: Dover.

Ueda, R. (1981). Naturalization and citizenship. In S. Thernstrom & A. Orlov & O. Handlin (Eds.), *Harvard encyclopedia of American ethnic groups* (pp. 734–748). Cambridge, MA: Harvard University Press.

Warner, W. L., & Srole, L. (1945). The social systems of American ethnic groups. New Haven, CT: Yale University Press.

Waters, M. C. (1990). *Ethnic options: Choosing identities in America.* Berkeley: University of California Press.

Waters, M. C. (1999). *Black identities: West Indian immigrant dreams and American realities.* Cambridge and New York: Harvard University Press and Russell Sage Foundation.

Wong, M. G. (1995). Chinese Americans. In P. G. Ming (Ed.), *Asian Americans: Contemporary trends and issues* (pp. 58–94). Thousand Oaks, CA: Sage.

Zhou, M. (1997). Growing up American: The challenge confronting immigrant children and children of immigrants. *Annual Review of Sociology, 23,* 63–95.

Zhou, M., & Bankston, C. L. (1998). *Growing up American: How Vietnamese children adapt to life in the United States.* New York: Russell Sage Foundation.

Zolberg, A. R. (1995). From invitation to interdiction: U.S. foreign policy and immigration since 1945. In M. S. Teitelbaum & M. Weiner (Eds.), *Threatened peoples, threatened borders: World migration and U.S. policy* (pp. 117–159). New York: W. W. Norton.

Zolberg, A. R., Suhrke, A., & Aguayo, S. (1989). *Escape from violence: Conflict and the refugee crisis in the developing world.* New York: Oxford University Press.

Commentary

Convergence and Divergence in the Developmental Contexts of Immigrants to the United States

Andrew J. Fuligni

R umbaut succeeds in demonstrating that the manner in which immigrants adapt to American society is not uniform and can depend to a great extent upon the age at which they come to this country. As such, the chapter produces findings that the impact of major social and historical events on individuals' life course trajectories has much to do with the developmental period during which these events occur. For the individuals involved, packing up and leaving one's native society for another can seem to be as life-altering an experience as more commonly studied historical events such as war and dramatic economic change. The nature of individuals' internal psychology and external social context can be dramatically different on both sides of the immigration event, potentially resulting in a sharp alteration in the life course. As the findings demonstrate, however, the magnitude and direction of the alteration can depend upon how far along the life course the act of immigration occurs. It would seem, therefore, that for many developmental outcomes Rumbaut would need to change his original axiom of "origins shape destinies" to become "origins *and* timing shape destinies."

As Rumbaut acknowledges, the available data do have limitations and caution is required before the findings can be considered definitive. Most notably, the Current Population Survey (CPS) data are not longitudinal and the results regarding the age of immigration could reflect differences that would have placed individuals on the same life course trajectories regardless of whether immigration ever occurred. There may be preexisting differences in skills, motivation, and cultural orientation between individuals and families who come to this country at different ages. For example, if the average age at which children come to the United States with their families is approximately 7 or 8 years (as suggested by the data from Rumbaut [Rumbaut, this volume] Children of Immigrants Longitudinal Study [CILS]), what does that say about the minority of families and children that come to this country when the children are very young or much older? Are there group differences in human or social capital? Does the timing of immigration along the life course reflect different preferences or choice patterns among individuals and families? These questions could be partially answered by more probing analyses of the CPS and CILS data, as well as other data sets, and seem to be important ones to answer in order to best understand Rumbaut's findings. Another limitation of the findings is that the CILS analyses are based upon all ethnic groups combined, and it would be reassuring to know that the different ethnic groups do not vary much in terms of age of immigration, thereby avoiding a confound between age of immigration and national origin.

Addressing these limitations would help to clarify the findings and provide more confidence in their reliability, but I do not expect further analyses to change the conclusions substantially. The data presented by Rumbaut are fairly convincing and will likely hold up under further scrutiny: age of immigration does make a difference for many developmental outcomes. The question we are left with, then, is "Why?" Why would age of immigration make a difference in the life course trajectories of immigrants? I shall attempt to provide here at least a partial answer to this question by considering how the proximal, functional environments of immigrants vary according to the age at which they enter this country. Contexts such as schools, families, and peers play significant roles in shaping developmental outcomes such as educational attainment, language ability and usage, and risky and criminal behavior. Therefore, it is possible that age of immigration shapes the life course of the foreign born through its effects on these critical developmental contexts. In the discussion below, I attempt to characterize what these developmental contexts are like for the 1.00, 1.25, 1.50, and 1.75 generations. This exercise suggests that the primary developmental contexts are quite similar for generations 1.00 and 1.25 but that there is a greater distance between the contexts of these groups and those of generation 1.50 and 1.75, who in turn experience more similar school, family, and peer environments. These patterns of convergence and divergence in contexts, in turn, likely explain some of the similarities and differences in developmental outcomes among the different cohorts of immigrants.

GENERATION 1.00

According to Rumbaut's typology, generation 1.00 represents the cohort of the foreign born who entered the United States at 18 years or age or older. These individuals have spent the majority of what has traditionally been considered their formative years in their native societies. Their developmental contexts, therefore, are likely to be drastically different from those of immigrants who entered the United States at younger ages. For example, the schooling of most members of this immigrant group will have taken place in their native countries, which generally have much lower access to high school and postsecondary education than the United States. Only a minority of the population in most sending countries has received education beyond the primary school level (UNESCO, 1999). For example, Mexico has only 6 years of compulsory schooling as compared with 10 years in the United States, and less than 50% of the population attends secondary school. Generation 1.00, therefore, has not had the same access to education as the other cohorts and will inevitably have lower levels of educational attainment as compared with other groups. As Rumbaut noted in his analyses of the CPS data, perhaps the most notable trend across the different cohorts of immigrants is the rise in high school completion as the age of immigration declines.

Members of generation 1.00 also have had almost exclusive exposure to their native language for 18 or more years, with the extent of their exposure to English varying according to their country of origin. Language learning is heavily dependent upon age, and it is much more difficult to learn new languages beyond the juvenile years (Bloom, 1998). Members of generation 1.00, therefore, should be virtually fluent in their native languages and have more difficulty learning English upon arrival in the United States.

In addition to having different experiences prior to their arrival in the United States, the nature of the school, family, and peer contexts of generation 1.00 within this country is quite different from for other cohorts of immigrants. Schooling within the United States is unlikely to occur for these individuals because they arrive beyond the mandatory age of schooling in this country (i.e., 16 years), and their mature age and relative difficulty with the English language provide them with few options even if they wished to pursue secondary schooling (Mc-Donnell & Hill, 1993). In terms of the family context, generation 1.00 is less likely than other groups to come to the United States with members of their family of origin. As adults, members of generation 1.00 are more likely to be married and to have dependents in both the United States and their native countries, resulting in a need to seek gainful employment. In fact, the likely intention of much of generation 1.00 is to seek employment rather than education in the United States. Together, factors such as limited educational options and the immediate demands of supporting oneself and others means that additional educational attainment is unlikely upon this generation's arrival in the United States.

Finally, the family and peer contexts of generation 1.00 are unlikely to involve much use of the English language even in the United States. The adult family members who immigrated with generation 1.00 likely speak their native language to one another, and the peer group of this generation is composed of predominantly co-ethnic immigrants who also speak the native language to one another (Jia, 2004). Along with the increased availability of native language media in the United States (e.g., Spanish television channels, Chinese newspapers), the family and peer contexts of Generation 1.00 do not present many demands for learning the English language. As a result, the English language use, ability, and even preference scores of this generation will tend to be much lower than for other groups, whereas the reverse would be the case for their native language.

GENERATION 1.25

Even though members of generation 1.25 arrive in the United States before 18 years of age (between 13 and 17 years), they generally experience developmental contexts that are quite similar to those of generation 1.00 both before and after coming to this country. These individuals have received virtually all, if not all, of their schooling in their native country. The limited access to secondary schooling in most sending nations means that many immigrants who come in their mid to late teens are likely to have been out of school for a period of time before coming to the United States. In addition, those who enter after turning 16 years of age are not mandated to attend school in the United States. For those who do wish to continue their schooling in the United States, the educational options available to them are quite limited. The difficulties many of these individuals have with the English language make enrolling in regular school programs intimidating and unlikely, and the alternative educational programs available to them tend to be limited and of poorer quality (McDonnell & Hill, 1993). generation 1.25, therefore, can become caught between two educational systems: one in their native country that offers limited access and one in the United States that ostensibly offers greater access but nevertheless can be an unattractive and difficult option to pursue. As a result, the educational attainment of generation 1.25 should be fairly similar to that of generation 1.00.

Generation 1.25, like generation 1.00, also has had almost exclusive exposure to their native language for their childhood years. Members of this generation enter the United States well past the developmental period at which language learning is flexible, making it more difficult for them to learn English upon their arrival. In addition, the peer context of this generation after their arrival in the United States is likely to be composed of predominantly co-ethnic immigrants who speak their native language. Even among adolescents with the same ethnic background, recent immigrants have more difficulty becoming integrated into American-born peer groups because of their language difficulties, value differences, and lack of knowledge about American popular culture (Matute-Bianchi, 1991). Therefore, the limited English exposure of generation 1.25, like generation 1.00, channels them into language environments in the United States that do not present as many opportunities for developing English skills as other environments, leading generations 1.00 and 1.25 to possess levels of language usage, ability, and preference that are quite similar to one another.

Ironically, the same peer dynamics that prevent generation 1.25 from getting more exposure to English-speaking environments may protect them from getting involved in risky and criminal behavior. American adolescents generally engage in risky behavior such as delinquency, sexual activity, and substance use to a greater extent than do adolescents in immigrant's native societies (Coie & Dodge, 1998). Moderate levels of some of these activities are actually fairly normative among American peer groups. Immigrants who arrive in their mid to late teens, however, do not experience as much pressure to engage in such activities because they generally are not involved with the American-born peer groups that are more involved in risky behavior.

Finally, the family environment of generation 1.25 after arriving in the United States is also fairly similar to that of generation 1.00. Although unlikely to be married themselves, some members of generation 1.25 come to the United States without their family of origin, despite their legal status as minors, with the explicit intention of seeking employment to support family members back in their native countries. The family dynamics for those who do come with their parents and family of origin are likely to be quite different than for those who do not, but the end result in terms of educational attainment is likely the same. Immigrant parents overwhelmingly place a strong value on education, and generally have high aspirations for their children's eventual educational attainment (Fuligni, 1997). Their children generally hold the same beliefs and want to complete their high school education and perhaps pursue more schooling in order to fulfill their parents' dreams. At the same time, adolescents in immigrant families feel a strong sense of obligation to support and assist the family (Fuligni, 1998). Recent adolescent immigrants are of the age when they can seek paid employment, whether on a formal or an informal basis, and the needs facing many immigrant families can lead these teenage immigrants to work in order to help support their families. The continual need to work inevitably can interfere with the teenagers' ability to do well in school and keep up their attendance, leading to a greater likelihood of dropping out of school entirely. As a result, the educational attainment of generation 1.25 is more similar to that of generation 1.00 than would be expected given that their age of arrival makes schooling a greater possibility.

GENERATION 1.50

Generation 1.50, which arrives between the ages of 6 and 12 years, experiences much different developmental contexts than generation 1.00 and generation 1.25 because of their access to schooling and exposure to the English language. This generational cohort is different in that all of its members will have at least some schooling in the United States. The younger members of the cohort will have virtually all of their schooling in this country. As a result, these individuals are more strongly situated within the American educational pipeline that is directed toward the completion of a high school degree. That is not to say that all members of generation 1.50 can easily complete high school; many other barriers exist that can prevent members of immigrant and ethnic minority families from receiving a high school degree. Rather, generation 1.50 is in a much different position than generations 1.00 and 1.25 because they are not caught between two educational systems and can take advantage of the access to secondary schooling that is available in this country.

This generation also has the benefit of a family environment that can both value education and afford the children more opportunity to complete their schooling. Like the parents of generation 1.25, the parents of generation 1.50 both have high aspirations for attainment and place great importance on children's obligation to support, assist, and respect the family. The difference from generation 1.25 is that the primary obligation of generation 1.50 is to do well and complete school. The younger age of arrival of the members of generation 1.50 limits their ability to seek paid employment, thereby removing the potential conflict between their need to work and their desire to complete school. This generation does not have the same responsibility of providing economic support to others immediately upon their arrival in the United States, giving them the opportunity to concentrate on their studies and to become more integrated into the American educational system. This is not to say that the need to assist the family will not become an issue as members of this generation enter the mid to late teenage years, but the opportunity of these individuals to become more established in American schools could provide them with greater ability to handle the potential conflicts with their time and make their parents and families feel that there has been too much already invested in their American education to threaten their ability to complete high school degrees.

It is possible that there will be greater variation within this generation according to exact age of arrival than within other generations because the younger members will have entered United States schools at kindergarten or the first grade and the older members will have started American schools during middle and junior high schools. The older members of this generation may face similar challenges as do members of generation 1.25, such as more difficulty with the English language and the greater ability to seek paid employment, and the fact that schooling is not mandatory beyond the age of 16 years may lead more older members of generation 1.25 to drop out of school before receiving their high school degree. It may be worthwhile, therefore, to explore whether generation 1.25 is a particularly diverse cohort of immigrants because of the way the age range maps onto the ages of schooling in the United States.

Finally, the greater exposure of members of generation 1.50 to English and their younger age of arrival allow them to develop greater skills in the English language and can make it more difficult for them to retain the native language of their families. This can lead them to be more integrated into peer groups of American-born children, which in turn enables them to become further skilled in English and makes them prefer using English more than their family's native language. In the same way, however, greater involvement with American-born peer groups can eventually lead them to engage in greater experimentation with delinquency, sexual activity, and substance use.

GENERATION 1.75

Individuals who arrive in the United States between the ages of 0 and 5 years will experience developmental contexts that are virtually indistinguishable from those of American-born individuals with a single, yet important exception. These individuals will grow up in a family that is led by immigrant rather than American-born parents, which leads to an environment that can be quite different in terms of values and expectations. Immigrant parents place an extremely strong emphasis upon the importance of doing well in school and attaining high school and college degrees, more so than American-born parents (Fuligni, 1997). Immigrant parents also place a great importance upon children's obligation to do well in school and to not engage in risky behavior and get into trouble. As a result, members of this generation often do better in school and are less likely to engage in delinquency, sexual activity, and substance use than those with American-born parents (Harris, 1999).

Nevertheless, members of generation 1.75 are still more likely to get into trouble than members of generations 1.00, 1.25, and 1.50 because they are more likely to be integrated into peer groups of American-born children. generation 1.75 will have had exposure to English virtually their entire lives, leading them to have greater English ability and to demonstrate a strong preference for using English. Having grown up in the United States, members of this generation also have knowledge of American popular culture that would be equal to that of those who were born in the United States. As a result, they will have peers who, although predominantly of the same ethnic background because of the general ethnic cleavage in American peer groups, are not necessarily immigrants and who speak English and not the family's native language. In addition, these groups will be more likely to engage in risky behavior that leads generation 1.75 to be more likely to be involved in these activities than the other immigrant cohorts.

CONCLUSIONS

In summary, the developmental contexts of immigrants to the United States appear to show patterns of convergence and divergence that are represented in figure 2.1. The school, family, and peer contexts of generations 1.00 and 1.25 overlap with one another to a great extent, whereas there is greater difference between the contexts of these generations and those of generations 1.50 and 1.75. The true extent of the overlap of generations 1.50 and 1.75 is somewhat unclear due to the potentially high level of diversity within generation 1.50 itself. More detailed analyses of generation 1.50 according to specific age of arrival will shed more light on the developmental outcomes and contexts for this group.

The extent to which age of arrival determines the life course trajectories of immigrants testifies to both maturational and contextual causes. Maturation plays a significant role because of the limited developmental window within which language can be learned, and context plays a role because age of arrival places immigrants within different types of school, family, and peer contexts within the United States. Yet even these two sets of factors interact with one another, because the relative ability or inability to learn English upon arrival in the United States can determine the school and peer contexts in which immigrants will live their daily lives in their new society. Immigration, therefore, is a compelling example of the complexity which

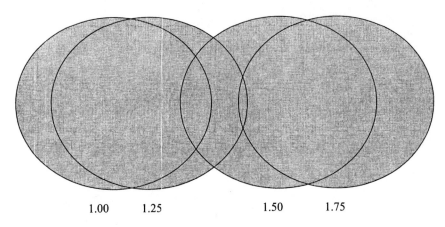

1.00   1.25   1.50   1.75

Figure 2.1   Generational overlap in developmental contexts.

major historical events can alter the life course trajectories of individuals.

REFERENCES

Bloom, L. (1998). Language acquisition in its developmental context. In R. S. Siegler, (Ed.), *The handbook of child psychology, Fifth edition. Volume 2: Cognition, perception, and language* (pp. 309–370). New York: John Wiley & Sons.

Coie, J. D., & Dodge, K. A. (1998). Agression and antisocial behavior. In N. Eisenberg (Ed.), *The handbook of child psychology, Fifth edition. Volume 3: Social, emotional, and personality development* (pp. 779–862). New York: John Wiley & Sons.

Fuligni, A. J. (1997). The academic achievement of adolescents from immigrant families: The roles of family background, attitudes, and behavior. *Child Development, 68,* 261–273.

Fuligni, A. J. (1998). The adjustment of children from immigrant families. *Current Directions in Psychological Science, 7,* 99–103.

Harris, K. M. (1999). The health status and risk behaviors of adolescents in immigrant families. In D. J Hernandez (Ed.), *Children of Immigrants* (pp. 286–347). Washington DC: National Academy Press.

Jia, G. (2004). The acquisition of English and maintenance of native language by immigrants in North America. In U. Gielen & X. Jaipaul (Eds.), *Advances in applied developmental psychology: Childhood and adolescence in cross-cultural perspective.* Ablex: Greenwood Press.

Matute-Bianchi, M. E. (1991). Situational ethnicity and patterns of school performance among immigrant and non-immigrant Mexican-descent students. In M. A. Gibson & J. U. Ogbu (Eds.), *Minority status and schooling: A comparative study of immigrant and involuntary minorities* (pp. 205–248). New York: Garland.

McDonnell, L. M., & Hill, P. T. (1993). *Newcomers in American schools: Meeting the educational needs of immigrant youth.* Santa Monica, CA: Rand.

UNESCO. (1999). *1999 UNESCO statistical yearbook* Paris, France: UNESCO.

Commentary

Immigration of Older Adults: Extending the Incorporation Typology

Gordon F. De Jong

HISTORICAL INFLUENCES ON LIVES AND AGING

Of all events that individuals may experience over their life course, immigration to a new country with a different cultural heritage surely ranks as one of the most traumatic. In terms of numbers, this transition is quite common in the United States, which receives more immigrants than any other country in the world—currently nearly 1,000,000 legal and an additional estimated 400,000 to 500,000 undocumented immigrants per year. It is in this context that Rumbaut addresses the important issue of immigration and the incorporation of generational cohorts in "Immigrant America." The goal is to evaluate relevant theories and suggest a typology for extending the "immigrant incorporation" focus from the younger generational cohorts of Rumbaut's findings to older adult immigrants.

Rumbaut has two major objectives. The first is to illustrate the importance of historical context for understanding the study of immigration and immigrant incorporation. I could not agree more with the motivation for this objective, and wish to extend this objective in two ways: (a) by highlighting the dramatic increase in legal immigration to the United States in recent years and (b) by documenting changes over the past decade in the number and ratio of children versus elderly immigrants.

THE DEMOGRAPHY OF U.S. IMMIGRATION

As shown in figure 2.2 from the Immigration and Naturalization Service (now the Department of Homeland Security Department, 2003), immigration has increased to over 1,000,000 people annually during the early years of the 21st century, a dramatic increase from the very low immigration of below 50,000 annually during the 1930s to mid 1940s period. Immigration was low during the Depression and World War II period due to both restrictive immigration policies and to poor economic conditions and World War II. An increase in immigration started soon after the end of World War II, and was spurred by the 1965 legislative changes in the restrictive U.S. immigration policy. The dramatic spike in immigration to over 1,800,000 in 1991 was a consequence of the Congressionally approved amnesty program for illegal immigrants in the late 1980s to early 1990s period (see figure 2.2). As these data show, the United States started the 21st century with high immigration levels that rival the pattern during the first 15 years of the 20th century—a similarity in historical context that is difficult to ignore. Whether or not a new era of restrictive immigration legislation will again be implemented in the 21st century is not known. But what is obvious is that immigrant incorporation is an increasingly salient issue for both research and public policy.

A second context to immigrant incorporation scholarship is re-

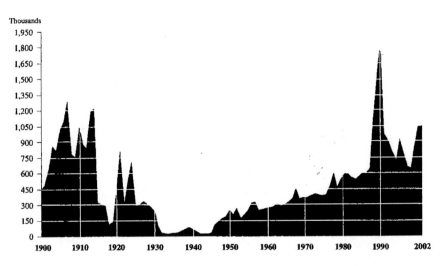

FIGURE 2.2   Immigrants admitted: fiscal years 1900–2002.

cent changing patterns in the annual number of child and elderly immigrants. Table 2.8 indicates that in the last decade the annual number of immigrants under the age of 15 has varied between a low of 129,000 to a high of 186,000, whereas the annual number of immigrants 60 years of age and over has ranged from 50,000 to just over 80,000. The number of immigrant children in 2002 was about the same as the number in 1992. Not so for elderly immigrants, where the number in 2002 was significantly higher than in 1992. This changing composition of the dependent immigrant population is apparent in the annual children/elderly immigrant ratios that declined from an average of nearly 2.8 children per elderly in the 1992–1996 period to 2.4 in the 1997–2002 period. Indeed the ratio was 2.1 children per elderly immigrants in 2002. While the largest number of immigrants to the United States are clearly of labor force age, the data in table 2.8 documents the change toward elderly immigrant, and their incorporation into American society is an increasingly salient issue.

The second objective Rumbaut attempts to enhance is the conceptual and methodological understanding of how immigrant incorporation influences lives and life courses by presenting a refined nativity by age at arrival typology of immigration and immigrant in incorporation studies. His emphasis is on the conceptualization of the second generation, and the empirical identification of second-generation populations. This objective addresses an important issue and is well reasoned,

TABLE 2.8   Number of Child and Elderly Immigrants Admitted to the United States, 1992–2002

Year	Age 15 and Under	Age 60 and Over	Child/Elderly Ratio
1992	169,551	62,151	2.7
1993	180,217	64,524	2.8
1994	164,995	62,806	2.6
1995	157,325	54,762	2.9
1996	186,362	66,966	2.8
1997	157,089	63,823	2.5
1998	129,291	50,368	2.6
1999	132,568	52,696	2.5
2000	151,894	61,591	2.5
2001	171,188	72,162	2.4
2002	168,817	80,756	2.1

Source: U.S. Government, Statistical Yearbooks of the Immigration and Naturalization Service, 1992–2001, and Yearbook of Immigration Statistics, 2002.

particularly for studies of children and youth incorporation as reflected in their educational, work, occupational, and income attainment trajectories in the United States. But as noted above, immigration to the United States now increasingly includes a sizable number of elderly immigrants. The remainder of this discussion will focus on two questions about the 3 immigrant lives and life course engendered by the changing demography of immigration context:

1. Are there useful theoretical perspectives for explaining and linking the determinants of elderly immigration with elderly immigrant incorporation?
2. Using Rumbaut's methodology for immigrant incorporation as a point of departure, can an incorporation typology targeting older adult immigrants be developed?

Explaining Elderly Immigration and Immigrant Incorporation

Immigration theory is largely bifurcated into those that focus on determinants of international migration, and those that focus on the assimilation of immigrants into new societies (i.e., Alba and Nee 1999; Massey 1999; Zhou 1999). Yet an integrated theoretical structure is not only important for understanding the historical context of forces shaping immigration flows, but also for determining the likelihood of successful or unsuccessful incorporation of immigrants in destination countries and communities. While not intended to be encompassing in scope, Table 2.9 identifies three frameworks in immigration scholarship that provide arguments about both the causes of immigration behavior and the assimilation consequences of immigration.

Although dominant theoretical perspectives in immigration scholarship, both macro- and microeconomic theories are primarily applicable to labor force age rather than child or elderly immigrant populations. Macroeconomic theory argues that the root cause of immigration is lodged in income inequalities across countries. However, this argument does not provide a basis for explaining which immigrants have successful or unsuccessful incorporation in destination countries. In contrast, microeconomic theory posits that immigration behavior of individuals results from the desire to maximize employment opportunities and wages, and that human capital attributes such as higher levels of educational attainment, prior occupational experience, and English language ability are fundamental to both predicting who moves and to successful assimilation in destination economies. Although largely applicable to younger working age immigrants, the mi-

TABLE 2.9   Theoretical Frameworks Linking Determinants of Immigration with Immigrant Incorporation.

Theoretical Frameworks	Determinants of Immigration	Immigrant Incorporation
Macro-and Microeconomic	National income inequalities; Maximizing employment and wage utility	Human capital attributes
Migrant Networks	Family and friend ties; Information flow; Sponsorships	Auspices and assistance
National Policies	Immigration quotas and preferences	Access to employment; Access to public program benefits; Refugee entitlements

croeconomic theory may apply to some older working age immigrants 4 whose immigration behavior is motivated by a desire for enhanced income for themselves and their families. The logic of this theory suggests that successful incorporation of older working age immigrants into the U.S. labor market is regulated by the same human capital attributes as for younger working-age immigrants—a fact that often puts older immigrant workers at a disadvantage because of their lower human capital accumulation in prior years.

More relevant to elderly immigration and immigrant incorporation are immigrant theoretical frameworks that focus on migrant networks and on U.S. immigration policies. Migrant network theory suggests that social capital garnered through ties with family and friends in destination locations in the United States are important determinants of immigration behavior. The major social processes underlying this argument include exchanges of information, remittances, sponsorship, and the social support obligations that extend beyond immediate family boundaries. These network ties thus facilitate immigration by lowering the social and fiscal costs of immigration behavior. Along with dependent children, elderly parents are important target individuals for network-driven immigration to the United States. This conclusion can be inferred from yearly U.S. Immigration and Naturalization

Service (1998) statistics, which show a remarkably similar increasing trend in the admission of children and elderly parents of U.S. citizens over the past 30 years. From this theoretical perspective, the incorporation of elderly immigrants is largely the responsibility of family and friends who function as patrons in providing assistance in aspects of well-being including housing, maintenance income, language, and social support. For many elderly immigrants, family and friend ties are both a necessary and a sufficient condition for U.S. immigration behavior and for immigrant incorporation.

The salience of migrant networks for elderly immigration and immigrant incorporation is complimented by the structure of U.S. immigration policy, which is based on four major principles: (a) family reunification, (b) needed labor force skills, (c) humanitarian needs, and (d) population diversity. Of these four, family reunification is by far the numerically dominant visa criteria in immigration quota legislation. For example, U.S. Immigration and Naturalization Service (2003) shows that in fiscal year 2001, of the1,064,318 legal immigrants to the United States, 63% entered as family-sponsored compared to 17% as employment-based immigrants. Humanitarian-based refugees and asylees accounted for 10%, whereas the remainder were diversity and other visa category immigrants. Thus the structure of the U.S. immigration policy strongly emphasizes family network sponsorship as a mechanism for obtaining immigration visas and for assigning legal responsibility for the support of immigrants during the early year immigrant incorporation process. Family network responsibility for immigrant incorporation was reinforced further by the Welfare Reform act of 1996, which severely restricted immigrants from receiving Temporary Assistance to Needy Families (TANF) and other public program benefits.

Extending the Incorporation Typology to Include Elderly Immigrants

How can the nativity by age at arrival methodological approach presented by Rumbaut be applied to elderly immigrants? Like for children and young adult workers, the incorporation of older adults is theorized to be fundamentally structured by the national cultural system and context of one's birth, and by the degree of socialization to U.S. society, measured as the age of arrival in this country. For purposes of a general typology, national cultural context is reduced to a dichotomy of native born versus foreign born, although refined empirical work clearly requires consideration of differences among either country-specific (i.e. Mexico, Philippines, Russia) or cultural context-specific (i.e.,

Asian, Hispanic, European) origin nativity. In the incorporation model for children and young adult workers, age at arrival is often considered a proxy indicator of formal education experiences in schools, early family socialization, and occupationally specific training. However, for older adults, age at arrival provides a proxy indicator for exposure to labor force participation, language acquisition, qualification for citizenship, and entitlements to U.S. government support programs.

Figure 2.3 presents a proposed extension of the incorporation typology for elderly immigrants. This typology identifies potentially key generational cohort factors that will affect elderly immigrant living arrangements, financial support, socioemotional well-being, physical health and disabilities, and government program service availability. Following Rumbaut's logic, the *1.0 first generational cohort* of elderly immigrants is composed of foreign born who were age 65 or older when they arrived in the United States. Almost certainly family-sponsored, network-based visa entrants, this population group has few government medical or financial program entitlements and only very limited labor force–based earning opportunities. While English language on arrival will vary with country of origin, language acquisition after arrival will depend heavily on the family context and social support networks. Wider language acquisition opportunities offered through employment situations will be limited. The well-being of the 1.0 first generation cohort of elderly immigrants is very heavily dependent on family members, many of whom are themselves younger first-generation immigrants.

The *1.33 and 1.67 first generation cohorts* of elderly immigrants is

---

GENERATIONAL COHORTS

1.0—Foreign born, 65+ when arrived in U.S.
1.33—Foreign born elderly, mid life arrival, worked less than 10 years in the U.S.
1.67—Foreign born elderly, early life arrival, worked 10+ years in the U.S.
2.0—Native born elderly of immigrant parentage.
3.0—Native born elderly of native parentage.

FIGURE 2.3 **Extending the incorporation typology to include elderly immigrants.**

composed of foreign born who arrived at a younger age. They have varying lengths of labor force participation experience (or are spouses of labor force participants), and are "aging in place" in the United States. The key difference between the 1.33 and the1.67 first generation cohorts is that the latter immigrant cohort qualification for Social Security entitlement benefits, which require 10 years (40 quarters) of earnings-generated (Social Security–covered) labor force participation. Time since arrival differences of 1.33 and 1.67 first generation elderly immigrants is also related to their likelihood of becoming citizens, their English language acquisition, and their continued reliance on family and friend networks for financial and social support. Indeed some 1.67 generation elderly immigrants may have arrived in the United States with employment-based as opposed to family-sponsored visas. As the typology suggest, successively higher elderly first generation cohorts are expected to have systematically improved immigrant incorporation and assimilation well-being indicators.

Despite the expected impact of age at immigration on the successful incorporation of elderly immigrants, nativity culture and nationality are hypothesized to have a lasting socialization-driven effect on elderly assimilation into U.S. society. This expectation is recognized in the Figure 2.3 typology by including the *2,0 (second generation elderly of immigrant parentage)* and *3.0 (third generation elderly of native parentage)* cohorts as comparison groups for 1.0, 1.33, and 1.67 first generation incorporation indicators. The issue goes beyond comparative citizenship and work status advantage of second- and third generation elderly for government health and financial support entitlement programs. It also involves possible countervailing elderly well-being forces such as generational cohort differences in the living arrangement of elderly, the spatial location of family members to assist in elderly care, possible elderly cumulative life-cycle health status advantage or disadvantage (epidemiologic health paradox), normative family obligations for elder care, and the family size–based number of children available for elder care support.

CONCLUSIONS

As Rumbaut concludes for younger generations, clarifying and specifying definitions and a methodological approach in the study of generations of elderly has practical as well as theoretical value. I have sought in my comment to not only highlight the significance of age-bounded generational cohorts in the study of elderly immigration and adaptation processes, but also to underscore the significance of changing immigration history and context on the lives and aging of elderly immigrants.

REFERENCES

Alba, R., & Nee, V. (1999). Rethinking assimilation theory for a new era of immigration. In C. Hirschman, P. Kasinitz, & J. De Wind (Eds.) *The handbook of international migration: The American experience.* New York: Russell Sage Foundation.

Immigration and Naturalization Service. (1998). *1996 statistical yearbook of the Immigration and Naturalization Service.* Washington, DC: Government Printing Office.

Immigration and Naturalization Service. (2003). *2001 Statistical yearbook of the Immigration and Naturalization Service.* Washington, DC: Government Printing Office.

Massey, D. S. (1999). Why does immigration occur? A Theoretical synthesis. In C. Hirschman, P. Kasinitz, & J. De Wind (Eds.), *The handbook of international migration: The American experience.* New York: Russell Sage Foundation.

U.S. Department of Homeland Security Office of Immigration Statistics. (2003). *2002 Yearbook of Immigration Statistics.* Washington, DC: Government Printing Office.

Zhou, Min. (1999). Segmented assimilation: Issues, controversies, and recent research on the new second generation. In C. Hirschman, P. Kasinitz, & J. De Wind (Eds.), *The handbook of international migration: The American experience.* New York: Russell Sage Foundation.

CHAPTER 3

Human Agency in the Transition from Communism: Perspectives on the Life Course and Aging*

Mikk Titma and Nancy Brandon Tuma

S ocialist states represented a unique experiment in building a state and society on the basis of ideological principles. The collapse of the Soviet empire and the transition from a socialist state and society have created new opportunities at every societal level through a series of traumatic changes. The results of the transition vary. Two structural changes, the development of a market society and the democratization of political processes, have been the object of most research on this transition. Perhaps we should say "transitions" in view of geographic variations. Our goal in this chapter is to examine the consequences of the societal changes associated with these transitions for people's lives and patterns of aging.

First, we consider social reproduction, the process by which mem-

*The research reported below was made possible in part by grant 199800085 from the Spencer Foundation and in part by National Science Foundation grants SBR-9710399 and SES-0115028. We also acknowledge the earlier support of National Science Foundation grant SES-9212936 because it enabled us to check, clean, and document the data from Waves 1-3 of "Paths of a Generation." We thank the Johann Jacobs Foundation for providing funds to collect the data in Wave 3. We thank our co-authors in previous research summarized here: Rein Murakas, Heili Pals, Kadi Roosma, Katerina Seryakova, Olga Tereshchenko, and Denis Trapido. We are grateful for the helpful suggestions of Glen H. Elder, Jr., and K. Warner Schaie. The statements made and the views expressed are solely the responsibility of the authors.

bers of one generation transmit certain qualities to their progeny. In sociology, social reproduction is usually studied by analyzing social mobility, the process by which parents transmit their social statuses to their children. More broadly, but related to social reproduction, scholars investigate the impact of social background on people's lives, as revealed in numerous outcomes, starting in childhood and continuing throughout adulthood.

Second, we consider the factors explaining income inequality in transitional societies. As might be expected, the transition from socialism increases income differences. It allows some people to become rich quickly but pushes many others into poverty. Here we are interested in factors that promote gains in earnings for some people while pushing other people down to the survival level.

Finally, we consider the success and failure of individuals, their pattern of aging, and the factors that influence differences in success. One obvious factor is age. People who were older than 50 when the transition began include many losers, whereas many young adults are winners. Older people lost most of the support formerly provided by the state and were unable to compete effectively with members of younger cohorts for the new economic opportunities. Young adults were at the right stage of life to seize the new opportunities and better their lives. They had an enormous advantage when compared with older cohorts and even younger cohorts whose members had not finished school when the transition began.

At our disposal are longitudinal data about the young men and women of the cohort that graduated in 1983–1984 from secondary schools in the Soviet Union and who now live in six of its successor states. We analyze data from the original baseline survey in 1983–1984 and from follow-up surveys in 1993–1994 and in 1997–1999 to identify factors affecting the life course and aging of young adults during the transition period.

We know that major historical events almost by definition are very influential, but it is challenging to develop a research design to study their effects (Elder & Pellerin, 1998). Rarely can one anticipate a major historical event and then formulate a plan to study it. We certainly did not anticipate the transition from socialism or design our study with this transition in mind. The "Paths of a Generation" (PG) project began in the early 1980s as a typical longitudinal study of individuals. Originally it had primarily a developmental approach to understanding early life careers. A secondary objective was the comparison of life careers of young adults in diverse regions of the USSR. But, fortunately for us, the PG cohort was born at a time that positioned it to become a major actor in the emergence of post-Soviet states and in the transition from the old Soviet party-state to new market-based societies. This historical accident let us expand our focus from the unfolding of life careers to a study of young adults' behavior in rapidly changing, transitional societies.

Comparing the object of our study to that of Elder (1974) in his famous book, *Children of the Great Depression,* we can identify some similarities and some differences. In all countries under consideration, the quality of life declined substantially for the average person, and this is similar to the situation in the United States during the Great Depression (Atal, 1999; Brainerd, 1998; Elder, Liker, & Jaworski, 1984; Milanovic, 1998). The decline in the quality of life induced by the transition from socialism was greatest for the older population. For part of the PG cohort, the great social changes accompanying the transition has also meant a worse quality of life than in the Soviet era. But for most members of this cohort, it has removed many former social constraints and brought new opportunities. The huge age variation in the effect of the transition from socialism appears to differ considerably from the less age-graded impacts of the Great Depression in the United States, though we know little about the latter.

In view of the historical events that occurred in the middle of our study, the focus of our research shifted to actions taken by members of the PG cohort that affect major outcomes in their lives (work careers, economic well-being, and family life) while basic foundations of society are changing. In this chapter we concentrate on the role of human agency on young adults' gains and losses during the early years of the transition. Previous research has shown that human agency is a potent factor that explains individual diversity on a variety of outcomes.

We first consider theories that offer explanations of the factors affecting gains and losses in social mobility, earnings, and success in transitional, post-Soviet societies. Next we provide basic information about the data at hand and our approach to the analysis. Finally, we summarize and discuss the results. We conclude with an overview of the main themes of our findings.

THEORETICAL FOUNDATIONS

Societal Context

Comparative historical and sociological research has established a basic link between human behavior and society. For individuals, the social environment involves especially social institutions and more broadly the sociocultural framework of the specific society in which they live. The link between society and human behavior is crucial to developing an understanding of individual behaviors. The macro-social factors of a stable society help to explain behavioral regularities. Historical events as major as the transfer from a communist system to a market-based society shake the institutional and the sociocultural underpinnings of people's beliefs and behaviors (Brinton & Nee, 1998). The emergence of a new institutional and sociocultural framework takes time, however. What happens in society in the short run may not be very important in explaining individual behavior if human agency has only secondary influence on people's actions.

Many studies explain current differences among transitional societies in eastern and central Europe in terms of their heritage—derived from the Austro-Hungarian or Russian empire. For example, development of a market-based, democratic society represents a slow and internally differentiated process in Russia, a huge country with a lengthy imperial heritage, where four or five generations lived under the Soviet system. On the other hand, transformation to a market-based democracy occurred quickly in tiny Estonia, which had a Germanic and Nordic heritage, and where only two generations had lived under Soviet rule and continued to have some limited access to the West through Finland even during the Soviet period.

We think that changes occurring in the transition are very important in understanding the behaviors of individuals in these societies. A comparison of the institutional and sociocultural frameworks can provide opportunities and producing actors in societies (Blau, 1994) reveals substantial differences in the social environment of young adults during the transition from communism in the late 1990s.

Human Agency

A common feature in the situations studied by us and by Elder (1974) in his analysis of people living during the Great Depression is that *human agency* is particularly important in explaining individual behavior in a period of rapid historical change. An emphasis on human agency is common in the social sciences and it represents a key principle of life course theory (Elder & Johnson, 2002). The whole tradition of historical narratives is oriented toward the deeds and personal characteristics of important actors in society (e.g., rulers and various elites). In political science, political actors are central in studies of political processes. In sociology, human agency is often described and identified with the concept of "social actor." This is especially true in qualitative sociological works (Shanahan & Elder, 2002), where the term "social actor" is used in the context of societal institutions, such as the family, religion, and so on.

This abstract definition of the meaning of human agency does not suffice for quantitative research. We need to understand the content of human agency so that it can be operationalized and observed empirically. The human agency approach distinguishes the individual from other people and from society. The social environment provides opportunities for social actors and deeply influences their behavior (Bynner & Silbereisen, 2000). It has an enduring effect on the formation of personality and on an individual's actions. Coleman (1986, 1990) and many others (e.g., Hollingsworth & Boyer, 1997) have shown that the linkage between individual actions and the social environment can be studied through the embeddedness of actions in the individual's social environment.

In our analyses, we study young adults whose personalities have already been formed and who have developed a system of beliefs about the world and about themselves. Consequently, their social actions are not spontaneous, unreflective reactions to their environment. The internal world of the individual is very complex, and it is justifiably studied by different disciplines. Because our data come from surveys, we know that we cannot use the theory of reasoned action (Fishbein & Ajzen, 1975) to specify the human agency approach. Our data do not contain measures of variables that would permit us to study the decision making of people and their ensuing actions. At the same time, we agree with Goldthorpe (2001) that the results of research should not be just statements that there are certain relationships among variables. These relationships are interpreted and explained within the context of existing theoretical approaches.

The human agency approach views the individual as an independent actor in society, distinct and distinguishable from other people and the social environment. Research on the main components of human agency requires that characteristics of the individual actors themselves be specified. For our purposes, these include education, abilities, and goals in life.

There is strong scientific evidence that education and abilities are consequential characteristics of individual actors in modern societies. These factors in human agency are elaborated in developmental psychology (Bandura, 1989), and are viewed in economics and sociology under the concept of human capital. Human agency and human capital address common phenomena but employ different theoretical frameworks. The human agency approach asks to what extent education and abilities explain individual *actions* and thus does not focus solely on the consequences of actions, as in the concept of human capital.

The next, also widely studied, characteristic of actors is the *goals* that they pursue. Here again the human agency approach under consideration overlaps with social psychological studies of people's motivations (cf. Brim, 1993). In studies of values and their impact on attainment, the most common goals are life plans and the evaluation of various goals in life or in work (Rosenberg, 1965). The achievement approach was initially developed by McClelland (1961). From another angle, it was studied in social stratification as status attainment (Blau & Duncan, 1967). With regard to goals and status attainment, the Wisconsin model (Sewell, Haller, & Portes, 1969) is especially noteworthy. Inglehart's (1990) "World Values Study" is particularly prominent in studies of values in political science. Our perspective on human agency considers the kinds of goals that are pursued in various actions and that thereby influence those actions and their results.

Individual abilities, education, and goals have important consequences for actions. However, some people are especially persistent in trying to achieve their goals and manage to use their abilities fully, whereas others do not concentrate on actions that would help them to achieve their goals. This individual characteristic has two distinct aspects. One entails the ability to mobilize oneself to act (i.e., willpower). The other involves decision making in accordance with available opportunities and circumstances in order to employ the most useful actions that will lead to desired goals.

Closest to the broad meaning of this characteristic of human agency are self-efficacy beliefs (Bandura, 1997) and the action control approach (Ajzen, 1985). Both perspectives are widely tested and accepted (Trafimow, Sheeran, Conner, & Finlay, 2002; Ajzen, 2002). A competing framework is provided by rational choice theory (Coleman, 1990). We chose to call this third aspect of human agency "*self-efficacy.*" One problem is to identify components of human agency that can be measured in surveys covering life careers. There are measures of it in studies covering behaviors related to health and habits, but to our knowledge, not in studies as broad-ranging as life careers.

We think human agency can be studied effectively only when individuals are social actors. In our view, individuals as social actors can be studied through four major characteristics: education, abilities, goals, and self-efficacy.

APPROACH TO DATA ANALYSES

When society is changing rapidly and radically, the sociocultural framework of a society is key. This is a most important consideration in comparative analyses of societies. Changes in the societal framework affect the available opportunities and the social environment of individual actors. From 1983 to 1990, members of the PG cohort lived in the Soviet Union, where their life opportunities were highly constrained as compared with those of their peers living in western democracies.

But these life opportunities were not similar throughout the Soviet Union. First of all, the sociocultural heritage in various regions differed, and many of these differences persisted under the Soviet regime. Second, the socioeconomic infrastructure also varied across regions of the Soviet Union. For example, Belarus developed an urbanized and industrial society during the Soviet era, but Tajikistan experienced only slow socioeconomic development, and the percentage of its population living in rural areas was still increasing at the end of Soviet era.

The main shared feature of the Soviet past was the common *political administrative regime*. This regime had political, economic, and cultural elites who sought to retain their advantages, power, and influence in post-Soviet societies. Not surprisingly, the new elites initially have come mainly from the former Soviet elite. In most post-Soviet countries, members of the former Soviet elite have been crucial actors in reshaping opportunity structures and the nature of social constraints.

Since 1990, the social and economic conditions under which members of the PG cohort live have become markedly different. The transition from the Soviet reality varied across the new post-Soviet countries. Those in our study—Estonia, Latvia, Russia, Belarus, Ukraine, and Tajikistan—were very different countries at the end of the 1990s. The opportunity structures and social constraints for the PG cohort have become much more varied across these new countries, paralleling the pre-existing dissimilarities in their sociocultural frameworks. The sociocultural climate is certainly important, as is the socioeconomic infrastructure that may be emerging or deteriorating; and the actual effectiveness of market reforms and the success (or lack thereof) of the elites who have been implementing societal changes.

We expect the life course and actions of the members of the PG cohort in various societies to vary in ways that correspond to the sociocultural and socioeconomic differences in their new societies. People who follow different social pathways are likely to age in different ways. For example, the fact that there is a larger percentage of entrepreneurs within the PG cohort in Estonia than in Belarus cannot be explained by differences in the characteristics of individuals in these two societies. Rather, the greater fraction of entrepreneurs in Estonia than in Belarus is primarily a result of differences in the opportunity structures of these two countries. As Elder (2003) wrote, contextual differences provide researchers with the opportunity to relate patterns of individual behavior to large-scale structures and groups.

Research on this change is difficult because official statistics in most of the new post-Soviet countries are not very reliable, arguably even less reliable than official Soviet statistics were in the past (Clem, 1986). Expert judgments and crude scales often furnish a more reasonable picture of these new societies than inaccurate official statistics. For example, in Estonia during the 1990s, roughly 20% of 17-year-olds had not completed the eighth grade, whereas the corresponding figure in the Soviet period was only a few percent. Deterioration in the percentage of youngsters who have not obtained a basic education had gone unreported by the official statistics of all post-Soviet countries. There is reason to believe that the decline in the percentage of youth obtaining a basic education is even greater in most post-Soviet countries than in Estonia.

We have not yet completed our analyses of the relationship between changing opportunity structures and the actions of members of the PG cohort in different countries. But the relationship between structural changes in society and the actual behavior of individuals is an extremely interesting and important topic. Structural changes (e.g., the implementation of private ownership, introduction of elections, changes in living standards) in the study countries are occurring at different rates and are not always moving in the same direction. These differences undoubtedly affect how members of the PG cohort in various countries deal with a multiplicity of life issues.

Consequences of Individual Action

Our next research task is to identify the important consequences of individual action through which human agency can be studied as a factor that explains individual behavior in transitional societies. In sociology, there is a strong tradition of viewing the intergenerational transmission of life opportunities as a major stabilizing process in most societies. In contrast, intragenerational mobility reveals the major gains and losses in one generation's lifetime. We have analyzed both inter- and intragenerational mobility, and among the various factors we have investigated are some that are relevant to human agency. Consider the following outcomes.

In all transitional societies, having an adequate income is a major problem for the large majority of people. As noted previously, material differentiation increased rapidly in transitional societies and is perceived by people in those societies as crucial to their lives (Flakierski, 1993).

In societies where the previous institutional framework has collapsed and a new one is emerging with large uncertainties, there is a high probability that real gains cannot be measured on a single dimension.

Under the very competitive and volatile situation of the early transition, attainment of a higher social position is a long-term goal that takes time to achieve. However, jobs and income are inescapable and immediate necessities for survival. We argue that individual strategies for living differ markedly and can be detected by cross-classifying the statuses of individuals in the workforce, their social position, income, and wealth.

The main focus of this study centers on factors that explain the differentiation of young adults by their stratum in society, as defined by three separate analyses: social stratum, total earnings, and overall social position. Naturally, the differentiation depends on the nature and speed of changes in specific societies. The manner by which human agency influences those outcomes, and the extent of that influence, is determined by the activities of elites who govern the countries we study. Variation within countries reveals the efforts of young adults and the impact of human agency operating among members of this age group. Are the factors explaining outcomes in transitional societies similar, or do country-specific developments have the predominant effect on the behavior of young adults?

This study is based on a *cross-national comparative* design, which has certain advantages. First, a comparative study enables researchers to discern the effects of higher-level work structures, such as national, social, political, and cultural arrangements, and to integrate structural and individual characteristics into a coherent whole (Kalleberg, 1988; Kalleberg & Berg, 1987). A comparative study of transitional societies with weakly established institutions and a fluidly changing situation is helpful for obtaining findings with greater generality. Secondly, a comparative approach can shed more light on class- and status-related inequality than can a similar study within a single country. Finally, a comparative study provides a better basis for generalizing about the relative impact of different factors, such as education, abilities and goals in explaining outcomes: social mobility, total earnings, and social position in transitional societies. Previous cross-national, comparative studies have found that the effects of proposed explanatory variables are not always consistent across national boundaries. We wish to discover the sources of differences in the effects of explanatory variables across post-Soviet countries.

HYPOTHESES

We compare social processes in the following post-Soviet countries: Belarus, Estonia, Latvia, Russia, Ukraine, and Tajikistan. As stated above, countries (regions in the case of large countries such as Russia and Ukraine) have distinctive sociocultural environments, constrain individuals' behaviors to a varying degree and in various ways, and provide different opportunities. During the early stages of transition within a country, the opportunity structure in capital cities and rural areas differs markedly, and urbanization varies greatly across countries. This leads to our first hypothesis:

Hypothesis 1

Type of country has strong effects on social mobility, income differentiation, and status in transitional societies. It is less clear whether type of country mainly affects the relative level of various outcomes (e.g., the level of income) or also affects the nature of the process leading to those outcomes. If the latter is true, then the effects of other variables will differ across countries.

Most studies in advanced Western democracies have found that social background broadly conceived has a considerable impact on the development of an individual's human capital and also affects access to social capital (e.g., social connections) and to cultural capital (e.g., class-based values). The transition from socialism is an opportune historical moment for social background to make a difference in people's lives, and to have a different impact than it had in a social system intended to prevent social inheritance. It is particularly important to examine the effect of family background on individual outcomes in the early transition because the former Soviet elite has lost the political-administrative basis for its advantageous position in most post-Soviet countries, allowing for the possibility of new elites and new patterns of social reproduction (cf. Nee, 1989). There are contradictory results on the ability of the former elite in former East European socialist societies to promote their offsprings' gains (Eyal, Szelenyi, & Townsley, 1998). We address this issue in post-Soviet countries (cf. Titma & Tuma, 2000).

Hypothesis 2

Social reproduction as indexed by family background and continuity played a minor role in social mobility, income differentiation, and social position in transitional societies. In modern societies, education is considered to be the most important characteristic describing overall individual development. Formal education provides general knowledge of the world, fosters a variety of specific skills, and develops the personalities of young people.

Hypothesis 3

Education has a strong effect on social mobility, income, and status in transitional societies. We have measures of youths' grades in school and their self-evaluations of their abilities shortly before they graduated from secondary school, as well as their completed education. The measures of grades in school and of self-evaluations of abilities enable us to study the impact of fairly specific abilities on the odds of advancing or failing during the early stages of the transition.

Hypothesis 4

Grades in school and abilities shortly before graduation from secondary school influence social mobility and social position in transitional societies. Human agency is guided in different directions by people's goals. Our data contain information on people's goals at three points in their lives. We have measures of their goals shortly before graduation from secondary schools, at the starting point of the transition when they were in their mid-twenties, and roughly 6 years after the transition had begun when they were in their early thirties.

Hypothesis 5

The goals of young people in secondary school influence their social mobility, income, and social position in transitional societies. Transitional societies have made people much more responsible for their own existence. Both state-provided social support and the power of various agents of social control have declined. This fact leads us to expect that human agency can be studied in transitional societies because individuals act, either by their own choice or through the force of their environment and their will to survive. A majority of young adults were engaged in the labor market, and as a consequence of their actions in the labor market, their labor market position and income relative to their peers changed radically.

We also consider *self-efficacy* in addition to abilities and goals. As a measure of self-efficacy, we use a variable showing how active respondents were in all kinds of work activities outside of a main job in 1991. There were two main strategies: One strategy followed by action-oriented young adults was to search for new opportunities and find new careers. The second main strategy was to hold on to one's current job in the belief that bad times will pass. The second strategy was typical among employees of large enterprises, who tended to believe that large enterprises could not fail. We expect that action-oriented young adults tended to be more successful than those who hoped that bad times would pass and who stayed in their previous jobs.

Hypothesis 6

Young adults in transitional societies who had multiple economic activities outside their main job in the Soviet era are more likely to be upwardly mobile and to have higher income than others.

DATA AND VARIABLES

We use data from the comparative longitudinal project, "Paths of a Generation" (PG), to address the issues outlined above. The PG project began as a study of the life careers of a cohort of 1983–1984 graduates from secondary schools in 15 regions of the Soviet Union (Titma & Tuma, 1995). The original sample was drawn using a two-stage stratified, clustered design. The stratification variables were the type of secondary school (general, specialized, vocational) and locality (regional capital, large city, town, village). In addition to the original base-year survey, there have been three follow-up surveys (in 1988–1989, 1992–1994, and 1997–1999). The four PG surveys have covered both factual items about people's lives (e.g., parental background, education, work, family history, political participation, income) and their opinions about various social and political issues. The most recent follow-up survey was conducted in 1997–1999 and used standardized,

TABLE 3.1 Main Characteristics of Countries in the Late 1990s

	Estonia	Latvia	Sverdlovsk (Russia)	Kurgan (Russia)	Kharkiv (Ukraine)	Belarus	Tajikistan
Population (millions)	1.477	2.445	4.670	1.107	3.184	10.235	6.112
Urban %	69	69	88	55	79	69	28
Rural %	31	31	13	45	22	31	72
Location	Baltic	Baltic	Urals	Urals	Ukraine	Between Poland & Russia	Central Asia
Titular	65%, 20% Russian	58%, 30% Russian	83% (country, no data on oblast)		74%, 21% Russian	78%, 13% Russian	65%, 25% Uzbek
GDP per capita 1998	$3,141	$2,646	$2,760	$1,260	Not Available	$2,070 (?)	$290
Market Orientation	Private-based economy	Private-based economy	Emerging market economy	State farms and local markets	Declining Soviet defense center	Command economy, small businesses	"Bazaar" economy

120

	1990	1991	1992, but not land	1993, but not land	1993, but not land	Limited	—
Private Ownership							
Culture	Nordic	Germanic	Russian	Russian	Ukrainian Russian	Clan based	
Religion	Lutheran	Lutheran	Russian Orthodox	Russian Orthodox	Ukrainian Orthodox/ Catholic	Russian Orthodox	Muslim
Political System 2000	Parliamentary rule	Parliamentary rule	Elected governor	Elected governor	Elected governor	Presidential rule Autocratic	Presidential rule Autocratic
Ruling Elite	Multiple sources	Multiple sources	Soviet era	Soviet era	Soviet era	Soviet era	Soviet era

face-to-face interviews. In the present study, we analyze data collected from approximately 12,000 respondents in six countries (Estonia, Latvia, Belarus, Tajikistan, two regions in Russia, and an important region in Ukraine). The response rate to the target sample in this wave ranged from 70 to 82% across these six countries.

Countries Studied

We furnish a short description of differences among the countries because they are important for understanding the social environments in which young adults in the PG study lived in the 1990s (see Table 3.1).

Estonia and Latvia are small Baltic countries. They gained independence after World War I, but were incorporated into the Soviet Union in 1939. Both countries are Lutheran by tradition and have been influenced historically by German culture. By the 1990s, about 70% of their populations lived in urban areas. Of post-Soviet countries, only the Baltic countries had developed market-based economies and had experienced real economic growth by 1998. Both Estonia and Latvia also succeeded in instituting democratic political processes.

Both Belarus and Ukraine became independent countries in 1991 and have had a strong Russian influence historically. Kharkiv oblast in Ukraine was the third largest center of the Soviet defense industry. Belarus was also heavily industrialized during the Soviet period. Russia is represented in our data by the Ural region. Sverdlovsk oblast was the most important center of the defense industry in the Soviet Union; Kurgan oblast is a relatively rural region to the east and somewhat to the south of Sverdlovsk oblast. Sverdlovsk oblast was market oriented, but it still had a command economy, which was declining. In the 1990s, Ukraine was in even worse shape economically than Russia. Belarus had a still functioning (though shrinking) command economy with almost full employment and social security still provided by the state. Its leadership adopted a strategy similar to China's, which is to say that the command economy was whittled away rather than suddenly abandoned.

Tajikistan represents Central Asia in our study. Its historical background is similar to that of Afghanistan. It is very mountainous and its population is not highly urbanized. It has levels of poverty and of people without jobs (i.e., joblessness) that are typical for countries in Central Asia. Following a civil war in the early 1990s, it developed a "bazaar" economy. According to Geertz (1978), this type of economy is characterized by an extreme division of labor, localized markets, and, more to the point of this chapter, "extensive traditionalization of occupation in ascriptive terms" (pp. 29–30).

There was a very clear difference between the Baltic countries with newly emerging elites and the other post-Soviet countries, in which local Soviet elites were still mainly in charge. Another distinctive feature was personal rule in all of the countries except the Baltic countries, which quickly installed parliamentary democracies.

Dependent Variables

Our outcomes include: intergenerational mobility (Titma, Tuma, & Roosma, 2003), intragenerational mobility between 1991 and 1997–1999, and total individual earnings in 1997. The intergenerational analysis used a 5-point scale based on a modified version of Erikson and Goldthorpe's (1992) class scheme; lower white-collar was the reference category. For the analysis of intragenerational mobility, we used a 9-point scale to measure social stratum and specified the semi-professional stratum as the reference category. Since respondents reported their earnings from all sources in the month before the interview in local currencies, we used official exchange rates and consumer-price indices for the six countries over time to convert the original reports of earnings in local currencies to equivalent amounts in constant U.S. dollars. The earnings of men and women were analyzed separately. In multivariate analyses, our dependent variable was the natural logarithm of the total earnings converted to U.S. dollars, plus one dollar, which was added to let us calculate the logarithm. We also report results from analyses of the educational process in the Soviet era (Tuma & Titma, 2003), of social position in transitional societies (Titma & Trapido, 2002), and of entrepreneurship (Pals & Tuma, 2004).

Measures of Human Agency

Four types of measures provide ways of thinking about and indexing human agency: education, abilities, goals in life, and self-efficacy.

First, we used two measures of education. The main one is completed formal education in years. In some analyses, we also included the type of secondary school from which respondents graduated because of the importance of secondary-school tracking on a person's life career.

Second, we included measures of abilities in some of our analyses. In the analysis of social stratum, we included grade point average

(GPA) in the eighth grade (the end of basic education), GPA at the end of secondary school, and self-evaluations of organizational skills and of manual skills.

Third, in analyses of social stratum, we included the goals that secondary school graduates had declared to be important to them, including plans to attend a university after secondary school graduation, the desire to be a leader, and the goal of having monetary rewards from work.

Our last measures pertaining to human agency were proxies for self-efficacy. We index it through measures of economic activity outside the main job before 1991. Such activities include part-time work, odd jobs, trading, making or growing things at home to sell, and so on. We included measures of these activities in analyses of social stratum and earnings

Other variables included in our analyses are control variables and are not important for the present discussion.

MODELS

In most analyses, we estimated regression or multinomial logistic regression models. Our study of earnings is an exception. A substantial fraction of the PG respondents reported no earnings. Omitting individuals with zero earnings from the analysis would be a form of sampling on the dependent variable and would lead to "sample selection bias" (Heckman, 1977; see also Berk, 1983). Consequently, we estimated multivariate tobit models (Long, 1997) of the logarithm of total earnings in our study of individuals' income. Tobit models include censored observations (i.e., cases with no salary or no earnings), as well as observations for which salary or earnings exceed zero, thereby avoiding the problem of sampling on the dependent variable.

FINDINGS

Country

Comparative, cross-national studies need to assess the importance of country differences. As seen in the results of analyzing respondents' social strata in 1997–1999 (table 3.2), Tajikistan differs markedly from all other countries. As noted earlier, in contrast to the other countries, it has a rural "bazaar" economy with an unusually high proportion of

TABLE 3.2 Multinomial Logistic Regression Analysis of the Social Strata of PG Respondents at 1997–1999 (Estonia, Latvia, Belarus, Kharkiv in Ukraine, Kurgan in Russia, Tajikistan; $N = 8,048$)

Predictor Variables	Own Business	Manager	Prof'l	Clerk	Sales, Service	Worker	Agric. Worker	Unskilled Laborer	No Job
	Effects of Stratum at 1997–1999 (relative to Semiprofessional)								
Regions									
Estonia	1.74***	.95***	-.07	-2.33***	.51***	-.08	.42*	.26	.25*
Latvia	1.54**	.53***	.26*	.59***	.78***	-.22	.88***	.24	.41***
Kharkiv (Ukr.).	.41	.47**	.14	.34	1.10***	.08	.52*	.28	1.25***
Kurgan (Rus.).	.39	.06	.05	.48*	.54***	-.37**	.44–	.34	.54***
Tajikistan	-1.66***	-1.77***	-.35*	.45	1.25***	-.56***	.85***	-.59*	1.13***
Urban-Rural									
Village	.23	-.04	.15	.02	-.06	-.49***	1.24***	.23.	.37***
Large City	.62***	.17.	22**	.24.	34***	.18	-.72***	.31*	.06
Nontitular Nationality	-.19	-.46***	-.32***	-.04**	-.11	.04	-.25	.14	.29***
Female	-1.99**	.12	.30	2.13***	1.23***	-1.56***	-.41	-1.13***	-.77***
Family Status									
Married	.60**	.71**	.14	-.05	.12	.08	.14	-.25	-.71***
Married Female	-.02	-.87**	.09	.22	.01	-.02	-.33	.16	1.22***
N of Children	.01	.13	.04	.34*	.29***	.10	.17*	-.02	.03
Female * N Children	.13	-.42***	-.25**	-.46**	-.39***	.01	.10	-.03	.22**

(continued)

125

TABLE 3.2 Multinomial Logistic Regression Analysis of the Social Strata of PG Respondents at 1997–1999 (Estonia, Latvia, Belarus, Kharkiv in Ukraine, Kurgan in Russia, Tajikistan; $N = 8,048$) *(continued)*

						Effects of Stratum at 1997–1999 (relative to Semiprofessional)			
Predictor Variables	Own Business	Manager	Prof'l	Clerk	Sales, Service	Worker	Agric. Worker	Unskilled Laborer	No Job
"Fundamental" School in Grades 1–8	-.13	.24	.14	.15	-.16	.23**	-.02	.12	-.19*
Secondary School Type									
Voc. Sec. School	-.11	.03*	-.02	.33	.01	.26*	.42**	.01.	.46***
Spec.Sec. School	1.05***	-1.23***	-1.17***	-1.32***	-.88***	-.43***	-.11	-.52***	-.87***
Acad. Sec. School	18	.02	.19	.19	-.15	-.54***	-.44	-.64**	.24
Abilities									
GPA in Sec. Sch.	.13	.11	.14***	-.06	-.01	-.01	.05	-.03	-.05
Years of Education	.25***	.44***	.58***	-.05	-.22***	-.32***	-.36***	-.40***	-.07***
Secondary School Behavior and Attitudes									
University plans	.21	.14	.12	.22	-.18	-.20*	-.68***	-.16	-.02
Time on Homework	-.18*	-.10	-.13**	-.06	-.04	-.07	-.11	-.19**	-.06
Manual Skills	.05	.18**	.08	-.01	-.09	.17***	.18***	-.04	.05
Organizational Skills	.62***	.21***	.10	-.27*	.13	-.14	-.14	-.20	-.12
Wanted to Be Leader	.34**	.18	.14	.22	.43***	.08	.27**	.05	.12
Work Should Lead to More Money	.39*	.21	-.07	.10	.26**	.11	-.03	-.08	.12
Economic Activities									
Outside Main Job 1992	.20*	-.07	-.02	-.21	-.02	-.11	-.05	-.04	-.10
N in Stratum	261	408	1,637	304	722	1,260	454	374	1,546

Notes: *$p < .10$; **$p < .05$; ***$p < .01$

peasants and jobless people and a relatively small proportions of managers and people having their own business. In contrast, Estonia and Latvia also differ substantially from the other countries, most prominently in offering greater opportunities for young adults to have their own business or to be a manager.

The opportunities to be an entrepreneur during the early transitional period were generally greater in the Baltic countries than elsewhere for adults of all ages. We are not suggesting that the Baltic countries have more managers overall; rather, the Baltic countries differed from the others in the availability of managerial positions to young adults who had no "Soviet history." Previous Soviet managers from older cohorts have succeeded in retaining their positions in other post-Soviet countries much more than in the Baltic countries. In the late 1990s, there were also somewhat more people with jobs in the Baltic countries than in the other countries, except for Belarus. Overall, our analyses suggest that it is sensible to use merged data from countries that have similar opportunity structures and similar cultural climates.

We have also examined country differences in intergenerational mobility in the final years of the Soviet Union (Titma, Tuma, & Roosma, 2003). The Baltic republics, the Russian and Ukrainian heartland, and Belarus had broadly similar mobility regimes, as well as similar effects of education and other variables, including parental background (see below).

In our analyses of earnings, we wanted to pool countries, if this would not suppress important differences in patterns of effects. Because of similarities in social, economic, and political circumstances, we wanted to combine the Estonian and Latvian samples, as well as the samples from the two Russian oblasts (Kurgan and Sverdlovsk) with the sample from the Ukrainian oblast (Kharkiv). Statistical tests assessed whether models estimated from data on the disaggregated research sites were significant improvements upon models estimated from the pooled data. These tests indicated that no important interaction effects were suppressed by the data aggregation. On the other hand, we found clear evidence that data from Tajikistan could not be combined with data from any other country, a finding that is consistent with our prior view of Tajikistan's distinctiveness. The aggregation of data from Belarus with data from Russia and Ukraine bordered on statistical significance. We therefore chose to analyze the data for Belarus separately because its leadership has maintained structures of the old Soviet system much more so than the leadership of the other countries.

The analyses revealed two main impacts of country differences on young adults' total earnings (see table 3.3). First, we found that the average level of total earnings varies across countries in the expected manner. Average total earnings were highest in Estonia and Latvia and lowest in Tajikistan. They were slightly higher in Belarus than in the Russian and Ukrainian oblasts, but these differences were not statistically significant. Second, we found significant country differences in the effect of having no job (i.e., of joblessness) on earnings. With higher incomes and therefore much to lose in the Baltic region, joblessness has a much more negative impact on the total earnings of young adults in these countries than elsewhere. Conversely, having a job has a greater positive effect on earnings in the Baltic countries than in the others. This pattern reflects the more rapid development of market economies in the Baltic countries and the increase of income differences associated with market economies.

Differences among the countries we studied during the early transition are apparent first of all because of new phenomena introduced by market reforms, namely, the opportunity to have one's own business and the opportunity to be jobless. In other respects, we have not yet found evidence of any large cultural and economic infrastructural differences in basic processes like educational attainment and social mobility. Thus, there is support for our first hypothesis, that there are country-level differences produced by the transition itself and not just preexisting cultural and infrastructural differences.

Social Reproduction and Family Background

Our second hypothesis states that the transition weakened social reproduction, and consequently family background is a minor factor in social mobility, income differentiation and status in transitional societies. Consider some results of our studies of intergenerational mobility.

In analyses of intergenerational mobility at the end of the Soviet era (Titma, Tuma, & Roosma, 2003), we found that mobility was very high in the European part of the USSR and that both education and gender had large effects on occupational stratum in 1991. Father's education (which we interpreted as cultural capital) had some effects, as more educated fathers were more likely to have children in professional occupations. Net of the effects of education, gender, and father's education, father's occupation had no noteworthy influences, except that the children of professionals were somewhat more likely to be professionals. Important, too, we found that parental participation in the nomenclatura (i.e., being one of the career functionaries chosen to fill positions in certain levels of the party-state hierarchy) had no significant impact on occupational stratum at the end of the Soviet era.

Not surprisingly, our results on mobility to social strata in 1997–1999 tell the same story as that at the end of the Soviet era. We again found that education and gender have the largest effects on social stratum. Official statistics show that conditions in transitional societies supported and possibly strengthened those gender differences in the labor market, which existed in Soviet society. We continue to find only minor effects of father's education on occupational stratum. But, interestingly, social stratum inheritance does become a significant factor in the Baltic countries in the late 1990s, especially among blue-collar and agricultural workers. Surprisingly, we found that inheritance within the lower strata is greater during the early transition than at the end of the Soviet era. At the same time, there is no apparent inheritance among managers, professionals, and other nonmanual workers (perhaps owing to the fluidity of the white-collar strata), net of education and gender effects.

These findings raise the question of why family background has such small effects on occupational stratum, net of the respondent's own education and gender. We note that our studies of the educational process in Soviet society discovered that social background mattered in post-secondary educational achievement in the Soviet Union, though not in a major way (Tuma & Titma, 2003). It should be noted, however, that a youngsters' educational opportunities were largely determined at the end of the eighth grade when students were assigned to a major secondary-school track. Of the various tracks, only general secondary school provided direct and ready access to post-secondary education. In general, the Soviet system had created state-run educational tracking that was linked to certain work careers and that did not incorporate parents as potentially influential actors in the education of their children. Consequently, it was difficult for parents to make a difference their offspring's educational attainment. We do not claim that the Soviet state produced a meritocratic educational system (which is one possible interpretation), but rather that parents' involvement in and impact on the development of their children's educational and work careers were more constrained than is the case in Western market societies.

Nevertheless, we found parental encouragement (especially by mothers) to be a very important factor for the continuation of post-secondary education. Fathers were less important in this respect than mothers; however, father's education did have a statistically significant effect on getting a university diploma, net of a student's own plans and

Table 3.3   ML Estimates of Tobit Models of the Log of Total Earning in 1997–1999.

Variables	All		Estonia & Latvia		Russia & Ukraine		Belarus		Tajikistan	
	M	F	M	F	M	F	M	F	M	F
Country										
Estonia (E)	5.20***	5.07***	5.24***	5.23***						
Latvia(L)	4.88***	4.94***	5.03***	5.18***						
Russia (R)	3.51***	3.37***			3.67***	3.32***				
Ukraine (U)	3.73***	4.05***			3.82***	3.96***				
Belarus (B)	4.17***	4.30***					3.96***	4.07***		
Tajikistan (T)	4.04***	3.03***							3.47***	2.85***
No Main Job*										
E	-3.83***	-4.62***	-3.68***	-4.61***						
L	-2.80***	-4.11***	-2.80***	-4.11***						
R	-2.42***	-2.94***			-2.69***	-3.07***				
U	-2.11***	.395***			-2.233***	-4.04***				
B	-2.63***	-3.40***					-2.15***	-3.04***		
T	-2.34***	-2.56***							-1.92***	-2.35***
Nontitular Nationality	-.12*	.02	-.28***	-.16	-.02	.22	-.17	-.01	.33	.32
Education (years)	.07***	.04**	.04**	.07**	.07**	-.002	.04	.07*	.09	.03
N of pre-1992 work activities outside main job	.21***	.52***	.16**	.35***	.14	.37**	.35**	.34*	.48***	1.46***
Married	.14	-.46***	.19	-.33***	.03	-.56***	.01	-.61***	.35	.45
Children	.24***	-.08	.15	-.19	.32*	.01	.20	.22	.33	-.43
Location										
Capital, major city	.29***	.10	.29**	.17	.34**	.17	.18	.004	.45*	-.25
Village, rural area	-.11	.01	-.06	.03	.10	.18	.12	.11	-.52*	-.72

130

Sector										
State-owned	.04	-.17	.08	.27	.01	-.01	.06	-.04	.06	.03
Shareholder	1.22	-.46	.31	.18	.18	-.14	.13	.004	.21	.04
Private	**2.30***	**.90**	.31	**.66**	.42*	.03	.29*	.003	**.56***	**.25**
Industry										
Agriculture	-.12	-.59	-.20	-.53	-.41	-.15	-.26	-.19	-.31*	-.26**
Manufacturing	.33	.13	.19	.05	-.10	.05	.04	.11	.004	.06
Service	.53	.30	.23	.04	.26	.20	-.07	.08	.05	.13
Education, Humanities	-.27	-.46	-.005	.08	-.17	-.25	-.20	-.17	-.17*	-.18*
Government	1.13*	**.18**	-.23	.32	**.28**	**-.19**	.23	.06	**.34**	**.002**
Occupational Group										
Unskilled Laborer	-.17	.27	-.03	-.19	-.35	-.28	-.1	-.30**	-.32**	-.28**
Farmer	-.07	-.20	.12	-.58	-.38	-.38	.19	-.16	-.05	-.26*
Worker	-.90	-.03	-.28	.09	.11	-.28*	-.34*	-.12	-.22*	-.18**
Salesperson	-.19	-.08	.01	-.83*	-.11	-.38	-.23*	-.10	-.07	.09
Clerk	-.07	.41	.13	.35	-.25	.65	-.02	-.20	-.07	.20
Professional	.93*	-.12	.08	.20	.20	.11	.06	.13	.13	.02
Manager	.40	-.91	-.30	.44	.43*	.12	.41*	.40***	.32**	.21*
Business-owner	—	.49	.25	.40	.22	.58*	.42*	.37**	.29	.27*
SE	2.38	1.68	1.45	1.01	1.87	1.70	1.58	1.22	1.78	1.48
N of observations	731	566	801	363	1,840	1,641	2,225	1,633	5,597	4,203
N left-censored	301	81	123	15	491	238	401	95	1,316	429
Log likelihood	-1,188	-1,031	-1,344	-519	-3,181	-3,027	-3,803	-2,633	-9,688	-7,402
Likelihood Ratio	343***	324***	449***	172***	957***	514***	1,936***	886***	4,095***	2,325***
R^2	.38	.45	.41	.37	.39	.27	.58	.42	.53	.43

Notes: $.01 < p < .05$; $.001 < p < .01$; $***p < .001$ (two-sided tests); **bold-face** denotes significant gender difference at the .05 level. Polytomous variables are dummy-coded, except for industry and occupation, which are effect-coded. Omitted categories are: For location, town; for sector, financed by state budget; for industry, other; for occupation, semiprofessional.

actions and other variables in our model. Thus, our analyses have shown that parental background had relatively weak effects on educational attainment during the Soviet period.

The intragenerational mobility of young adults in transitional societies is surprisingly high. Social reproduction and status attainment theories claim that statuses achieved in the past influence future attainment. According to most research on life careers, the period from the late 20s to the early 30s represents a crucial period for solidifying status achievement. Our results on intragenerational mobility (see table 3.4) are surprising because we found substantial upward *and* downward mobility during the 6 years following the collapse of the Soviet Union. In this historical period, the average number of job changes was greater for the PG cohort than it was over the entire lifetime of older generations. (On average, people in their 40s in Estonia during Soviet times had changed employers twice.) Intragenerational mobility in all post-Soviet countries was considerably higher than one would usually expect. Only workers (75%), agricultural workers (67%), and professionals (64%) had both a substantial degree of stability as well as considerable mobility. Mobility dominated over stability for all other occupational groups. Excluding Tajikistan and Belarus, the majority of the age cohort was mobile during the early transition. Even by standards of Western countries, the level of mobility during these first 6 years is very high.

Other analyses (Titma & Murakas, 1997; Titma & Tereshchenko, 1997) have found an amazingly high level of income mobility during the early transition. In the first stage of the post-socialist transition, people greatly valued monetary rewards. The most deprived members of the PG cohort were the poorest 40% in the Russian and Ukrainian regions (cf. Lokshin & Popkin, 1999). The ratio of the income (comparing those near the top with those near the bottom) was smallest in countries with the most developed markets, Latvia and Estonia, and in the one country that still retains a command economy, Belarus. This surprising finding results from the fact that a very large percentage of young adults in the Russian and Ukrainian regions and in Tajikistan earned almost nothing, and not from the fact that those near the top in these regions were exceedingly prosperous.

When we cross-classified the quintile of income at Wave 4 with the quintile of income in 1992 for Estonia (Tuma, Titma, & Murakas, 2002), we observed little stability in relative income; changes in relative income were almost random. Nearly 10% of the respondents moved from the top tenth to the bottom tenth, and nearly 10% moved from the bottom tenth to the top tenth.

TABLE 3.4 Social Mobility Between 1991 and 1997–1999

Social Stratum	Social Stratum in 1997–1999										
	Own Business	Manager	Professional	Semiprofessional	Clerk	Sales, Service	Worker	Agric. Worker	Unskilled Laborer	No Job	Row Total
Manager	30	34	3	1	2	1	1	1	1	1	4% (376)
Professional	18	29	64	4	8	7	1	2	3	11	18% (1,799)
Semiprofessional	10	7	5	65	9	8	3	2	6	11	15% (1,440)
Clerk	2	3	2	1	47	5	1	1	3	6	4% (423)
Sales or Service Worker	3	2	2	1	5	38	1	3	4	7	6% (628)
Worker	11	6	3	9	6	11	75	8	20	19	21% (2,046)
Agric. Worker	3	2	1	2	1	4	3	67	8	9	8% (780)
Unskilled Laborer	2	2	1	-	3	4	4	3	37	6	5% (470)
Jobless	21	15	19	15	19	22	11	13	18	30	19% (1,885)
Column Total N (= 100%)	299	464	1,883	1,331	355	913	1,548	625	448	1,981	9,847

Source: PG Respondents in Estonia, Latvia, Belarus, Kurgan in Russia, Kharkiv in Ukraine, Tajikistan.

Education

We next turn to the effects of completed education, which is the most widely studied component of human capital. At the end of the Soviet era, education was a strong predictor of occupational stratum, particularly of having a profession (Titma, Tuma, & Roosma, 2003), but not a strong predictor of income (Titma & Murakas, 1997; Titma & Tereshchenko, 1997).

Education is also a strong predictor of occupational stratum in 1997–1999, except that its effects on being a clerk or a semi-professional are similar. In 1997–1999, those with more education were most likely to be professionals and somewhat more likely to be managers, whereas those with less education were more apt to end up in sales or service, or in manual occupations. Broadly speaking, the pattern of effects of education on occupational stratum in 1997–1999 resembles the pattern at the end of the Soviet era, even though the economic situation in post-Soviet societies in the late 1990s was quite different from that prevailing during the Soviet era.

The effect of education on total earnings in the late 1990s for the societies we studied is large and positive. The effect is larger for men than for women when samples from all sites are combined, but the effect is larger for women than for men in the Baltic countries and Belarus. The only significant gender difference in the effect of education on income occurs in Russia and Ukraine, where it implies a higher rate of return from education for men than for women.

After gender, education is the second strongest predictor of social position in the Baltic countries in 1997–1999 (Titma & Trapido, 2002). Having low education raises the likelihood of being unemployed or poor, as one would expect. Having high education increases the chances of being a professional (as one would expect), as well as the chances of being a manager, an owner of property, or an entrepreneur. Education is beginning to differentiate among young adults in transitional societies as it does in advanced Western societies. To be educated matters among young adults, who are now the most successful age group in post-Soviet societies. There is clear support for our third hypothesis, that in transitional societies, education has a strong impact on the outcomes under consideration.

Abilities

We next turn to our fourth hypothesis, which states that abilities (measured shortly before graduation from secondary school) influence social mobility and status in transitional societies. Grade point average has a highly significant positive effect on the likelihood of being a professional, but no effect on the likelihood of being in any other occupation (see table 3.2; Titma & Trapido, 2002). In other research (Tuma & Titma, 2003), we found that GPA in secondary school is a strong predictor of eventually obtaining a university diploma. Self-evaluations of abilities before graduation from secondary school (roughly 15 years before 1997–1999) are a better predictor of ending up in other statuses than are school grades. Having organizational skills in secondary school increases the chances of being an owner of a business, a manager, or an entrepreneur in 1997-1999 (Pals & Tuma, 2004; Titma & Trapido, 2002). Interestingly, having manual skills in secondary school raises the chances of being a manager as well as the odds of being a manual or agricultural worker. Again, our results show that abilities, as indicators of human agency, can be empirically measured more broadly than simply as years of formal education.

Goals

Our fifth hypothesis states that goals in secondary school influence social mobility, income, and status in transitional societies. In our research to date, the strongest evidence about the impact of goals is found in our studies of the educational process. After type of secondary school, plans to attend post-secondary schools represent the strongest predictor of an actual attempt to obtain a post-secondary education. Plans for post-secondary education also raise the chances of obtaining a post-secondary diploma (Tuma & Titma, 2003). As shown in table 3.2, plans to attend university after secondary school have significant negative consequences for being a manual or agricultural worker in 1997–1999, but do not have a significant impact on holding any other status in 1997–1999. At the same time, the goal of being a leader in the future has a large and statistically significant effect on the likelihood of becoming a business owner or a sales/service worker. There is a similar pattern of effects for having monetary rewards as a goal in work. Thus our fifth hypothesis is well supported by the data; youthful goals (namely goals in secondary school) have had a lasting influence on young adults' outcomes in transitional societies.

When the transition started, members of the PG cohort were in their late 20s. During this period of life, people in modern industrial societies usually put their work careers and family lives on some clear path that will provide a basic framework for their lives over the next 20 years or so. But in transitional societies, a great many young men and women changed their work and income. These changes destabilized their work careers and profoundly affected all other aspects of their lives, including their family lives (resulting in a sharp decrease in the birthrate and a surge in divorces). In our first analyses of Estonian data, we thought that the destabilization of work activity resulted from a rapid shift of people to the private sector. But further analyses revealed that destabilization also occurred in post-Soviet societies where the command economy just collapsed without the accompaniment of any appreciable development of the private sector.

Self-Efficacy

We investigate the sixth hypothesis about the importance of self-efficacy by examining the impact of having been engaged in economic activities outside their principal job before 1991. We think that those who were motivated to search for work opportunities outside their principal job prior to 1991 are the ones with above average self-efficacy. We hypothesized that this variable would influence both their social position and their income in 1997–1999.

As the results in Table 2 show, this kind of activity indeed significantly increased the odds of having one's own business in 1997-1999. It was also a strong predictor of being an entrepreneur in 1997-1999 (Pals & Tuma, 2004). It was also a strong predictor of total income, especially in Tajikistan. Notably, in all countries except Belarus, it was stronger predictor of income for females than for males. Many young women chose to stay in their principal job, but those who had been active in the past in seeking ways to earn money outside their principal job had higher income gains. This finding is important for considering past actions as part of the measurement of human agency. We find support for our sixth hypothesis. It encourages us to recommend the study of self-efficacy and action processes as a whole through multiple variables in the future.

CONCLUSIONS

As a cohort, young adults in post-Soviet societies are winners because of their fortunate historical timing. The transformation of their society occurred at a time when they were ready for action and were better positioned to seize new opportunities than were members of other age cohorts. We cannot study cohort differences because our sample consists only of the age cohort born in the 1960s whose members graduated from secondary school early in the 1980s. However, the lives of members of this cohort, from 1991 to the late 1990s, underscores the importance of several aspects of human agency.

A major purpose of longitudinal studies and life course research on agency is to understand the impact of events early in life on subsequent life outcomes. This study of the PG cohort provides an opportunity to investigate the effect of early life careers during the period of the Soviet party-state, when respondents ranged in age from 17 to 26 years old. Thus, the young people we studied had made many important life decisions prior to the collapse of the Soviet party-state. When members of this cohort reached the age of 27 years, most of their choices had to be made under social and economic conditions that differed markedly from the conditions prevailing during their youth.

The labor market status of many young adults during the period 1991 to 1997–1999 changed markedly from remaining in a well-established occupational career, to new opportunities, such as being an entrepreneur, or to new hardships, such as becoming unemployed. Considering income, a scatterplot revealed major movements at an early stage of the transition, both from the bottom to the top, and vice versa. In terms of intragenerational mobility, we discovered that a majority of young adults were upwardly or downwardly mobile, except in Belarus and Tajikistan. We conclude that under conditions of societal transition, young adults' careers showed even greater mobility than that typically found across ages 17 to 26, the period during which basic career patterns are usually established.

However, according to official statistics, the careers of young adults in their 30s had begun to stabilize during the late 1990s. In the next few years, either people's occupational strata and their socioeconomic situations will become stabilized at current levels, or there may still be improvement in opportunities, allowing those who were losers in the mid-1990s to cut their losses, and possibly also become "winners." From relatively uniform socioeconomic conditions when the Soviet Union collapsed, the members of the PG cohort have traveled on socially new and different paths. Some have become very wealthy and have achieved considerable economic influence; others have become impoverished. We would expect differences in subsequent aging for those who are following such different paths. What factors tend to put people on one life path or another? As changes have been so rapid and diversity in young adults' lives has been so great, one can study the factors affecting life careers more readily than is possible in stable societies.

A comparative approach directs us to differences among countries as one of the most important influences on the outcomes we have studied. First of all, whatever policies were pursued after the collapse of Soviet Union, the command economy collapsed virtually everywhere (with the possible exception of Belarus), leading to a corresponding decline in the quality of life and impoverishment for a portion of young adults everywhere. Even Belarus with a still functioning command economy in 1998 did not entirely avoid these adverse effects. Surprisingly, sociocultural and socioeconomic differences had relatively moderate effects on outcomes such as income differentiation, social mobility, and social position in the labor market.

We found that country of residence had the largest effect on young adults' average earnings. The difference in income between the top decile and the bottom decile (and the top and bottom quintiles) was greater among young adults in regions of Russia and Ukraine than in the Baltic countries between 1991 and 1997–1999. This can be explained by the economic disintegration of Soviet Union. People in the bottom strata in Russia and Ukraine were much worse off than members of the elite in those places. But these elites were not better off in the Baltic countries. The availability of new opportunities brought about by privatization, the introduction of private ownership, and the possibility for entrepreneurial activities was linked with economic reforms after the collapse of the Soviet Union. In our analyses, differences between countries reflect recent economic reorganization with only one exception, Tajikistan. This country is unique in its influence on young adults, for reasons that require a deeper, historically rooted explanation.

Human agency as a factor explains outcomes in the lives of young adults best in the Baltic and least well in Tajikistan and Belarus. This younger generation has greater opportunities in Baltic countries than in the others. In contrast, this generation experienced fewer opportunities to be managers in Russia, Ukraine, and Belarus, not to speak of their options to engage in entrepreneurial activities. Evidence of human agency is hard to identify when individuals are highly constrained in their actions by culture and social institutions.

In this region of drastic change, social background had very little effect on outcomes for young adults in transitional post-Soviet countries. Human agency proved to be a stronger factor than social background. This result can be explained by the fact that the Soviet state ran the educational system in a way that greatly limited parents' actions to influence children's education. Another explanation is that young adults' attributes were more consequential in a difficult and rapidly changing social environment, where choices were hard and risky.

Education is a major characteristic in the development of the individual in modern societies, and indeed we found completed education to be an important predictor of social stratum, both in the final years of the Soviet Union and continuing into the early stages of the transition. Education also has important effects on income. This well studied factor emerged rapidly, especially in the Baltic countries.

It is surprising that youths' evaluations of their own abilities shortly before secondary school graduation help to predict their labor market status and income under the new market conditions. Self-evaluated abilities in secondary school have statistically significant effects on the odds of being an entrepreneur or manager. In general, our resources in the 1980s did not allow us to have better measurements of abilities. Even today, such studies are costly. For future research, it seems important to use the results of psychological research on abilities in quantitative studies of life careers.

Personal goals as a factor were well represented in our surveys, and again we can trace their influence, measured before graduation from secondary school, on life outcomes. We found that life plans are very strong predictors of attempts to attend post-secondary schools and to gain a post-secondary diploma. In addition, the goal to become a leader raised the odds to be an entrepreneur or manager in the new market-based society.

The last factor in this study was self-efficacy, indexed by past activities of young adults outside their main job (i.e., in the so-called second economy). Those activities revealed how individuals acted when labor market opportunities were opening up. Efforts at using economic opportunities outside the main job before 1991 increased the chances in 1997–1999 of being an entrepreneur, having a higher income, and having a higher social position in transitional societies. We interpreted previous economic activities in the second economy as measures of self-efficacy. This indicator of human agency deserves more research in transitional societies.

Above-average gains during the early post-Soviet transition for young adults born during the late 1960s occurred during a major societal transformation from a command economy under a party-state to a market economy under a democratic state. To retain these gains in the future, however, members of this cohort will need to compete with members of cohorts born more recently. Those born since 1980 enter adulthood in societies governed in varying degrees by market rules, whereas the younger cohort born since 1990 has been socialized in new post-Soviet systems. In theory, cohorts born since 1980 should be

better prepared to succeed than the cohort born in the late 1960s. In
actuality, things are more complicated.

The transformation of post-Soviet states pushed many people into
poverty. Hardship led to sharply lower birthrates, much higher rates of
divorce, and higher rates of mortality. Though less well known, members of cohorts educated in post-Soviet states also have lower educational attainment on average than in the recent Soviet past. Secondary
education was compulsory in the Soviet Union. But state support of education plummeted in post-Soviet societies. In the Baltic countries, for
example, where support for education is greatest, compulsory education has been officially reduced from secondary education to basic education (roughly equivalent to ninth grade). Unless the situation
changes, a fourth of post-Soviet cohorts will receive less than a basic education with another fourth completing their basic education, a
marked decrease from the last decades of the Soviet era. Although secondary education for all Soviet youths was more fiction than reality in
Central Asia, more than 80% of those born in large cities and in the
western part of the Soviet Union completed secondary school in the
1980s.

In the western parts of the former Soviet Union, the size of birth
cohorts during the 1990s fell by almost a half, quite aside from the
small fraction of secondary school graduates in these cohorts. Consequently, the fortunate cohort born in the late 1960s that we studied
may not face nearly as much competition from younger cohorts as
might normally be expected. However, the most educated and successful members of the cohort born in the late 1960s may indeed face
tough challenges from the more educated sector of younger cohorts,
with their better prepartion for getting ahead in a market society.
Shrinking numbers of youths entering the labor force today are likely
to increase the demand for people to do manual and the simpler nonmanual jobs.

Except in Tajikistan, most members of the cohort we studied
have had few children, and many of them have experienced a divorce. Rising living costs, limited housing opportunities, and few
adult children who can help them can make life hard when people
reach the age of retirement. Support for the elderly in post-Soviet societies has shriveled and prospects for improved support do not seem
to be in the offing. If so, our fortunate cohort may find that their
good luck runs out when they become older. The historical window
of opportunity that they had may not give them much aid or comfort
in old age.

REFERENCES

Ajzen, I. (1985). From intentions to action: A theory of planned behavior. In J. Kuhl & J. Beckmann (Eds.), *Action control: From cognition to behavior* (pp. 11–39). Berlin: Springer-Verlag.

Ajzen, I. (2002). Perceived behavioral control, self-efficacy, locus of control and the theory of planned behavior. *Journal of Applied Social Psychology, 32,* 665–683.

Atal, Y. (Ed.). (1999). *Poverty in transition and transition in poverty: Recent developments in Hungary, Bulgaria, Romania, Georgia, Russia, Mongolia.* New York: Berghahn Books.

Bandura, A. (1989). Human agency in social cognitive theory. *American Psychologist, 44,* 1175–1184.

Bandura, A. (1997). *Self-efficacy: The exercise of control.* New York: W. H. Freeman and Company.

Berk, R. A. (1983). An introduction to sample selection bias in sociological data. *American Sociological Review, 38,* 386–398.

Blau, P. M., & Duncan, O. D. (1967). *The American occupational structure.* New York: John Wiley and Sons.

Blau, P. M. (1994). *Structural contexts of opportunities.* Chicago: University of Chicago Press.

Brainerd, E. (1998). Winners and losers in Russia's economic transition. *American Economic Review, 88* (5, December), 1094–1116.

Brim, G. (1993). *Ambition: How we manage success and failure throughout our lives.* New York: Basic Books.

Brinton, M. C., & Nee, V. (Eds.). (1998). *The new institutionalism in sociology.* New York: Russell Sage Foundation.

Bynner, J., & Silbereisen , R. K. (Eds.). (2000). *Adversity and challenge in life in the new Germany and in England.* New York: St. Martin's Press.

Clem, R. S. (1986). *Research guide to the Russian and Soviet census.* Ithaca, NY: Cornell University Press.

Coleman, J. S. (1986). Social theory, social research and a theory of action. *American Journal of Sociology, 91,* 1309–1335.

Coleman, J. S. (1990). *Foundations of social theory.* Cambridge, MA: The Belknap Press of Harvard University Press.

Elder, G. H., Jr. (1974, 1999). *Children of the Great Depression: Social change in life experience.* Boulder, CO: Westview Press.

Elder, G. H., Jr. (2003). The life course in time and place. In W. R. Heinz & V. W. Marshall (Eds.), *Social dynamics of the life course: Transitions, institutions, and interrelations* (pp. 57–71). New York: Aldine de Gruyter.

Elder, G. H., Jr., & Johnson, M. K. (2002). The life course and aging: Challenges, lessons, and new directions. In R. Setterstein, Jr. (Ed.), *Invitation to the life course: Toward new understandings of later life* (Part II, Chapter 2 pp.49–81). Amityville, NY: Baywood Press.

Elder, G. H., Jr., Liker, J. K., & Jaworski, B. J. (1984). Hardship in lives: Depression influences from the 1930s to old age in postwar America. In K. Mc-Cluskey & H. Reese (Eds.), *Life-span developmental psychology: Historical and generational effects* (pp. 161–201). New York: Academic Press.

Elder, G. H., Jr., & Pellerin, L. A. (1998). Linking history and human lives. In J. Z. Giele & G. H. Elder, Jr. (Eds.), *Methods of life course research: Qualitative and quantitative approaches* (pp. 264–294). Thousand Oaks, CA: Sage.

Erikson, R., & Goldthorpe, J. H. (1992). *The constant flux: A study of class mobility in industrial societies.* Oxford, UK: Clarendon Press.

Eyal, G., Szelenyi, I., & Townsley, E. (1998). *Making capitalism without capitalists: class formation and elite struggles in post-communist Central Europe.* London, UK: Verso.

Flakierski, H. (1993). *Income inequalities in the former Soviet Union and its republics.* Armonk, NY: Sharpe.

Fishbein, M., & Ajzen, I. (1975). *Belief, attitude, intention and behavior. An introduction to theory and research.* Reading, MA: Addison-Wesley.

Geertz, C. (1978). The bazaar economy: Informationand search in peasant marketing. *American Economic Review, 68*(2), 28–32.

Goldthorpe, J. H. (2001). Causation, statistics, and sociology. *European Sociological Review, 17,* 1–0.

Heckman, J. J. (1977). Sample selection bias as a specification error. *Econometrica, 47,* 153–161.

Hollingsworth, R., & Boyer, R. (Eds.). (1997). *The embeddedness of institutions.* New York: Cambridge University Press.

Inglehart, R. (1990). *Culture shift in advanced industrial societies.* Princeton, NJ: Princeton University Press.

Kalleberg, A. L. (1988). Comparative perspectives on work structures and inequality. *Annual Review of Sociology, 14,* 203–225.

Kalleberg, A. L., & Berg, I. (1987). *Work and industry: Structures, markets, and processes.* New York: Plenum Press.

Lokshin, M., & Popkin, B. M. (1999). The emerging underclass in the Russian Federation: Income dynamics 1992–96. *Economic Development and Cultural Change, 47,* 803–829.

Long, J. S. (1997). *Regression models for categorical and limited dependent variables.* Thousand Oaks, CA: Sage Publications.

McClelland, D. (1961). *The achieving society.* New York: The Free Press.

Milanovic, B. (1998). *Income, inequality, and poverty during the transition from planned to market economy.* Washington, DC: World Bank.

Nee, V. (1989). A theory of market transition from redistribution to markets in state socialism. *American Sociological Review, 54,* 663-681.

Pals, H., & Tuma, N. B. (2004). Entrepreneurial activities in post-Soviet societies: Impacts of social psychological characteristics. *International Journal of Sociology, 34,* 11–38.

Rosenberg, M. (1965). *Society and adolescent self-image.* Princeton, NJ: Princeton University Press.

Sewell, W. H., Haller, A. O., & Portes, A. (1969). The educational and early occupational attainment process. *American Sociological Review, 34*(2), 82–92.

Shanahan, M. J., & Elder, G. H., Jr. (2002). History, agency, and the life course. In L. J. Crockett (Ed.), *Nebraska symposium on motivation (Life course perspectives on motivation)* (pp. 145-186). Lincoln, NE: University of Nebraska Press.

Titma, M., & Murakas, R. (1997). Impact of maketization on income inequalities. In Titam, M. (Ed.), Sotsial'noye rassloyeniye vozrastnoy kogorty: Vypuskniki 80-x v postsovetskom prostranstve. Proyekt "Puti pokoleniya") [Social Stratification of an Age Cohort (Graduates of the 1980s in the Post-Soviet Countries. Project "Paths of a Generation")], Published jointly by the Institute of Sociology of the Russian Academy of Sciences (Moscow) and the Center for Social Research in Eastern Europe (Tallinn, Estonia). Moscow. Pp. 146–185.

Titma, M., & Terestsenko, O. V. (1997). Subjective and objective factors of age cohort distribution on income. In Titam, M. (Ed.), Sotsial'noye rassloyeniye vozrastnoy kogorty: Vypuskniki 80-x v postsovetskom prostranstve. Proyekt "Puti pokoleniya") [Social Stratification of an Age Cohort (Graduates of the 1980s in the Post-Soviet Countries. Project "Paths of a Generation": The third stage)] (pp. 146–185). Moscow: Institut Sotsiologii RAN.

Titma, M, & Trapido, D. (2002). Prediction of success in post-communist societies: Evidence from Latvia and Estonia. *Society and Economy, 24*(3), 297–331.

Titma, M, & Tuma, N. B. (1995). *Paths of a generation: A comparative longitudinal study of young adults in the former Soviet Union.* Technical report, Department of Sociology, Stanford University, Stanford, CA.

Titma, M, & Tuma, N. B. (2000). *Modern Russia.* Boston, MA: McGraw-Hill.

Titma, M, Tuma, N. B., & Roosma, K. (2003). Education as a factor in intergenerational mobility in Soviet society. *European Sociological Review, 19*(3), 281–297.

Trafimow, D, Sheeran, P., Conner, M., & Finlay, K. A. (2002). Evidence that perceived behavioral control is a multidimensional construct: Perceived control and perceived difficulty. *British Journal of Social Psychology, 41,* 101–121.

Tuma, N. B., & Titma, M. (2003). The educational attainment process in the former Soviet Union: Factors promoting women's success. Paper presented at the August 2003 meetings of Research Committee 28, New York University.

Tuma, N. B., Titma, M., & Murakas, R. (2002). Transitional economies and income inequality: The case of Estonia. In B. J. Wejnert (Ed.), *Transition to democracy in Eastern Europe and Russia: Impact on politics, economy and culture* (pp. 111–140). Westport, CN: Praeger Publishers.

Commentary

Life Course Analysis in the Context of Failed Institutional Change in Post-Communist Societies

Victor Nee

The rich and suggestive findings regarding the transition process in post-Soviet societies draw on an extraordinary longitudinal data set that documents the workaday experiences of former Soviet citizens before and during a period of far reaching transformative change. In general, we know very little about the lives of ordinary citizens during periods of major societal disruptions, especially on the scale experienced in the former Soviet Union. Following the collapse of the Soviet Union, the great expectations for a rapid and smooth transition to a Western-style capitalist economy quickly ran aground as the big-bang approach to establishing simultaneously democratic institutions and market capitalism faltered. The new states lacked the bureaucratic capacity to implement the ambitious program of institutional innovations charted by reformers in their effort to promote rapid large-scale institutional change. Far from the smooth transition to capitalism, transition economies in the former Soviet Union stumbled into a serious and prolonged economic depression.

Reformers in new states were ill-prepared for the unanticipated consequences of failed economic policies. There ensued a calamitous descent into conditions arguably worse than even those found in some of the poorest and least developed economies of the world, characterized by very high unemployment, a precipitous drop in fertility, dangerously high infant mortality, massive breakdown of social services and health care, and so on. In light of these conditions, it is remarkable that Titma and Tuma persisted in their efforts to extend their baseline survey conducted in 1983–1984 to collect follow-up life course data in 1993–1994 and 1997–1999. The extraordinary historical context of economic and institutional involution in itself draws much deserved attention to their research findings.

Understanding how ordinary social actors manage during hard times is the focus of their study. Not surprisingly Titma and Tuma turn to Glen Elder's (1974) life course study of the effect of the Great Depression in the United States on ordinary lives to locate their central theme: understanding human agency during uncertain times. Titma and Tuma's discussion of human agency does not fully clarify the theoretical underpinnings for their assertion that human agency is best understood by examining variables such as educational attainment, ability, stated goals, and perceived self-efficacy. The problems facing ordinary citizens of post-communist Russia in making career decisions, securing earnings, and managing family life were complicated by the unusual circumstances created when neither the preexisting nor the still to be consolidated post-communist institutional order provided a credible framework for stable expectations.

Institutions comprise a system of interrelated informal and formal elements—custom, shared beliefs, conventions, norms, and rules—governing social relationships within which actors pursue and fix the limits of legitimate interests. These social structures provide a conduit for collective action by facilitating and organizing the interests of actors and enforcing principal agent relationships. It follows from this that rapid transformative institutional change involves not simply remaking the formal rules, but fundamentally it entails the realignment of interests, norms and power. The variables they draw on to be sure are useful, even though they may not take fully into account the problems facing Russian citizens stemming from the enormous uncertainties they faced in the breakdown of large institutional structures of the polity and economy.

Recently a colleague at Cornell returned from a summer's sojourn in Estonia and Latvia and vividly described very harsh conditions of decline and stagnation based on participant observation research. Survey data tend to shed a softer light on the same conditions in these post-communist societies, as can be seen in Titma and Tuma's somewhat bland style of reporting of conditions in post-communist Russia and the Baltic states. For example, Titma and Tuma write "we found significant country differences in the impact of joblessness on earnings. Joblessness has a much more negative impact on total earnings of young adults in the Baltic countries than elsewhere. . . . Thus, there is support for our first hypothesis, that there are country differences produced by the transition itself and not just by preexisting cultural and infrastructural differences."

Notwithstanding, the advantage of survey data is to identify and confirm structural patterns that would not be picked up in observational studies in the natural setting. Titma and Tuma's finding that father's education has only minor effects on occupational attainment is consistent with similar findings reported by Whyte and Parish (1984) in their analysis of life courses during the Cultural Revolution in urban China. It supports the view of a breakdown of predictable chances for social mobility caused by catastrophic disruption of societal institutions. The lack of evidence supporting inheritance for the working classes and for managers, professionals, and service workers also is not surprising in light of the disruption caused by the collapse of Soviet institutions, followed by severe economic depression and exacerbated by the inability of reformers to sustain a credible commitment to building during the 1990s a viable institutional framework to realize their goals for a market democracy. The finding of greater than expected churning in labor markets and large fluctuations in relative earnings for young people is also consistent with the view that post-Soviet societies during the early 1990s had yet to reestablish normalcy in labor markets.

Titma and Tuma uncovered findings that point to the gradual emergence of a new market society. They find support for the proposition advanced by market transition theory that returns to investments in education tend to improve to the extent reward is linked to individual performance. Their findings with respect to returns to education are consistent with other studies of market transition (e.g., Nee & Cao, 2004). Similarly their finding that ability is related to higher educational attainment and to becoming an entrepreneur is also consistent with what one would expect in the emergence of a market society. The link between stated goals and entering entrepreneurial and service sector careers suggest more predictability in the emergent mobility regime over time. Young enterprising young people who seek opportunities outside of their main job are more likely to discover new structures of opportunities as entrepreneurs. Together these findings are consistent with the view that by the end of the decade of the 1990s, post-communist Russia was evolving social institutions that offered some return to normalcy evident in predictability of chances stemming from investments in human capital and individual enterprise to search out new opportunities in the emerging market economy.

When International Monetary Fund and other Western economists traveled to eastern Europe and the former Soviet Union to advise reformers at the onset of market reforms, they consistently emphasized establishing capitalism by designing sweeping changes to implement Western-style economic institutions. Such emphasis on legislating new rules of economic action overlooked the realities of power and interests vested in existing institutional arrangements and longstanding personal relationships of the political elite. The trial-and-error approach taken by reformers in China has allowed for a more successful approach to economic transition. "The contrast between Russia's transition, as engineered by the international economic institutions, and that of China, designed by itself, could not be greater: While in 1990 China's gross domestic product (GDP) was 60 percent that of Russia, by the end of the decade the numbers had been reversed. While Russia saw an unprecedented increase in poverty, China saw an unprecedented decrease" (Stiglitz, 2002, p. 6). What we are missing in their account is the larger story of failed institutional change in Russia's transition from communism to a market economy. Titma and Tuma might have done more to interpret their finding in light of comparison with studies of other transition societies.

All in all Titma and Tuma provide a thoughtful and well-executed empirical study drawing on an extraordinary data set that investigates the effect of the calamitous process of societal breakdown and regeneration during the transition to a market society in former Soviet societies. I look forward to subsequent research reports from the Titma and Tuma research team.

REFERENCES

Elder, G., Jr. (1974). *Children of the Great Depression: Social change in life experience.* Chicago: University of Chicago Press.

Nee, V., & Cao, Y. (2004). Market transition and the firm: Institutional change and income inequality in urban China. *Management and Organization Review 1*, 23–56.

Stiglitz, J. (2002). *Globalization and its discontents.* New York: W.W. Norton.

Whyte, M. K., & Parish, W. L. (1984). *Urban life in contemporary China.* Chicago: University of Chicago Press.

Commentary

Social Change and Individual Development: A Challenge-Response Approach

Rainer K. Silbereisen, Matthias Reitzle, and Martin Pinquart

B eginning in the late 1980s and early 1990s, dramatic changes took place in the former USSR and the countries of the former Eastern Bloc. An example of such change is the reunification of Germany, an event that belongs to a series of social and political transformations in many countries, though the fact that two formerly divided states merged peacefully is a unique historical event. When this event occurred, the strong position of the social and behavioral sciences in the West, together with a buoyant economy, enabled the coordination of large-scale research programs to exploit this unprecedented situation for a better understanding of how rapid social change would impact institutions and people.

The metaphor of a giant "experiment of nature" was coined, though one has to keep in mind that differences derived from East-West comparisons could not be solely attributed to the "treatment" of social change. Instead, existing differences in terms of national peculiarities, traditions, and habits had to be considered, as well as social and political trends that were evolving prior to reunification. It would have been preferable if data gathered in the East and West prior to reunification could have been exploited and followed up after reunification. Unfortunately, with very few exceptions, this was not the case. To study the role of reunification it was therefore necessary to conduct cohort comparisons with samples drawn after the fact.

Fortunately, this situation differs in a few ongoing studies, one of them concerning the former USSR. Similar to the Berkeley and Oakland studies that were begun a few years preceding to the Great Depression in the late 1920s, and that allowed Elder and his colleagues (e.g., Elder, 1974; Elder & Caspi, 1992) to investigate the role of this tremendous experience on the life-course decades later, Mikk Titma was lucky to have available a large longitudinal research program that could be expanded beyond the collapse of the USSR and the formation of new national states on its former territory. More precisely, he was able to use the longitudinal data on a cohort of young people who graduated from school in 1983–1984 and who were followed up until 1997–1999. This data set offered the opportunity to examine young adults' lives during the period of rapid social change that culminated in the collapse of the USSR in 1990, and subsequent changes until the turn of the century.

As Titma and Tuma report, they had a large set of representative panel data at their disposal, with tolerable attrition rates despite the long period covered by their study. Crucial for an investigation of how the social and political transformation affected people's lives, however, is the fact that participants came to the threshold of adulthood under the conditions of the former USSR, then had to adapt to entirely new circumstances in one of six successor states that differed not only from the former USSR but were also vastly different from each other. As Titma and Tuma graphically illustrate, economic conditions as well as cultural and historical background make a big difference when comparing, for example, Estonia, with its centuries of tradition of free trade and its rapid assimilation to principles of democracy and market economy, and Tajikistan with a tradition of tribal loyalties and a "bazaar economy" that operates as a barrier against modernization and economic growth.

In sum, these differences and distinctions formed the backdrop against which young people had to renegotiate their lives. The highly standardized educational system may have homogenized young people with respect to educational resources. However, differences in the modes and consequences of their adaptational efforts to the new conditions can, at least partly, be attributed to personal attributes such as self-efficacy (Bandura, 1995), embedded in the larger institutional context of the legal and economic incentives for entrepreneurial activities.

For us, the most impressive common thread in Titma and Tuma's findings is their observation that success under the new economic and political conditions can be predicted by individuals' accumulation of human and social capital, providing adequate opportunities for initiative and self-realization, prior to the collapse of the communist system. The term "adequate" here refers to simple matters, such as the predictability of political conditions for individuals' decisions and investments, security with respect to one's assets and physical health, and the like. With regard to these criteria, the Baltic states may represent more favorable environments for individual development than many other successor states of the former USSR. Irrespective of these contextual differences, however, it seems to be the young people in particular who were more likely to adapt successfully to rapidly changing conditions. This finding supports the idea of greater plasticity during the "sensitive years" of young adulthood (cf. Alwin, 1994).

Titma and Tuma's conceptualization of their research program shows some interesting similarities, but also differences, to the research endeavors that we have pursued in the aftermath of German reunification. In addition, we utilized a survey approach including large samples from former East and West Germany and placed particular emphasis on biographical transitions and age-graded achievements in adolescence and young adulthood. Even though the core of our research is not longitudinal, it still captures the effects of ongoing sociopolitical change by comparing cohorts of same-aged young people in 1991 and 1996. With the time span between the two surveys, we covered a period of major transformations. Moreover, with the retrospectively gathered biographical data and data on psychosocial competencies we were also able to extend our scope to the period prior to reunification. Furthermore, we were able to access longitudinal data on East German adolescents with data collected prior to and after German reunification.

CORNERSTONES OF TRANSFORMATION RESEARCH

An examination of some of the differences between our work and that of Titma and Tuma's will provide a better understanding of what has been accomplished. The first point concerns the nature and conceptualization of social and political changes in the "Transition from Communism" study. The authors, at least implicitly, refer to the concept of modernization to describe the transformation from a traditional to a more modern or "westernized" society. Changes are expected to occur in a unidirectional fashion approaching a final goal that, in contrast to a command economy based on the reign of a one-party system, may be defined as a market economy based on democratic institutions.

Similar views prevailed in the beginning of German research on reunification. The breakdown of the East German political system was attributed to a lack of differentiation into well-coordinated social institutions better suited to meet the new challenges of globalization than the directive top-down management prevailing in the former German Democratic Republic (GDR). Because of the influx of Western TV programs, the failures of the Eastern system became increasingly obvious and undermined the loyalty of GDR citizens. In addition, the severe and economically motivated travel restrictions as well as the lack of high quality consumer goods increasingly fostered proneness for political protest and social unrest that ultimately lead to the collapse of the GDR. Based on this scenario, the theory of a "modernization catch-up" (Zapf, 1996) predicted that the introduction of West German legal, economic, and social institutions, by virtue of its incentives and options, would result in massive changes in individual behavior and quality of life within a brief period.

This model, corrected by reality, is now regarded by social and behavioral scientists as rather naive, at least within the German context. The alternative position was to predict a multidirectional and occasionally chaotic course of change, an expectation confirmed by actual events. But many consequences of the transformation proved unpredictable. Sometimes a surprising coexistence of the old and new was observed, and the pace of change and adaptations revealed vast dissimilarities for different ecological niches and individual capabilities. An organizing principle for approaching this complex pattern of transformation effects can be derived from broader concepts that are subsumed under challenge-response models by our sociological colleagues (Best, 2003; Boudon, 1986).

Transformation effects can roughly be ordered into a fourfold table along two dimensions. With regard to individuals, the first dimension is defined by persistence of old behaviors versus readiness for change of behaviors and orientations rooted in the past. The second dimension refers to institutions and is located along the dimension of the rigidity versus the flexibility of the new institutional order and corresponding expectations for individuals' behaviors and orientations. The resulting table with four cells is reminiscent of similar schemes in research on the acculturation of immigrants (Berry, 1997): Basically, the manner in which "old" individuals and "new" institutions match defines the four different modes of adaptation to social change. Each of these cells, for example, the one combining discontinuity of individuals' behavior patterns with flexibility in the behavioral expectations of the new institutions, forms an opportunity structure for individuals' actions that clearly facilitates innovation as a result of social change.

In the course of social change, more than one or even all of the above-mentioned opportunity niches may arise concurrently. Each niche holds a particular set of challenges and threats perceived in different ways by different individuals. It is these perceptions that initiate what Elder refers to as "control cycles" (Elder & Caspi, 1992). The concept of control cycles is similar to psychological concepts that describe and explain how individuals deal with challenges in general, for example, by pursuing primary or secondary control strategies (Heckhausen & Schulz, 1995) or by exerting problem-focused and/or emotion-focused coping behaviors (Lazarus & Folkman, 1984).

Applying the fourfold actor by institution table to Titma and Tuma's study, the situation prevailing in the new Baltic states would most likely fit into the cell characterized by high individual readiness for change with regard to past behaviors and orientations and flexibility of the new institutions, a combination evoking innovation. In contrast, the situation in Tajikistan is probably best characterized as a combination of individuals' clinging to old behaviors and orientations combined with a rigid new order, a combination encouraging submission as the modal way of adaptation to social change. These general directions of social change effects, of course, do not preclude inter-individual differences in adaptive efforts and outcomes. However, the fourfold actor by institution table helps to distinguish between different social change scenarios before turning to individual differences within these scenarios.

We conclude then that the modus operandi of social change at the aggregate level results from a multitude of constellations among features of the past and the present that are not static givens but are subject to dynamic change. The malleability of these constellations may well be the primary reason that the course of social change and its effects often turn out less unidirectional and less predictable than was previously assumed.

THE ROLE OF INDIVIDUAL RESOURCES: SELF-EFFICACY

Individuals pursue goals concerning their own development. These goals result from the complex processing of information on opportunities, normative expectations, one's capabilities and, importantly, one's beliefs that the individual's actions can lead to the desired results. Individuals' agency is of utmost importance because abrupt social change often requires actions for which established behavioral models and templates are not available. Agency, however, is bolstered by efficacy beliefs. This line of argument suggests that individuals with higher self-efficacy are better able to cope with new and unprecedented demands.

Rather than employing an established measure of self-efficacy beliefs, Titma and Tuma had to rely on a behavioral indicator as an indirect measure of "self-efficacy." They used an index of activities outside the individuals' principal occupation prior to 1991, including part-time and odd jobs, producing and growing food and other objects at home to sell or trade, and so forth. The rationale for this indirect measure may be that those persons who engage in numerous quasi-commercial activities outside their regular jobs also believe in the success of their endeavors. Although this particular index is intuitively appealing, it still awaits psychometric validation. It is crucial that the index refers to commercial types of behavior outside the individual's principal occupation before dramatic changes occurred. In this case, this agency measure might actually capture a personal disposition rather than a forced reaction to the strains of social change. Nevertheless, the results show that high levels of entrepreneurial agency were a precursor of significant self-employment toward the end of the 1990s under the new conditions. The situation in Eastern Germany was quite similar soon after the West German deutsche mark was introduced.

Commercial behaviors also predicted higher income levels, especially in Tajikistan, where conditions after the breakdown of the USSR were presumably more unfavorable than, for example, in the Baltic states. This finding shows that individual agency bears the potential, at least partially, to offset even unfavorable conditions which gridlocked many individuals by persisting in their old orientations within a scenario of rigid new institutions. Because the index used by Titma and Tuma is indirect, it will be necessary to use more established measures to evaluate the role of self-efficacy as a moderator more definitively. Additionally, their index did not clearly refer to the period prior to the occurrence of the social and political changes; hence, the direction of effects remains somewhat obscured.

In our own research on self-efficacy we had a sample that was initially interviewed 4 years prior to reunification in 1990, and that was followed up at regular intervals for 5 years after reunification. Because of the young age of the participants (12 years at Wave 1, 18 years at Wave 7) the self-efficacy measure used in this study referred to academic activities and peer relationships. We were able to confirm our hypothesis that higher self-efficacy before reunification would correspond to higher levels of psychological well-being after reunification.

Moreover, Pinquart, Silbereisen and Juang (2004) found support for their buffering hypothesis. They predicted that higher self-efficacy would protect people against negative effects of perceived reunification-related challenges and threats, such as economic hardship due to parental unemployment or the closing of former state-run youth clubs. The rationale behind this assumption is that higher self-efficacy is known to allow individuals to seize opportunities and pursue goals even under conditions that would normally discourage adaptive efforts. There was also a relationship between decline of one's economic and personal situation and lower levels of psychological well-being. Moreover, more detailed analysis showed that this relationship was especially strong for those with a low sense of self-efficacy (see Figure 3.1).

The role of self-efficacy was also assessed in the context of political reorientation. Those who were strongly committed to the political system of the former GDR were urged to change their values fundamentally, and were often sanctioned for their previous political engagement. Against this backdrop, we were interested in whether high levels of self-efficacy would buffer against the negative effects that a strong

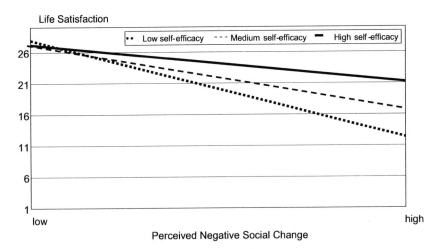

FIGURE 3.1 Associations of perceived social change with post-unification life-satisfaction in adolescents with high, medium, and low levels of pre-unification self-efficacy.

Note. High (low) levels of self-efficacy were defined as one standard deviation above (below) the mean.

identification with the old political system could potentially have on adolescents' psychological well-being after reunification. Adherence to the old system was assessed a few months before the fall of the Berlin Wall, at a time when many East Germans had already reduced their identification with the former system and when some were even leaving East Germany. Maintained identification, as understood in our study, was found only among hard core supporters of the old regime. High level identification with the Communist system, within the first 2 years of German reunification, however, was associated with an increase in psychological distress only in a subgroup that scored low on self-efficacy prior to reunification. On the other hand, moderate to high self-efficacy was not followed by a significant increase in psychological distress for those who identified with the GDR system (Pinquart, Juang, & Silbereisen, 2004).

Persistence of old orientations was a source of conflict only among those young people who did not believe in their ability to master new demands. Whether self-efficacy would have offset the negative effects of an ideological adherence to the old system among older adults, however, remains questionable. For young people, still in their impressionable years, identification with the old system may have simply been an attitude, whereas for older people it had become the basis of social status and a source of gratifying experiences.

In sum, when self-efficacy was formed years before reunification it seemed to generate long-term positive effects by consolidating the psychological well-being even when they were confronted with obstacles and difficulties imposed by the new order. We were not able to distinguish clearly, however, between perceived challenges and objective changes after reunification. Consequently, it remains unclear how self-efficacy precisely mediates the process of adaptation to social change. Self-efficacy may have helped individuals to gain some advantage from the changes despite the obstacles they experienced, or it may have helped individuals to perceive even aversive consequences of change more favorably. There were some indications in our data that the effects of high self-efficacy were not restricted to more positive cognitions, but that they also corresponded to factual advantages. Individuals with high prereunification self-efficacy beliefs, for example, were less likely to become unemployed in the first years of German reunification, even when controlling for school achievement and parental socio-economic status (Pinquart, Juang, & Silbereisen, 2003).

At any rate, Titma and Tuma's study on the changes in the former USSR, as well as our studies on the former East Germany, demonstrate that self-efficacy is a critical personal resource for favorable development under changing and unpredictable conditions. Admittedly, challenges in the course of German reunification were, on average, milder than those experienced during the restructuring of the former USSR. In East Germany, many (especially members of the younger generation) met new opportunities rather than constraints; (e.g., in terms of access to higher education). In any case, the fact that similar effects were observed despite differences in the social change scenarios and in the operationalizations of measures in the two studies is encouraging. That self-efficacy measured for the rather limited academic domain revealed such profound effects may indicate that academic self-efficacy was successfully generalized to other behavioral domains. This is a crucial point because self-efficacy with regard to public action was certainly not promoted during the decades of Communist rule. All in all, our results fit the results of research on profound social changes in other countries, such as the Iowa farm crisis (Conger & Elder, 1994). These social changes also had severe consequences for individuals' development even though they were not as fundamental as the large-scale societal transformation that occurred in the former Eastern Bloc countries. Similar to findings in our studies, this research depicts the role of self-efficacy in diminishing the magnitude of perceived economic stress (Conger, Jewsbury-Conger, Matthews, & Elder, 1999).

COHORT COMPARISONS ACROSS REGIONS AND AGE GROUPS

The characteristics of the social and political changes and of individual properties as exemplified so far can be located in a fourfold grid comprised of dimensions that apply to many "transformation societies" of central and eastern Europe. This grid is derived from the more general idea of a challenge–response model (Best, 2003). In this particular case, it is made up of the juxtaposition of old versus new on the part of individuals' behaviors and orientations (persistence vs. discontinuity) and of rigidity versus flexibility of the new legal, economic, and social order. The location of actors or respondents to social change in this fourfold grid provides an understanding of the modes and directions of their actions in adapting biographical pathways to rapidly changing or changed institutional contexts. Though an abstract heuristic, this model has far-reaching implications for the design and the measures of empirical studies dealing with social change and its effects on human development at the individual level.

Quite obviously, the matrix of individual behaviors and institutional expectations needs to be represented in the design. For example, one indicator of the flexibility of the new institutional context is whether the previously learned occupation is still in demand under the new system. In a unified Germany, Middendorff (2000) analyzed the career success of East German students who had graduated in 1986–1987 in East Germany, that is, about 3 years before the fall of the Berlin Wall. In 1991, career success clearly depended on whether their occupation was still needed within the changed societal conditions. Not surprisingly, former teachers of Marxism-Leninism fared worst, despite all of them having also taught a second, less ideologically grounded subject. About 70% had to leave their former jobs, and 40% switched to a job for which no university education was required. Similarly, about one third of the graduates in economics showed downward mobility, compared to less than 4% of physicians.

Most research conducted on the consequences of German reunification was far less explicit with respect to concrete contextual demands and individual behavior orientations. Most often, Eastern and Western samples were compared in terms of nominal comparisons (Bronfenbrenner & Morris, 1998) (i.e., without any fine-grained breakdowns into smaller regions with allegedly different opportunity structures and without operationalized measures of these presumed regional differences). Furthermore, most studies did not measure the degree to which different individuals were actually affected by the demands and challenges of the new institutions.

In this respect, Titma and Tuma's approach is not all that different from the prevalent German research on reunification. However, they had the opportunity to study different regions that were quite distinctive in terms of their pre-USSR history, culture, and post-USSR economic development and legal regulations. At the institutional level, this is certainly an advantage compared to the simpler situation in Germany where reunification did not create a multitude of institutionally different scenarios. Unfortunately however, they do not have data on how individuals were differentially affected by these conditions.

The single-cohort design used by Titma and Tuma does not allow comparisons by age cohort. Elder's model of the impact of social change, particularly his life stage principle (e.g., Elder & Caspi, 1992), proposes that the developmental pathways of even adjacent cohorts may take completely different directions as a function of age-related differences in resources and opportunities at the time when marked social change occurs. Elder (1974) demonstrated that the consequences of the Great Depression were less severe for male adolescents than for male children. The former were more able to cope and were better adjusted throughout their lives. In part this was due to immediate advantages in a situation of crisis. For example, male adolescents who had to contribute to the family income and who may even have taken over part of their fathers' former responsibilities, were granted autonomy earlier than was usual at that time. After World War II, they became eligible for the G.I. Bill, granting them free access to college and higher education, which created a basis for successful careers. The situation was quite the opposite for females. Adolescent girls suffered from a lifelong disadvantage as compared to those females who were still children at the time of the Great Depression.

In our own research regarding German reunification we focused systematically on the role of age, cohort, and gender. We included male and female adolescents and young adults between the ages of 13 and 29. Because development during these life stages is strongly influenced by normative expectations of the educational context, we differentiated between students and graduates of vocationally oriented and college-preparatory schools. Data were analyzed from two age-equivalent samples, one surveyed in 1991 and one in 1996. These years demarcate important cornerstones in the process of reunification. By 1991, the new West German institutions were set in place. Of major concern for young people was the complete restructuring of the East's formerly unitary school system into a three-tier system that introduced the concept of preselection into educational pathways as early as after fourth grade. Particularly for those in the two vocationally oriented school tiers, the school-to-work transition became a matter of individual initiative and responsibility to a much higher degree than for their predecessors in the former GDR school system.

In 1991, the East's economy remained almost unaffected by the German reunification because many formerly state-owned production plants survived unchanged until they were either sold or closed down. In the following years, the economy deteriorated rapidly so that 1996 was characterized by high unemployment despite politicians' overoptimistic promises that accompanied the social and political changes. In sum, 1991 was characterized by a merely formal change to the Western system. Those in our age bracket had spent their formative years predominantly or even entirely under East German conditions. In 1991, these cohorts were not yet confronted with the full blast of the economic restructuring. In 1996, things had definitely changed. It is true that a larger portion of the age range studied had school and vocational training experiences under the new auspices of unified Germany, which can be regarded as an advantage. Conversely, they faced a definitely more difficult labor market compared to the situation in

1991. This was reflected in Reitzle and Silbereisen's (2000a) finding that in 1996, 20- to 29-year-old young adults from vocationally oriented school tracks had achieved financial self-support, the crucial cornerstone en route to adulthood, significantly later compared with their same-aged predecessors in 1991 who had automatically achieved financial independence on completion of vocational training in the former GDR. The difference in the timing of financial self-support between the cohorts surveyed in 1991 and 1996, respectively, could partly be "explained away" by two indicators representing structural change in the East. First, being in some kind of training at the time of assessment was supposed to reflect newly emerged options and demands for education. Second, having ever been unemployed before the achievement of self-support, or before the survey if financial independence was not yet accomplished, was thought to reflect newly emerging constraints of the labor market. The two predictors together accounted for roughly one third of the timing difference between young adults surveyed in 1991 and 1996 thus indicating that delay in financial independence can, at least in part, be directly attributed to structural change in the form of new options as well as constraints.

Another topic raised by Titma and Tuma deserves some further consideration. They refer to the fact that young people are especially flexible in response to new challenges. This notion resonates with the more general theme of the formative years. For example, earlier research (Alwin, 1994; Glenn, 1980) has shown that particularly basic political attitudes, worldviews, and values may still change during adolescence, but become more stable during the adult years. Against this backdrop, it could be expected that East German adolescents should adapt more quickly and more easily to the political changes after reunification compared with young adults in their late 20s. This implies, broadly speaking, a shift to a greater preference for individualistic values and a turning away from collectivist values fostered by institutions of socialization and the media.

Indeed, Reitzle and Silbereisen (2000b) found that the existing, albeit moderate, differences in value preferences between East and West German adolescents and young adults (age 15 to 29) measured in 1991 became attenuated in 1996, particularly among members of younger birth cohorts who were 15 to 19 years-old in 1991, and 20 to 24 years old in 1996. It was, however, not the East Germans' increased preference for individualistic values that rendered them more similar to their Western counterparts, but their decreasing preferences for collectivist values such as family safety, social order, politeness, and respect for tradition.

CONCLUSION

Titma and Tuma's study is an example of social change paralleling an ongoing longitudinal study on individual development. This may be considered an advantage insofar as one has some kind of individual pre-post measures gathered before and after demarcating events of social change. Crucial measures concerning individuals' resources were collected three years before the former USSR formally finished to exist. Ideally, the measured resources such as formal education or self-efficacy represent personal assets that were not themselves created by newly emerging societal conditions. Quite obviously, these individual assets contributed to successful development in a completely altered context. Still, one has to keep in mind that it was education accomplished in the socialist system that now turned out beneficial under the rules of an emerging market economy. In a similar vein, we also found that higher educational levels achieved in the former GDR were related to career success after unification. In sum, high levels of formal education per se as well as self-efficacy beliefs seem to be helpful universals with regard to successful adaptation in changing contexts.

One could, however, ask whether these beneficial effects are restricted to comparably young people at the beginning of their transitions into adulthood. Given the age homogeneity of Titma Tuma's samples, it is difficult to pursue a strategy of nested comparisons (Shanahan & Elder, 1997) in order to establish differential effects of social change (e.g., according to individuals' status in the life course). For example, the positive effects of formal education may vanish with increasing age if the labor market operates with implicit age limits and offers hardly any opportunities for people beyond age 50, as holds true in the German case. In addition, the cohort comparisons in our research showed that younger people exert a somewhat greater readiness for change (e.g., with respect to their value preferences). As already known from Elder's research, it is the patterning of individuals' position in the life-course and their resources on the one hand, and opportunities and constraints provided by changing contexts on the other hand, that exerts long-term influences on development.

In order to fully understand individuals' adaptation in the research on effects of social change, variability must exist on both the individual and the contextual aspects. On the person's site, variability with regard to life stage is but one example, and self-efficacy is not the only resource one may think of. Family support and being embedded in social networks represent further viable candidates. In this vein,

Titma and Tuma's behavioral indicator of self-efficacy is not clearly defined as a merely psychological property. Instead, individuals' engagement in multiple commercial activities outside their major occupations could result from a blend of their efficacy beliefs and their embeddedness in supportive social networks. Following this line of reasoning, persons' apparent continuity could partly be confounded with continuity of supportive proximal contexts.

As the successor states of the former USSR pursued rather different political and economic pathways, a great amount of variability exists on the macro-contextual level. In other words, there are different shades of social change potentially creating positioning as well as patterning effects between different regions of the former Soviet Union. Going beyond comparisons between the eastern and western parts of Germany, we increasingly consider regional similarities and differences within each part of Germany. For developmentalists, however, it is not the political borders that are demarcating the psychologically relevant research entities. Instead, changing macro-contexts can be mapped along operationalized and actually measured aggregate properties that are deemed influential on individual development. Even within these rather homogenous settings, however, for different persons social change may unfold in a completely different fashion. Consequently, a further desiderate for future research is the measurement of individual experiences of social change. This is a still unfulfilled task in most of the research on social change and human development, of course originating in the unpredictability of the direction and nature of particularly sudden economic and societal changes.

Our research program on German reunification was begun under great time pressure. No social scientists anticipated the fall of the GDR. Consequently, we had to decide on a research paradigm very quickly, one that turned out to be a medley of acculturation research and Elder's approach to family stressors, such as economic hardship embedded in a larger scenario of rapid social change. With regard to acculturation, we had learned from Feldman and Rosenthal (1990) that immigrants adapt their timetables for developmental tasks and biographical transitions in a highly differential manner. Normative expectations that are deeply rooted in one's culture of origin will take years or even generations to adjust to the host culture's standards. In contrast, issues that are dictated by the pragmatics of everyday life will change rapidly. Based on this view, and given the fact that the transfer of social institutions from West to East produced some kind of acculturation pressure without actually moving from early on the people, we expected changes at the individual level to happen at a highly differential pace.

Elder's work equipped us not only with a general model of how new challenges will be handled via control cycles based on an evaluation of the situation and limited by the resources available, it also alerted us to the possibility (and as it turned out, actually to the fact) that the way of mastering new challenges is also a function of the life stage in which the affected individuals are located. Furthermore, his view opened the way to a more general challenge-response model serving as a blueprint for the multidirectional changes one could expect. The persistence of behavioral orientations nourished before reunification and the rigidity in the implementation of the new order form a backdrop against which individuals attempt to negotiate their goals for development that are, of course, also shaped by numerous other influences, such as biological maturation and personal aspirations beyond the social forces already mentioned.

This general outline can be specified for the age groups and cohorts we have been investigating. Concerning the transition into work roles, the new institutional order established in former East Germany was very rigid. The Western educational system was implemented overnight without permitting a smooth transition with intermediate regulations. Instead, all schools had to follow the new guidelines with respect to curriculum, teacher training, and even everyday routines, such as teaching styles and achievement evaluation (Little, Oettingen, Stetsenko, & Baltes 1995). For children at the beginning of their school careers, such changes did not really form challenges or barriers, because there is no substantial amount of prior experiences to conflict with the new regulations. This example illustrates the more general principle that rigidity of the new order can be outweighed by the individuals' malleability.

In sum, the effects of social change as they were studied are multifacetted (e.g., Reitzle & Silbereisen, 2000a, 2000b), depending on whether structural constraints were directly imposed or not (for an overview, see Juang, Reitzle & Silbereisen, 2000; Silbereisen, 2000; Silbereisen & Youniss, 2001). A vivid example is young adults' timing of financial self-support. The early self-support of young Easterners surveyed in 1991 mirrored the narrow but secure pathways from school to work in the former GDR. The later self-support of the successive cohorts surveyed in 1996 could, at least in part, be directly attributed to the new challenges of social change in the form of unemployment and the need for further qualification. The value study, on the other hand, showed that adaptations are easier to accomplish if one is still young and void of an extensive learning history in an outdated context—at least insofar as the later cohorts of young adults may have encountered the tougher conditions, but nevertheless had the advantage of still being in their formative years. Furthermore, our research indicated that high levels of self-efficacy seem to be an asset for successful adaptation over and beyond being at an advantageous stage in the life cycle.

In our view, future research on the role of social and political changes on personality development needs to bear in mind that the challenges so central in our general framework are actually confounded with a host of other conditions, such as differences in cultural traditions, value orientations, and economic systems. To find out what indeed is specific to the changes under scrutiny, at least as long as one lacks an explanatory concept at this level, the systematic comparison across a number of cases is of high heuristic importance. For instance, we deem a coordination of existing research endeavors, which would bring together that described by Titma and Tuma and the one we are part of as very fruitful. However, there are other countries and regions of interest that may also not yet be the focus of social science research, in part, because they do not permit open access.

Next, it is of utmost importance to design studies so that they are resonant of the major insights in the workings of social change that Elder and colleagues (e.g., Elder, 1974; Elder & Caspi, 1992; Elder & O'Rand, 1995) have published: it is a resource-consuming process of regaining control under the burden of multiple challenges that unfold over time and is basically shaped by what the actors have to bring to the situation. In this regard, a number of major moderating effects are known and need to be addressed, such as age, cohort, and gender.

Though we believe our own research to have been adequate in this regard, there are two major additions we want to suggest. One refers to individual potentials that help to cope with the challenges of social change. A prominent example is self-efficacy which, however, needs to be operationlized and measured as an unambiguous psychological property of the person. The other refers to the challenges themselves—we need to accurately measure the actual load of aversive or benign strains that individuals face in the course of economic and societal changes. Only then would research on social change get closer to definite conclusions about cause and effect. A clear dose-response relationship among opportunities, adversities and behaviors would give credit to the assumption of a causal association.

REFERENCES

Alwin, D. F. (1994). Aging, personality, and social change: The stability of individual differences over the adult life span. In D. L. Featherman, R. M. Lerner, & M. Perlmutter (Eds.), *Life-span development and behavior* (Vol. 12, pp. 135–185). Hillsdale, NJ: Erlbaum.

Bandura, A. (1995). Exercise of personal and collective efficacy in changing societies. In A. Bandura (Ed.), *Self-efficacy in changing societies* (pp. 1–45). Cambridge, UK: Cambridge University Press.

Berry, J. (1997). Immigration, acculturation, and adaptation. *Applied Psychology: An International Review, 46,* 5–68.

Best, H. (2003). Der langfristige Wandel politischer Eliten 1867–2000: Auf dem Weg der Konvergenz? [The long-term change of political elites 1867–2000: On the way of convergence?]. In S. Hradil & P. Imbusch (Eds.), *Oberschichten—Eliten—Herrschende Klassen* (pp. 369–399). Opladen: Leske + Budrich.

Boudon, R. (1986). *Theories of social change: A critical appraisal.* Berkeley: University of California Press.

Bronfenbrenner, U., & Morris, P. A. (1998). The ecology of developmental processes. In W. Damon & R. M. Lerner (Eds.), *Handbook of child psychology. Volume one: Theoretical models of human development* (pp. 993–1028). New York: Wiley.

Conger, C., & Elder, G. H., Jr. (1994). *Families in troubled times: Adapting to change in rural America.* New York: De Gruyter.

Conger, R. D., Jewsbury-Conger, K., Matthews, L. S., & Elder, G. H. (1999). Pathways of economic influence on adolescent adjustment. *American Journal of Community Psychology, 27,* 519–541.

Elder, G. H., Jr. (1974). *Children of the Great Depression: Social change in life experiences.* Chicago: University of Chicago Press.

Elder, G. H., Jr., & Caspi, A. (1992). Studying lives in a changing society: Sociological and personological explorations. In R. A. Zucker, A. I. Rabin, J. Aronoff, & S. Frank (Eds.), *Personality structure in the life course* (pp. 276–322). New York: Springer.

Elder, G. H., Jr., & O'Rand, A. M. (1995). Adult lives in a changing society. In K. S. Cook, G. A. Fine & J. S. House (Eds.), *Sociological perspectives on social psychology* (pp. 452–475). Needham Heights, MA: Allyn & Bacon.

Feldman, S. S., & Rosenthal, D. A. (1990). The acculturation of autonomy expectations in Chinese high schoolers residing in two Western nations. *International Journal of Psychology, 25,* 259–281.

Glenn, N. D. (1980). Values, attitudes and beliefs. In O. G. Brim, & J. Kagan (Eds.), *Constancy and change in human development* (pp. 596–640). Cambridge, MA: Harvard University Press.

Heckhausen, J., & Schulz, R. (1995). A life-span theory of control. *Psychological Review, 102,* 284–304.

Juang, L., Reitzle, M., & Silbereisen, R. K. (2000). The adaptability of transitions to adulthood under social change: The case of German unification. *European Review of Applied Psychology, 50,* 275–282.

Lazarus, R., & Folkman, S. (1984). *Stress, appraisal, and coping.* New York: Springer.

Little, T. D., Oettingen, G., Stetsenko, A., & Baltes, P. B. (1995). Children's action-control beliefs about school performance: How do American children compare with German and Russian children? *Journal of Personality and Social Psychology, 69,* 686c700.

Middendorff, E. (2000). *Individueller Lebenslauf und gesellschaftlicher Umbruch* [Individual life-course and societal upheaval]. Halle: Martin Luther University Halle.

Pinquart, M., Juang, L. P., & Silbereisen, R. K. (2003). Self-efficacy and successful school-to-work transition: A longitudinal study. *Journal of Vocational Behavior, 63,* 329–346.

Pinquart, M., Juang, L. P., & Silbereisen, R. K. (2004). Changes of psychological distress in East German adolescents facing German unification: The role of commitment to the old system and of self-efficacy beliefs. *Youth & Society, 36,* 77–101.

Pinquart, M., Silbereisen, R. K., & Juang, L. (2004). Moderating effects of adolescents' self-efficacy beliefs on psychological responses to social change. *Journal of Adolescent Research, 19,* 340–359.

Reitzle, M., & Silbereisen, R. K. (2000a). The timing of adolescents' school-to-work transition in the course of social change: The example of German unification. *Swiss Journal of Psychology, 59,* 240–255.

Reitzle, M., & Silbereisen, R. K. (2000b). Adapting to social change: Adolescent values in Eastern and Western Germany. In J. Bynner & R. K. Silbereisen (Eds.), *Adversities and challenge in life in the new Germany and in England* (pp. 123–152). Houndmills: Macmillan.

Shanahan, M. J., & Elder, G. H., Jr. (1997). Nested comparisons in the study of historical change and individual development. In J. Tudge, M. J. Shanahan, & J. Valsiner (Eds.), *Comparisons in human development. Understanding time and context* (pp. 109–136). New York: Cambridge University Press.

Silbereisen, R. K. (2000). German unification and adolescents' developmental timetables: Continuities and discontinuities. In: L. Crockett & R. K. Silbereisen (Eds.), *Negotiating adolescence in times of social change* (pp. 104–122). Cambridge: Cambridge University Press.

Silbereisen, R. K., & Youniss, J. (2001). Families and development in childhood and adolescence: Germany before and after reunification. Special Issue of the *American Behavioral Scientist, 44.*

Zapf, W. (1996). Zwei Geschwindigkeiten in Ost- und Westdeutschland [Eastern and Western Germany at different pace]. In M. Diewald & K. U. Mayer (Eds.), *Zwischenbilanz der Wiedervereinigung: Strukturwandel und Mobilität im Transformationsprozess* (pp. 317–328). Opladen, Germany: Leske und Budrich.

CHAPTER 4

Job-Search Strategies in Time and Place: A Study of Post-Service Employment Among Former Russian Army Officers*

**David E. Rohall, V. Lee Hamilton,
David R. Segal, and Jessica Y. Y. Kwong**

L ife-course theory orients the study of human lives in historical times, reflecting the fact that historical events affect the people going through them in different ways depending on their life circumstances. The theory links structural conditions influencing individuals' reaction to personal resources that can be mobilized to cope with events. In addition, the time in our lives in which an event occurs can influence how we react to it. That is, certain events have more or less impact on us depending on the flow of our life course. Life course theory is unique in that it includes the concept of human agency in choice making (Elder, 1994). Some events will affect some people

*This research was funded by the National Science Foundation (Sociology Program) under grants SBR-9402212, 9411755, and 9601760 and the Army Research Institute under contract DASW 0100K16. The views expressed here are those of the authors, not necessarily those of the National Science Foundation, The Army Research Institute, or any other agency of the U.S. government. Please direct all correspondence to David E. Rohall, Department of Sociology, Western Illinois University, Macomb, IL 61455.

more than others, depending on the resources they bring to bear and the choices they make during those events.

One such event is organizational downsizing. Downsizing affects individuals in a number of ways. The loss of a job entails a major loss of income and can impact an individual's sense of identity and self-worth (Broman, Hamilton, & Hoffman, 2001; Hamilton, Hoffman, Broman, & Rauma, 1993; Kessler, Turner, & House, 1988). Even after finding new work, leavers must cope with change in a significant part of their lives. Such change is probably more severe in institutions like the armed services where employment is often considered more than "just a job"; it is a way of life (Moskos & Wood, 1988).

A considerable amount of research has focused on the role of the military in the life course. Some of this research has focused on life course factors that lead to military service (e.g., Woodruff, 2003). To a greater extent research has focused on the post-military sequels of service during wartime (Elder, 1987; Elder, Gimbel, & Ivie, 1991), and particularly exposure to combat (Elder & Clipp, 1988).

The analyses in this chapter focus on the Russian military and the experiences of a generation of officers who were commissioned in the Soviet Army during the Cold War but experienced interrelated historical changes that included the collapse of the Soviet regime and the end of the Cold War in Europe. They were then left in an army where their profession carried less prestige and their jobs were less secure due to large-scale downsizing efforts. The goal of this chapter is to assess the effects of job-search strategies on the quality of post-service employment. This study incorporates the life-course approach by examining the role of time, in terms of career stage, and place, the region in which the downsizing occurred, in re-employment strategies.

AN ARMY IN TRANSITION

The Soviet military had been manned primarily by conscripts (Jones, 1985). However, the nucleus of the armed forces was a professional officer cadre that was regarded as militarily effective and had high social status and a relatively high degree of professional autonomy (Segal & Schwartz, 1981). By contrast, in post-Soviet Russia, the Army has been characterized as at best "a deprofessionalising territorial defense force . . . with a decreasing ability even to provide security for the territory of the Russian federation" (Herspring, 2002a, p. 208). Perhaps most importantly for our concerns, however, professional officers were privileged in their post-service lives relative to other Soviet citizens—and this privilege has been evaporating.

The Soviet government had maintained a comprehensive system of non-contributory old-age retirement and veterans' pensions funded primarily by the government and by state-owned enterprises, based upon laws passed in the 1950s and 1960s. Civilians could not retire until age 60 unless they were disabled. In the mid-1980s, almost 14 million old-age civilian pensioners were receiving pensions below the "under provisioning" (poverty) level of 70 rubles per month. About 12 million old-age pensioners continued to work, primarily in low paying jobs. Many retirees achieved a degree of financial relief by living with their children. In 1988, just before the fall of the Soviet regime, about a million civilian pensioners lived alone, in almost total neglect and near destitution (Zickel, 1991).

However, there was also a "special pension" system, awarded for outstanding service to the state. In the late 1980s, for example, retired members of the Communist Party administrative elite were receiving pensions that ranged from 250 to 450 rubles per month. Military retirees were covered by a similar program. Unlike civilian Soviet workers, officers could retire after 25 years of service, regardless of age, at which point their pension was 50% of their salary. Where civilians' old-age pensions were keyed to their salaries up to a ceiling of 120 rubles, military pensions were keyed to years of service with no ceiling, and went up to 75% of salary (Jones, 1985). Moreover, unlike the American military officer corps, Soviet officers were not required to retire early if they did not advance in rank. Junior lieutenants could serve until they were 40 years old, mandatory retirement went up to age 60 for major generals (the norm for civilians); above this rank, officers were effectively exempt from mandatory retirement. In addition, officers who resisted retirement were put to work in civil defense, the Voluntary Organization for Cooperation with the Army, Aviation, and the Fleet (DOSAAF), moved into the Ministry of Defense as inspectors, or became faculty or administrators at military academies.

In 1988 and 1989, the State Committee for Labor and Social Problems developed a new pension law to replace the laws of the 1950s and 1960s. It anticipated a guaranteed subsistence wage, an increased ceiling on old-age pensions, and regular cost-of-living increases. It was anticipated that it would become effective in 1991. However, in 1989 the Soviet Union that more than two generations of Russians lived under collapsed (Collins & Waller, 1982; Galtung, 1992; Segal, 1992), and the minimal infrastructure for pension support that had been planned went down with it.

DOWNSIZING THE RUSSIAN ARMED SERVICES

The Russian military underwent major organizational downsizing in the mid-1990s—a process that was common among armed forces cross-nationally at that time (Segal & Babin, 2000). Unlike the parallel process in the United States, where if a military base was closed or a unit deactivated the personnel would be reassigned, the downsizing of the Russian military was more like a plant closing. If a base was deactivated, or a position declared redundant, the incumbent officers lost their jobs. Between 1990 and 1993, the number of Russian military personnel declined from 3.4 million to 2.3 million; the current size of the Russian armed services is just over 1 million officers and enlisted personnel (1.16 million), over half of whom are conscripts (Myasnikov, 2003). The goal is to reduce the armed services by half, with most of the cuts coming out of the Russian Ground Forces, its Army (Interfax, 2001). Hence, organizational downsizing in the armed services will continue to be a significant "turning point" in the life course of many Russian soldiers, particularly in the Army, over the next decade (Elder, Gimbel, & Ivie, 1991).

Given the transitions in Russia's armed services following the fall of the Soviet Union, organizational downsizing in the Russian Army may actually be a positive turning point in officers' lives. While unemployment is always a concern for workers asked to leave a job as a result of downsizing, staying in a bad organization may represent something even worse to the worker (Milkman, 1997). Current information regarding the conditions of daily life in the Russian services continues to show corruption in the Russian officer corps, low levels of discipline, and large numbers of soldiers deserting (Herspring, 2002b). Investigators have found soldiers being fed with dog food in place of stew (Meek, 1998), and many garrisons let their heat and electricity bills go unpaid; such conditions have helped contribute to a breakdown in soldiers' morale (Ball, 1996). The poor conditions of life in service also impact finances because, by some estimates, families of contract servicemen are paid only 78% of income of an average Russian family (Galaiko, 2001). Consistent with these reports, prior research using the data set from the current study shows that former officers, those who left army service and found new employment, reported better living conditions and well-being than officers who stayed in service after a period of downsizing (see Rohall, Hamilton, Segal, & Segal, 2001).

EMPLOYMENT TRANSITIONS: FINDING A JOB

Military service can act as a turning point in finding work after leaving service. Sampson and Laub (1996) show how overseas duty and in-service military education enhanced the employability of American servicemen after World War II. That is, having military experience increased the occupational status, job stability, and economic well-being of men who had been in service during the war compared with men without such experiences. This effect was especially strong among those who had joined the services earlier in life and those who had a history of delinquency. Laub and Sampson's work in this volume shows similar results for Korean veterans. Hence, the authors found both direct effects of military service on the occupational well-being of former servicemen as well as interactive effects, based on when they joined the services and their backgrounds prior to service.

Strong and Weak Ties

Sampson and Laub's (1996) work demonstrates the influence of military service on American soldiers after World War II. The context of the transition from military to civilian labor in Russia is somewhat different, notably because Russian officers are not serving in war and entered service voluntarily; they wanted to be in service. They also had more education prior service than the Sampson and Laub samples. Thus, Russian officers in modern times are coping not only with changing jobs but also with changing careers. In addition, these officers are not entering an expanding economy like the World War II and Korean War generations.

Unlike their civilian counterparts, many military jobs, notably in combat-related specialties, cannot easily be transferred to the civilian context. (Imagine, for example, how tank commanders or artillery specialists might use their skills in the civilian context—outside of the defense industry, there is little carry-over.) Even if the military provided personal and professional growth opportunities, such skills would not necessarily be enough to overcome larger structural problems in the Russian economy.

Finding work may also be hampered because the networks and

ties traditionally used to find civilian work are less accessible for military personnel, who have most of their contacts still in service. This distinction is important because traditional social science research has focused on the role of "weak ties" in finding work after losing a job (see Granovetter, 1973, 1995). Weak ties refer to distant friends or acquaintances who are connected to the job seekers through other people; hence, the seeker has little or no direct contact with the potential employer. Rather, a bridge between the knowledgeable intermediary and the employer is made. In some sense, the "strong tie," someone who knows the job seeker very well, should be more beneficial to the job seeker because he or she is more motivated to help the seeker. However, Granovetter (1973) argues that, "those to whom we are weakly tied are more likely to move in circles different from our own and will thus have access to information different from that which we receive" (p. 1371). Thus, for job seekers, the *quantity* of ties is argued to be more important to finding work than the *quality* of those ties.

Granovetter's (1973) earlier research supports his contention that weak ties are more important than strong ties for finding work. He reports that of people who find work through contacts, 84% reported seeing their contacts rarely or occasionally. Only 17% reported seeing their contact often. Hence, "strength" is defined here as how often people meet or get together. However, Granovetter's (1995) more recent work combines both strong and weak ties in assessing job-searching strategies. He finds that 56% of the professional, technical, and managerial workers experiencing job transition in New England report finding work via personal ties (both strong and weak), followed by another 19% who found jobs through formal means (e.g., ads or employment agencies), and 26% through direct application and the rest via miscellaneous other ways (differences due to rounding). And personal ties not only produce jobs, they are also associated with finding better jobs: workers who found jobs via networks (strong or weak) were more satisfied with their work and reported higher incomes than those who found work through other means.

Similar findings have been cited in non-Western samples. Bian's (1997) study of more than 1,000 Chinese adults found that almost half (45%) got their job assignments using help from another person, similar to other western samples. (Unlike Western employment systems, jobs were until recently assigned to adults by the Chinese government.) Further, 45% of the personal ties were indirect in nature—they used intermediaries or "weak ties," especially if they were older candidates. Not surprising, helpers of higher status were able to obtain better jobs for job seekers than helpers in less prestigious positions. Hence, it may be not so much the fact that personal ties produce better jobs, as the fact that people that initiate such strategies have contacts in higher places.

Subsequent research on the relative effects of strong and weak ties shows mixed results regarding the long-term importance of weak versus strong ties in finding a job. That is, in some cases, strong ties may be as or more important than weak ties in finding a good job (Marsden & Hurlbert, 1988; Montgomery, 1992). For instance, during times of great uncertainty and change in society, such as the current Russian economy, strong ties may be more useful to finding work than weak ties.

Prior to the fall of the Soviet Union in the early 1990s, much like in the Chinese system, many jobs were obtained through the government. While informal economies always helped support workers in finding more favorable assignments, research on the current Russian economy suggests that there is an increase in the size and scope of such informal economies (Ledeneva, 1998). Employers and workers regularly rely on "favors" and informal commitments in order for the economy to maintain itself. Gerbner (2004) has recently noted that in the face of governmental collapse, "Russians often rely on close circles of intimates and networks of people with whom they trade favors" (p. 27). Hence, the Russian economy seems particularly open to the personal-ties system of finding work with the incorporation of a capitalist economy.

But Yakubovich and Kozina's (2000) study of job acquisition in four Russian cities, using Granovetter's paradigm, shows little support for the notion that the use of personal ties increased during the time of economic transition. Rather, the authors argue that an informal economy of personal ties existed both before and after the fall of the Soviet Union, despite changes in the nature of the work available and the necessary qualifications for the new jobs. These findings are important because they suggest that we should not expect that the changing Russian economy will produce an economy based more on personal ties than any other economy.

In sum, both Eastern and Western samples emphasize the importance of personal ties in finding work during a period of job transition. The use of such ties seems to be relatively stable after the fall of the Soviet Union. Given the dramatic changes going on in the Russian society and culture, we predict that workers who used personal ties, especially strong ties, to find work will report finding better jobs than those individuals using more formal methods of finding work.

Strategies in Time

The role of time is essential to life course theory; timing provides another context to understanding reactions to life events. For instance, Hardy, Hazelrigg, and Quadagno (1996) present an analysis of ending careers in the automobile industry shows differential reactions to retirement decisions, depending on the timing of that event. Although many workers were comfortable with their retirement decisions, others were less satisfied, notably those who decided to retire early as part of corporate "buy-out" plan. Hence, many workers in this study chose to leave the industry, but the decision was more satisfying for some than others.

Older workers may also view downsizing differently than their younger counterparts, seeing it as a sign of a larger failure in society (Newman, 1985, 1986). Many workers simply blame poor management for the decline of a business, or the failure of the state, as with the case of Russian officers, most of who trained under the auspices of a much larger, stronger Soviet empire. Whereas downsizing is generally deemed as more difficult for older workers than younger ones, there may be other advantages to leaving work at an older age or later career stage. According to Granovetter's (1995) work, generally speaking, older job seekers are much more likely to use personal ties to find work than younger workers. Hence, older workers may get better, higher paying jobs because they use different strategies to obtain those jobs. Alternatively, they may have more access to a larger network of contacts or have higher-ranking contacts, simply by virtue of the time that they have vested in the economic system. On the other hand, potential employers may feel that they will get relatively few years of work from an older "new worker" relative to younger new employees before they have to retire them with pensions.

The role of age is particularly important for the life course paradigm that tries to account for the intersection of historical events and individual lives (Elder, Gimbel, & Ivie, 1991). If losing a job through downsizing represents a major "turning point" in the life course vernacular, how someone responds to such an event is affected partly by the social conditions under which that change occurs and partly by the personal resources an individual can utilize to manage those changes. According to the "personal-ties" paradigm, age can serve as a resource, yielding better or more elaborate networks of contacts. In our study we have chosen to focus on the closely related variable of career stage (military rank), as it is most directly linked to the resources and prospects of these officers. Therefore, we predict that higher ranked (older) soldiers will find better jobs than their lower ranked (younger) counterparts, although we recognize that younger workers may have offsetting advantages in the labor market.

Strategies in Place

The place downsizing occurs may be important for a number of reasons. First, place represents job conditions. For instance, seeking work in a marketplace with high unemployment may make finding a job nearly impossible, regardless of strategy (Leana & Feldman, 1992). Place is a particularly important concern given the large span of the Russian countryside—as well as the diversity of those places.

The focus of this chapter is on the lives of officers who left the service. How did they manage the loss of work and start a new life after leaving service? Our data suggest that there are variations in reactions to downsizing by region. Other research supports this finding, showing that reform is regionally concentrated (Zisk, 2000). Downsizing in more urban areas has generally been more successful than in rural areas. Hence, we predict that place will play an important role in the quality of work found after leaving service, and specifically, that former officers in more urban areas will find better jobs than those in more rural areas.

METHODS

Our study of downsizing is based on interviews of 1,798 Russian officers in 1995 from seven military districts across the Russian countryside. Army lists were used to randomly sample officers who were expected to leave because their jobs, units, or bases were being closed within 3 to 6 months, and a roughly equal sample of officers who were expected to stay. About 85% (1,536) of the officers from the first wave of interviews were re-interviewed 18 months later. When we conducted our second wave of surveys in 1997, we found that the downsizing process had gone more slowly than we (or the Russian Army) had anticipated; many of the soldiers we had expected to be retired were still in service, whereas many of those who left had originally been expected to remain in service. The slow pace of the downsizing was due in part to the fact that the army did not have the financial resources to provide the pension and housing benefits that the new Russian legislature had passed into law (Rohall et al., 2001).

The goal of this analysis is to examine re-employment among officers who left service by Wave 2 (555 or 36% of the 1,536 interviewed at Wave 2). Only 431 of these departed officers, or 78%, actually found work. (While that makes 22% of officers who left service "unemployed," we estimate that the actual long-term unemployment is below 15%, once time out of service is controlled. That is, it took 3 to 6 months for most officers to find work and a substantial number of the officers listed as unemployed in this study had only been out for 1 or 2 months.) Hence, most of our analysis will focus on these 431 former officers.

Independent Variables

Our primary goal is to understand employment patterns of former officers who found work after leaving service, especially the quality of jobs that they found, and the methods used to obtain those jobs given their life stage and location.

Strategy: Ways of Finding Work

Respondents were asked to report the means they used to obtain their current employment, from the following list:

"From someone who worked here before"
"From one of your relatives"
"From a friend"
"From an acquaintance"
"Through a newspaper ad"
"Through the employment agency or employment services"
"You just came here and asked whether there was a job"

Responses were 1 "yes" and 2 "no" and respondents could report all that applied. These responses were then recoded into their respective categories using Granovetter's paradigm. Respondents who marked "Yes" to either the first or fourth questions, but not the others, were coded as using a "weak" tie to find work; respondents who marked "yes" to items two or three but not the others were coded as using a "strong" tie to find their current work. Respondents who reported using ads, and agency, or direct means were coded using "other" means of finding work. Finally, some respondents had used both weak and strong ties, or both formal and informal means of finding work. For instance, 66 or 16% of the sample reported using at least one weak and one strong tie in finding work.

It is interesting that almost all of our officers used at least one form of strategy listed in our survey. In addition, very few of them used more than one or two strategies. Notably, those officers that used formal means, of any kind, of finding work rarely employed personal ties, of any kind, to find work. Given fiscal concerns after leaving service, one would think that all strategies would be employed to find work. We did not find this to be true in our study.

Time: Career Stage

Former rank will be used to represent career stage in this case. Age is highly correlated with rank in the military; older soldiers generally have higher rank than younger soldiers. However, age is an ascribed status while rank is an achieved status, making the latter a form of resource, possibly signifying access to different types and/or number of social relationships. We divided rank into three categories: warrant officers to senior lieutenants, captains to majors, and lieutenant colonels to generals. These correspond to relatively new officers, mid-career officers, and career officers.

Place: Location of Downsizing Event

Respondents were downsized at different locations throughout the Russian countryside, ranging from major urban centers like Moscow to rural areas like the Far East. Most of our sample were released from the St. Petersburg region (31%), followed by the Far East and Volga regions (both 17%), Kaliningrad (12%), Moscow (11%), Trans-Baikal (9%), and the Urals (4%).

Control Variables

Several variables will be controlled in the higher level analysis presented later; they include prior work experience, access to savings, and marital status. Former officers were asked, "Have you ever held a civilian job?" as part of the first wave of interviews. Responses were coded into a dummy variable with 0 "no" and 1 "yes." At Wave 2 officers were asked: "Tell [me] please, does your family have any savings?" Responses were also coded as a dummy variable with 0 "no" and 1 "yes." Marital categories were reduced to 0 "single, widowed, divorced" and 1 "married." Education is not controlled because almost all officers have completed some higher education (e.g., college or cadet school).

Dependent Variables

Army-Civilian Job Comparisons

Our first measure of job quality asks respondents to compare their current job with their former Army positions, indicating whether their current position is 1 "much better in the Army," 2 "a little better in the Army," 3 "the same," 4 "a little better now," or 5 "much better now." Dimensions of comparison include:

"Your opportunities for advancement"
"Your salary"
"Opportunities to use your abilities"

These items were combined into a single scale, producing a Cronbach's alpha of .72, with a mean of 2.24, showing that on average, these respondents tended to think their Army jobs had been a bit better.

Income

Our second measure of job quality is household income, since job income was not available. Preliminary analysis showed no significant effects of spousal working status on outcomes. Only 302 respondents reported their income in this survey. The average income reported was 2,062 rubles per month, or about $82 American dollars.

RESULTS

The first set of results is designed to give the reader a sense of officers interviewed in our data. We will initially review who found work by time (i.e., the career stage of officers who left service) and location (the region in which they were released). A second set of analyses will address the quality of work found by job-search strategies, career stage, and region.

Leaving Service and Finding Work

Our data show that downsizing is not evenly distributed among officers' ranks or locations. Most of those leaving service were senior officers (colonel to generals), with 49% leaving service, as compared to 37% of mid-career officers and 31% junior officers ($\chi^2 = 22.847$, $p <$ .001) (see table 4.1). However, career stage had little effect on actually

Table 4.1 Downsizing Conditions by Rank at Time Leaving Service

Rank	Downsizing Status*			Employment Status**		
	Organizational Survivors (n)	Left Service (n)	Total (n)	Employed (n)	Unemployed (n)	Total (n)
WO to Senior Lieutenant	68.7	31.3	100.0	79.3	20.7	100.0
	26.9	20.0	24.3	20.4	18.5	20.0
	(244)	(111)	(355)	(88)	(23)	(111)
Captain to Major	63.1	36.9	100.0	76.9	23.1	100.0
	56.5	53.9	55.5	53.4	55.6	53.9
	(512)	(299)	(811)	(230)	(69)	(299)
Colonel to General	50.8	49.2	100.0	77.9	22.1	100.0
	16.6	26.1	20.2	26.2	25.8	26.1
	(150)	(145)	(295)	(113)	(32)	(145)
Total	62.0	38.0	100.0	77.7	22.3	100.0
	100.0	100.0	100.0	100.0	100.0	100.0
	(906)	(555)	(1461)	(431)	(124)	(555)

*Entire sample, Pearson χ^2 = 22.847, $p < .001$. ** Leavers only; Pearson χ^2 = .267, $p < .875$.

finding a job. Seventy-nine percent of junior, 77% of mid-career officers, and 78% of senior-level officers found work after they left service. Hence, the career timing of departure from service seems to have little bearing on finding work after leaving service.

It seems clear that higher-ranking officers were more likely to use potential downsizing as a reason to leave service through legitimate reasons, such as retirement. Data from the first wave of data collection support this contention, showing that higher-ranking officers report that they plan to retire at much higher rates than junior officers (55% vs. 29%). Perhaps they are also less likely to want or need a job, too. Our analysis will focus on those officers who sought and obtained jobs after leaving service, regardless of prior rank. However, even this group of older soldiers may be less concerned about job conditions than their junior counterparts, since they may look forward to pensions and other benefits of leaving service at a later career stage.

Location of downsizing, however, affected both whether our respondents left service and whether they found a job. For instance, almost 50% of the former officers in the Urals region left service as a result of downsizing, followed closely by the Far East, where 43% left service (see table 4.2). But more metropolitan areas like Moscow and St. Petersburg also saw large proportions of officers leaving service (43% in both cases). The Baikal region saw the smallest percentage of downsized soldiers with only 28% leaving service.

Proportions leaving service by region do not necessarily translate into ease or difficulty of finding work after a period of downsizing. The highest unemployment rates in our sample include the Volga and Kaliningrad regions, both with 33% unemployment rates. The lowest unemployment rates are in the Far East (11%) and St. Petersburg (12%). Our prediction that the best areas for re-employment would be more urban is partially supported; they are mostly urban (Moscow and St. Petersburg), with the exception of the Far East. The worst areas of unemployment are rural or semi-rural areas (i.e., Volga, Urals, and Kaliningrad).

Strategies, Time, Place, and Job Comparisons

What role do job-search strategies play in obtaining good work after leaving military service? Our analysis shows a direct correlation of job-search strategies to job comparisons with their former army jobs (see table 4.3, Model 1) ($F = 3.25$, $p < .05$). The use of formal means (e.g., ads or agencies) to find work is associated with the lowest mean score (2.1). The use of strong ties and mix of both strong and weak ties are

Table 4.2 Downsizing Conditions by Location at Time of Leaving Service

Location	Downsizing Status*			Employment Status**		
	Organizational Survivors (n)	Left Service (n)	Total (n)	Employed (n)	Unemployed (n)	Total (n)
St. Petersburg	56.8	43.2	100.0	87.6	12.4	100.0
	22.2	27.6	24.2	31.1	15.3	27.6
	(201)	(153)	(354)	(134)	(19)	(153)
Moscow	56.9	43.1	100.0	78.0	22.0	100.0
	8.6	10.6	9.4	10.7	10.5	10.6
	(78)	(59)	(137)	(46)	(13)	(59)
Kaliningrad	68.4	31.6	100.0	66.7	33.3	100.0
	17.9	13.5	16.2	11.6	20.2	13.5
	(162)	(75)	(237)	(50)	(25)	(75)
Volga	63.6	36.4	100.0	67.0	33.0	100.0
	20.4	19.1	19.9	16.5	28.2	19.1
	(185)	(106)	(291)	(71)	(35)	(106)
Far East	56.7	43.3	100.0	89.3	10.7	100.0
	12.1	15.1	13.3	17.4	7.3	15.1
	(110)	(84)	(194)	(75)	(9)	(84)
Urals	51.2	48.8	100.0	75.0	25.0	100.0
	2.3	3.6	2.8	3.5	4.0	3.6
	(21)	(20)	(41)	(15)	(5)	(20)
Trans-Baikal	72.0	28.0	100.0	69.0	31.0	100.0
	16.4	10.5	14.2	9.3	14.5	10.5
	(149)	(58)	(207)	(40)	(18)	(58)
Total	62.0	38.0	100.0	77.7	23.0	100.0
	100.0	100.0	100.0	100.0	100.0	100.0
	(906)	(555)	(1461)	(431)	(124)	(555)

*Entire sample, Pearson χ^2 = 21.385, $p < .001$. ** Leavers only, Pearson χ^2 = 30.027, $p < .001$.

Table 4.3　Effects of Job-Search Strategies, Time, and Place on Job Comparisons†

Source	Model 1: Main Effects				Model 2: Interaction Effects			
	Type III Sum of Squares	df	Mean Square	F	Type III Sum of Squares	df	Mean Square	F
Independent Variables								
Job-Search Strategies	5.64	4	1.41	3.25**	3.03	4	.76	2.08*
Rank Prior to Downsizing	6.51	2	3.26	7.51***	1.70	2	.85	2.34*
Region of Downsizing	8.21	6	1.37	3.16***	4.70	6	.78	2.15**
Strategies * Rank					3.40	8	.43	1.17
Strategies * Region					15.49	21	.74	2.03***
Control Variables								
Savings (1=have savings)	2.73	1	2.73	6.30	1.65	1	1.65	4.54**
Prior Work Experience (1=have experience)	.91	1	.91	2.10*	.004	1	.004	.01
Marital Status (1=married)	.03	1	.03	.08	.07	1	.07	.18
Error	112.28	259	.43		72.01	198	.36	
Total	1498.94	275			1498.94	275		
Corrected Total	135.85	274			135.85	274		

†ANOVA Analysis, Model 1 R Squared = .173 (Adjusted R Squared = .126), Model 2 R Squared = .470 (Adjusted R Squared = .266)
* $p < .10$, ** $p < .05$, *** $p < .01$

associated with the highest job comparison scores (2.4 and 2.5, respectively). Thus, the use of strong ties results in better jobs relative to those held in the Army. The use of only weak ties is associated with a score between those extremes (2.2).

Career stage or rank is also associated with job comparison (Table 4.3). Senior officers (i.e., Lt. Colonel and above) who left the service report significantly *lower* job comparison scores (2.0) compared to mid- (2.2) and junior-level officers (2.5) ($F = .7.51$, $p < .01$). It appears that junior officers are more satisfied with their new jobs, relative to what they left behind in the Army. We had predicted that older soldiers might report more favorable job-comparison scores than younger soldiers, partly because they have better job contacts. However, it is also likely that they had more difficulty getting jobs with as much authority and prestige as they had had in the Soviet Army, while younger soldiers had greater opportunities for upward mobility. The post-Soviet military held less prestige and job conditions were much worse for newer soldiers than older ones. Hence, any civilian job may have seemed better than their old jobs in the Army.

The location of downsizing is also related to job comparisons. The places with the worst scores for good civilian jobs as compared to the Army job include the Far East (2.0) and Baikal regions (2.0), two of the more rural areas ($F = 3.16$, $p < .01$). In contrast, St. Petersburg and Kaliningrad show the highest comparison scores (2.4 and 2.5, respectively). Given the size of the St. Petersburg economy, we are not surprised that former officers found good jobs there. Kaliningrad, however, is a virtual island, existing outside the Russian borders near Poland. However, it is close to some large population centers that may have provided good jobs, in addition to access to the Polish economy.

Some of our control variables also had an effect on outcomes. Not surprising is the fact that prior work experience is also associated with better jobs, at least with job comparisons (table 4.3, Model 1). It is difficult to know the role of savings in these models. Having savings is associated with better job comparisons and higher incomes. Savings may be a proxy for better money management, representing personal ability. Thus, having such ability is likely to make a person more employable (human capital) or elite status and networks (social capital).

Strategies, Time, Place, and Income

Our data also show the effects of job-search strategies on income. Much like the previous analysis, the use of formal strategies is associated with the lowest incomes (1,677) ($F = 2.80$, $p < .05$) (Table 4.4,

Table 4.4 Effects of Job-Search Strategies, Time, and Place on Income†

	Model 1: Main Effects				Model 2: Interaction Effects			
Source	Type III Sum of Squares	df	Mean Square	F	Type III Sum of Squares	df	Mean Square	F
Independent Variables								
Job-Search Strategies	9997025.97	4	2499256.49	2.80**	6322817.38	4	1580704.35	1.87
Rank Prior to Downsizing	97632.59	2	48816.29	.05	21489.31	2	10744.65	.01
Region of Downsizing	32116904.60	6	5352817.43	6.01***	17398351.80	6	2899725.30	3.42**
Strategies * Rank					9465837.38	7	1352262.48	1.60
Strategies * Region					22121533.21	20	1106076.66	1.31
Control Variables								
Savings (1 = have savings)	16123891.02	1	16123891.02	18.10***	8489166	1	8489166.96	10.02**
Prior Work Experience (1=have experience)	503654.04	1	503654.04	.56	3590071.79	1	3590071.79	4.24*
Marital Status (1=married)	187567.45	1	187567.45	.21	345170.96	1	345170.96	.41
Error	248266874.17	279	890562.27		184754220.60	218	847496.43	
Total	1557364625.00	295			1557364625.00	295		
Corrected Total	301729986.95	294			301729986.95	294		

†ANOVA Analysis, Model 1 R Squared = .177 (Adjusted R Squared = .132), Model 2 R Squared = .388 (Adjusted R Squared = .174)
* $p < .10$, ** $p < .05$, *** $p < .01$

Model 1). Further, the use of strong ties is associated with the highest incomes (2,183). The regions of Baikal and the Far East show the lowest incomes (1,437 and 1,483, respectively) ($F = 6.01$, $p < .01$). To summarize, strong ties produce jobs that are more satisfying and have higher levels of incomes. But where officers left service is also associated with the re-employment experience.

Intersections of Strategies with Time and Place

Most of our analyses have shown the direct effects of job-search strategies (over time and place) on the job outcomes of former army officers. Life-course theory suggests that these factors may intersect, that strategies may be more or less important, depending on the personal lives of men and their social contexts. Our data show a small interaction effect between strategies and location on job comparisons ($F = 2.03$, $p < .01$) (Table 4.3, Model 2), but not income levels (Table 4.4, Model 2).

These data show that strong ties have more impact on job comparisons in some locations than in others. Strong ties produced the best jobs in places like Kaliningrad (3.0 [the only place in which new jobs, on average, were seen as comparable to former army jobs]), St. Petersburg (2.6), and Baikal (2.6). It is difficult to know why such an interaction occurred. The worst location for strong ties is in the Far East (1.9). We would have predicted that strong ties may be more important in more rural areas, with fewer jobs. But the findings are not that clear, since Baikal is included in one of the better areas for the use of strong ties. This result deserves further research and analysis.

DISCUSSION

The data presented in this chapter give us a unique view of former Russian Army officers at a significant turning point in their lives. They were leaving army service and forced to find new work in an unstable economy. Our data suggest that the method used to find those jobs helped determine their quality in comparison with former army jobs and income levels. Former officers who used strong personal ties to help them find work report better job-comparison ratings and higher incomes than former officers using other methods, including formal means (e.g., ads and agencies) as well as weak ties (e.g., acquaintances).

But life course incorporates the role of real time and place in analyzing life changes (Elder, 1994). In our study, both factors had a large ifluence on job outcomes. Former officers at an earlier career stage report much better jobs relative to prior army employment, perhaps because older officers left better military jobs than the younger ones. Similarly, officers released in more remote areas like the Baikal and Far East report lower job comparison levels and income. Hence, career stage (time) and place are important to understanding the effects of downsizing on job quality in our sample.

We also explored the nexus between job-search strategies over time and place. Do some strategies work better at different career stages or locations? Our data show some evidence that job-search strategies can vary in their impacts by location: former officers with strong social ties report varying outcomes by location. However, our findings are not clear in this area; strong ties are more effective in some urban areas (e.g., St. Petersburg) but also in more rural or distant ones (e.g., Baikal). Perhaps future research can elaborate on these findings, the economic and personal conditions of these areas that make strategies more or less effective.

Our findings support much of the literature on job strategies generally as well as in the context of the modern Russian economy. If the use of strong ties to find work represents the importance of an informal economy in Russia as Ledeneva (1998) suggests, then our findings support this idea. The former officers in this sample were most likely to use personal ties, particularly strong ties, to find work after leaving military service. In this sense, these officers reacted to their job transition as both white and blue-collar workers do in most parts of the world: turning to friends, family, and acquaintances for information about or access to different jobs. Formal means played a very small role in their transition from the military to civilian economic sectors. Similarly, very few members of our sample employed a mixture of personal and formal means of finding work.

The strategy for finding work also seems to have an effect on the quality of jobs former officers obtained after leaving service. Supporting the work of Granovetter (1995) and others, finding work via personal ties (especially strong ties, unlike Granovetter's 1973 argument) is associated with the better quality of work. In our case, quality includes subjective and objective ratings of those jobs—both subjective comparisons of their new jobs to their army ones and objective income levels. Interestingly, although previous analyses of these data show that officers who left the Russian Army reported better mental health and higher quality of life than those who stayed, this analysis shows that on average, they do not think their current civilian jobs are as good as the army jobs they left.

CONCLUSION

Our data give us a glimpse of an interesting group of men at a significant juncture of their lives. It is clear that most of our respondents are actively seeking out a new life in the civilian world but they have employed different strategies to obtain that life. And those strategies have an influence on the outcomes of their new lives. But the when and where of their starting point has an impact, too.

We originally hypothesized that workers who used personal ties, especially strong ties, to find work would report finding better jobs than those individuals using more formal methods of seeking employment. Findings generally supported this hypothesis with the use of formal means of finding work (e.g., ads or agencies) associated with the lowest job-comparison scores, comparing civilian and military employment conditions. Similarly, using strong ties to secure jobs is associated with the highest income scores. Hence, using personal ties, especially strong ones, is associated with getting better civilian jobs after leaving the military.

We also hypothesized that higher ranked (older) soldiers may find better jobs than their lower ranked (younger) counterparts, ostensibly because they may have had better links to jobs in the civilian contexts. However, we found the opposite of what we had predicted: senior officers (i.e., Lt. Colonel and above) who left service reported significantly *lower* job comparison scores, relative to their mid- and junior-level counterparts. Indeed, junior officers seemed to find the best jobs, in terms of job-comparison ratings. No differences were found in income between ranks, suggesting that younger officers are happier, though no better paid than the older workers.

These findings show that aging processes must be understood in context of historical circumstances. In the Russian case, the modern, Western-style economy seems better suited for younger, more technologically prepared workers. Alternatively, leaving military service at a younger age makes lower-ranking officers less distant from the demands of the civilian economy, hence more prepared to work in it. In either case, middle- and higher-ranking officers seem less prepared for the modern Russian economy, even though they left at a higher rate than their younger counterparts.

Finally, we hypothesized that place would play an important role in the quality of work found after leaving service, that former officers in more urban areas will find better jobs than those in more rural areas. Our findings generally support this hypothesis. The places with the worst job-comparison scores and income levels include the Far East and Baikal regions. These findings should be examined with some caution, however, since there can be great variation in social conditions with each of the regions included in these analyses.

Life course theory argues that these factors may intersect, that strategies may be more or less important to people, depending on their personal lives and their social contexts. Our data show a small interaction effect between strategies and location on job comparisons but not income levels, with strong ties having more impact on job comparisons in some locations more than in others. It is difficult to determine exactly why such strategies would have different effects in these areas without considerable examination of the economic, social, and political differences in these regions. Perhaps some economies are better suited for some methods than others, simply because of the nature of available jobs. Our data does not allow such analyses but future research should attempt to make such connections. The intersection of job-search strategy with time and place needs further research.

Future research should also address these issues by further examining the meaning of work to the Russian people. This task may be particularly difficult among the military forces in which there is a totally different system of rank and job specifications than occurs in the civilian world. But this dilemma will have to be addressed as the Russian military continues to shrink over the next decade—to a much larger degree than it did in the 1990s. It is also clear that future Russian officers cannot assume that they can rely on military pensions when they get older as many did prior to the fall of the Soviet Union. Hence, more of these types of employment transitions will occur in the future and they will be more difficult, if not desperate. We hope that our research helps to initiate a dialogue on the special conditions in which job transitions occur from military to civilian sectors in times and places of profound social change.

REFERENCES

Ball, D. Y. (1996). How reliable are Russia's officers? *Jane's Intelligence Review* (May), 204–207.

Bian, Y. (1997). Bringing strong ties back in: Indirect ties, network bridges, and job searches in China. *American Sociological Review, 62,* 366–385.

Broman, C. L., Hamilton, V. L., & Hoffman, W. S. (2001). *Stress and distress among the unemployed: Hard times and vulnerable people.* New York and other locations: Kluwer Academic Publishers.

Collins, R., & Waller, D. (1992). What theories predicted the state breakdowns and revolutions of the Soviet bloc? *Research in Social Movements, Conflicts and Change, 14,* 31–47.

Elder, G. H., Jr. (1987). War mobilization and the life course: a cohort of World War II veterans. *Sociological Forum, 2,* 449–473.

Elder, G. H., Jr. (1994). Time, human agency, and social change: Perspectives on the life course. *Social Psychology Quarterly, 57*(1), 4–15.

Elder, G. H., & Clipp, E. C. (1988). Combat experience, comradeship, and psychological health. In J. P. Wilson, Z. Harel, & B. Kahana, (Eds.), *Human adaptation to extreme stress: From the holocaust to Vietnam* (pp. 131–156). New York: Plenum.

Elder, G. H., Gimbel, C., & Ivie, R. (1991). Turning points in life: The case of military service and war. *Military Psychology, 3,* 215–231.

Galaiko, V. (2001). A stone rolling down the mountain: Still trying to make sense of Russia's military reforms. *Versty,* February 22.

Galtung, J. (1992). Eastern Europe fall 1989—What happened and why? *Research in Social Movements, Conflicts and Change, 14,* 75–97.

Gerbner, N. T. (2004). When public institutions fail: Coping with the dysfunctional government in the post-Soviet Russia. *Contexts, 3,* 20–28.

Granovetter, M. S. (1973). The strength of weak ties. *American Journal of Sociology, 78,* 1360–1380.

Granovetter, M. S. (1995). *Getting a job: A study of contacts and careers* (2nd ed.). Chicago and London: The University of Chicago Press.

Hamilton, V. L., Hoffman, W. S., Broman, C. L., & Rauma, D. (1993). Unemployment, distress, and coping: A panel study of autoworkers. *Journal of Personality and Social Psychology, 65,* 234–247.

Hardy, M. A., Hazelrigg, L., & Quadagno, J. (1996). *Ending a career in the auto industry: "30 and out."* New York and London: Plenum.

Herspring, D. (2002a). De-professionalising the Russian armed forces. In A. Forster, T. Edmunds, & A. Cottey (Eds.), *The challenge of military reform in postcommunist Europe* (pp. 197–210). Houndmills: Palgrave Macmillan.

Herspring, D. (2002b). Putin and military reform: Some first hesitant steps. *Russia and Eurasia Review, 1,* 7.

Interfax. (2001). Russian defense ministry sources outline radical armed forces' cuts this year. January 25.

Jones, E. (1985). *Red army and society: A sociology of the Soviet military.* Boston, MA: Allen and Unwin.

Kessler, R. C., Turner, J. B., & House, J. S. (1988). Effects of unemployment on health in a community survey: Main, modifying, and mediating effects. *Journal of Social Issues, 44,* 69–85.

Leana, C. R., & Feldman, D.C. (1992). *Coping with job loss.* New York: Lexington Press.

Ledeneva, A. V. (1998). *Russia's economy of favours.* Cambridge, UK: Cambridge University Press.

Marsden, P. V., & Hurlbert, J. S. (1988). Social resources and mobility outcomes: A replication and extension. *Social Forces, 66,* 1038–1059.

Meek, J. (1998). An army on dog food. *The Guardian Weekly,* July 12.

Milkman, R. (1997). *Farewell to the factory.* Berkeley and Los Angeles: University of California Press.

Montgomery, J. D. (1992). Job-search and network composition: Implications of the strength of weak ties hypothesis. *American Sociological Review, 57,* 586–596.

Moskos, C. C., & Wood, F. R. (Eds.). (1988). *The military: More than just a job?* Washington, D.C.: Pergamon-Brassey's.

Myasnikov, V. (2003). Where can Russia contract servicemen?: The military reforms may be stalled by a shortage of personnel. *Vremya,* January 30.

Newman, K. S. (1985). Turning your back on tradition: Symbolic Analysis and moral critique in a plant shutdown. *Urban Anthropology, 14,* 1–3.

Newman, K. S. (1986). *Falling from Grace: The Experience of Downward Mobility in the American Middle Class.* New York and London: The Free Press.

Rohall, D. E., Hamilton, V. L., Segal, D. R., & Segal, M. W. (2001). Downsizing the Russian Army: Quality of life and mental healthy consequences for former organizational members, survivors, and spouses. *Journal of Political and Military Sociology, 29,* 73–91.

Sampson, J., & Laub, H. (1996). Socioeconomic achievement in the life course of disadvantaged me: Military service as a turning point, circa 1940–1965. *American Sociological Review, 61,* 347–367.

Segal, D. R. (1992). From convergence to chaos: theoretical perspectives on the transformation of industrial societies. *Research in Social Movements, Conflicts and Change, 14,* 1–11.

Segal, D. R., & Babin, N. (2000). Institutional change in armed forces at the dawning of the 21st century. In S. Quah & A. Sales (Eds.), *International Handbook of Sociology* (pp. 218–235). London, UK: Sage.

Segal, D. R. & Schwartz, J. (1981). Professional autonomy of the military in the United States and the Soviet Union. *Air University Review, 32,* 21–30.

Woodruff, T. (2003). *Influence of the life course on the development and salience of soldier identity.* Unpublished M.A. thesis, Department of Sociology, University of Maryland, College Park.

Yakubovich, V. & Kozina, I. (2000). The changing significance of ties: An exploration of the hiring channels in the Russian transitional labor market. *International Sociology, 15,* 479–500.

Zickel, R. E. (Ed.). (1991). *Soviet Union: A country study.* Washington: Government Printing Office.

Zisk, K. M. (2000). Putin and the Russian military. *Ponars Policy Memo, 155.* Stable URL: www.csis.org/ruseura/ponars/policymemos/pm_0155.pdf.

Commentary

Job Search in the New Russia by Former Soviet Army Officers

Mikk Titma

R ohall and colleagues' study on Russian Army officers' employment outcomes in the mid-1990s is remarkable, especially for
having surveyed members of this important subgroup of Russian society. Every military service is secretive, but historically Russians
in particular have sought to hide from public view the Army, their basic
tool for empire building.

With both an inner and outer empire, the officer corps of the Soviet era was the largest in Russia's entire history. Military officers were
very proud of their important role in Soviet society and indirectly in
the world. Consequently, for the officer corps, the most significant historical event was not the collapse of the Communist system but the end
of the Soviet Empire, which followed after Yeltsin's fight with Gor-
bachev for power in 1991. The dismantling of the Soviet empire deeply
shocked the officer corps. The sharp decline in their homeland's position in terms of land area, population, and military might means that
Russia cannot be a major world power in the foreseeable future. The
size of the military machine needed to sustain present-day Russia is
vastly smaller than the one required by the Soviet empire. Major downsizing of the military in general and the officer corps in particular has
been the inevitable result.

The Soviet system prepared people for a particular occupation in
its command economy, and most people retired from the same place
of employment where they first entered the workforce. Because salary
differences were relatively small, and because labor shortages were se-

vere from the 1970s onward, official Soviet propaganda labeled people who changed jobs as "letuny" ("flyers") and looked down on them. But, after the command economy collapsed, many people's jobs were eliminated, and the state did not find new jobs for them. Further, the state provided almost no financial support for the unemployed. People accustomed to the Soviet system needed to learn that they must find jobs for themselves.

The abrupt change in mental outlook required by this new situation, as well as the new material deprivation, was extremely difficult for the Soviet people. Younger persons developed a new outlook most quickly. Residents of large cities and members of small work units also learned fairly rapidly to look for new jobs.

In the section "Downsizing the Russian Armed Services," Rohall et al. briefly compare the Soviet and American officer corps, primarily using other groups in Russian society as their point of reference. Military officers were present in large numbers in every committee of the Communist Party of the Soviet Union (CPSU), from the Central Committee of the CPSU at the top, to committees at lower levels. With the collapse of the Soviet empire, the officer corps lost its elite status. Officers have been removed from political power in the new Russia. They have become ordinary military officers similar to that given to military officers in democratic countries in the West. Loss of their former political role in society has been a definite blow to the officer corps.

Russia's army still uses conscription to recruit ordinary soldiers. As in the Soviet army, today's army officers in Russia live separately from and under vastly better circumstances than the conscripts. The living situation of army officers in Russia and their relationship to rank and file soldiers is quite different from that of their counterparts in America's professional army

The understanding that the state had practically abandoned the military, which had historically been its main tool for expanding and controlling the empire, came as an unexpected surprise to military officers. As an important part of the Russian elite throughout history, military officers were not prepared for their new and much less important role in society, let alone for the end of their military careers. The military in the Soviet Union never imagined that they might need to find new jobs. It was much harder for officers than for others in the military because officers were overwhelmingly family men and usually the family's only breadwinner. In this situation, most tended to wait in the hope of better times. Not a few of them are still waiting in military areas to solve their job and living problems.

In the section "Emplyment Transitions: Finding a Job," Rohall and colleagues discuss the problem of military officers engaged in searching for new jobs. Russian officers had great difficulty overcoming their loyalty to the military profession. Their entire education and training had prepared them to expect a 25-year career. In Soviet society, no other profession was so clearly oriented to a specific career and had such limited qualifications for any other type of work. Their main asset was leadership and combat training, although some had engineering training and other technical knowledge. Their training was a potential asset during the first few years of the transition, but was no longer very useful by 1995 when Rohall et al. collected their data.

Officers were kept in the Army too long; they were not given a chance to leave, and they thereby missed the best period during which to look for new jobs appropriate to their qualifications. Compared with other professional and occupational groups, they had less freedom to take advantage of new opportunities resulting from marketization to move to new jobs. Like many engineers and workers in large factories, most of them were either forced to wait, or deliberately chose to wait, until bad times were over. It was unimaginable to employees of a factory with 10,000 workers that it could be eliminated, and it was equally unimaginable to military officers that their military units would be disbanded.

Like most of the defense industry, Soviet army bases were located outside large cities. More specifically, military compounds were usually located some distance away from neighboring small towns or villages. Their location was the result of a deliberate strategy to maintain military secrecy. This strategy effectively isolated military units from local populations.

The authors rightly include location in their analyses because job availability in Russia has varied radically with location. To get a job, an officer also needs to live where there are job openings. The officer corps began to be actively downsized after Russian troops returned from the Soviet outer empire in 1994 when Russia's Defense Ministry realized it lacked the resources needed to maintain a large officer corps. As is typical in collapsing industries, no one worked very hard to find new jobs for those put out of work. No special program was created to provide new jobs for officers pushed out of a military career. In practice, officers just ceased to be paid and had only some miserable place to live with their families. Hence, it was the human factor (that is, individual agency) that decided every person's fate.

For the theoretical framework for their analyses, the authors chose Granovetter's (1973) well-known distinction between *strong* and *weak* ties, which has been used in many other studies in the United States.

Granovetter and others have found weak ties to be surprisingly important in achieving labor market advantages in the United States. As a
modern society, the United States has a population that is geographi-
cally highly mobile. Professionals are especially ready to move to jobs
in other regions. In contrast, heads of small businesses and many people engaged in local markets stay in one place fairly permanently.

Most historical societies have had different job-search situations.
Strong ties, especially family linkages, are more effective than weak ties
in finding a job—especially in finding a good job. Officers located in a
military compound in Russia who are actively searching for a job cannot easily use weak ties to find new jobs. An officer in a compound lives
and works among fellow officers and conscripts in the same environment who may even be looking for a job themselves. Usually military
downsizing in Russia has been executed through elimination of an entire military unit, not by a partial reduction of the officer corps. In
practice, weak ties can be useful in finding a job only if a large city can
easily be reached from the military compound. In general terms, Russians, like most Americans, easily form contacts and weak ties with
other people. But this is not true in small towns or in typical Russian
villages in Siberia or the south of Russia. Such communities do eagerly
welcome newcomers.

More useful in helping unemployed military officers with finding
new jobs are former fellow officers with whom an officer had formed a
strong tie earlier in his military career—former officers who currently
are better located than the officer seeking a new job. Afghanistan veterans provide a good example. Their organization throughout Russia
has been an important source of help to Afghanistan veterans in finding jobs. Similar kinds of ties may exist among fellow graduates from
the same military academy.

Another major way to find a job is through ties to the family of the
officer or his wife. Family ties have an extremely important advantage
in Russia. As a real housing market did not exist in Russia in the 1990s,
and began to emerge only around 2002, family ties have often been a
means to obtain a temporary living place and probably have helped
many people to find a permanent place to live, as well as to find a new
job. With the sharp decline in living conditions in the 1990s, traveling
a long distance was hard even for those in the military. The Army
helped somewhat with long-distance travel, but not much.

Employment agencies that advertised promised a lot but provided
little. As a rule, they operated on the principle of pay first, then offer a
promise. But when overall unemployment was huge, a promise was
often just a promise. It is very important to consider that until 1999,

many employees of Russian factories and offices were formally employed but were not paid. Thus, military downsizing occurred when much of Russia's population had no paid jobs. Consequently, military officers had to compete for jobs in a situation not unlike that in the United States during the Great Depression. Weak ties offer very little help when job vacancies are very rare. According to Rohall et al.'s citations of Russians sources, personal ties have helped Russians find jobs before and after the collapse of the Soviet Union, but strong ties are ordinarily more useful than weak ties. Consequently, the authors expect military officers who used personal ties, especially strong ties, to report having found better jobs than those who used impersonal means to find new jobs.

The section on "Strategies in Time" has a rather misleading title because it actually discusses age and life course stage. The authors state that "according to the 'personal-ties' paradigm, age can serve as a resource, yielding better or more elaborate networks of contacts. . . . Therefore, we predict that higher ranked (older) soldiers may find better jobs than their lower ranked (younger) counterparts, although we recognize that younger workers may have offsetting advantages in the labor market."

In the United States, being older can be an asset within the context of the "personal ties" paradigm. But under the conditions of the transition from a command economy to a market economy, I doubt that being older is an asset. To perform a multiplicity of tasks reliably, especially in small businesses, requires a very different work ethic from the ethic formed by a "command economy." Observations of common labor practices in transitional countries have revealed that private businesses prefer younger people who do not have the habits of work acquired in a command economy. Employees without these old-style work habits tend to more effective laborers in a market economy. Consequently, the people hit the hardest by the economic transition have been those in their forties or older. Being older has not been an advantage.

Our own analyses have revealed some important factors that favored the success of young adults in general. In the 1990s, risk taking was a very important factor in success during the transitional period (Titma & Trapido, 2002; Titma & Tuma, this volume). Those trying different jobs or having multiple sources of income ended up with higher incomes and also with higher status in the labor market. For officers, the avenue to success most suitable to their qualifications was to find work in a security firm or in law enforcement. The major risk they needed to take was to migrate from where their military unit was located to one of the larger cities where jobs in security services and law enforcement were available. Entrepreneurial activity was a less common path, but it offered the possibility of even greater success in the labor market (Pals & Tuma, 2004). For officers to turn their back on their chosen life career was a difficult as well as risky choice. This was especially true for middle-aged or older officers with an established career. It was easier for younger officers who were not yet deeply involved in military life.

I agree with the authors that a higher military rank may have helped a former military officer get a higher-paying job, but it should not be interpreted as evidence that age per se was an asset. It was having a higher rank that gave better-paying job opportunities, not older age. The authors' data allow them to test this hypothesis by using age and military rank as distinct independent variables.

Rohall et al.'s section "Methods" is interesting because their data provide opportunities for various kinds of analyses. Their data are remarkable because 1,798 officers in 7 locations were interviewed in 1995. After 18 months had passed, 1,536 of the 1,798 (85%) were re-interviewed, a remarkably high follow-up rate. Of those re-interviewed, 555 had left the army. Table 4.1 of their study reports information about 1,461 individuals who were interviewed twice. Of these, 295 were colonels or generals; 811 were captains or majors; and 355 were lower-level officers. Re-interviewing 555 officers who had left military service is an amazingly large number, even if the officers still lived near their original military compound. They did more extensive analyses of the 431 of the 555 officers who had not only left military service but had actually found a new job. Because more than a third of the 431 former officers who had found a new job lived in the St. Petersburg or Moscow regions, examining the association between success in job search and weak ties seems reasonable as these huge metropolitan areas are the places where weak ties are most likely to have been helpful.

They distinguished four types of ties used in finding work: only weak ties (acquaintances or former coworkers), strong ties (relatives or friends), both weak and strong ties, and impersonal ties (having used ads, employment agencies, or direct application). As independent variables, they used career stage defined by three ranks (lower or senior lieutenant; captain or major; colonel or general), location (7 regions), and the officers' combined evaluation of his new job. They combined the officers' evaluations of their new jobs' monthly salary, advancement opportunities, and opportunities to use their abilities. They also controlled marital status, having savings, and prior work experience in some analyses. For some unexplained reason, they did not control the basic division in how they originally selected their sample of officers, namely, whether or not the officer belonged to a unit that expected to be disbanded "soon" at the time of the first interview. The methods used for their analyses allow them to compare different categories of respondents. Readers would have appreciated more attention to estimation of models that test hypotheses about officers' use of various methods of job search as well as whether different types of ties used in job searching affected the quality of the jobs that ex-army officers had obtained. Their use of ANOVA (Table 4.4) appears to have the latter aim but suffers from several methodological difficulties. Most important, their sample size is too small to justify the large number of interactions included in their analysis. In addition, they include savings measured *after* the new job had been obtained as a control variable, but a post-measure of savings could be a consequence of the new job as easily as a cause. Still more clearly, their simple comparison of means within categories in the section "Results" is not an adequate basis for drawing conclusions about the causal relationship between two variables.

It must also be noted that their comparison of different regions of Russia (Table 4.2) does not have a sound basis because in some regions the number of respondents is small, not to mention the numbers in various categories of Employment Status (less than 10 respondents in some instances). It would have been better to aggregate regions with similar places that had larger numbers of respondents. For example, four reasonable groupings based on opportunities for new jobs would be Moscow + St. Petersburg, the Far East + Trans-Baikal, the Volga + Ural regions, and Kaliningrad.

In the section "Results," the authors conclude that "career stage had little effect on actually finding a job." This statement is overly strong given that the numbers of unemployed respondents as well as the numbers in each of the three main military ranks are not large. Something can be concluded about regional differences when there are sufficient respondents in a region. For instance, in the Moscow, St. Petersburg, and Far East regions, the numbers were the largest in the data and the percentages of those downsized were similar. In contrast, the authors' claim that "almost 50% of the former officers in the Urals region left service as a result of downsizing" arouses skepticism since they interviewed only 41 respondents in that region. Similarly, it is hard to be confident about their claim that "the career timing of the departure from service seems to have little bearing on finding work after leaving service." To find this claim credible, readers need to be given much more information about the sample, its distribution across military ranks, sample losses in the follow-up interview, and the numbers of officers who were really forced to leave military service and who left voluntarily.

Beyond their methodology, there are also some questions about their conclusions. It is odd to expect that the new nonmilitary jobs of colonels and generals would offer higher salaries or better opportunities for advancement or use of their abilities. The higher a person's position, the harder it is to move to an even better position. The comparison of an officer's new job with his position in the military should be interpreted differently for officers who had different military ranks. It is very questionable whether former generals found jobs with higher salaries or better "opportunities to use your abilities." It is also not plausible to expect that a younger officer's assessment of his opportunities in a new, nonmilitary job are comparable to the career prospects he could have anticipated in the former Soviet army.

The "Discussion" section gives a broader explanation of Rohall and colleagues' results. They state that "former officers using strong personal ties to help them find work report better job-comparison ratings and higher income than former officers using other methods, including formal means . . . as well as weak ties." The importance of strong personal ties in many areas of social life, including situations where there is corruption among the social networks of elites, not to mention politicians, is a well-known phenomenon. Granovetter's (1973) findings in the 1970s that weak ties are important among middle-class Americans was a surprising result confirmed by considerable subsequent research. It points to the uniqueness of American society and its job market. In most of the world, strong personal ties clearly dominate in the labor market, and Russia is therefore not unusual in this. In Russia, the officer corps is largely isolated from the rest of society, which inevitably makes weak ties less relevant in searching for a new job.

The different avenues used to find work were strongly influenced by the fact that the situation in Russia's emerging job market in the 1990s was comparable with that in the early 1930s in the United States. In both situations, people were desperate to find any paid job, and weak ties could offer little help.

This work is significant as it gives a rare view of the world of Russia's officer corps, which is usually very hidden from view. It gives a picture at the lowest point in modern times of the Russian military, when even officers in the high and middle ranks were forced in mass out of the profession they had proudly held.

REFERENCES

Granovetter, M. S. (1973). The strength of weak ties. *American Journal of Sociology, 78*, 1360–1380.

Pals, H., & Tuma, N. B. (2004). Entrepreneurial activities in post-Soviet societies: Impacts of social psychological characteristics. *International Journal of Sociology, 34*, 11–38.

Titma, M., & Trapido, D. (2002). Prediction of success in post-communist societies: Evidence from Latvia and Estonia. *Society and Economy, 24*(3), 297–331.

Commentary

The More Things Change: Coping with Transition in the New Russia

Regina Smyth

Military reform and in particular, demilitarization, is among the most serious challenges facing transitional democracies (Barany, 1997). Yet, the forced retirement of over a half million officers in the Russian Federation continues to unfold without major political or social upheaval. This pattern of military quiescence reflects a hundred years of military culture and the perpetuation of informal coping mechanisms developed during the Soviet era. Moreover, it is borne out of the lack of orchestrated demands on the new democratic regime structure and the regime's willingness to use nondemocratic, rather than effective response, to quiet dissent. As such, the relationship between the new Russian state and its retired officers is an important case study of the impact that individual choices can have on the process of democratic consolidation.

Continuity in mass and elite behavior between the Soviet and post-Soviet periods is best observed at the individual level, whereas the consequences of these choices can be observed at the national level. In my own work on Russian candidate behavior, ample evidence shows that Communist Party networks developed in the late Soviet period remain central to Russian politicians' strategic choices regardless of their party affiliation. We might expect the same of military officers. Yet, despite the import of the phenomena of demilitarization, analysts rarely get a look at the individual-level behaviors and attitudes that explain the relative quiescence (or lack thereof) among officers forced out by mili-

tary downsizing. Rohall and colleagues explore the reemployment patterns of military officers and illuminate why the forced retirement of a
significant portion of the post-Soviet officer corps has not provoked
widespread protest or political change in the Russian Federation. The
persistence of non-state coping strategies, together within minimal political organization, and concentrated power at the top undermined
the capacity of officers' to work through new regime structure to demand political change in the form of response to their demands.

As Rohall and colleagues point out, the picture that emerges from
these data raises interesting questions about the implications of the
findings for the meaning of work to officers trained in a different system and for reemployment trends as military reform moves forward.
The unique data also raise questions about the lack of state response to
the problems provoked by military reform, the effect of international
organizations in retraining, and the generalizability of the 1997 findings as military reform accelerates.

INTERPRETING THE DATA: THE LARGER CONTEXT

To fully interpret the implications of Rohall et al.'s findings for the future and for the more general pattern of re-employment tactics in the
new market economy it would be useful to define more clearly the
population from which the sample was drawn. Russian military demobilization is an enormous project—between 1995 and 2002 416,500 officers resigned. They were replaced by 244,000 officers, most of whom
were trained in military academies. Yet, numbers do not provide a
complete picture of the dilemmas and opportunities resulting from a
pattern of downsizing defined by generational, service, temporal, and
regional components.

Protracted Reform: Getting Out While the Getting Is Good

In the period since these data were collected, there have been two initiatives to step up military reform. The first occurred in 1998; the second initiative began during Putin's honeymoon with the military and
was prompted by the sinking of the Russian submarine *Kursk* in 2000.
These initiatives included cuts in the officer corps estimated at 50,000
individuals. As Rohall et al. report, military downsizing continues to be
hampered by political struggles at the highest levels and a lack of funding to pay growing pension bills. Today, despite the massive reform already undertaken, the Russian military remains an inverted pyramid

with a great number of colonels, suggesting that demobilization will continue for some time.

In order to generalize about the conclusions reached on the basis of these data we must ask: Does this sample from relatively early in the reform process reflect the population of officers now or in the future? Clearly, some evidence suggests that the composition of the early sample of retirees is skewed toward those with the most usable skills in the new market economy. According to Zisk (1999), more than 80% of the officers who retired in the early stages of reform did so before regulations required them to do so. Russian Ministry of Defense statistics suggest that 37% of all officers under the age of 40 resigned, many were just out of military school. It is possible that these officers left because they had reliable networks and usable skills that advantaged them in the transitional job market. Moreover, while there were serious attempts to shed mid- to high-level officers there has been a shortage of essential lower-level officers. These contrasting data support Rohall et al.'s finding that those officers who left early reported better living conditions than those who hung on until they were forced to leave. As such, these data may present the best possible picture of reform and patterns of life transition.

Regional Patterns of Military Downsizing

Russian military reform is regionally concentrated (Zisk, 2000). A report of demobilized army divisions suggests that downsizing has profoundly affected the Siberian and Far Eastern regions but not the urban centers of St. Petersburg and Moscow (although there has been a demobilization of heavy tank units around the capital). As a result, the degree to which this constituency was aided in their transition to civilian life depended largely on regional coffers and regional opportunities. In other words, the veracity of general claims would be contingent on how the regions included in this sample measure up to the other subjects of the Federation.

Russian statistical evidence suggests that this sample reflects both a specific time frame and regional concentration. Russian state statistics from approximately a year after these data were collected hint that these data overestimate the re-employment rates of retired officers. First, as predicted by the structure of reform, statistics show significant variation in re-employment from regional to region. Not surprisingly, unemployment among retired officers was much lower in Moscow than in the outlying regions or *oblasts*. Second, the success rates reported in the paper surpass the 60 to 70% figures reported by Ministry of Labor.

On the bright side, national labor statistics also indicate that 22 to 25% of retired officers are entrepreneurs—a category that does not show up in the study (Antonenko, 2000). Overall, a concise placement of the study within the national sample and a stronger recognition of its temporal limits would provide a clearer interpretation of Rohall and colleagues' reported findings. Similarly, a comparison with national statistics compiled by the Russian Department of Defense and Ministry of Labor would also help to situate the findings in the larger picture.

THE SOVIET LEGACY: POLITICAL DEMANDS AND STATE RESPONSE

Despite the scope of the problems facing retired officers, there is little concerted demand for a state response to the problem (Busza, 2000; Taylor, 1998; Zisk, 1999). The retiring officers are fragmented, divided by rank, age, and region. In large part, political pressure from retired officers is not national but is channeled through regional governors. During the Yeltsin era, strong regional governors, many of whom were building political machines, were obvious allies for these officers as they made demands on the central state. They fought with the Ministry of Defense over base closings much as regional representatives in the United States did in the early 1990s. Since 2000, President Putin's centralizing reforms severely limited this access point for retired officers. At the national level, the pressure also has been muted. Military leaders are profoundly divided by generation, branch, levels of support for reform, different military doctrines, and a bifurcated (civilian and military) command structure. There is strong evidence that President Putin exacerbated these tensions at the top ranks through his appointments and policies (Zisk, 2000). The lack of leadership, coupled with the regional pattern of reform, means that the capacity of downsized officers to organize on a national level or press demands on the central state is limited. Moreover, these officers do not have a clear venue through which to press their demands on government. The apparatus charged with issues of downsized officers is labyrinthine, including offices in the Ministry of Labor and Social Development's Department of Social Problems of Retired Servicemen, the Ministry of Defense, the Union of Veterans, a special commission that reports directly to the presidential apparatus, and the State Duma.

Despite these numerous obstacles, retired officers did attempt to organize on the national level. The state quashed nascent organizations, such as the Union of Officers, mostly through coercion and intimidation. More recently, a number of proto-political party organizations such as the Union to Support the Army sprang up. To date, these organizations remain quite small as they compete against each other and against a large number of nationalist/patriotic party organizations spawned by the electoral process. Thus, while retired officers run and win office at the regional level, they have not had the same success in national politics (Busza, 1999; Taylor, 2000, 2002). At the very top, Putin's strong verbal and budgetary support won him overwhelming support among current and retired officers in the 2000 presidential elections. This trend continued in the March 2004 presidential race as the Kremlin ensured that no credible rival could credibly challenge Putin.

Without immediate pressure from the retired officers, the Russian state that provoked demobilization has ignored the problems it created. The state continues to put out more immediate fires within the military, including the inability to recruit new members at the junior officer level, stop brutal hazing or *dedovshchina,* and provide housing and wages. Conditions are so dire that a recent poll conducted by the Ministry of Defense and reported in *Izvestiya* revealed that fewer than 50% of currently serving officers wished to remain in the military, a sentiment echoed in the retired officers' relatively high satisfaction levels reported by Rohall et al. The state also faces the more general problem of aiding the civilian population through wrenching economic restructuring. It is telling that while the Ministry of Defense planned to institute a retraining program targeted at the officer corps during 1998 through 2002, the actual program was not realized. Thus, as the data reveal, few retired officers rely on state-sponsored employment agencies to find jobs.

The lack of Russian state intervention on behalf of its officers is particularly puzzling because the international community does appear to be concerned with post-military retraining. This concern is well founded. Though there has been little open protest or threat of coup, the lack of support for retired officers has significant social costs. Several specialists argue that the ills that plague the military are just a microcosm of those that plague the general population. Participation in crime is on the rise and is hinted at in a paper that finds that many re-employed officers work in the business of private security. Antonenko (2000) cites an internal study that shows that some officers are approached by organized crime organizations before they retire. A large number of post-military families live in poverty. Finally, there are international ramifications in the inability of a young, retired military corps to find work at home. The effective transformation of soldiers into civilian entrepreneurs grew more urgent in the highly charged era of the war on terror. Soviet and Russian-era military consultants to Middle East governments retired and reestablished their connections under private consulting companies and remain active in training and weapons procurement (Antonenko, 2001).

State-sponsored aid from Europe and Japan targeted the officer corps retraining programs, many of which were also regionally concentrated. For example, Japanese aid efforts were concentrated in the Far Eastern regions of the country and provided employment opportunities in large firms that traded with Russian partners. In 1997 the British Ministry of Defense initiated a program in six Russian regions with an annual budget of $2 million a year. The European Union established its own program to aid officers in remote regions. Interestingly, despite overtures from the EU, the U.S. Department of Defense has not provided direct aid to retired officers, though NATO did launch a regional retraining support program in 2002. This program included a module that mapped the availability of services from the U.S. government. In addition, USAID ran a relatively small housing program for demobilized officers.

Nongovernmental efforts matched these state-sponsored programs. The Open Society Institute (OSI)was among the first to participate in retraining efforts, beginning in 1996. OSI created its *Partners* program, which provided both retraining and the infrastructure necessary for military officers to put their skills to use in the new business environment. Later, the Eurasia Foundation funded a program in the region of Khabarovsk run by the Far Eastern Institute of International Relations. Coordination among these programs is a goal of the International Institute for Security Studies, which engaged in a number of activities to boost the effectiveness of these programs, including conferences to build ties among aid efforts and Russian officials. Unfortunately, the role of state and nongovernmental organizations' (NGO) assistance in life transformation is new to the scene and is not measured directly by this survey instrument. It is an interesting and important aspect of political change that might be measured in future work.

THE SOVIET LEGACY AND THE ROLE OF INFORMAL NETWORKS

As Rohall et al. note, reliance on informal networks was a hallmark of daily life under the Soviet regime. In the economic realm, the unpredictable patterns of production and trade in the shortage economy forced individuals to rely on each other to meet daily needs (Ledeneva, 1998; Shlapentokh, 1989). Networks were particularly strong in the labor market where both personal and organization-based linkages abounded but there was no infrastructure for finding new jobs. The continued reliance on informal networks in the post–Soviet period as a source of job mobility among retired officers is not unique to society. Some scholars have argued that these personal networks are more valuable in the post-socialist context than under state socialism (Sik & Wellman, 1999). Not only are the conditions of uncertainty and shortage replicated in the transition, but the infrastructure of a market economy has not yet emerged and the state has not stepped up to fill the void.

Similarly, the skill sets of officers are not the same. Military reformers have long argued that there is lack of technological and management skills in the upper levels of the officers corps. As General Aleksandr Lebed, who struggled in his role as governor of the region of Krasnoyarsk before his death, said, "I was in the military for twenty six years. I left five years ago and found myself in another world. I very quickly realized that that world had no need of all the skills and knowledge that I'd acquired in the past and I began to get rid of them one-by-one" (in Taylor, 2002). Thus, as Rohall and colleagues note, it is wrong to assume that all officers have access to the same type or quality of networks. Similarly, Baev (2002) argues that the late Soviet-era officer corps was isolated from civilian networks, a situation that would not serve them well in the transition. Finally, Zisk (1999, 2000) argues that junior officers possessed greater skills and experience in technology and management. As such, the skill sets of the more junior officers better matched the demand of the labor market and they have left in droves to capitalize on these opportunities (Zisk, 1999, 2000). Since the priorities of the Soviet state privileged industrial production over the service economy, there is a perpetual shortfall of labor in the new Russian service sector. Moreover, the demise of the behemoth Soviet-era enterprises generated a further demand for service-oriented employees, particularly in terms of information technology and security.

By ignoring generational differences in training, the authors mischaracterize the strength of networks and skill sets across groups by following U.S.- or Western-based assumptions about force structure. For example, Rohall et al. hypothesize that senior officers should rely more heavily on well-developed informal networks and should fare better in the job market. These expectations are not borne out by the data. For Russia watchers, the finding that technologically savvy junior officers fair better than their senior colleagues is not surprising. The same problem may occur in the categorization of post-military employment based on Western assumptions. Although it is difficult to assess from the information in the text, there is some sense that jobs are misclassified. For example, "doctor" is quite a low-paid, low-status profession in Russia. More generally, the meaning of the evidence presented is difficult to assess since Rohall et al. failed to report the variance along with means. It may be that the difference in means across groups was not significant in a number of cases due to high levels of within group variation.

A fascinating follow-up to this research would be an inquiry into the structure of different networks and their cross-over value into civilian life. Establishing accurate assessments of patterns of networks and skill levels is critical to understanding both the potential impact of future reforms and the larger relationship between military officers and the civilian population. There is some evidence that those officers who have not yet left are the ones who most fear facing the uncertainty of the labor market (Zisk, 2000). These new waves of retirements will come at a difficult time. In 2003, the Russian Ministry of Labor released a dire report claiming a growing unemployment crisis across the Federation (February 18, 2003, at Pravda.ru). A new wave of surveys should reveal a much more dismal picture of the re-employment and job satisfaction levels among officers.

CONCLUSION

In the end, these data show more continuity in individual coping mechanisms during the transition than breaks with the behaviors common to the Soviet past. Moreover, the evidence suggests why these patterns persist beyond the old political and economic regime and in fact, coexist with emerging institutions. As in the Soviet era, personal networks are substitutes for state aid structures and they are necessary because the state does not want to or is unable to meet citizens' demands. These strategies relieve pressure on the state to respond to acute needs of its population. As with the larger population, the Russian state is unwilling or incapable of providing the resources to recapture the skills and experiences of well-trained segment of the population, missing a valuable catalyst for economic change. These data provide strong support for a managed democracy definition of the new Russia: a relatively weak state that relies increasingly on coercion and informal mechanisms to maintain stability and support.

REFERENCES

Antonenko, O. (2000). The social costs of Russian military reform: Redefining priorities for US assistance. *PONARS Policy Memo 152.* Stable URL: http://www.csis.org/ruseura/ponars/policymemos/pm_0152.pdf

Antonenko, O. (2001). Russia's military involvement in the Middle East. *Middle East Review of International Affairs Journal, 5*(1), 31–46.

Baev, P. K. (2002). The plight of the Russian military: Shallow identity and self-defeating culture," Armed Forces and Society, vol. 29, no. 1, pp. 129-146

Barany, Z. (1997). Democratic consolidation and the military: The East European experience. *Comparative Politics, 30*(1), 21–43. Stable URL: http://links.jstor.org/sici?sici=0010-4159%28199710%2930%3A1%3C21%3ADCATMT%3E2.0.CO%3B2-1

Shlapentokh, V. (1989). *Public and private life of the Soviet people. Changing values in post-Stalin Russia.* Oxford, UK: Oxford University Press.

Sik, E., & Wellmann, B. (1999). Network capital in capitalist, communist, and post-communist countries. In B. Wellmann (Ed.), *Networks in the global village: Life in contemporary communities* (pp. 225–253). Boulder, CO: Westview Press.

Taylor, B. (2000). The Duma and military reform. *PONARS Policy Memo 154.* Stable URL: http://www.csis.org/ruseura/ponars/policymemos/pm_0154.pdf

Taylor, B. (2002). Strong men, weak state: Power Ministry officials and the Federal districts. *PONARS Policy Memo 248.* Available through the CSIS website: http://www.csis.org/ruseura/ponars/policymemos/pm_0284.pdf

Zisk, K. M.(1999). Institutional decline in the Russian military: Exit, voice and corruption. *Ponars Policy Memo 67.* Stable URL: http://www.csis.org/ruseura/ponars/policymemos/pm_0067.pdf

Zisk, K. M. (2000). Putin and the Russian military. *Ponars Policy Memo 155.* Stable URL: http://www.csis.org/ruseura/ponars/policymemos/pm_0155.pdf

CHAPTER 5

Coming of Age in Wartime: How World War II and the Korean War Changed Lives*

John H. Laub and Robert J. Sampson

INTRODUCTION

It is accepted wisdom that historical events influence individual behavior. What is less well known is precisely *how* historical events influence individual behavior. As Elder and Caspi (1990) point out:
"the challenge for any study of lives in a changing society is to keep
both individual and environmental variations in the picture" (p. 202).
This chapter explores the mechanisms underlying the influence of military service during the World War II and Korean War era. We examine
the effect of military service on men's lives and aging using data from a
classic longitudinal study of a large group of disadvantaged, delinquent adolescents raised during the Great Depression in the city of
Boston and followed up at age 25 and again at age 32 (see Glueck &
Glueck, 1950, 1968).

In our previous work with these data, we concluded that marriage,
work, and military service represent "turning points" in the life course
and are crucial for understanding the processes of change in behavior,

---

*An earlier version of this chapter was prepared for the Penn State Conference on the
Historical Influences on Lives and Aging, October 13–14, 2003. We thank the editors
for their comments and suggestions and Elaine P. Eggleston for her superb research assistance.

especially criminal activity, over time (for more details see Sampson & Laub, 1993). Although a wide range of experiences have been associated with the notion of a turning point, Rutter (1996) warns that turning points should not be equated with major life experiences or expectable transitions (see also Clausen, 1998; Maughan & Rutter, 1998). First, some transitions may lead to no change in life trajectories. Second, some transitions merely accentuate preexisting characteristics rather than promoting change. Despite these difficulties, Rutter concludes "there is convincing evidence" of turning point effects defined as change involving "a lasting shift in direction of life trajectory" (1996, p. 621). Thus, in our view, the turning point idea reveals the interactive nature of human agency and life events such as marriage, work, and serving in the military. Nevertheless, more needs to be learned about the mechanisms underlying turning points in the life course. Our new work focuses on the potential of such structural turning points in tandem with agency to promote within-individual change in behavior (for more details see Laub & Sampson, 2003).

This chapter seeks to illuminate *why* institutions like the military have the potency to reshape life course trajectories for those from disadvantaged backgrounds and previously involved in crime. We draw on newly collected data from our follow-up study of the delinquent sample from the Gluecks' study as these men approached age 70. Although our sample and data are unique, we believe our research can make a contribution to the understanding of both the immediate and long-term effects of historical events, such as military service during wartime.

MILITARY SERVICE AND LIFE COURSE CHANGES

In a previous examination of the influence of the military, we argued that military service is a turning point in the transition to young adulthood (Sampson & Laub, 1996; see also Elder, 1986; Elder, Gimbel, & Ivie, 1991). Specifically, using quantitative data from the Gluecks' study, we found strong evidence that military service in the World War II and Korean War era fostered long-term socioeconomic achievement among men raised in poverty areas of Boston during the Great Depression.

Military service during World War II stands out as the defining moment for an entire generation, touching the lives of three in four American men and yielding one of the largest social interventions in U.S. history—the G.I. Bill of Rights. Our results revealed that overseas duty, in-service schooling, and G.I. Bill training at ages 17 to 25 generally enhanced subsequent occupational status, job stability, and economic well-being, independent of childhood differences and socioeconomic background. The benefits of the G.I. Bill were also larger for veterans stigmatized with an officially delinquent past, especially those who served in the military earlier rather than later in life (see Sampson & Laub, 1996, for more details).

Additional evidence, although limited, suggests that the military presents a unique setting for men with a disadvantaged background in the form of a criminal record. As illustrative of this research, Mattick (1960) compared the recidivism rates of men paroled to the army with those of a group of civil parolees, and found that the rates of recidivism among army parolees were much lower. An 8–year follow-up revealed lasting positive effects of the Army experience: The recidivism rate for the army parolees was 10.5%, compared with the national average of 66.6%. Mattick, however, could not identify aspects of the Army experience that may have accounted for this difference.

More recently, Bouffard and Laub (2004) addressed whether serving in the military facilitated desistance from crime using data from Shannon's 1942 and 1949 birth cohort data from Racine, Wisconsin (Shannon, 1994), Wolfgang's 1945 birth cohort data from Philadelphia, Pennsylvania (Wolfgang, Figlio, & Sellin, 1994), and the National Longitudinal Survey of Youth (Center for Human Resource Research, 1995). Men in these samples served during different historical periods from the beginning of the Vietnam War to the early period of the all-volunteer force. The results revealed that delinquents, particularly serious delinquents, who entered the military were more likely to discontinue their offending after they left the military. Moreover, this finding was not conditioned by historical era (see Bouffard & Laub, 2004 for more details).

Our age-graded conceptualization of the life course suggests that military service sets in motion a chain of events (or experiences) in individuals' lives during the transition from adolescence and young adulthood, which progressively shape future outcomes. What is it about the military that facilitated change in behavior, especially for those who were involved in crime prior to entering?

First, military service exemplifies change by removing disadvantaged youths from prior adverse influences (for example, bad neighborhoods, delinquent peers) and social stigma (for example, a criminal record). As Elder (1986) argued, war and serving in the military can profoundly affect a person's development by introducing a major source of discontinuity in the life course (see also Elder, Gimbel, &

Ivie, 1991). Caspi and Moffitt (1993) also point out that the military is a strong situational transition because it includes institutional discouragement of previous responses and provides clear direction and novel opportunities for behavioral adaptation.

Beginning with basic training, the military provides both education and socialization designed to reorient newcomers to a world with different rules and structures. Past accomplishments and past deficits alike have diminished influence. Thus a prominent feature of serving in the military is the "knifing off" of past experience and its potential for reorganizing social roles and life opportunities (see Brotz & Wilson, 1946; Janowitz, 1972). As one former delinquent told us, "The military cured me. It took a young hoodlum off the street. My neighborhood in East Boston was a jumping off place for jail."

Second, the military provides opportunities such as in-service training and subsequent training or education under the G.I. Bill. In this way military service may offer additional structural benefits that in turn enhance later attachment to work and marriage, which may in turn encourage desistance from crime. As we see in our life history narratives described below, the military provided a bridging environment that introduced disadvantaged men to both in-service and post-service on-the-job training and education (Browning, Lopreato, & Poston, 1973; Cutright, 1974).

In short, similar to marriage and work, but more by conscious design, the military changes routine activities, provides direct supervision and social support, and allows for the possibility of identity change. In addition, the military setting provides qualities often missing from the homes of disadvantaged men, such as firm discipline, cooperative relations or teamwork, strong leadership, social responsibility, and competent male models for emulation (Elder, 1986). The military also entails new options and experiences, especially travel to diverse places and corresponding exposure to all sorts of people and situations—varied backgrounds, talents, interests, goals, and even new conceptions of meaning (Elder, 1986; Elder & Hareven, 1993). For instance, one former delinquent we interviewed talked about his surprise at the extent of segregation by race in the service. Growing up in a racially and ethnically diverse Boston neighborhood, it never occurred to him that there was segregation. In his own words, this experience in the service demonstrated how "incredibly naive he was at twenty-odd years of age."

For some, the military even provided basic necessities—food, shelter, and clothes, for example. One man we talked to said, "I liked the uniform. It seems like it's [the military] altogether different from my childhood. From what I went through." For some, the attraction of the military was so great that they went to great lengths to enter. One former delinquent wanted to join the Marines to get away from his father, and he was so desperate to get away that he signed up under another name because he was on parole at that time.

Of course, serving in the military has its downside as well. Some men were seriously injured in the military, affecting their lives dramatically. According to Elder (1986), veterans least likely to benefit from the military experience were those who served in combat, who were wounded or taken captive, or who observed killing by others. War-induced trauma can undermine the stability of marriage or can result in avoiding marriage altogether. Using data from the Terman study, Pavalko and Elder (1990) examined the effects of mass mobilization in World War II and found that veterans were more likely to divorce than nonveterans. Similarly, Laufer and Gallops (1985) suggested that trauma resulting from combat heightened the risk of marital instability. Clearly, the tragic consequences of military service cannot be ignored, nor can the wider historical context of war be neglected. Consistent with life course theory, we are thus careful to situate claims about serving in the military in its historical context.

HISTORICAL CONTEXT

Historical context, especially growing up during the Great Depression and World War II era, heavily influenced the objective opportunities and the subjective "worldview" for the men in our study (for more details see Laub & Sampson, 2002). The historical embeddedness of particular turning points (for example, early marriage and children; lack of education and geographic mobility; military service and the G.I. Bill of Rights) cannot be overstated. Although not necessarily reflected in the lives of the men we have studied, this period of history was marked by less mass alienation and crime than today, low unemployment, increasing national wealth, expansion of the occupational structure, and, for some, the G.I. Bill of Rights with its occupational and educational training.

We believe this historical time period is a particularly interesting one in which to think about crime and deviance as well as more general developmental patterns over the life course (for example, the adolescence-to-adulthood transition). For example, drugs like crack cocaine were not even known in this period, and the level of criminal violence, especially gun use, was below present-day levels. Pervasive alcohol abuse, coupled with the virtual absence of other drug use (for example, cocaine), suggests a strong period effect. As already noted, perhaps one of the major forces in the lives of the men we interviewed was the military. These men were also in a position to take advantage of numerous opportunities offered by the G.I. Bill of Rights (see Modell, 1989). As Modell (1989) has argued, "the dominant lasting effect of the war seems to have been the economic forces it unleashed, and the personal optimism and sense of efficacy that it engendered" (p. 162). As discussed in more detail below, we found this to be especially true for the men who desisted from crime in adulthood.

THE GLUECKS' UNRAVELING JUVENILE DELINQUENCY DATA

The Gluecks' prospective study of the formation and development of criminal careers was initiated in 1940 and involved a sample of 500 delinquents and 500 nondelinquents born between 1925 and 1935. The delinquent sample contained "persistent delinquents" recently committed to one of two correctional schools—the Lyman School for Boys in Westboro, Massachusetts and the Industrial School for Boys in Shirley, Massachusetts. The nondelinquent sample was drawn from the public schools in the city of Boston. Nondelinquent status was determined by criminal record checks as well as through a series of interviews with key informants (e.g., parents and teachers). The Gluecks' sampling procedure was designed to maximize differences in delinquency—an objective that by all accounts succeeded (see Glueck & Glueck, 1950). For example, approximately 30% of the delinquent group had a juvenile court conviction at age 10 or younger, and the average number of convictions for all delinquent boys was 3.5 (Glueck & Glueck, 1950).

A unique aspect of the Unraveling Juvenile Delinquency (UJD) study was the matching design whereby the 500 officially defined delinquents and 500 nondelinquents were matched case-by-case on age, race/ethnicity, intelligence, and neighborhood SES. The delinquents averaged 14 years, 8 months and the nondelinquents 14 years, 6 months when the study began. As to ethnicity, 25% of both groups were of English background, another fourth Italian, a fifth Irish, less than a tenth American, Slavic, or French, and the remaining were Near Eastern, Spanish, Scandinavian, German, or Jewish. And, as measured by the Wechsler-Bellevue Test, the delinquents had an average IQ of 92 compared to the nondelinquents of 94.

The matching on neighborhood ensured that both delinquents and nondelinquents grew up in "underprivileged neighborhoods"—

slums and tenement areas—of central Boston. Given the similarity in neighborhood conditions the areas were in essence matched on delinquency rate along with poverty. Overall, then, the 1,000 male participants in the UJD study were matched on key criminological variables thought to influence both delinquent behavior and official reactions by the police and courts. That 500 of the boys were persistent delinquents and 500 avoided delinquency in childhood and adolescence thus cannot be attributed to residence in urban slum areas, age differences, ethnicity, or IQ.

The original sample was followed up at two different points in time—at age 25 and again at age 32 (see Glueck & Glueck, 1968). This data collection effort took place from 1949 to 1965. Extensive data are available for analysis relating to family life, schooling, employment history, military experiences, recreational activities, and criminal histories, for the matched subjects from ages 11 to 17, 17 to 25, and 25 to 32. More important, data are available for 438 of the original 500 delinquents (88%) and 442 of the original 500 nondelinquents (88%) at all three interview waves. When adjusted for mortality, the follow-up success rate is approximately 92%—relatively high by current standards (e.g., Wolfgang, Thornberry, & Figlio, 1987). The low attrition rate is testimony to the Gluecks' rigorous research strategy, but also to lower residential mobility and interstate migration rates in the 1940s and 1950s compared to today. It should be noted, though, that the follow-up of criminal histories and official records covered 37 states—the most common involving California, New York, New Hampshire, Florida, and Illinois (Glueck & Glueck, 1968).

ARCHIVAL LIFE RECORDS

A wealth of data on social, psychological, and biological characteristics, family life, school performance, work experiences, and other life events were collected on the delinquents and nondelinquent controls in the period from 1940 to 1965. These data were gathered through an elaborate investigation process that was developed by the Gluecks and employed with great success in their earlier research studies (Glueck & Glueck, 1930, 1934a, 1934b). Data gathered by the Gluecks in the UJD study included interviews with the subjects themselves and their families as well as interviews with key informants such as social workers, settlement house workers, clergymen, school teachers, neighbors, employers, and criminal justice and social welfare officials (Glueck &

Glueck, 1950). An important component of this process is what the Gluecks called the home investigation. This consisted of an interview with family members and offered an opportunity for the investigator to observe the home and family life.

These interview data were supplemented by field investigations that meticulously culled information from the records of both public and private agencies that had any involvement with the individual subject or the family as a whole. These data verified and amplified the case materials gathered during the home investigation. For example, a principal source of record data was the Social Service Index in Boston, a clearinghouse for every contact between a family and every welfare or social agency in the Boston area. Similar indexes from other cities and states were utilized where necessary. For information on criminal activity, the Gluecks collected data from the Massachusetts Board of Probation, which maintained a central file of all court records from Boston courts since 1916 and for Massachusetts as a whole from 1924. These records were compared and supplemented with records from the Boys' Parole Division in Massachusetts. Out-of-state arrests, court appearances, and correctional experiences were gathered through correspondence with equivalent state depositories and federal agencies like the Federal Bureau of Investigation.

In short, the Gluecks' strategy of data collection focused on multiple sources of information that were independently derived from several points of view and at separate times. The Glueck data represent the comparison, reconciliation, and integration of these multiple sources of data (Glueck & Glueck, 1950; Vaillant, 1983). It should be noted that the level of detail and the range of information sources found in the UJD study will likely never be repeated given contemporary research standards on the protection of human subjects.

Along with the extensive quantitative data coded by the Gluecks' research team, the case records from the Gluecks' study contained a wealth of "richly descriptive qualitative details" (Riley, 1994, p. 2). Kidder and Fine (1987) have distinguished two types of qualitative data. The first referred to as "big Q" includes fieldwork, participant observation, or ethnography. The chief characteristic of big Q is that "it consists of a continually changing set of questions without a structured design" (Kidder & Fine, 1987, p. 59). The second type of qualitative data is "small q," which "consists of open-ended questions embedded in a survey or experiment that has a structure or design" (Kidder & Fine, 1987, p. 59). The Gluecks' qualitative data are of the second variety. For each subject in the Gluecks' study, qualitative data can be found in several parts of the case file including:

1. detailed handwritten interviews with the subjects and their families conducted by the Gluecks' research team
2. interviewer narratives that were produced for each subject at each interview including detailed information on tracing and locating each subject
3. interviews conducted with key informants including teachers, criminal justice officials, and employers
4. volumes of miscellaneous notes and correspondence relating to family and school experiences, employment histories, military service, and the like

Given the time period during which the Glueck study was conducted, a majority of the men served in some branch of the military (67% overall). This time span covered specific military actions, such as the last few years of World War II and the stationing of troops in Japan and West Germany (1944–1945) and the Korean War (1950–1953) (Glueck & Glueck, 1968). Data were collected on the military experience for each of these subjects during the Wave 2 investigation (age 25). The sources of information that were used included records from the specific branch of military service in question (e.g., Army or Navy), Selective Service, State Adjutant General, Veterans Administration, and Red Cross, in conjunction with interviews with the subject. The availability of rich data on military experiences reflects the unique historical circumstances of the Gluecks' study.

FINDING THE GLUECK MEN AT AGE 70

Our follow-up study of the Glueck men at age 70 consisted of three major tasks: (a) the collection of criminal records, both at the state and national levels; (b) the collection of death records, both at the state and national levels; and (c) finding a subset of the original delinquent subjects and interviewing them. In this chapter, we focus on the life history interviews we collected from the Glueck men.

Life History Interviews

We believe that life history narratives, more so than any other methodology, enables us to capture the heterogeneity of life course experiences and uncover the dynamic processes surrounding salient life course events, turning points, and criminal offending (see Laub & Sampson, 2003, for more details).

Initially our strategy for selecting interviewees was driven by the vagaries of funding. More precisely, selection of the men to be interviewed was influenced by a grant to study violence. With support from the Harry Frank Guggenheim Foundation, we identified eight distinct trajectories of violent criminal behavior across three stages of the life course (juvenile < 17, young adult 17–32, and middle/later adulthood 32–70). We sought to capture variation in dynamic trajectories of violence across the life course. In order to do this, our target was to interview at least five individuals in each of the eight groupings for a minimum total of 40 interviews. We eventually conducted life history interviews with 52 men, well beyond our target.

As it turned out, there were not enough men in certain trajectory groups, and in other cases the data on violence were overlapping with predatory offending against property (for example, burglary). We therefore collapsed and revised our classification to be more parsimonious and reflective of offending patterns in the data, regrouping the 52 men we interviewed into five working categories: (a) persistent violent or predatory offenders ($N = 14$), (b) nonviolent juvenile offenders who desisted in adulthood ($N = 15$), (c) juvenile violent offenders who desisted in adulthood ($N = 4$), (d) intermittent offenders with an onset of violence in later adulthood ($N = 5$), and (e) intermittent offenders with an onset of violence in young adulthood and desistance in middle age, or those showing an erratic offending pattern over their entire life course ($N = 14$).

For the interviews, we developed a modified life history calendar (see Freedman, Thornton, Camburn, Alwin, & Young-DeMarco, 1988) to help subjects place major life events (for example, marriages, divorces, residential moves, jobs) in time. The life history calendar is an important visual aid that allows the subject and the researcher to contextualize objective events. From the life history calendar, one learns the number of events, their timing, sequence, and duration.

Along with the life history calendar, we used an open-ended interview schedule that covered a variety of life course domains and brings into focus retrospective views of one's own life course (Clausen, 1993). Specifically, we asked the Glueck men to reflect about their educational and work experiences, military service, family relationships, living arrangements, neighborhood characteristics, and social activities including both official and unofficial involvement in crime and violence and alcohol/drug use. Of particular interest are the questions regarding the subject's assessment of his own life, specifically whether he saw improvement or a worsening since childhood, adolescence or young adulthood, and the self-evaluation of turning points in one's life course and their relationship to criminal activity and various life course transitions (for example, marriage, divorce, military service, residential change, and the like).

Although life history narratives with a long retrospective window should be used with caution (see Henry, Moffitt, Caspi, Langley, & Silva, 1994; Janson, 1990), a "catch-up study" such as ours really has no alternative. The key is to ensure that the data collected are valid and reliable, regardless of whether they are collected prospectively or retrospectively, or are quantitative or qualitative (Scott & Alwin, 1998). The strength of our approach is that we combined life history narratives with extensive institutional records, as well as with data in the Glueck archives, to ascertain validity and reliability of the narratives.

We believe that the narrative data are accurate from the actor's point of view, precise in their detail, and full of breadth (see Becker, 1996). As previously argued, qualitative interviews provide a unique perspective often lacking in criminological research (see also Becker, 1966; Katz, 1988). We expect that these life history narratives will provide important clues regarding the course of adult development from the vantage point of the actor, which cannot be obtained from statistical tables. Of course, these interviews do not provide a full life review, but they provide a rich supplement to the quantitative data we have collected in our follow-ups of official criminal histories and death records, and recoding of information extracted from the original files in the Gluecks' study.

NARRATIVES REGARDING MILITARY EXPERIENCES

The first set of life history narratives come from men who desisted from crime in adulthood. In fact, some of these men identified serving in the military as a turning point in their life course. The idea of military service as a turning point is also consistent with the quantitative data we collected from the desisters, which reveals that several of the men had a successful tour of duty in the military. Specifically, of the 19 men we interviewed, 13 served in the military and received an honorable discharge, one man served and received a dishonorable discharge, and the remaining five men did not serve in the military at all.

> In our interview, Victor highlighted the idea of military service as a turning point: I'd say the turning point was, number one, the Army. You get into an outfit, you had a sense of belonging, you made your friends. I think I became a pretty good judge of character. You met

some good ones, you met some foul balls. And things along that line. There was more of a spirit of camaraderie there, togetherness, you know, you come to rely on the friends you make, you know. And even if you didn't like the guy you wouldn't throw him to the dogs. There's no question that the fittest survive and you have to learn to get along with everybody.

The timing of the military experience for this cohort of men, who were raised during the Great Depression, is crucial as well. Serving in the military in the 1940s represents something different from the military today. Patriotism and pride in the military during the World War II era were abundant. But even more significant, the military offered clothes, shelter, meals, discipline, and structure to men who had little. Several men we talked to about the military mentioned food. One man we call John recounted to us:

I thought a turning point was joining the Navy. Oh, sure, everybody squawked about the food. And I'm laughing myself, because I had nothing. Where the hell can you have roast beef on a Monday for supper and then have roast pork? If we had roast beef [in Boston], we had it once a month. So I appreciated it. Like I said I only had a couple of bad meals. Like on a Sunday night, that bologna . . . we used to call it. Every other meal, even breakfast, was good. That was my turning point.

For more on what the military offered to disadvantaged youth, we turn again to Victor's interview:

Well, number one, you had guys that were coming out of the Depression. They got out of school and there were no jobs around, that was number one. And a lot of my friends, they're a little older than I am, a lot of those jumped into the National Guard to pick up a few extra bucks and they got a uniform. A lot of guys went into the service in WWII, a lot of them didn't know what three squares a day was. And I can remember a picture I saw in *Life Magazine* pertaining to that. It showed a black from Georgia going back home on leave and everybody's just sitting on the porch and they're feeling his uniform and everything else. They never saw threads like that. He's got shoes on, you know? But, like I say, put three meals on the table.

Another man we interviewed further added that the military taught him to control his temper, the value of helping others, and the need to follow orders. As a man we call William pointed out: "They teach you that you can be your own boss as long as you do what the

other people want you to do." One man we call Henry, who we interviewed at age 69, told us that he "learned a lot of responsibility there
[in the military] and . . . how to follow orders." Victor told us, "then
the Army too in those days didn't take any shit." He continued, "If you
want to be a wise ass, they had ways of taking care of you. Like I can remember, going out to the obstacle course and dig a 6 by 6. That's 6 feet
square, 6 feet deep. He'd throw a newspaper in and then I buried it up.
Then he would say, 'What was the headline? Dig it up, and take a look.'
Shit details, KP, things like that. They had a way of getting back at you."

It is also important to note that the military offered something
concrete to men when they returned to civilian life—the G.I. Bill. The
importance of this voluntary "aftercare" program should not be under-
estimated (see Sampson & Laub, 1996). To illustrate, we examine
John's experience in the military. While on parole at the age of 17,
John enlisted in the Navy. He received important skill training as an
electrician in the Navy, a career he would eventually work in all of his
life. When he left the service, he used the G.I. Bill. But even more important for John was the fact that his veteran status overrode his ethnic
status in joining the union. John explained:

> I worked for [name of company] the last four months of '41. I went
> to the service from there. Congress passed a law saying that anybody
> leaving their job voluntarily would come back to the same place—
> regular seniority. And I went back there [in 1945] and they were
> non-union. In 1946 they had to go union because they had a bank
> that they couldn't get on the job unless they were a union shop. And
> they went "Hey, sign me up." I happened to be one of the guys there
> who was working there as non-union and then I got into the union.
> At the time with my name, which looks real Italian—I'm not Ital-
> ian—it was an Irish union. "What are you, Ginzo?" But I got in the
> union. They took 200 veterans. The VA made them do it. I was about
> the 180th or something like that, that close. That was 1947. I was an
> apprentice for four years. You had to be an apprentice in the union.
> So I had my license at the end of three years. I was just hanging for a
> year—but I was getting the G.I. Bill, which paid up to five cents
> under an hour. In other words if I was getting $1.80 an hour at the
> time, I can get up to $1.75 with the G.I. Bill. It was pretty good; it was
> helpful with four kids. My biggest help was the G.I. Bill of Rights. It
> raised my pay up to five cents under what a journeyman would make.

Thus, we see that military service has the potential to be a transformative experience, especially for those from disadvantaged and delinquent backgrounds. For some men, the military provided the opportu-

nity to learn a new set of skills, both technical as well as interpersonal, in a new and different environment. Moreover, the military provided a "bridge" called the G.I. Bill that allowed disadvantaged men with a criminal record to access jobs, technical training, and even housing to facilitate their efforts to start anew.

The second set of narratives about the military come from men who persisted from crime across much of their life course. Unlike the desisters who pointed to turning points in their lives such as marriage, work, and the military that helped move them away from crime, turning points are absent or take different forms in the lives of persistent offenders. In fact, only 7 of the 14 persistent offenders served in the military at all. Among those who served, 4 received a dishonorable discharge.

Supporting the idea of continuity of antisocial behavior over the life course (see Sampson & Laub, 1993, 1996), the persistent offenders we interviewed had difficulty in the military. For most, the military was, upon reflection, a big mistake. Some of the men tried to enter the military through fraudulent means (most commonly using an assumed name or reporting their age to be older than it was). Others who entered legally went AWOL or generally disregarded orders. For example, one man was in the military for a little more than 6 months and spent most of this time in the guardhouse. Perhaps a man we call Buddy said it best. "Yeah, I was in the navy and the army but I got kicked out of both of them. I just couldn't conform. I couldn't handle any kind of regulation. When somebody told me to do something, if I didn't think it was right I'd tell them to go and fuck themselves."

For some the timing of the potential turning point, in this case, serving in the military, seemed to have made a difference in retrospect. For example, a man we call Maurice said, "As for a change, I think what happened when I was 17 in the army made things worse for me. That was down. That was really the downer, what happened there. Because I think if I had been able to go into the service after the war had ended and I would have been serving as the peace thing instead of actually being in the war. I might have liked it. I might have learned to accept discipline, which was hard for me to accept. I might have been able to continue my education while I was in the service."

Even among persistent offenders though some men pointed to the military as their turning point. One man stated, "Oh, the military helped me a lot. Gave me an education. Helped me know right from wrong, discipline. Be neat and clean. Yeah. In other words, the Marine Corps was like a mother and father to me . . . like a closely knit family."

The final set of life history narratives we present come from men who displayed a zigzag or intermittent offending pattern over the life course. In many ways, the experiences of these men are similar to the experiences of men who desisted from crime. Of the 19 men in this category, 12 served in the military and 8 of these received an honorable discharge. For example, in the life of a man we call Allen, the military was a transformative experience. "I think it was kind of important. It taught you basically how to get along with different types of people, you know, like blacks and whites, . . . there were a lot of Filipinos in my outfit. Just getting along with different cultures. I found it good."

Some of the men reflected on the military as a missed opportunity. The best illustration of this comes from a man we call Art who desisted from crime after age 30. Art received a Bad Conduct Discharge from the Navy. This is somewhat surprising because Art went into the service early (at age 17) plus he was assigned to overseas duty. According to our previous quantitative analyses these are two of the key elements of a successful transition from the military to adulthood (Sampson & Laub, 1996, see also Elder, 1986). Clearly Art's is not a simple story regarding the military and desistance from crime. Art also had opportunities for skill development, although he admits that he did not take advantage of those prospects. Of course, his Bad Conduct Discharge prohibited him from using the G.I. Bill. Nevertheless, Art regarded the military experience as an important event in his life, albeit its full potential was unrealized.

At age 70, he said, "It was an important role. But I mean . . . I wasn't smart enough to take advantage of it, because I rebelled against the discipline. And as far as I can tell, the B.C.D. was a bad decision. All I got it for was for mouthing off. I had a summary court martial, not a general, and I swear the reason I got it was because I gave the planning officer a smart answer." Again, this shows Art's inability to function in situations demanding conformity and rule abiding behavior. But at his age 70 interview, Art understood this aspect of his life. Reflecting on his regrets, he said, "Well, in the first place, I wouldn't have got in trouble with the law, okay, for one thing. I wouldn't have been so smart when I was in the service. And I wouldn't have gone over—when I was a kid I wanted to go over—they say, 'No liberty.' I says, 'See you later.' Boom, I go, you know what I mean? I think my attitude would have changed. But in retrospect, hindsight is better than foresight."

For Edmund, his reported turning point was a specific incident in the service—getting wounded. Edmund served in the Navy during World War II and in the Army during the Korean War. He told us that "after I was wounded I was changed." He reflected further, "I don't know, I settled down more after I got wounded. I guess I got the hell scared out of me so many times. I guess, I wasn't as wild, I used to be a wild kid."

Other men were not so lucky. Mickey, for example, had remarkable marital stability (49 years), residential stability (18 years) and home ownership, and long-term job stability (more than 20 years with one company), yet he developed a drinking problem as a way of medicating the pain from a war-related disability. During World War II, Mickey was hit in the head with shrapnel from an exploding hand grenade. He lost an eye, among other serious head injuries. He told us, "The pain would just rip the hell out of me. I was loaded with shrapnel in the skull, on the nerve systems. . . . I'd take the medication and drink. Anything to get rid of the pain." Mickey was arrested at least eight times for drunkenness and he was arrested once for assault and battery at the age of 31. Eventually Mickey did give up drinking and smoking—about 15 years before we met him at the age of 70.

Perhaps the most tragic life story we heard came from Carlo. Although he desisted from crime in later adulthood, Carlo seemed to be quite negatively affected by his stint in reform school as an adolescent, which in turn affected his experience in the military. He told us that he was "beaten up, scarred, and torn up" by his experiences in reform school. For instance, he said his teeth were broken when the guards punched him in the face. He also recounted a trip to the dentist in which the dentist said, "open your fucking mouth you bastard," and he pulled three teeth without any novocaine. He concluded "I hate fucking people like that. I can't forget things."

These experiences became aggravated in the military during World War II. At the age of 18, Carlo entered the Army with enormous hostility and aggression. In his words, he "started to kill human beings." He further stated that "killing allowed me to get my anger and frustration out." The negative effects of the war experience continued when he returned to the States. In his file in the Glueck archive, the Gluecks' researcher reported that after he came out of the service Carlo claimed "he started to push people around just like we did over in Germany, but he . . . found out he could not get away with it over here." In adulthood, Carlo was arrested for domestic violence with his first wife, was identified as an "excessive drinker" in his Glueck file, and it was reported that he had difficulties on the job. Apparently, he did not get along with his bosses and he deliberately "loafed" to avoid paying child support. In our interview at age 70, Carlo stated that he carried his bad memories for a long time, although he tried to forget them. He talked repeatedly of his hatred of the State—"the bastards"—

for what they did to him and for their failure to respond to his cries for help.

CONCLUSION

Serving in the military changes individual behavior and its effects can be realized throughout the life course. One of our goals was to identify the mechanisms by which the military changes individuals and to understand the life course changes that result. To accomplish this goal, we drew on a rich set of life history narratives collected from a group of men at age 70 who grew up disadvantaged and delinquent and who came of age during World War II and the Korean War.

What have we learned from our life history narratives? Perhaps the most important aspect of serving in the military is the process of "knifing off" individuals from their immediate environment and offering them a new script for the future (see Caspi & Moffitt, 1995; Elder, Gimbel & Ivie, 1991). Overseas duty was particularly effective in knifing off past social disadvantage (e.g., poverty and exposure to deviant peers) as well as stigmatization by the criminal justice system (e.g., arrest and incarceration). In addition, the military provided the men a daily routine that provided both structure and meaningful activity. The result was that the men found themselves in new situations that accorded both supervision and monitoring as well as new opportunities for social support and growth. Finally, the military offered the men an opportunity for identity transformation. In the larger view, for these men, the military can be seen as a structurally induced turning point that served as the catalyst for sustaining long-term behavioral change. As Howard Becker noted a long time ago:

> A structural explanation of personal change has implications for attempts to deliberately mold human behavior. In particular, it suggests that we need not try to develop deep and lasting interests, be they values or personality traits, in order to produce the behavior we want. It is enough to create situations which will coerce people into behaving as we want them to and then to create the conditions under which other rewards will become linked to continuing this behavior. (1964, pp. 52–53; see also Becker, 1960)

Our work here using qualitative life history data, when coupled with our earlier work using quantitative data (Sampson & Laub, 1996), tell a consistent and important story. Military service in the World War

II and Korean War era provided American men from economically disadvantaged and delinquent backgrounds with an unprecedented opportunity to better their lives through on-the-job training and further education. In particular, the G.I. Bill was a powerful macro-induced opportunity that offered a chance to economically disadvantaged and officially stigmatized youths to redirect their lives in a new context where their past did not count. However, as revealed in our narratives, for some men serving in the military can backfire, leading to pain and destruction in the shaping of an individual's adult life course.

Of course, turning points and developmental change are bound by historical context. The men in the Gluecks' study entered the adult labor market during the 1950s and 1960s, in a period of expanding economic opportunities, and were able to take advantage of numerous benefits offered by the G.I. Bill. Prospects for current cohorts appear to be less promising. Indeed, large cohorts of disadvantaged and delinquent youths are now coming of age without access to macro-level interventions such as military service and the G.I. Bill. Instead, lower-income cohorts today face an additional disadvantage in the form of radically altered policies of criminal justice that block the reintegration of offenders into society, particularly the "war on drugs" and unprecedented increases in the incarceration of young black males (see Sampson & Laub, 1993; Tonry, 1995). In this context, we need to ask what we can do to deflect the trajectories of disadvantaged youth who are involved in delinquency so as to improve their life chances in adulthood.

REFERENCES

Becker, H. S. (1960). Notes on the concept of commitment. *American Journal of Sociology, 66,* 32–40.

Becker, H. S. (1964). Personal change in adult life. *Sociometry, 27,* 40–53.

Becker, H. S. (1966). Introduction. In C. R. Shaw, *The jack roller: A delinquent boy's own story* (pp. v Janson, 1990; viii). Chicago: University of Chicago Press.

Becker, H. S. (1996). The epistemology of qualitative research. In R. Jessor, A. Colby, & R. A. Shweder (Eds.), *Ethnography and human development: Context and meaning in social inquiry* (pp. 53–71). Chicago: University of Chicago Press.

Bouffard, L. A., & Laub, J. H. (2004). Jail or the army: Does military service facilitate desistance from crime? In S. Maruna & R. Immarigeon (Eds.), *After crime and punishment* (pp. 129–151). London: Willan Publishing.

Brotz, H., & Wilson, E. (1946). Characteristics of military society. *American Journal of Sociology, 51,* 371–375.

Browning, H. L., Lopreato, S. C., & Poston, D. L., Jr. (1973). Income and veteran status: Variations among Mexican Americans, Blacks, and Anglos. *American Sociological Review, 38,* 74–85.

Caspi, A., & Moffitt, T. E. (1993). When do individual differences matter? A paradoxical theory of personality coherence. *Psychological Inquiry, 4,* 247–271.

Caspi, A., & Moffitt, T. E. (1995). The continuity of maladaptive behavior: From description to understanding in the study of antisocial behavior. In D. Cicchetti & D. J. Cohen (Eds.), *Developmental psychopathology, volume 2: Risk, disorder, and adaptation* (pp. 472–511). New York: Wiley.

Center for Human Resource Research. (1995). *NLS user's guide.* Columbus, OH: Ohio State University.

Clausen, J. A. (1993). *American lives: Looking back at the children of the Great Depression.* New York: Free Press.

Clausen, J. A. (1998). Life reviews and life stories. In J. Z. Giele & G. H. Elder, Jr. (Eds.), *Methods of life course research: Qualitative and quantitative approaches* (pp. 189–212). Thousand Oaks, CA: Sage Publications.

Cutright, P. (1974). The civilian earnings of White and Black draftees and nonveterans. *American Sociological Review, 39,* 317–327.

Elder, G. H., Jr. (1986). Military times and turning points in men's lives. *Developmental Psychology, 22,* 233–245.

Elder, G. H., Jr., & Caspi, A. (1990). Studying lives in a changing society: Sociological and personological explorations. In A. I. Rabin, R. A. Zucker, R. A. Emmons, & S. Frank (Eds.), *Studying persons and lives* (pp. 201–247). New York: Springer.

Elder, G. H., Jr., Gimbel, C., & Ivie, R. (1991). Turning points in life: The case of military service and war. *Military Psychology, 3,* 215–231.

Elder, G. H., Jr., & Hareven, T. K. (1993). Rising above life's disadvantage: From the Great Depression to war. In G. H. Elder, Jr., J. Modell, & R. D. Parke (Eds.), *Children in time and place: Developmental and historical insights* (pp. 47–72). Cambridge: Cambridge University Press.

Freedman, D., Thornton, A., Camburn, D., Alwin, D., & Young-DeMarco, L. (1988). The life history calendar: A technique for collecting retrospective data. *Sociological Methodology, 18,* 37–68.

Glueck, S., & Glueck, E. (1930). *500 criminal careers.* New York: A.A. Knopf.

Glueck, S., & Glueck, E. (1934a). *Five hundred delinquent women.* New York: A. A. Knopf.

Glueck, S., & Glueck, E. (1934b). *One thousand juvenile delinquents.* Cambridge, MA: Harvard University Press.

Glueck, S., & Glueck, E. (1950). *Unraveling juvenile delinquency.* New York: The Commonwealth Fund.

Glueck, S., & Glueck, E. (1968). *Delinquents and nondelinquents in perspective.* Cambridge, MA: Harvard University Press.

Henry, B., Moffitt, T. E., Caspi, A., Langley, J., & Silva, P. A. (1994). On the 're-membrance of things past': A longitudinal evaluation of the retrospective method. *Psychological Assessment, 6,* 92–101.

Janowitz, M. (1972). Characteristics of the military environment. In S. E. Ambrose & J. A. Barber, Jr. (Eds.), *The military and American society: Essays and readings* (pp. 166–173). New York: Free Press.

Janson, C-G. (1990). Retrospective data, undesirable behavior, and the longitudinal perspective. In D. Magnusson & L. R. Bergman (Eds.), *Data Quality in Longitudinal Research* (pp. 100–121). Cambridge: Cambridge University Press.

Katz, J. (1988). *Seductions of crime. New York:* Basic Books.

Kidder, L. H., & Fine, M. (1987). Qualitative and quantitative methods: When stories converge. In M. M. Mark & R. L. Shotland (Eds.), *Multiple methods in program evaluation* (pp. 57–75). San Francisco: Jossey-Bass.

Laub, J. H., & Sampson, R. J. (2002). Sheldon and Eleanor Glueck's Unraveling Juvenile Delinquency Study: The lives of 1,000 Boston men in the twentieth century. In E. Phelps, F. F. Furstenberg, Jr., & A. Colby (Eds.), *Looking at lives: American longitudinal studies of the twentieth century* (pp. 87–115). New York: Russell Sage Foundation.

Laub, J. H., & Sampson, R. J. (2003). *Shared beginnings, divergent lives: Delinquent boys to age 70.* Cambridge, MA: Harvard University Press.

Laufer, R. S., & Gallops, M. S. (1985). Life-course effects of Vietnam combat and abusive violence: Marital patterns. *Journal of Marriage and the Family, 47,* 839–853.

Mattick, H. W. (1960). Parolees in the army during World War II. *Federal Probation, 24,* 49–55.

Maughan, B., & Rutter, M. (1998). Continuities and discontinuities in antisocial behavior from childhood to adult life. In T. H. Ollendick & R. J. Prinz (Eds.), *Advances in clinical child psychology* (Vol. 20, pp. 1–47). New York: Plenum Press.

Modell, J. (1989). *Into one's own: From youth to adulthood in the United States, 1920–1975.* Berkeley: University of California Press.

Pavalko, E. K., & Elder, G. H., Jr. (1990). World War II and divorce: A life-course perspective. *American Journal of Sociology, 95,* 1213–1234.

Riley, M. W. (1994). Data on age-related structural change: Challenges to ICPSR. *ICPSR Bulletin, 15,* 1–6.

Rutter, M. (1996). Transitions and turning points in developmental psychopathology: As applied to the age span between childhood and mid-adulthood. *International Journal of Behavioral Development, 19,* 603–626.

Sampson, R. J., & Laub, J. H. (1993). *Crime in the making: Pathways and turning points through life.* Cambridge, MA: Harvard University Press.

Sampson, R. J., & Laub, J. H. (1996). Socioeconomic achievement in the life course of disadvantaged men: Military service as a turning point, circa 1940–1965. *American Sociological Review, 61,* 347–367.

Scott, J., & Alwin, D. (1998). Retrospective versus prospective measurement of life histories in longitudinal research. In J. Z. Giele & G. H. Elder, Jr. (Eds.), *Methods of life course research: Qualitative and quantitative approaches* (pp. 98–127). Thousand Oaks, CA: Sage Publishers.

Shannon, L.W. (1994). *Juvenile delinquency and adult crime, 1948–1977 [Racine, Wisconsin]: Three birth cohorts* (computer file). Conducted by University of Iowa, Iowa Urban Community Research Center; 2nd ICPSR edn. Ann Arbor, MI: Inter-university Consortium for Political and Social Research.

Tonry, M. (1995). *Malign neglect—Race, crime, and punishment in America.* New York: Oxford University Press.

Vaillant, G. E. (1983). *The natural history of alcoholism.* Cambridge, MA: Harvard University Press.

Wolfgang, M. E., Figlio, R., & Sellin, T. (1994). *Delinquency in a birth cohort in Philadelphia, Pennsylvania, 1945–1963* (computer file). Conducted by University of Pennsylvania, Wharton School; 3rd ICPSR edn. Ann Arbor, MI: Inter-university Consortium for Political and Social Research.

Wolfgang, M. E., Thornberry, T. P., & Figlio, R. (Eds.). (1987). *From boy to man, from delinquency to crime. Chicago:* University of Chicago Press.

Commentary

Time, Race, and Gender Differences in the Effects of Military Service on Veteran Outcomes*

David R. Segal

L aub and Sampson have made a significant contribution to our understanding of the effects of serving in the military on the subsequent life trajectories of those who serve. Their initial analysis of the Gluecks' data on poor White males of European background, who grew up in Boston during the Great Depression, showed that service in World War II or the Korean War fostered socioeconomic achievement (Sampson & Laub, 1996). Their current effort, reviewing criminal records and death records, and locating and re-interviewing a subset of the original respondents at the age of 70, allowed them to explore long-term criminological outcomes, and to present personal narratives that gave voice to the respondents themselves, and explores issues of how and why military service had the effects that it did.

I am not about to try to teach John Laub or Glen Elder anything about World War II veterans (see Elder, 1986). Rather, I want to reflect on how generalizable the findings from this World War II cohort are,

*Preparation of this commentary was supported in part by the U.S. Army Research Institute for the Behavioral and Social Sciences under contract DASW 0100K0016. The views herein are those of the author and do not necessarily represent those of the Army Research Institute, the Department of the Army, or the Department of Defense.

and to encourage the collection of similar follow-up and narrative data from other veteran populations. The Glueck data are different from the data used in many other analyses of World War II veterans, and World War II and Korea were different from many other wars.

The results of three decades of research on what happens to veterans upon their return to the civilian labor force are mixed, but they suggest that the returns to military service (or the costs of military service) vary by race and ethnicity, gender, and period of military service. Among male veterans, those who served during the periodsat the time of conscription during for World War II and the Korean War—our largest proportional mobilizations—tend to do better in terms of subsequent civilian socioeconomic status than their peers who did not serve (Fredland & Little, 1985; Little & Fredland, 1979; Martindale & Poston, 1979; Villemez & Kasarda, 1976). By contrast, those who served during the Vietnam War tend to do less well than their peers who did not serve (Berger & Hirsch, 1983; Cohen, Segal, & Temme, et al., 1986,; 1992; Teachman & Call, 1996). The evidence suggests that whereas veterans of World War II and Korea had access to educational benefits through the G.I. Bill that were not more broadly available, and which yielded returns through occupational attainment and income, federal aid for higher education was decoupled from military service during the Vietnam era, and non-veterans could get similar benefits without delaying their education and entry into the civilian labor force to serve in the military. Since the 1960s, federal aid for higher education has largely been a G.I. Bill without the G.I.

World War II was the first war that was extensively studied by sociologists and manpower economists, but one can infer that benefits tied to military service affected the life course of participants in earlier wars, and did so differentially. There was a great deal of immigration from Europe in the decade prior to the Civil War, and the Union Army had an extremely international flavor. The disability and survivors benefit program that veterans of that army eventually received, largely because of political lobbying by the Grand Army of the Republic, became America's first old-age insurance program and may have affected the well-being of members and their families (Segal, 1989; Vinovkis, 2003). In contrast, one of the largest ethnic groups fighting for the confederacy were Mexican Americans, who came to their status not through immigration, but rather through the annexation of the Republic of Texas. By virtue of their regional location, they received no benefits.

The Consequences consequences of military service are less clear with regard to the post–Vietnam War volunteer force. Cohen, Warner, and Segal (1995) suggest that the Vietnam veteran disadvantage in education continued into the current era, regardless of ethnicity or gender. Conversely, Teachman and Call (1996), controlling for the selectivity of the military, found that White male veterans of the all-volunteer force (AVF), when it began in 1973, received an educational benefit, but that it did not affect post-service income or occupational prestige. Indeed, evidence shows this educational benefit persisted into later AVF years, but income was negatively affected in these years. Teachman and Call (1996) suggest further that African American veterans of the early AVF years suffered an educational decrement, which disappeared in the later AVF years but did not affect occupational prestige or earnings in either period. Phillips, Andrisani, Daymont, and Gilroyet al (1992), however, found that White non-Hispanic male AVF veterans gained an advantage in earnings (which is not shared with minority male veterans) over their non-veteran counterparts. Though these studies suggest that during the AVF period minority veterans did not fare well, in the aggregate, military service seems to have been more beneficial to minority male veterans than to White male veterans, particularly during periods of conscription (Angrist, 1990; Browning, Lopreato, & Poston,et al., 1973; Cutright, 1974; DeTray, 1982; Poston, 1979; Xie, 1992).

In contrast to these conflicting findings on socioeconomic attainment, and speaking more directly to their present study, Bouffard and Laub (2004) found that men from three different samples, who served from the Vietnam War to the current all-volunteer force, were more likely to discontinue serious delinquency than were men who did not serve.

We know less about female veterans, largely because with the exception of World War II, relatively few women served in the American military prior to the end of conscription in 1973. Although hundreds of thousands of women served in the American armed forces in World War II, the U.S. Census did not collect data on women's military experience until 1980 and did not ask about period of service. Thus, early studies that used census data to study effects on women of military service were unable to control for important factors. Poston, Segal, and Butler (1984) did find that White and African American women veterans who served between 1944 and 1980 earned more than their non-veteran counterparts. However, they were not able to look at when the women veterans served. Warner's (1985) study of women veterans aged 17 to 24 found no relationship between veteran status and earnings for White or minority women, but the women in her sample may not have had time to transition into the civilian labor force or complete schooling that might eventually increase their earnings. DeFleur and Warner

(1985) claim that women veterans of the AVF period seem to be advantaged relative to their non-veteran peers in terms of earnings, but their results are more suggestive than definitive.

Mangum and Ball (1987) examined male and female veterans of the AVF-era with regard to their ability to transfer their military skills to the civilian labor market and the impact of this transfer on post-service earnings. They found that women veterans were somewhat more able to transfer their skills, but that in terms of earnings, women veterans benefit less than men from their service. Mehay and Hirsch (1996) also reported that women veterans received a wage penalty for their service, relative to non-veterans, and that this penalty was greater for White women than for minority women. Prokos and Padavic (2000) also found that young female veterans are at a disadvantage in terms of earnings, whereas older women veterans, and particularly African American women and women with low levels of education, did benefit from their service. Most recently, Cooney, Segal, Segal, and Falk (2003) found that African American women veterans did not differ from their non-serving civilian counterparts in terms of earnings and family income, but that White non-Hispanic women veterans suffered economic penalties relative to similar non-serving women.

The statistical findings on the effects of military service on men and women of varying racial and ethnic groups are mixed. Interviews and personal narratives such as those presented by Laub and Sampson (2003) might enable us to understand the how and why of these dynamics.

REFERENCES

Angrist, J. D. (1990). Lifetime earnings and the Vietnam era draft lottery. *American Economic Review, 80,* 313–336

Berger, M. C., & Hirsch, B. T. (1983). The civilian earnings experience of Vietnam-era veterans., *Journal of Human Resources, 18,* 455–479.

Bouffard, L. A., & Laub, J. H. (2004). Jail or the army: Does military service facilitate desistance from crime? In S. Maruna & R. Immarigeon (Eds.), *After crime and punishment.* London: Willan Publications.

Browning, H. L., Lopreato, S. C., & Poston, D. L., Jr. (1973). Income and veteran status: variations among Mexican Americans, blacks, and anglos. *American Sociological Review, 38,* 74–85.

Cohen, J., Segal, D. R., & Temme, L. V. (1986). The educational cost of military service in the 1960s. *Journal of Political and Military Sociology, 14,* 303–319.

Cohen, J., Segal, D. R., & Temme, L. V. (1992). The impact of education on Vietnam-era veterans' occupational attainment. *Social Science Quarterly, 73,* 397–409.

Cohen, J., Warner, R. L., & Segal, D. R. (1995). Military service and educational attainment in the all-volunteer force. *Social Science Quarterly, 76,* 88–104.

Cooney, R. T., Segal, M. W., Segal, D. R., & Falk, W. W. (2003). Racial differences in the impact of military service on the socioeconomic status of women veterans. *Armed Forces & Society, 30,* 53–86.

Cutright, P. (1974). The civilian earnings of white and black draftees and nonveterans. *American Sociological Review, 39,* 317–327.

DeFleur, L. B., & Warner, R. L. (1985). Socioeconomic and social psychological effects of military service on women. *Journal of Political and Military Sociology, 13,* 195–208.

DeTray, D. (1982). Veteran status as a screening device. *American Economic Review, 72,* 133–142.

Elder, G. H. Jr. (1986). Military times and turning points in men's lives. *Developmental Psychology, 22,* 233–245.

Fredland, J. E., & Little, R. D. (1985). Socioeconomic status of World War II Veterans by race. *Social Science Quarterly, 66,*(1985), 533–551.

Laub, J. H., & Sampson, R. J. (2003 October). Coming of age in wartime: How World War II and the Korean War changed lives. Paper presented at the Penn State Conference on Historical Influences on Lives and Aging, University Park, PA. Oct. 13-14.

Little, R. D., & Fredland, J. E. (1979). Veterans status, earnings, and race. *Armed Forces & Society, 5,* 244–260.

Mangum, S. L., & Ball, D. E. (1987). Military skill training: Some evidence of transferability. *Armed Forces & Society, 13,* 425–441.

Martindale, M., & Poston, D. L. (1979). Variations in veteran/non-veteran earnings patterns among World War II, Korea, and Vietnam cohorts. *Armed Forces & Society, 5,* 219–243.

Mehay, S. L., & Hirsch, B. T. (1996). The postmilitary earnings of female veterans. *Industrial Relations, 35,* 197–207.

Phillips, R. L., Andrisani, P. J., Daymont, T. N., & Gilroy, C. L. (1992). The economic returns to military service. *Social Science Quarterly, 73,* 379–396.

Poston, D. L. Jr. (1979). The influence of military service on the civilian earnings patterns of blacks, Mexican Americans, and anglos. *Journal of Political and Military Sociology, 7,* 71–88.

Poston, D. L., Jr., Segal, M. W., & Butler, J. S. (1984). The influence of military service on the civilian earnings patterns of female veterans: Evidence from the 1980 census. In *Women in the United States Armed Forces: Progress and Barriers in the 1980s* (pp. 52–71). Chicago: Inter-University Seminar on Armed Forces & Society.

Prokos, A., & Padavic, I. (2000). Earn all that you can earn: Income differences between women veterans and non-veterans. *Journal of Political and Military Sociology, 28,* 60–74.

Sampson, R. J., & Laub, J. H. (1996). Socioeconomic achievement in the life course of disadvantaged men: Military service as a turning point, Circa 1940–1965. *American Sociological Review, 61,* 347–367.

Segal, D. R. (1989). *Recruiting for Uncle Sam: Citizenship and military manpower policy.* Lawrence: University Press of Kansas.

Teachman, J. D., & Call, V. R. A. (1996). The effect of military service on educational, occupational, and income attainment. *Social Science Research, 25,* 1–31.

Villemez, W. J., & Kasarda, J. D. (1976). Veteran status and socioeconomic attainment. *Armed Forces & Society, 2,* 407–420.

Vinovkis, M. (2003, October). *Aging in changing communities.* Paper presented at the Penn State Conference on Historical Influences on Lives and Aging, University Park, PA. Oct. 13-14.

Warner, R. L. (1985). The impact of military service on the early career. Unpublished Doctoral Ph.D. Ddissertation, Washington State University.

Xie, Y. (1992). The socioeconomic status of young male veterans, 1964–1984. *Social Science Quarterly, 73,* 379–396.

Commentary

Military Service and Emotional Maturation: The Chelsea Pensioners*

Carolyn M. Aldwin and Michael R. Levenson

Military service has been studied primarily by clinicians examining the effects of combat exposure on posttraumatic stress disorder (PTSD) (cf., Keane, Zimering, & Kaloupek, 2000). As Laub and Sampson remind us, however, military service can also serve as a turning point for troubled youths. Our purpose is to examine Laub and Sampson's hypothesis that military service contributes to the psychosocial development of youths, using a sample of older British veterans, the Royal Hospital Chelsea Brigade, informally known as the Chelsea Pensioners.

Laub and Sampson do a nice job of describing the factors that contribute to making military service a turning point. These include

- Removal from negative environments
- Change in routine activities

*We would like to thank Brigadier General A. G. Ross, OBE, for providing access to the men of the Royal Chelsea Hospital; Dr. Kathy Parkes for providing an invitation to Oxford University, which enabled this research; and Dr. Karen Sutton for her help in data collection. Special thanks for our Chelsea Pensioner guides: Gareth Evans, Arthur E. Jeffery, Edward P. Lee, and Noel Daly. Correspondence concerning this commentary should be addressed to Professor Carolyn Aldwin, Department of Human & Community Development, University of California, Davis, One Shields Avenue, Davis, CA 95616. cmaldwin@ucdavis.edu.

- Direct social support/supervision
- Provision of discipline and leadership
- Encouragement of teamwork
- Provision of male role models
- Allowance of identity change and new meaning
- Promotion of job skills—especially through the G.I. Bill

Though psychologists tend to attribute antisocial behavior to individual predispositions or perhaps family dynamics, from a sociological point of view, the broader environment may promote antisocial behavior, whether it be in the immediate neighborhood (cf., Runyan, 1978) or through particular microcultures (Levenson, 1992). Removal of individuals from such negative environments constitutes a major step toward eliminating antisocial behavior. Similarly, substitution of new routines for older, more destructive behavior patterns is also an effective way of changing antisocial behavior. Drill sergeants and other non-commissioned and commissioned officers are male role models who provide direct supervision and social support, insisting on discipline and modeling leadership. Further, a recruit is encouraged to abandon his or her previous identity, through changes in dress, hairstyles, and sometimes even names by adopting informal nicknames. A group identity is reinstated through teamwork. For example, Stouffer (1945) noted that most soldiers fire their weapons in combat not through a sense of personal duty but rather through a desire to support their platoon.

This type of personality change may sometimes be short-lived. Once back in the original environment, individuals can return to previous identities and habits. However, the G.I. Bill has provisions for job training and education, which permit upward mobility and a more permanent escape from toxic environments.

Laub and Sampson attribute the turning point characteristics of military service primarily to environmental change and socioeconomic opportunities. Indeed, they quote Becker: "A structural explanation of personal change has implications for attempts to deliberately mold human behavior. In particular, it suggests that we need not try to develop deep and lasting interests, be they values or personality traits, in order to produce the behavior we want. It is enough to create situations which will coerce people into behaving as we want them to and then to create the conditions under which other rewards will become linked to this continuing behavior." (Becker, 1964, pp. 52–53).

However, as Laub and Sampson note, not everyone benefits from military service, which suggests some interaction with personality or other individual difference variables. In part, we intend to argue that military service (and other institutionalized turning points such as college education) can result in emotional maturation, which underlies the ability to take advantage of potential turning points to result in meaningful personality and social change.

EMOTIONAL MATURATION

Currently there is no accepted definition of emotional maturity (Tilton-Weaver, Vitunski, & Galambos, 2001). Earlier, more psychodynamic definitions equated it with coping abilities, especially the ability to adapt to change (e.g., Menninger, 1963). Some equate it with ego development (Bauer & McAdams, 2004); others base it on personal strivings (Sheldon & Kasser, 2001). Helson and Srivastava (2001) developed four criteria for emotional maturity: competence, generativity, ego development, and wisdom (defined as practical wisdom, i.e., expertise and competence). Emotional maturity is conceptually similar to but subtly different from emotional intelligence, which involves sensitivity to and understanding of both one's own emotions and that of others in the social environment (Goleman, 1995).

We identified six criteria for the type of emotional maturity youths can develop as they enter adulthood, especially those who participate in such liminal social organizations such as military service, higher education, or apprentice work positions. We based these criteria partially on the literature but also on informal discussions with high ranking military officers who described their observations about the impact of military service, including combat, on the young men and women in their command.

A major component is emotional maturation is *increased emotional stability*. Roberts, Caspi, and Moffitt (2001) describe a general increase in emotional stability and mastery from late adolescence to the early 20s. McCrae et al. (1999) also observed these general developmental trends in a large multinational study. The development of emotional stability allows one to cope in a calmer, more thoughtful fashion with problems and counterbalances—the type of impulsivity that so often gets youths into trouble. Presumably, individuals who are capable of regulating their own emotional reactions to problems are less likely to seek external means of emotion regulation such as cigarettes, alcohol, and drugs, both licit and illicit (cf., Aldwin, 1994).

Arnett (2001), in his study of the transition to adulthood, identified the *ability to accept responsibility for own actions* as one of the hallmarks of adulthood. Conversely, emotionally immature individuals are more likely to blame others for their problems. The difficulty with this stance, or course, is that it blocks individuals from sincerely examining the sources of problems and from undertaking any sort of personal change that might prevent the occurrence of problems. The classic example is blaming bad grades on personal dislike by teachers or professors rather than acknowledging poor study habits.

Arnett (2000) also identified the *ability to self-generate goals and goal-directed behaviors* as one of the criteria for being considered an adult. Brandstädter (1999), also identified the ability not only to self-generate goals as an important ingredient in his theory of self-development, but also to modify those goals according to environmental demands. In other words, an individual who is emotionally mature should be able to have enough self-understanding to develop his or her own goals, rather than unthinkingly accept goals set by others such as parents. Further, individuals must have sufficient ego development and general competence to be able to identify possible pathways to those goals, recognize and cope with barriers, and identify alternative pathways and/or goals if initial attempts do not work out. Cultures may differ in the amount of autonomy they allow young adults to display in developing those goals, but eventually the emotionally mature individual needs to develop and display some autonomy in goal setting, whether within the initial framework generated by parents or in new settings.

The military officers of the Chelsea Pensioners to whom we spoke identified two additional goals. The first was the ability to accept critical feedback. This has a certain degree of face validity. Again, any sort of self-improvement requires the ability to accept critiques of one's efforts. This facilitates the development and refinement of skills in any type of endeavor, whether it involves academic, career, interpersonal, athletic, or spiritual goals. This should not be confused with subservience or abasement or tolerance of abuse, but rather involves the ability to decode fairly complex social and emotional signals to differentiate between constructive feedback and simple domination, as well as a certain amount of objective self-knowledge to evaluate the accuracy of the feedback.

Given that military practices typically rely on group endeavors, it is not surprising that these officers also identified the ability to work in a group setting as an important component of emotional maturity. Although the tendency of the general public is to assume that military operations are highly hierarchical, in truth field units need to be able to operate relatively independently, within the set goals and the rules of engagement. The ability of small units to operate independently, however, requires a high degree of cooperation and trust among the unit members. Thus, it is reasonable to posit that the ability to work in a cooperative manner in order to achieve collective goals is also a major component of emotional maturity.

Thus, emotional maturity contains what at first glance appears to be opposite elements. One must be emotionally stable, but capable of generating sufficient motivation to sustain the achievement of goals. Moreover, one also needs to be autonomous in setting one's own goals and in taking personal responsibility for one's own actions, but be able to work collectively and to accept critiques from others. Further reflection, however, reveals that these elements do constitute a legitimate, if complex, pattern. Sufficient autonomy and emotional stability may actually make it easier to work in groups and accept constructive critiques of one's work. In other words, defensiveness is an indication of emotional instability and uncertainty, which makes working in groups and criticism from others highly threatening. Counter-intuitively, it is mature autonomy that allows individuals to work cooperatively.

Liminal or transitional institutes such as the military, colleges, and apprenticeships, then, should provide the correct blend of structure and freedom to promote the development of emotional maturation. Clearly, there are individual differences in the readiness and/or capacity of individuals for this type of emotional development, however. We propose that emotional maturation is the mediating variable through which turning points such as military service may change individuals lives and promote future socioeconomic and personal development. To examine this issue, we draw upon data collected from the Chelsea Pensioners, a military brigade of retired British Army enlisted men who filled out surveys on their military experience and current levels of PTSD and health.

CHELSEA PENSIONERS

The Royal Chelsea Hospital Brigade was begun by King Charles II and Nell Bligh in the 18th century as a means of providing for retired army enlisted men. It is open to anyone who served in the British Army as a non-commissioned officer or private, and is not restricted to career military men. The only other restriction is that the men are not supposed to be currently married or have any dependents. The Chelsea Pensioners, as they are known, are required to give up their government pensions and in return receive free housing, food, clothing, and medical care for life. They do retain private pensions or other sources of income.

In many ways, the Royal Hospital Brigade is a self-governing institution. There is a general who heads the Brigade, but the pensioners have a great deal of responsibility for the running of the institution and staff the office, museum, and guard house. They also organize the annual Royal Chelsea Flower Show, which is a major source of income, and also one of the premier flower shows in England, opened by a parade presided over by the Queen of England, their current patron.

The facility consists of 18 wards of approximately 20 residents each; each ward is supervised by a master sergeant and a staff sergeant. The wards are graded by level of ability, with two functioning as infirmaries for the more impaired. Each resident has a small private wooden cubby hole, with just enough foom for a bed, a desk, and a dresser. There is a main dining hall, which is decorated by plaques commemorating the major battles in which the pensioners have participated. There is also a chapel, a pub, and a museum on site.

Qualitative Observations

We spent a considerable amount of time at the facility, conducting pilot interviews with the men, both formally and informally over meals and drinks at the pub. It was clear that the men took enormous pride in being Chelsea Pensioners. There were a number of men who were recipients of awards comparable to the medal of honor, and were considered to be military experts of considerable renown. The pensioners were often invited to address military and non-military organizations all over the world.

The British military is organized differently than the U.S. military, which consciously seeks to integrate soldiers from different areas of the country. In contrast, the British military is based upon regional militias, like the Welsh Fusiliers, often headed by specific members of the British royalty. The men were proud of their units and geographic areas and often spoke with thick regional accents.

As such, the pensioners represented a cross-section of British working class men, born in the early decades of the 20th century. A number of the men we spoke with were boy soldiers. It was expected that boys in orphanages, due either to parental bereavement or extreme indigence, would join the military in early adolescence, often to serve as messengers, paramedics, or musicians. Our informants told us that rates of illiteracy were high. It was also clear that the lack of a G.I. Bill seriously impeded economic upward mobility. It was sur-

prising to us that men who were highly decorated, widely acknowl-
edged war heroes would return after the war to jobs as day laborers
or other types of manual labor. The major job aspiration seemed to
be buying a small pub. Some of the men reported severe financial difficulties prior to joining the brigade; others were comfortably middle
class but greatly enjoyed the comaraderie and prestige of the Chelsea
Pensioners.

Many of the men had been career military and had seen very high
levels of combat, participating in the many wars in Europe, Asia, and
Africa occasioned by the breakup of the British empire. Part of the instrument we had developed in the NAS sample (see below) had asked
the men to detail their tours of duty. British soldiers, however, were
transferred every 2 years, usually traveling by ship for months, and it
was too difficult to ask them to detail all of their transfers. Nonetheless,
they had vivid memories of their combat experiences, often recount-
ing horrific stories of deaths and suffering, but there were also many
humorous and adventurous tales as well.

Nonetheless, the pensioners were not very psychologically mind-
ed. Even the most sympathetic did not understand why we were interested in the long-term effects of combat exposure. As one of our
primary informants said, "Why are you interested in whether I've seen
dead men? Of course I've seen men die in combat. I'm a soldier.
That's what happens. To tell you the truth, when I see a man die in
battle, I'm much more worried about plugging the hole than worry-
ing about the poor sod." This man regularly drank four pints of ale at
lunch. Indeed, the pub was very much a center of the Pensioners' social lives, and quite high levels of alcohol consumption seemed to be
common. Some men complained that there was little to do other
than drink at the pub, but others were very active both inside and
outside the community.

Quantitative Study

Sample and Procedure

We distributed anonymous questionnaires via the men's mailboxes.
Approximately one third (90 men) responded, who ranged in age
from 68 to 92 ($M = 79.25$, $SD = 6.24$). Five of these men requested and
received assistance in filling out their questionnaires, generally due either to visual or motor impairment. The men entered the service between the ages of 14 and 30 ($M = 18.17$, $SD = 3.35$); 19 men (21.6%)
were boy soldiers, and the rest entered as privates. Their average

length of service was more than 20 years ($M = 21.81$, $SD = 7.95$, range = 2 – 39); 81% had achieved the rank of sergeant by their discharge. Two thirds of the men (66.7%) reported having been in major battles, 9 (10%) were POWs, and nearly half (48.1%) reported having a military-related disability. Most men were World War II veterans, although there was one from World War I and a fifth (22.1%) reported their last combat experience after World War II.

As noted in the qualitative section, education rates were very low. Nearly a fifth (18.6%) had no school certificate, indicating less than an eighth grade education; two thirds had an army certificate, indicating that they completed the equivalent of a GED in the military. Fewer than 10% of the men had any higher education.

After their military service, about half of the men were blue collar workers, with the modal response (23.85%) being civil servants (e.g., policemen and firemen). Ten men were office workers, and an additional 26.16% were small businessmen or managers; only one reported being a professional. On average, the men had resided at the Royal Hospital Chelsea for a relatively long time ($M = 6.16$ years, $SD = 5.82$). Approximately a fifth (19.3%) had been there a year or less, but 15.7% had been there 10 years or more, with the longest resident reporting a stay of 30 years.

Measures

The men filled out a number of questionnaires that had also been administered to the Normative Aging Study Men (see Aldwin, Levenson, Spiro, 1994). The Combat Exposure Scale (Keane, Fairbank, Caddell, Zimering, Taylor & Mora, 1989), includes 7 items, rated on a 5-point likert scaling, which assesses the degree to which individuals have participated in war zone activities. The Mississippi Scale (Keane, Caddell, & Taylor., 1988) was used to assess PTSD symptoms and includes 35 items, rated on a 5-point likert scale, which tap affective, cognitive, and behavioral symptoms. We also used the British version of the SF-36 (Jenkinson, Layte, Wright, & Coulter, 1996). In this study we utilized the self-rated 5-point item, (5 = excellent health and 1 = poor health). However, the main focus of this study is on the Desirable and Undesirable Effects of Military Service scale, which was developed by Aldwin et al. (1994), based upon earlier work by Elder and Clipp (1989). This scale includes 28 items, using 4-point likert scaling. All scales were summed, using Michigan scoring to correct for missing data.

Results

For illustrative purposes, Table 5.1 compares the means and standard deviations on the scales of primary interest for both the NAS men and the Chelsea Pensioners. The qualitative observation that the pensioners had seen a great deal of combat was borne out by the quantitative data: they had seen nearly three times as much combat and were nearly four times as likely to have perceived negative aspects of their military experience. They were also slightly more likely to suffer from PTSD. However, they were also more likely to have perceived desirable experiences stemming from their military service.

Table 5.2 presents frequencies for the desirable experiences items. (Unfortunately, an error in the skip pattern for the desirable experiences scale lead to 20 of the men skipping that scale. This could not be corrected by Michigan scoring. Mean substitution only weakened the results.) More than 85% of the men reported greater discipline and reliability, as well as learning to cope with adversity. A similar percentage reported learning cooperation and teamwork, and nearly 80% reported becoming more independent. Thus, a large percentage of the Chelsea Pensioners reported developing the components of emotional maturity identified earlier. Not surprisingly, more than 80% reported developing more positive feelings about themselves. In contrast, only about two thirds of the men reported improving their life through education or better job skills. This suggests that the military did form a positive environment for emotional maturity, which could not be completely explained through the development of better career opportunities.

Which is not to say that the Chelsea Pensioniers did not experience a considerable amount of hardship. Indeed, as reported earlier, they did perceive a much higher rate of undesirable experiences. Table 5.3 lists the frequencies for those items. More than half reported

TABLE 5.1 Comparison of Chelsea Pensioners with NAS Men

	NAS Men (N = 1,287)		Chelsea Pensioners (N = 90)	
	M	SD	M	SD
Combat exposure	5.63	9.42	15.46	6.93
Desirable	27.29	8.51	38.64	11.12
Undesirable	6.83	6.15	24.35	7.83
PTSD	57.81	10.19	64.67	12.04

TABLE 5.2   Percentage Reporting Desirable Military Experiences

Item	Percent (%)
Lifelong friends	98.6
Broader perspective	77.1
Learned to cope with adversity	88.2
Greater self-discipline, dependability	86.8
Became more independent	78.6
Improved life chances through education	67.6
Value life more	83.6
Positive feelings about the self	82.9
Became more patriotic	63.8
Clearer direction and purpose in life	60.0
Better job skills and options	63.8
Rewarding memories	84.3
Learned cooperation, teamwork	86.8
Appreciate peace more	82.9

TABLE 5.3   Percentage Reporting Undesirable Military Experiences

Item	Percent (%)
Economic problems for me or my wife	42.5
Disrupted my life	43.6
Lonely for my wife and children	44.5
Delayed career, put me behind my age mates	16.9
Combat anxieties, apprehensions	47.4
Hurt my marriage	22.4
Waste of time, boredom	20.5
Misery, discomfort	53.2
Loss of friends	60
Loss of my good health	30.0
Separation from loved ones	57.1
Drinking problem	22.4
Bad memories or nightmares	26.0
Death and destruction	40.5

misery and discomfort, as well as separation from loved ones. Slightly less than half reported economic problems, being lonely for wives and children, and that it disrupted their lives. Interestingly, less than 20% reported being put behind age mates.

To determine whether emotional maturation and career advancement constituted separate categories of desirable effects, we factor analyzed the 14 desirability items using principle axis extraction, hypothesizing two factors. However, a scree test suggested that there were two or three factors, and the three factor oblique solution was most interpretable, accounting for 66.69% of the data. Table 5.4 lists the factor loadings for that solution. It should be noted that the factor structure should be considered exploratory, given the relatively small sample size.

However, it makes a good conceptual sense. The first factor reflects emotional maturation, and consists of six items with factor loadings ranging from .80 (learned to cope with adversity) to .34 (became more independent). A seventh item, positive feelings about the self, was a double loader with the second factor (.42 vs. −.47). However, it was conceptually more similar to the first factor, so we decided to group it with the first factor. The second consisted of four items reflecting change in values, including value life more (−.81) and appreciate peace more. Again, there were two double loaders. Became more

TABLE 5.4   Analysis of the Desirable Military Experiences Scale

	Factor Loadings		
	1	2	3
Learned to cope with adversity	0.80		
Greater self-discipline, dependability	0.79		
Broader perspective	0.71		
Learned cooperation, teamwork	0.67		
Lifelong friends	0.51		
Became more independent	0.34		
Value life more		−0.81	
Appreciate peace more		−0.70	
Rewarding memories		−0.58	
Positive feelings about self	0.42	−0.47	
Became more patriotic		−0.46	0.36
Better job skills and options			0.73
Improved life chances through education			0.60
Clearer direction and purpose in life		−0.42	0.57

patriotic clearly reflected values, and thus was left on the values factor. Clearer direction and purpose in life, however, were conceptually more similar to the third factor. This factor reflected career advancement, that is, better job skills and training (.73), improved life chances through education (.60), and clearer direction and purpose in life (.53). These items were summed and unit weighted to create three subscales: maturity, values, and skills.

Table 5.5 shows the correlations among combat exposure, these three subscales, PTSD symptoms, and self-rated health. As can be seen, combat was positively associated with PTSD symptoms ($r = .28$, $p < .05$) and negatively with self-rated health ($r = -.35 < .01$). It was also associated with lower skills ($r = -.32$, $p < .01$). This subscale was the only one to be associated with health ($r = .35$, $p < .01$). That is, the better the skills learned in the military, the better the self-reported health in later life.

We also explored whether the desirable experiences moderated the effects of combat exposure on both PTSD symptoms and health in later life, using hierarchical regressions with computed interaction terms. The predictor variables were centered to reduce multicollinearity. Two of the six equations indicated that there were moderating effects. The change in R^2 (.08) for the interaction between values and combat exposure was significant for self-rated health ($F(1, 58) = 6.053$, $p < .05$). Graphing the interaction term indicated that increases in values appeared to be protective of self-rated health, primarily under high combat exposure (Fig. 5.1).

There was also a trend for emotional maturity to moderate the effect of combat exposure on PTSD symptoms, with the interaction term accounting for 5% of the variance ($F(1, 60) = 3.427$, $p = .067$). As Figure 5.2 indicates, it would appear that emotional maturity was primarily effective under relatively low combat experiences; high combat levels overwhelmed the effect.

TABLE 5.5 Correlations

	Mature	Values	Skill	PTSD	Health
Combat	0.03	−0.10	−0.32**	0.28*	−0.35*
Mature		0.68***	0.64***	−0.11	0.12
Values			S0.60***	0.03	0.18
Skill				−0.21	0.35*
PTSD					−0.44*

$*p < .05$, $**p < .01$, $***p < .001$.

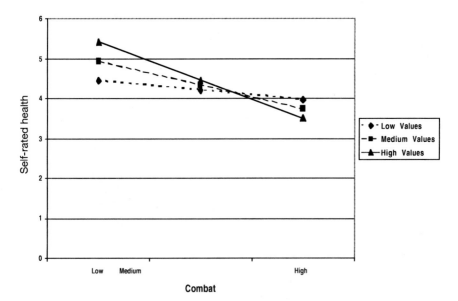

FIGURE 5.1 Interaction between combat and values on self-rated health.

SUMMARY AND DISCUSSION

The Chelsea Pensioners are a unique sample, consisting largely of non-commissioned officers who served in the major wars of the 20th century. Not only did they serve in World War II and Korea (as well as World War I), they also witnessed the often violent breakup of the British empire, serving in such locales as India and Burma. They reported very high levels of combat exposure, and a relatively high percentage were disabled due to their war service. Ten percent of the sample had been prisoners of war, primarily during World War II, while 20% had been boy soldiers, entering the military as young adolescents.

This study is consistent with others that have found long-term effects of combat exposure (Kahana,1992; Spiro, Schnurr, & Aldwin, 1994). In particular, retrospective reports of combat experiences were positively associated with higher levels of PTSD symptoms in later life, as well as poorer self-rated health. However, it would be a mistake to assume that their military experience was completely negative. Rather, they reported high levels of desirable experiences stemming from their military service.

Exploratory factor analyses suggested that there were three basic categories of desirable experiences: emotional maturation, values, and

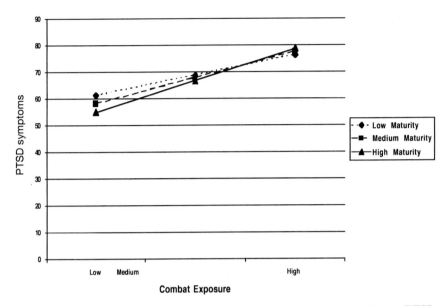

FIGURE 5.2   Interaction between combat exposure and maturity on PTSD symptoms.

increases in skills. We had hypothesized that emotional maturation consists of both increased autonomy and independence, as well as increased ability to cooperate with others. Indeed, the emotional maturation factor did reflect this seeming contradiction. The men reported learning to cope with adversity, and to cooperate with others, as well as becoming more disciplined and independent. On the values subscale, the men indicated valuing life and peace more, as well as becoming more patriotic. In support of Laub and Sampson's hypotheses, the men also reported benefiting from education and increased job skills, even though Britain did not have the equivalent of the G.I. Bill.

The correlates of these attitudes presented an interesting pattern. Only increased job skills was associated with better self-reported health. Presumably, this increase in education and job skills allowed the men a degree of upward social mobility, and higher SES levels are associated with better health (Adler & Snibbe, 2003). However, the other two subscales appeared to moderate the effect of combat. Values appeared to moderate high levels of combat, whereas emotional maturity was more effective at lower levels. This findings are all the more impressive because they were found in this relatively small sample.

A limitation of this study wase the sample size, especially in the multivariate analyses. The sample was by no means representative, but rather was a very special sample of British working-class non-commissioned officers who witnessed most of the major battles of the early to mid-20th century. These men displayed much pride in their military service, and were often quite comfortable in a setting in which they often took a very active role in running. They were especially proud of their royal patronage, and the quite astonishing success of the Chelsea Flower Show, which is routinely sold out for months in advance. They also served as a reservoir of knowledge, and current military officers from around the Commonwealth would routinely visit for consultations. Some of the residents were also asked to give lectures worldwide.

The Chelsea Pensioners retained their regional identification and often had thick accents reflecting their original counties or shires. This sometimes made it difficult to understand some of the oldest residents. One resident, a Yorkshireman, had a particularly thick accent. We told one of our guides that we couldn't understand this man, and he said, "That's alright, luv. We can't understand him either." This was typical of the good-natured banter we witnessed among the men.

As an institution, the Royal Hospital Chelsea Brigade is unique. It is not a nursing home, although it does have two infirmaries for residents who need higher levels of care. It is in someways similar to a continuum of care facility, in that it is an open institution with residents who often are not disabled in any way. It differs, however, in that the residents actively participate in running the organization. As mentioned earlier, the residents do most of the routine tasks, including intake of new residents, office work, running the museum, organizing the flower show, and so on (but not the cooking or cleaning). They remain a military unit, even in retirement, and often take great pride in that. They may actually provide a model for cooperative elder housing. Their shared experience, however, and perhaps the emphasis on cooperation and teamwork that they learned in the military, may be a necessary ingredient for the success of this type of endeavor.

This preliminary model of emotional maturation also needs to be tested and replicated in other samples. Clearly, the increased level of education and job skills did help at least some of the Chelsea Pensioners, supporting Laub and Sampson's contention, but it would be a mistake to reduce this maturational effect to simply change in situations, as Becker (1964) suggests. Rather, there was an increased level of emotional maturation, as well as a marked change in values, which is also characteristic of positive turning points in people's lives.

REFERENCES

Adler, N. E., & Snibbe, A. C. (2003). The role of psychosocial processes in explaining the gradient between socioeconomic status and health. *Current Directions in Psychological Science. 12,* 119–123.

Aldwin, C. M. (1994). *Stress, coping, and development: An integrative approach.* New York: Guilford.

Aldwin, C. M., Levenson, M. R., & Spiro, A., III. (1994). Vulnerability and resilience to combat exposure: Can stress have lifelong effects? *Psychology and Aging, 9,* 33–44.

Bauer, J. J., & McAdams, D. P. (2004). Growth goals, maturity, and well-being. *Developmental Psychology, 40,* 114–127.

Becker, H. S. (1964). *The other side; perspectives on deviance.* New York: Free Press of Glencoe.

Brandtstädter, J., Wentura, D., & Rothermund, K. (1999). Intentional self-development through adulthood and later life: Tenacious pursuit and flexible adjustment of goals. In J. Brandtstädter & R. M. Lerner (Eds.), *Action and self-development: Theory and research through the life span* (pp. 373–400). Thousand Oaks, CA: Sage.

Elder, G., & Clipp, E. (1989). Combat experience and emotional health: Impairment and resilience in later life. *Journal of Personality, 57,* 311–341.

Goleman, D. (1995). *Emotional intelligence.* New York: Bantam Books.

Helson, R., & Srivastava, S. (2001). Three paths of adult development: Conservers, seekers, and achievers. *Journal of Personality & Social Psychology, 80,* 995–1010.

Jenkinson, C., Layte, R., Wright, L., & Coulter, A. (1996). *The U.K. SF-36: An analysis and interpretation manual.* Oxford University: Health Services Research Unit.

Kahana, B. (1992). Late-life adaptation in the aftermath of extreme stress. In M. Wykel, E. Kahana, & J. Kowal (Eds.), *Stress and health among the elderly* (pp. 4–34). New York: Springer.

Keane, T. M., Caddell, J. M., & Taylor, K. L. (1988). Mississippi Scale for Combat-Related Postraumatic Stress Disorder: Three studies in reliability and validity. *Journal of Consulting & Clinical Psychology, 52,* 889–891.

Keane, T. M., Fairbank, J. A., Caddell, J. M., Zimering, R. T., Taylor, K. L., & Mora, C. A. (1989). Clinical evaluation of a measure to assess combat exposure. *Psychological Assessment, 1,* 53–55.

Keane, T. M., Zimering, R. T., & Kaloupek, D. G. (2000). Posttraumatic stress disorder. In M. Hersen & A. S. Bellack (Eds.), *Psychopathology in adulthood* (2nd ed.) (pp. 208–231). Needham Heights, MA: Allyn & Bacon.

Levenson, M. R. (1992). Rethinking psychopathy. *Theory and Psychology, 2,* 51–71.

McCrae, R. R., Costa, P. T., Jr., Pedroso de Lima, M., Simoes, A., Ostendorf, F., Angleitner, A., et al. (1999). Age differences in personality across the adult life span: Parallels in five cultures. *Developmental Psychology, 35,* 466–477.

Menninger, K. A. (1963). *The vital balance; The life process in mental health and illness.* New York: Viking Press.

Roberts, B. W., Caspi, A., & Moffitt, T. E. (2001). The kids are alright: Growth and stability in personality development from adolescence to adulthood. *Journal of Personality & Social Psychology, 81,* 670–683.

Runyan, W. M. (1978). The life course as a theoretical orientation: Sequences of person-situation interactions. *Journal of Personality, 46,* 552–558.

Sheldon, K. M., & Kasser, T. (2001). Getting older, getting better? Personal strivings and psychological maturity across the life span. *Developmental Psychology, 37,* 491–501.

Spiro, A., III, Schnurr, P., & Aldwin, C. M. (1994). Combat-related PTSD in older men. *Psychology and Aging, 9,* 17–26.

Stouffer, S. A. (1949). *The American Soldier.* Princeton, NJ: Princeton University Press.

Tilton-Weaver, L. C., Vitunski, E. T., & Galambos, N. L. (2001). Five images of maturity in adolescence: What does "grown up" mean? *Journal of Adolescence, 24,* 143–158.

CHAPTER 6

Well-Being of Low-Income Adults in a Period of Historical Changes in Welfare and Employment Policies*

Aletha C. Huston, Rashmita S. Mistry, Johannes M. Bos, and Mi-Suk Shim

M ost research investigating welfare and employment policies is concerned primarily with drawing conclusions about the positive or negative impacts of public policy. But, major policy changes constitute important historical events with potential impact

*This project was supported with a grant from the U.S. Department of Health and Human Services, Office of the Assistant Secretary for Planning and Evaluation, (grant 01ASPE374A), and an NICHD Postdoctoral Research Fellowship (grant 1 U01 HD37558) to the second author. The opinions and conclusions expressed herein are solely those of the authors and should not be construed as representing the opinions or policy of any agency of the federal government. The New Hope Child and Family Study was conducted in collaboration with the MacArthur Network on Successful Pathways Through Middle Childhood and was supported by the John D. and Catherine T. MacArthur Foundation, the William T. Grant Foundation, the Annie E. Casey Foundation, and the National Institute for Child Health and Human Development. The larger program evaluation was conducted by the Manpower Demonstration Research Corporation under a contract with the New Hope Project, Inc., and was supported by the Helen Bader Foundation, the Ford Foundation, the State of Wisconsin Department of Workforce Development, and the U.S. Department of Health and Human Services.

We thank the participating families and children for their time and interest.

on the developmental course of adult lives. This chapter conceptualizes adult development in the framework of Elder's (1998) life course theory, in which individual change over time is a result of age-related and life stage factors as well as secular, historical changes in the context surrounding the individual. In Elder's (1974) classic work on adults born in two cohorts during the 1920s, he examined two major historical events—the Great Depression and World War II—as influences on the life course. Both had lifelong effects on the careers and economic well-being of men and women, and those effects differed depending on cohort (i.e., the age at which historical events occurred) and prior occupational experience (e.g., professional vs. working class jobs).

HISTORICAL CHANGES IN WELFARE AND EMPLOYMENT POLICY

We examine a major public policy change in the 1990s as an influence on adults' trajectories of income from different sources and on their material and psychological well-being. In 1996, the system providing cash supports to low-income parents in the United States changed dramatically with the passage of the Personal Responsibility and Work Opportunities Reconciliation Act (PRWORA). Entitlements to Aid to Families with Dependent Children (AFDC) were ended, and a new system of Temporary Assistance to Needy Families (TANF) was introduced. Among its provisions were a lifetime limit of 5 years of support and strong inducements to seek and maintain employment. One of the major goals of the law was to move families from "welfare to work," and states were given broad latitude in setting up programs to accomplish this goal. The provisions of the law are described in depth by Greenberg et al. (2002).

In the years from 1995 to 2000, rates of employment among single mothers increased, and the number of people receiving cash assistance (AFDC or TANF) declined markedly (U.S. Department of Health and Human Services, 2003). Moreover, by 2000, poverty among single mothers had been reduced (Haskins & Primus, 2002). In Milwaukee, the site of this study, this was a period of exceptionally low unemployment (the rate fluctuated between 5.0% and 3.6%), making it generally easier for people to obtain and hold jobs. These patterns suggest that welfare reform in the context of a strong economy succeeded in increasing employment, reducing the number of people receiving welfare, and increasing income of single parents.

During the same period that welfare reform took place, *work supports* for low-income parents were increased. Earnings supplements in the form of the federal Earned Income Tax Credit (EITC), first established in 1975, were increased considerably in the 1990s. During the study period, the maximum federal benefit changed from $3,110 in 1995 to $3,888 in 2000, and the State of Wisconsin, where our study was conducted, offered a benefit that was approximately 25% of the federal benefit, depending on family size. Moreover, changes in the federal rules and funding for child care assistance and Medicaid were designed to decouple these programs from cash assistance—that is, to make them available to income-eligible parents who were not receiving cash assistance through welfare programs.

All of these policy changes had dramatic effects on Wisconsin's caseloads and the allocation of funds. In Milwaukee, the number of people receiving AFDC dropped from over 35,000 in 1995 to 21,400 in 1997—a decline of 41 percent—before the Wisconsin version of welfare reform was fully implemented (Pawasarat, 2000). By 2000, only 5,427 adults were receiving cash assistance, and another 3,180 were receiving case management designed to help them obtain employment. The purpose of the study reported here was to examine individual differences among adults who experienced these historical policy changes. We ask three broad questions: (a) How did individual patterns of total income and income from different sources (earnings, earnings supplements, food stamps, and cash assistance) change over the period in which welfare reform was implemented? (b) Are these patterns of income level and change related to adults' material and psychological well-being? (c) Do adults of different ages have different patterns of income, and does the relation of income to well-being differ for people of different ages?

Income and Adult Well-Being

Both absolute levels of poverty and changes in income are related to the social and emotional well-being of adults. On average, adults with lower incomes have poorer physical and psychological health than do adults with higher incomes (Belle, 1990; McLoyd, 1998; Radloff, 1977). Declines in family income lead to stress and material hardship that can impact the psychological well-being of parents (Conger & Elder, 1994; Elder, 1999; McLoyd, 1998).

For those working at low wage jobs, increasing work hours is the principal means of increasing income. More income from earnings is likely to improve material well-being, but it may have both positive and negative consequences for physical and psychological well-being. For example, many low-income workers have irregular and nonstandard hours, which can create stress and family difficulties, including problems parenting and managing daily family activities (Edin & Lein, 1997; Henly, 2003; Presser, 2004).

Earnings supplements are defined here as public funds that are contingent on earnings—that is, funds that supplement wages in some fashion. In this study, the major earning supplement was the EITC, which is a refundable tax credit based on the amount of earned income. In the late 1990s, the maximum EITC benefit was available for parents with annual incomes from about $12,000 to $16,000; it declined gradually for higher incomes, reaching 0 at about $30,000. Half of our sample was also eligible for earnings supplements from the New Hope Project during the first 3 years of the study. These supplements was added to the EITC when total earnings plus EITC did not reach a level that exceeded the federal poverty threshold.

Earnings supplements can increase family income with public funds that reward employment and are relatively free of the stigma associated with "welfare." Earnings supplements increase the return on work without requiring longer hours. In some cases parents who receive supplements may elect to reduce the total number of hours worked throughout the year, based on the total earnings cap. Although individuals have the option to receive the supplement throughout the year or to take it as a lump sum as part of their annual tax return, most elect the lump sum option. They use the money to catch up on expenses, to pay debts, and to purchase big-ticket items such as household appliances (Romich & Weisner, 2002).

One premise of welfare reform was that income from earnings would be more beneficial for individuals and families than would income from welfare. Although the reasons for this assumption are generally not well articulated, it appears to be based on the idea that welfare carries a stigma or that it leads to laziness, disengagement from the world of work, and disorganized family routines. The problem in evaluating this notion is that parents receiving welfare, particularly over extended periods, are more disadvantaged in many ways than are poor working parents. Moreover, as the number of welfare recipients declined following 1996, it is likely that those adults entering or remaining in the welfare system had more serious barriers to employment (e.g., poor physical or mental health, low skill levels, family caregiving responsibilities) than did the average welfare recipient in 1995.

There were fewer restrictions on eligibility for food stamps than for cash assistance following the 1996 legislation, so more people continued to receive food stamps even while employed than cash assistance. Moreover, food stamps are clearly linked to a basic need, so there may be less social stigma attached to using them. For these reasons, we examined food stamps separately from cash assistance.

CURRENT STUDY

In this report, we present *nonexperimental* analyses of longitudinal data collected from 1995 to 2001 as part of the evaluation of New Hope, a work-based anti-poverty program conducted in two high-poverty areas of Milwaukee (see Bos et al., 1999). The New Hope study had a random assignment design, testing a policy that provided wage supplements and subsidies for child care and health care to full-time workers. It provides a rich source of data for nonexperimental analyses of the changes brought about by welfare reform, in part because program group members' eligibility for New Hope ended in 1997 and 1998 during the time that Wisconsin's version of welfare reform, Wisconsin Works (W-2), was being implemented. Moreover, all sample members, whether they were in the program or control group, were subject to the same welfare policies and changes. Administrative data on employment, earnings, earnings supplements, food stamps, and cash welfare receipt are available for program- and control-group adults for an entire 5-year period. Extensive information about material hardship and psychological well-being was collected in individual interviews in 1997 and 1998 and 2000 and 2001, approximately 2 and 5 years after parents applied for the New Hope program.

We asked the following research questions: (a) How did total income and income from different sources (earnings, cash assistance, food stamps, and earnings supplements) change over time from 1995 to 2000, during a period of rapid change in welfare and employment policies affecting low-income single mothers? (b) Did the patterns of income and income change predict material and psychological well-being for low-income single mothers at the end of the 5-year period under study? (c) Did the source of income (earnings, cash assistance, food stamps, or earnings supplements) predict material and psychological well-being? d) Did mothers of different ages experience different patterns of income over these years, and did they respond differently to the changes that occurred?

DESIGN AND METHODS

New Hope

The New Hope program was conducted in two high-poverty areas of Milwaukee between 1994 and 1998, families were followed up in 1997 and 1998 and 2000 and 2001. Any adult (age 18 or over) with an income below 150% of poverty was eligible to participate. Applicants were randomly assigned to the program or control groups. For 3 years following random assignment, the program group was eligible for wage supplements, child care subsidies, and health care subsidies whenever they worked full time (30+ hours/week). Program group members also had access to high quality case management. If they were unsuccessful in finding full-time employment, they could work in minimum-wage community service jobs. The hours in these jobs counted in determining eligibility for New Hope benefits, and the earnings counted toward the federal and state EITC, unlike earnings in similar jobs under W-2. Enrollment in the program took place from July 1994 through December 1995; hence, program group members reached the end of eligibility for New Hope benefits between July 1997 and December 1998.

Wisconsin Works (W-2)

New Hope functioned in the broader context of welfare programs in the state of Wisconsin and the city of Milwaukee. In 1994 Wisconsin's governor announced that AFDC would end in Wisconsin. A welfare reform known as Pay for Performance, which tied receipt of AFDC benefits to work, began in 1996. After the federal welfare reform legislation was passed in 1996, all prior programs were replaced by Wisconsin Works (W-2), which was implemented statewide in 1997 and 1998. Under this program, all recipients and applicants for TANF are required to complete Personal Responsibility contracts and Employability Plans that specify the employment activities to be required as a condition for receiving assistance (see http://www.CLASP.org).

According to W-2 policies, an individual who is deemed employable does not get immediate cash grants but does receive assistance in finding a job or assistance with different types of transitional employment. Participants who do not find employment are eligible for several types of short-term subsidized employment, including trial jobs (subsidies paid to employers), community service jobs (wages paid by state), and transitional placements. Individuals with barriers to employment receive cash grants (ranging from $518 per month in 1996 to $673 per month in 2000 with no adjustment for family size), but they are required to participate in employment-related services. This participation is designed to be like work; individuals lose $5.15 per hour for each hour of nonparticipation.

The New Hope program group members were *not* exempt from the requirements of the local welfare system, and they were eligible for any of its benefits if they qualified. Hence, both program and control group members experienced a number of policies designed to increase employment and reduce welfare receipt throughout the 5-year period. Moreover, because a participant's eligibility for New Hope ended after 3 years, the two groups experienced identical policy environments during the approximately 2 years before the follow-up in 2000 and 2001.

Sample

The New Hope Child and Family Study (CFS) was initially designed to assess impacts on families and children in early and middle childhood as part of the larger New Hope study. All adults in the larger New Hope sample who had at least one dependent child between the ages of 1 and 10 at baseline ($N = 745$) constituted the CFS sample. The income patterns we report herein were calculated on administrative data for all 745 sample members.

Individual interviews were conducted in 1997 and 1998, 2 years after random assignment, with 578 parents, and in 2000 and 2001 and 5 years after random assignment, with 545 parents. There were approximately equal numbers of program and control group members, and there was no evidence of differential attrition for program and control parents. For the analyses presented here, households with more than one adult ($n = 85$) were eliminated because we did not have income data for other adult household members. Another 21 men were eliminated because gender could affect the results and there were too few males to do gender comparisons. The resulting sample was composed of 439 single women.

At baseline, when they entered the New Hope study, the parents' average age was 29.4 years; slightly over half (55%) were African American; and 29% were Hispanic. About half of them had a high school diploma or GED. The majority had a history of employment, but most had earnings of less than $5,000 in the previous year. Approximately 80% were receiving public assistance at baseline (i.e., AFDC, Medicaid, and/or food stamps).

Data Sources

All applicants for the New Hope program completed a Baseline Information Form providing information about previous employment, income, family characteristics, and attitudes about work and welfare. We obtained administrative data from the state of Wisconsin for quarters of employment, reported earnings, and receipt of AFDC, TANF, and food stamps for the 5 years after random assignment as well as 1 year prior to random assignment. Data on New Hope payments were obtained from New Hope administrative records. Because individual tax returns are not available for research, we used a procedure for estimating Earned Income Tax Credits received over the 5-year study period that was developed in cooperation with the Wisconsin State Department of Taxation (see Appendix H in Bos et al., 1999). Extensive face-to-face individual surveys were conducted with sample members at 2 and 5 years after random assignment.

HOW INCOME, EARNINGS, EARNINGS SUPPLEMENTS, FOOD STAMPS, AND CASH ASSISTANCE CHANGED OVER TIME

We first describe the economic circumstances and changes experienced by all sample members ($N = 745$) during the years in which welfare reform transformed the public assistance environment in Wisconsin, developing specific measures of income level and *change* over time. Because the income measures were derived from administrative data sources, certain income sources are not included, such as earnings by other household members, earnings from casual or informal employment, earnings outside the state of Wisconsin, child support, income from renters or boarders, gifts and in-kind support from friends and relatives, and sources of public assistance for which no administrative data were available. (For example, Supplemental Security Income, General Assistance, and child care subsidies). Fortunately, analyses of the relative importance of these additional income sources have shown that they contribute relatively little *on average* across all the families in this sample (Bos et al., 1999), even though they can make a big difference for individual families at a specific point in time.

Earnings and public assistance data (food stamps and cash assistance) are reported in quarters, resulting in 20 data points over a 5-year period. Although EITC benefits are often paid in a lump sum annually, we spread them out over the year. For each sample member, the

---

Earnings and Income Data Sources:

- Baseline information form
- State of Wisconsin Unemployment Insurance Records
- State of Wisconsin AFDC/W2 payment data
- State of Wisconsin Food Stamp payment data
- State of Wisconsin EITC data (includes Federal EITC)
- New Hope program data on earnings supplements and community-service jobs

---

starting point for these 20 quarters of data is the quarter following the date of random assignment (i.e., entry into the New Hope study). Those entry dates ranged from August 1994 through December 1995. Hence, the 2-year anniversary (the end of Quarter 8) occurred between August 1996 and December 1997, which corresponds to the period of implementation of Wisconsin Works (W-2). The 5-year anniversary, and the end of follow-up for everyone, occurred between August 1999 and December 2000.

We describe income data across the entire 5-year follow-up period (Q1–20) and for the last three years of follow-up (Q9–20) separately. During the first 2 years of follow-up, sample members experienced large increases in earnings and reductions in welfare receipt. Such changes may partly reflect the fact that, although most sample members were not working full-time at baseline, they applied for a program requiring full-time work. Even without welfare reform, many of these individuals might be expected to leave public assistance and increase employment on their own.

Because such a large one-time change may have effects on parental and family well-being that are different from those associated with more gradual changes in employment and family income, we analyzed changes in family income and earnings *after* the first 2 years of follow-up for each family (i.e., Q9–20). This period also corresponds more closely to the post–W-2 welfare environment in Wisconsin. Still another advantage was the fact that the first individual interview was conducted after 2 years, so we could examine increases or decreases in well-being between Quarters 9 and 20 in relation to changes in income during that same time interval.

Calculation of Levels and Changes in Different Forms of Income

We summarized the income data for the 20 quarters of follow-up using PROC MIXED in SAS to estimate *for each adult* a quadratic function of change. This function describes the pattern of these variables as a combination of a baseline level (the intercept), a linear change (the slope), and a quadratic moderation of this change. Thus, for example, for a hypothetical person, an intercept of 500, a slope of 500, and a quadratic coefficient of –12 would imply that this person started out with quarterly income of $500, added on average $500 to this every quarter, but saw this increase get progressively smaller every quarter. The result is a positive trend in average income that levels off over time.

After fitting such lines to people's income profiles we saved the coefficients and used them in subsequent analyses to estimate effects on measures of well-being. This enabled us to distinguish the effects of different initial *levels* and different patterns of *increases or decreases* in income on well-being outcomes.

Trajectories For Quarters 1–20: Total Income and Earnings

Table 6.1 shows the estimated regression coefficients that describe patterns of earnings and total income for all sample members during the full 5-year period. The average initial earnings intercept was $1,476, and there was a significantly positive earnings slope, at $108. The quadratic term is –$1.99, which offsets some of the increase, especially in later quarters. (For example, in Quarter 20, this term reduces estimated earnings by 20 × 20 × –1.99 = $796, compared to an increase of

TABLE 6.1 Estimated Intercepts and Slopes of Income and Earnings

	Quarters 1–20		Quarters 9–20	
	Earnings	Total Income	Earnings	Total Income
Intercept	1,476***	3,384***	2,229**	3,338***
Slope	108***	–15	60**	–2
Quadratic slope	–1.99**	1.22†	–0.51	1.96
Sample size		745		

Notes: A two-tailed *t* test was used to assess the statistical significance of each coefficient. Statistical significance levels are indicated as ***$p < .001$, **$p < .01$, *$p < .05$, and †$p < .1$.

108 × 20 = $2,160, from the slope coefficient, resulting in a total esti-
mated gain of $1,364.) The result is an earnings trend that slopes up
significantly, but whose slope flattens out over time.

Meanwhile, total income went down slightly in the earlier quarters with
a slope coefficient of –$15, but increased toward the end of follow-up,
shown by a positive quadratic slope of $1.22. This suggests that short-
term reductions in public assistance income initially more than offset
increases in earnings and earnings-related income, but as earnings
continued to grow, the balance turned positive by the last year of follow-up. Figure 6.1 shows these patterns.

In this analysis, we are concerned with how *individual* patterns of
income impact individuals' material and psychological well-being. For
such analyses to be successful, there must be significant variation in the
individual slopes and intercepts. There is large variation in the estimated individual slopes for income. Figure 6.2 shows the distribution
of individual slopes for total income. It has pronounced tails at the bottom and top, showing that approximately 25% of the sample (101 individuals) had income slopes showing either reductions greater than
$500 a quarter or gains greater than $400 a quarter. Closer examination of these individuals' income trajectories reveals that these large
slope coefficients were often accompanied by large quadratic coefficients as well, meaning that their income trajectories had pronounced

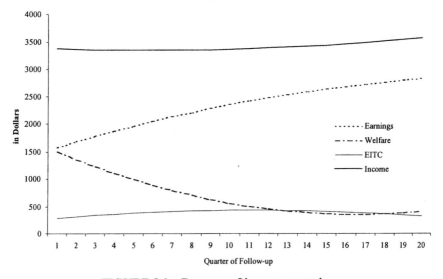

FIGURE 6.1   Patterns of income over time.

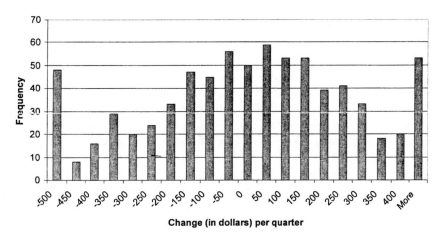

FIGURE 6.2   Distribution of income slopes, Q1–20.

U-shapes over time. This either signifies a very rapid increase in income that subsequently plateaus or a very significant reduction in income, which subsequently remains at 0. Especially with the latter group of sample members data problems are a potential concern, because it is possible that sample members moved out of state or got a job that was not covered by unemployment insurance, which would make their income invisible in our analyses.

Setting aside the tails of the distribution shown in figure 6.2, the overall distribution of income slopes shows a very regular profile that is only slightly skewed toward income growth. Summing the negative bars and excluding the tails on both sides, more than 43% of the sample actually had a negative income slope during the follow-up period.

Trajectories for Quarters 9–20

In table 6.1 we show the results from similar analyses for Quarters 9–20. For these analyses we excluded the first 2 years of data, but otherwise estimated regression models that were identical to those used for the Q1–20 models presented earlier. The average individual slopes, as well as the accompanying quadratic slopes were smaller than those for the full 20 quarters. Earnings have a continued upward slope, and total income also increases, albeit slightly. During the last years, earnings constituted a larger proportion of total income than it did in the first 2 years.

Patterns of Earnings Supplements, Food Stamps, and Cash Assistance

The procedures using continuous estimates of dollar amounts were not appropriate for earnings supplements, food stamps, and cash assistance because the major sources of variation resulted from receiving or not receiving these sources of income rather than from the specific amounts received. For example, the average income from cash assistance dropped over time, largely because fewer people were receiving any AFDC or TANF. Hence, for Q1 through Q8 and for Q9 through Q20, we classified each individual as (a) receiving no income from cash assistance (no receipt), (b) receiving cash assistance for four or fewer quarters (short term), or (c) receiving cash assistance for 5 or more quarters (long term). Similar classifications were formed for earnings supplements and food stamps (see table 6.2).

The frequencies of AFDC/TANF receipt demonstrate the dramatic shift in the number of people receiving cash assistance over the 5-year period of the study. Only 12% of the sample members never received cash assistance in the 5 years, but another 41% received no cash assistance after Quarter 8. In contrast, 58% of the sample members were long-term recipients in the first 2 years, compared with 17% in the last 3 years. The changes in food stamp receipt were less dramatic, dropping from 72% long-term recipients in Q1–8 to 56% in Q9–20. The majority of the sample members received earnings supplements for most quarters, and there was little change in the number of people receiving these supplements over the 5-year period. However, because earnings increased and the maximum EITC credit increased over the 5-year period, the amount of the earnings supplement also increased for most people. Few of the sample members had sufficient income to reach the point of diminishing returns on the EITC.

MATERIAL AND PSYCHOLOGICAL WELL BEING

Measures

Economic Well-Being

In the 2- and 5-year surveys, parents were asked several questions to assess their material and financial well-being. The *material hardship* index included six questions asking whether the family had been without utilities, medical care, housing, or other necessities because of

TABLE 6.2 Number of People Receiving AFDC/TANF, Food Stamps, and Earning Supplements in Quarters 1–8 and 9–20

	Q9 to Q20											
	AFDC/TANF				Food Stamps				Earning Supplement			
Q1 to Q8	No Receipt	Short-Term	Long-Term	Total Total	No Receipt	Short-Term	Long-Term	Total Total	No Receipt	Short-Term	Long-Term	Total
No receipt	52	3	0	55	32	6	5	43	33	17	36	86
Short-term	98	21	11	130	43	16	21	80	15	18	58	91
Long-term	81	108	65	254	29	64	223	316	17	66	179	262
Total	231	132	76	439	104	86	249	439	65	101	273	439

lack of financial resources; the total was the proportion of items answered "yes" (Mayer & Jencks, 1989). *Financial health* included nine items assessing participants' degree of financial stability and ownership of such assets as a car, a savings account, or cable TV; the total score was the proportion of "yes" responses. *Satisfaction with standard of living* was one question on which the participant rated her or his satisfaction on a 5-point scale from 1 = unhappy to 5 = happy. *Sustainability* comprised five items assessing how capable parents felt to manage their lives and secure resources for their families, using a 5-point scale.

Health and Psychological Well-Being

Depressive symptoms were measured on the 20-item CES-D asking how often in the last week the respondent had felt a range of depressive symptoms; each item had a 4-point scale ranging from 0 = rarely or none to 3 = most or all (Center for Epidemiological Studies—Depression scale; Radloff, 1977). The score on this scale is a total rather than an average; on national norms a score of 16 is the cut-off above which scores suggest serious depression. General stress was a single item asking parents how much of the time they had felt stressed in the past month on a 4-point scale with 1 = none and 4 = almost all. *Financial worry* included five questions asking how much the respondent worried about paying bills and lacking money for important needs (e.g., for food and housing); items were 5-point scales from 1 = not at all to 5 = a great deal. *Overall health* was a single item rating the parent's overall health relative to others her age on a 5-point scale of 1 = poor to 5 = excellent. *Substance abuse* was assessed in two items asking how many days in the past month the parent or others worried about their use of drugs or alcohol on a 5-point scale with 1 = on no days and 5 = almost every day. These items did not include mere use of such substances, but asked specifically about expressed concern regarding drug and alcohol use. Hope was assessed with the State Hope Scale (Snyder et al., 1996), which includes agency—"belief in one's capacity to initiate and sustain actions" and pathways—"belief in one's capacity to generate routes" to achieve goals. Each of the six items has a 4-point scale from 1 = strongly disagree to 4 = strongly agree. *Social support* was measured with six items asking to what extent parents felt they could count on the support of others using a 5-point scale from 1 = not at all true to 5 = always true.

RELATIONS OF INCOME DYNAMICS TO MATERIAL AND PSYCHOLOGICAL WELL-BEING

We use the individual estimates of absolute level (i.e., intercept) and rate of change (i.e., slope) in total income to predict measures of well-being at the end of the study period. Table 6.3 shows the 0-order correlations of income intercept and slope with the parent outcomes and baseline characteristics. Table 6.4 shows the means of the well-being and baseline characteristics for each category of cash assistance, food stamps, and earnings supplements.

Baseline Differences

In all analyses, the following baseline variables were controlled in order to equate individuals statistically on preexisting characteristics that might affect both economic outcomes and well-being: membership in the program or control group, age of parent, ethnic group (African American, Hispanic, or other), family size (number of children), parent's education (years of completed schooling), employment history (months in full-time job in prior 12 months), earnings history (earnings in past 12 months), and AFDC receipt during the past 12 months. The correlations of these variables with the income variables (table 6.3) and the mean differences associated with different income sources (table 6.4) help to describe the groups under study.

Not surprisingly, absolute levels of income were higher at both Q1 and Q9 for people with more education and histories of more employment and higher earnings and, at Q1 only, for those who had received more AFDC, but none of these characteristics predicted changes in income over time. Women with more children had higher incomes than those with fewer children, especially at Q1, but their incomes declined over time, apparently as a result of reduced earnings and reduced cash assistance. Women whose youngest child was older were slightly more likely than those with very young children to increase their income, probably because they had fewer barriers to employment.

The means in table 6.4 are purely descriptive, but they provide some information about the baseline characteristics of people with different income sources. Women receiving cash assistance and food stamps, particularly those in the long-term group, had lower levels of education and work experience, younger children, and larger families than those who did not receive these forms of assistance.

TABLE 6.3   Zero Order Correlations of Dependent Variables and Baseline Characteristics with Income Variables

	Total Income Q1–20		Total Income Q9–20	
	Q1 Intercept	Q1–20 Slope	Q9 Intercept	Q9–20 Slope
Dependent Variables				
Material hardship	–0.105**	–0.050	–0.196***	0.028
Financial health	0.125*	0.083†	0.266***	0.022
Satisfaction with standard living	0.023	0.071	0.137**	–0.036
Sustainability index	0.059	0.053	0.152**	–0.024
Depression	–0.104*	–0.004	–0.115*	0.011
General stress	–0.004	–0.035	–0.087†	0.062
Financial worry	–0.122*	0.006	–0.155**	0.066
Overall health	0.100*	–0.119*	0.009	–0.029
Substance abuse	–0.026	–0.055	–0.074	–0.039
Hope	0.098*	0.022	0.154**	–0.044
Availability of supportive others	–0.023	0.000	0.035	–0.021
Baseline Characteristics				
Membership (program or control)	0.130**	–0.044	0.045	–0.013
Parent's education	0.029	0.069	0.135**	0.028
Ethnic group (African American)	0.046	– 0.022	0.034	–0.032
Ethnic group (Hispanic)	0.036	0.024	0.036	0.025
Earning history	0.154**	0.060	0.142**	0.049
Employment history	0.150**	0.031	0.125**	0.046
AFDC receipt during past 12 months	0.099*	–0.065	–0.0 15	–0.0 15
Parent's age	0.044	0.009	–0.019	–0.034
Family size	0.283 ***	–0.106 *	0.079 t	–0.067
Age of youngest child	–0.053	0.093†	0.036	0.059

Notes: Statistical significance levels are indicated as †$p < .10$, *$p < .05$, **$p < .01$, and ***$p < .001$; all two-tailed.

TABLE 6.4 Means on Dependent Variables and Baseline Characteristics for People with Different Income Sources

	Q1–8 Means								
	AFCD/TANF			Food Stamps			Earnings Supplment		
	None	Short-term	Long-term	None	Short-term	Long-term	None	Short-term	Long-term
Dependent Variables									
Material hardship	0.67	0.89	1.22	0.63	0.94	1.14	1.33	1.19	0.92
Financial health	0.55	0.54	0.43	0.58	0.53	0.45	0.45	0.48	0.48
Satisfaction with standard of living	3.89	3.77	3.72	3.79	3.75	3.75	3.53	3.78	3.82
Sustainability index	3.19	3.06	2.91	3.13	3.02	2.96	2.82	2.95	3.06
Depression	14.65	12.91	16.99	15.19	12.90	16.18	17.56	17.82	13.96
General stress	2.33	2.35	2.63	2.35	2.33	2.58	2.66	2.51	2.46
Financial worry	2.26	2.28	2.78	2.24	2.25	2.69	2.81	2.66	2.45
Overall health	3.58	3.61	3.39	3.53	3.59	3.44	3.36	3.54	3.49
Substance abuse	1.01	1.02	1.05	1.01	1.03	1.04	1.03	1.09	1.01
Hope	3.09	3.01	2.98	3.03	2.97	3.01	2.91	2.93	3.06
Availability of supportive others	3.16	3.14	2.94	3.18	3.07	3.00	2.99	3.09	3.02
Baseline Characteristics									
Membership (program or control)	0.51	0.51	0.50	0.53	0.51	0.50	0.21	0.46	0.61
Parent's education (years)	12.00	11.51	10.98	12.16	11.78	11.01	11.40	10.97	11.32
Ethnic group (African American)	0.60	0.49	0.65	0.63	0.49	0.62	0.60	0.65	0.58
Ehnic group (Hispanic)	0.25	0.34	0.21	0.19	0.34	0.24	0.19	0.24	0.28
Earning history	3.82	2.58	2.04	3.79	2.50	2.22	2.10	2.60	2.46
Employment history	8.15	3.81	2.38	8.30	3.48	2.89	2.67	3.88	3.69
AFDC receipt during past 12 months	3.76	4.58	4.82	3.42	4.51	4.81	4.36	4.69	4.67
Parent's age	3.02	2.86	2.72	2.98	2.86	2.76	2.78	2.86	2.79
Family size	2.07	2.13	2.32	1.95	2.13	2.30	2.16	2.21	2.27
Age of youngest child	4.89	3.58	3.39	4.89	3.72	3.44	3.58	3.81	3.59

(continued)

TABLE 6.4 (continued)

	Q9–20 Means								
	AFCD/TANF			Food Stamps			Earnings Supplment		
	None	Short-term	Long-term	None	Short-term	Long-term	None	Short-term	Long-term
Dependent Variables									
Material hardship	0.85	1.06	1.64	0.64	1.03	1.23	1.32	0.94	1.03
Financial health	0.53	0.46	0.33	0.59	0.53	0.41	0.43	0.46	0.49
Satisfaction with standard of living	3.80	3.79	3.55	3.96	3.79	3.66	3.55	3.86	3.76
Sustainability index	3.12	3.00	2.57	3.15	3.14	2.88	2.78	3.02	3.03
Depression	14.28	15.97	18.31	13.50	13.65	16.96	17.77	14.80	15.18
General stress	2.42	2.50	2.80	2.36	2.43	2.60	2.68	2.51	2.47
Financial worry	2.33	2.73	2.96	2.25	2.46	2.72	2.71	2.45	2.57
Overall health	3.52	3.63	3.11	3.53	3.48	3.45	3.25	3.52	3.51
Substance abuse	1.01	1.05	1.08	1.01	1.01	1.06	1.04	1.03	1.04
Hope	3.01	3.08	2.83	3.04	2.98	2.99	2.85	3.03	3.03
Availability of supportive others	3.08	3.06	2.81	3.11	3.18	2.94	3.03	3.02	3.03
Baseline Characteristics									
Membership (program or control)	0.51	0.44	0.59	0.54	0.48	0.50	0.31	0.55	0.53
Parent's education (years)	11.48	11.13	10.83	11.71	11.28	11.07	10.91	11.29	11.34
Ethnic group (African American)	0.50	0.69	0.72	0.42	0.59	0.67	0.62	0.46	0.64
Ehnic group (Hispanic)	0.32	0.17	0.17	0.36	0.26	0.21	0.18	0.37	0.23
Earning history	2.71	2.22	1.88	3.09	2.43	2.14	2.57	2.31	2.43
Employment history	4.49	2.72	1.97	5.13	3.53	2.85	3.68	3.14	3.63
AFDC receipt during past 12 months	4.51	4.63	4.92	4.09	4.51	4.88	4.32	4.82	4.61
Parent's age	2.89	2.67	2.75	2.87	2.78	2.78	2.91	2.94	2.72
Family size	2.17	2.34	2.24	2.03	2.12	2.36	2.22	2.25	2.23
Age of youngest child	3.77	3.35	3.73	4.16	3.66	3.41	3.89	3.77	3.52

Relations of Income Level and Change to Well-Being

Using an ordinary least square (OLS) regression-based approach, we tested two models for each measure of well-being assessed at the end of 5 years. The income predictors in the Q1–20 analysis were Quarter 1 intercept and Q1–20 slope estimates of total income, entered as predictors in Model 1. In a second model, we added cash assistance, food stamp receipt, and earnings supplements in Q1-Q8 as categorical variables (no assistance or short term, with long term as the omitted variable) as well as parallel categorical variables representing these three sources of income during Q9–20. The Model 2 analyses including different sources of income allowed us to distinguish the effects of both level and change of total income while determining whether income source was also a predictor. Model 2 controls for income source. There is no separate term for earnings because earnings constitute the income remaining after the other sources are controlled. That is, the coefficients for income in these analyses largely reflect the effects of earnings. Table 6.5 exhibits the results of these analyses.

A second set of analyses was identical except that they were limited to Q9–20. The income variables in the second analysis were Q9 intercept and Q9–20 slope estimates of total income; the categorical variables for cash assistance, food stamps, and earnings supplements during Q9–20 were included in Model 2 (see table 6.6).

Total Income Level

People with higher total incomes at both the beginning of the study and by Quarter 9 had generally better material well-being at the 5-year survey. They reported less material hardship, better financial health, more satisfaction with their standard of living, and, at Q9, better ability to sustain and balance their family's needs. People with higher incomes also reported somewhat better psychological well-being. They reported fewer depressive symptoms, less financial worry, and higher levels of hope. Income at Q9 was a little more consistently related to later well-being than was income at Q1.

Income Change

People whose incomes improved over the entire 5-year period reported less material hardship, better financial health, and slightly more satisfaction with their standard of living at the end of that period than did adults whose incomes did not improve or declined. Income

TABLE 6.5 Regression Coefficients for Income Intercept and Slope from Q1–20 with Controls for AFDC/TANF, Food Stamp Receipt, and Earnings Supplement Receipt

	Model 1		Model 2		Quarters 1–8					
	Intercept	Slope	Intercept	Slope	Never AFDC	Short-Term AFDC	Never FS	Short-Term FS	Never ES	Short Term ES
5-year outcome										
Material hardship	-0.0185***	-0.0509*	-0.0139*	-0.0433†	-0.2431	-0.1046	0.0706	0.1499	0.1818	0.1474
	(.0055)	(.0253)	(.0056)	(.0251)	(.3167)	(.1749)	(.3060)	(.1908)	(.2046)	(.1841)
Financial health	0.0036	0.0121**	0.0030**	0.0105*	-0.0331	0.0600	0.0545	-0.0343	0.0276	0.0386
	(.0010)	(.0043)	(.0010)	(.0045)	(.0703)	(.0364)	(.0717)	(.0407)	(.0373)	(.0279)
Statisfaction with standard of living	0.0073†	0.0327†	0.0050	0.0303	0.4565*	0.0451	-0.6122*	-0.2074	-0.2194	0.0243
	(.0043)	(.0187)	(.0043)	(.0194)	(.2082)	(.1536)	(.2418)	(.1879)	(.1615)	(.1275)
Sustainability	0.0048	0.0212	0.0012	0.0147	0.2970	0.0872	-0.2925	-0.1757	-0.1017	-0.0553
	(.0033)	(.0117)	(.0034)	(.0153)	(.2052)	(.1148)	(.2192)	(.1366)	(.1092)	(.1045)
Depression	-0.0941*	-0.1646	-0.0468	-0.1257	-2.1549	-2.3519†	2.4302	-0.4354	1.6839	2.8755†
	(.0448)	(.1974)	(.0453)	(.2137)	(2.8344)	(1.4078)	(3.0957)	(1.5295)	(1.5746)	(1.4706)
General stress	-0.0026	-0.0024	0.0010	0.0024	-0.1339	-0.1484	0.0056	-0.1162	0.1015	0.0383
	(.0036)	(.0156)	(.0039)	(.0164)	(.1670)	(.1259)	(.1837)	(.1378)	(.1372)	(.1077)
Financial worry	-0.0148**	-0.022.2	-0.0108*	-0.0257	-0.3252	-0.2636	0.0352	-0.0657	0.1983	0.1006
	(.0048)	(.0222)	(.0050)	(.0221)	(.3287)	(.1756)	(.3462)	(.1831)	(.1623)	(.1532)

Overall health	0.0033	−0.0424*	0.0003	−0.0519**	0.3445	0.2706†	−0.1320	−0.0448	0.0757	0.1715
	(.0044)	(.015)	(.0048)	(.0196)	(.2963)	(.1638)	(.3177)	(.1744)	(.1693)	(.1315)
Substance abuse	−0.0016	−0.0063	−0.0011	−0.0064	−0.0380	−0.0052	0.0239	0.0366	0.0195	0.0808†
	(.0011)	(.007)	(.0009)	(.0050)	(.0291)	(.0292)	(.0376)	(.0388)	(.0295)	(.0466)
Hope	0.0044*	0.0026	0.0021	−0.0001	0.2781†	0.0271	−0.2982†	−0.1188	−0.0646	−0.1019
	(.0022)	(.01(0))	(.0022)	(.0100)	(.1424)	(.0720)	(.1588)	(.8628)	(.0781)	(.0680)
Availability of supportive others	−0.0019	−0.001:6	−0.0036	−0.0092	0.1226	0.2414†	−0.0503	−0.1634	−0.0391	0.0983
	(.0031)	(.010)	(.0034)	(.0155)	(.2883)	(.1233)	(.2878)	(.1380)	(.1290)	(.0998)

Notes: All analyses include the following covariances: New Hope experimental status, parent's education; parent age; race/ethnicity; having received AFDC in the prior year; having been employed full-time in prior year; earnings in prior year; number of children in the household; and age of youngest child. The omitted categories for AFDC/TANF, food stamps, ane EITC were long-term receipt, defined as 5–8 quarters in Q1–8 and 5–12 quarters in Q9–20. Model 1 did not include controls for AFDC, Food Stamp Receipt, and EITC. Model 2 included these sources of income. Coefficients for Quarters 9–20 categories were not presented here, since they are very close to those in table 6.6 (see table 6.6). Statistical significance levels are indicated as †$p < .10$, *$p < .05$, **$p < .01$, and ***$p < .001$.

TABLE 6.6 Regression Coefficients for Income Intercept and Slope from Q9–20 with Controls for AFDC/TANG, Food Stamp, and Earning Supplement Receipt

	Model 1		Model 2		Quarters 1–8					
	Intercept	Slope	Intercept	Slope	Never AFDC	Short-Term AFDC	Never FS	Short-Term FS	Never ES	Short Term ES
5-year outcome										
Material hardship	-0.0151***	0.0080	-0.0143***	0.0084	-0.05991*	-0.5640*	-0.2854	0.0248	0.0699	-0.1588
	(.0036)	(.0176)	(.0034)	(.0174)	(.2505)	(.2245)	(.1903)	(.1872)	(.2012)	(.1518)
Financial health	0.0034***	0.0017	0.0031***	0.0007	0.0935	0.0889**	0.1077**	0.0805*	0.0027	-0.0086
	(.0007)	(.0038)	(.0007)	(.0036)	(.0374)	(.0316)	(.0391)	(.0335)	(.0345)	(.0303)
Satisfaction with standard of living	0.0082**	-0.0145	0.0078*	-0.0133	0.0505	0.1768	0.2378	0.0935	-0.0932	0.0807
	(.0030)	(.0130)	(.0030)	(.0133)	(.1774)	(.1618)	(.1498)	(.1424)	(.1582)	(.1238)
Sustainability	0.0058*	-0.0069	0.0043†	-0.0067	0.4573***	0.3773**	0.0149	0.0970	-0.1502	0.0375
	(.0024)	(.0101)	(.0024)	(.0103)	(.1394)	(.1310)	(.1155)	(.1041)	(.1297)	(.0914)
Depression	-0.0612*	0.0385	-0.0538	0.0255	-2.2314	-1.2605	-1.1907	-2.1788	1.4396	-1.0808
	(.0308)	(.1568)	(.0325)	(.1621)	(1.9629)	(1.8024)	(1.6815)	(1.3324)	(1.5821)	(1.3512)
General stress	-0.0043†	0.0198†	-0.0024	0.0229†	-0.2615*	-0.2757*	-0.0815	-0.0279	0.2305†	0.0762
	(.0024)	(.0117)	(.0026)	(.0121)	(.1468)	(.1375)	(.1313)	(.1069)	(.1299)	(.1067)
Financial worry	-0.0099**	0.0231	-0.0104**	0.0228	-0.5845**	-0.1826	-0.1824	-0.0685	-0.0649	-0.2685*
	(.0034)	(.0162)	(.0033)	(.0158)	(.1903)	(.1813)	(.1648)	(.1554)	(.1744)	(.1292)
Overall health	-0.0018	-0.0145	-0.0038	-0.0140	0.4656	0.5530**	-0.0275	-0.1169	-0.2295	0.0356
	(.0029)	(.0142)	(.0030)	(.0148)	(.2008)	(.1857)	(.1615)	(.1553)	(.1605)	(.1364)

Substance abuse	-0.0011 (.0007)	-0.0027 (.0025)	-0.0012 (.0007)	-0.0030 (.0029)	-0.0658 (.0545)	-0.0290 (.0543)	-0.0098 (.0272)	-0.0249 (.0217)	-0.0117 (.0429)	-0.0252 (.0359)
Hope	0.0035* (.0015)	-0.0077 (.0067)	0.0023 (.0015)	-0.0069 (.0071)	0.1478 (.1039)	0.2345* (.0926)	-0.0255 (.0803)	-0.0806 (.0744)	-0.1518 (.0815)	0.0186 (.0667)
Availability of supportive others	0.0010 (.0023)	-0.0087 (.0112)	0.0009 (.0024)	-0.0077 (.0116)	0.1108 –.. (.1377)	0.1718 (.1323)	0.0552 (.1276)	0.1732 (.1116)	-0.0036 (.1250)	-0.0037 (.0995)
Change from 2 to 5 years										
Material hardship	0.0020 (.0054)	0.0076 (.0221)	0.0052 (.0054)	0.0094 (.0222)	-0.6355* (.2743)	-0.3029 (.2600)	-0.0029 (.2276)	0.1456 (.2382)	0.3835 (.2725)	-0.1546 (.1754)
Satisfaction with standard of living	0.0091* (.0038)	0.0344† (.0185)	0.0081* (.0041)	0.0293 (.0190)	0.0234 (.2277)	0.0172 (.2016)	0.1045 (.2078)	0.1001 (.1953)	-0.0660 (.1927)	-0.1550 (.1598)
Depression	0.0061 (.0336)	-0.0796 (.1617)	0.0030 (.0357)	-0.0885 (.1674)	0.8796 (1.8382)	1.3273 (1.7102)	0.0866 (1.7068)	-2.4166 (1.6559)	-0.2377 (1.5881)	0.0281 (1.4889)
General stress	-0.0038 (.0033)	-0.0031 (.0145)	-0.0017 (.0035)	0.0002 (.0145)	-0.0604 (.1818)	-0.1535 (.1756)	0.0784 (.1606)	-0.2150† (.1291)	0.2387 (.1713)	0.2053 (.1341)
Financial worry	0.0039 (.0039)	0.0181 (.0194) (0041)	0.0040 (.0196)	0.0171	-0.3718 (.2277)	-0.0951 (.2115)	-0.0068 (.1848)	-0.1944 (.1818)	-0.0677 (.1821)	-0.1843 (.1656)
Hope	0.0021 (.0019)	-0.0083 (.0089)	0.0019 (.0020)	-0.0091 (.0092)	-0.0460 (.1155)	-0.0042 (.1036)	0.0030 (.0970)	0.0514 (.0978)	-0.0267 (.1052)	-0.0529 (.0789)

Notes: All analyses include the following covariances: New Hope experimental status, parent's education; parent age; race/ethnicity; having received AFDC in the prior year; having been employed full-time in the prior year; earnings in prior year; number of children in the household; and age of youngest child. The omitted categories for AFDC/TANF, food stamps, ane EITC were long-term receipt, defined as 5–8 quarters in Q1–8 and 5–12 quarters in Q9–20. Model 1 did not include controls for AFDC, Food Stamp Receipt, and EITC. Model 2 included these sources of income. Statistical significance levels are indicated as †$p < .10$, *$p < .05$, **$p < .01$, and ***$p < .001$. −

275

change was not, however, related to psychological and physical well-being, with one exception. People whose incomes had improved reported lower overall health levels than those whose incomes had not improved. For the most part, the association of income level and income change with adult well-being remained when the source of income was controlled, suggesting that it is overall income rather than type of income that is important.

Changes in income after Q9 were not related to any of the indicators of material well-being or to most of the indicators of psychological well-being, perhaps because the changes during this period were less dramatic than those during the first 2 years after the study began. There was a tendency for income improvement to predict *higher* levels of general stress in this period, but no other significant relations appeared.

Fixed-effects Models Predicting Change in Outcomes from 2 to 5 Years

Even with controls for baseline variables, relations of the economic variables to adult well-being may be conjointly influenced by "unobserved" or omitted variables. Moreover, adult psychological well-being could affect income as well as being affected by it. Therefore, firm conclusions about the causal direction of effects are not warranted. We attempted to limit the influence of omitted variables by examining the relations of the predictors to the *increase or decrease* in a particular outcome across two time points (from the 2-year to the 5-year survey). For a subset of the well-being measures—those for which there were identical measures in both the 2-year and 5-year surveys—we calculated *change scores* (5-year score minus 2-year score) reflecting the change in each individual's score across the two time points. Positive values indicate increases across time; negative values indicate decreases. By regressing the economic predictor variables for Q9–20 on the change scores, we test whether the intercepts and slopes of the economic variables were systematically related to *changes* in the outcomes across the two survey administration time points.

As table 6.6 indicates, the only significant relation of income to changes in well-being occurred for satisfaction with standard of living. Adults with higher incomes at Q9 and those whose incomes improved from Q9–20 reported a greater increase in satisfaction over three years than did those with lower Q9 incomes and those whose incomes did not improve. Income change did not, however, predict changes in other indicators of material well-being, depressive symptoms, general stress, financial worry, or hope.

Sources of Income

Three sources of income were examined: cash assistance, food stamps, and earnings supplements. The regressions shown in tables 6.5 and 6.6 indicate that, during the first 8 quarters of the study, before W-2 was fully implemented, there were relatively few differences based on the source of income. In a few instances, people who received long-term cash assistance differed from those who received no assistance or short-term assistance, but the patterns were weak (Table 6.5).

The picture is quite different during Q9–20, when welfare reform was fully implemented (table 6.6). Compared with women who received no cash assistance or short-term assistance (less than 1 year), those who received long term assistance during this period (more than 1 year) had more material hardship, less adequate financial health, and less ability to sustain their family's basic needs. They reported more general stress, more financial worry, less adequate overall health, and less hope that they could meet their goals. Although the difference in depressive symptoms was not significant, it is noteworthy that the mean level for women receiving long-term cash assistance was 18.3, well above the cut-off of 16 that indicates a risk of clinical depression (table 6.4). In the fixed effects analysis they reported a greater increase in material hardship from Year 2 to Year 5 than people who had not received cash assistance.

It appears that those individuals remaining in the welfare system after W-2 was implemented were considerably more materially deprived than were people who left welfare. This finding may indicate that the people remaining in the welfare system were those with the highest levels of disadvantage and barriers to employment. This interpretation would suggest that the system worked to cull out people who could become "self-sufficient," retaining only the most disadvantaged cases. It is also possible that the welfare system precluded combining earnings with welfare income, making it difficult for welfare recipients to increase their overall resources. Unlike most other states, Wisconsin did not allow people to keep part of their welfare grant if they earned money; in fact, people who were deemed employable did not receive immediate cash grants, though they could receive food stamps.

Age and Life Stage of Participants and Income Change

One premise of life span theory is that historical events, in this case a dramatic change in policies, might affect individuals differently depending on the life stage at which they experience the events. We can define life stage by the adult's age, but two life stage indicators—family size and children's ages—may also influence women's responses to changes in the public assistance system. The 0-order correlations show no significant relations between parents' ages and income or income change, but both family size and the age of the youngest child in the family were associated with income (table 6.3) and with public assistance (table 6.4). Women with large families had higher incomes in Q1, but they gained less over time than did women with smaller families.

This pattern suggests that women of different ages had about the same likelihood of benefit or harm from the policy changes of the late 1990s, but that women with older children and those with fewer children were more likely than those with younger children or large families to succeed at achieving income gains through earnings and leaving the cash assistance system. Income gains were least likely for women whose youngest child was very young, perhaps because they were likely to move out of the cash assistance system without increasing their earnings as much as women with older children did. (The means in table 6.4 suggest that women with younger children moved out of cash assistance; the mean age of youngest child for people never receiving cash assistance in Q1–8 was almost 5 years old; the mean for those never receiving assistance in Q9–20 was 3.77, about the same mean as that of long-term recipients.)

We also tested the hypothesis that absolute levels of income and income change affected women of different ages differently by adding interactions of age with income intercept and with income slope to each of the regressions on the well-being measures shown in tables 6.5 and 6.6 (interactions not shown). Only two of a large number of interactions were significant at the .05 level; the most parsimonious interpretation is that these occurred by chance.

DISCUSSION

In this chapter, we have asked the following questions: (a) How did total income and income from different sources (earnings, cash assistance, food stamps, and earnings supplements) change over time from 1995 to 2000, during a period of rapid change in welfare and employment policies affecting low-income single mothers? (b) Did the patterns of income and income change predict material and psychological well-being for low-income single mothers at the end of the 5-year period under study? (c) Did the source of income (earnings, cash assistance, food stamps, or earnings supplements) predict material and psychological well-being? (d) Did mothers of different ages and life stages experience different patterns of income over these years, and did they respond differently to the changes that occurred?

Changes in Income over Time

The years from 1995 to 2000 were a period of major policy changes in welfare and employment policies, producing a dramatic shift from welfare to work in our sample that mirrors national trends. Average earnings increased markedly, and the number of people receiving cash assistance declined considerably. Changes in earnings were most pronounced in the first 2 years from 1995 to 1997. During the last 3 years, when the Wisconsin welfare program was fully implemented, earnings increased slightly, and the number of people receiving cash assistance declined steeply. There was less change in receipt of food stamps, so many people were still receiving some in-kind benefits, suggesting that some features of the safety net remained in place even as cash assistance dropped precipitously. There was little change in the number of people receiving earnings supplements, probably because eligibility for supplements was based on earnings. Even with earnings supplements, however, average total incomes increased very little. This pattern is consistent with national data showing that the shift from welfare to employment did not substantially increase total incomes. Many families traded welfare for work, but continued to be poor (Greenberg et al., 2002).

The changes in income that we observed between 1995 and 1997 occurred before full implementation of the 1996 law, raising questions about whether the policy change was responsible for our observed economic changes. Although the 1996 legislation provides a clear time point defining a policy change, we have already noted that related changes occurred more gradually during the 1990s—large increases in the EITC benefit from 1993 to 2000, decoupling of child care and health care assistance from AFDC, and a strong economy with low unemployment. Many welfare policy changes also began well before 1996, particularly in Milwaukee where such programs as Pay for Performance were implemented. People in the community knew that welfare reform was coming as a result of widespread publicity about impending changes. At a more local level, the New Hope program, which began in 1994 and 1995, provided another source of employment incentives and rewards for the half of the sample that was randomly assigned to the program. The intervention, which ended after 3 years, increased employment and income and reduced welfare receipt for half the sample.

Because the sample were all applicants for New Hope, the overall increase in earnings and decline in cash assistance, particularly during the first 2 years of the study, would be expected to occur without any intervention. People applying for a work-based program are self-selected likely to be work-ready, but at a low point in normally fluctuating patterns of employment. Even without any intervention, one would expect an initial burst of increased employment among both program and controls. For a variety of reasons, then, work was more rewarding and rewarded as a result of several new policies in the context of an economy with low levels of unemployment. By contrast, cash welfare was less available, more onerous, and less stable. It is still noteworthy, however, that there were fewer changes in income from 1997 to 2000, after full implementation of Wisconsin's welfare reform. The number of people receiving cash assistance dropped, but average earnings improved relatively little. Changes in the cash assistance system succeeded in removing large numbers of people from the welfare rolls, but did not consistently lead them into lucrative employment.

How Did These Changes Affect Adult Lives?

These average trends disguise a wide range of individual variation in patterns of income. Almost half of the sample experienced reductions in income over the 5 years. Income levels and changes did predict families' material well-being and financial health. Even though many individual characteristics were controlled in these analyses, it is possible that other unobserved variables contributed to both income level and well-being. However, income increases over the subsequent period, which were partly reflected in higher income levels at Q9 made added contributions to parents' material well-being, financial health, and satisfaction with their standard of living. Higher income parents at Q9 were less likely to report such indicators of material hardship as eviction from housing, unmet medical and dental needs, and utility shutoffs; they were more likely to have such financial supports as a bank account, a credit card, a car, a loan from a bank, and money set aside for an emergency.

Income increases in the final 3 years did not predict most indicators of material well-being, perhaps because these increases were smaller than those in the first 2 years. Increasing income during this period did, however, lead to increases in satisfaction with standard of living. Overall, these findings suggest that increasing income contributed to the financial security and well-being of these single-parent families, and decreasing income reduced their material security, independently of other family characteristics.

Income also predicted psychological well-being at both Q1 and Q9. People with higher incomes had lower levels of depressive symptoms, general stress, and financial worry, and they were more optimistic about their future possibilities. Again, it is possible that people with better psychological adjustment were better able to adjust to the changes in policy that required them to increase employment and to forsake cash assistance. This interpretation is supported by the fact that there were few associations of income change with psychological well-being, and those that occurred were not positive. People whose incomes increased reported worse overall health and slightly higher levels of stress. Given the fact that income increases occurred primarily through earnings, this finding may indicate that extensive employment has some costs in the form of health problems and stress.

Sources of Income

As we have noted repeatedly, the policy changes of the late 1990s were not intended to increase total income, but to shift the families' sources of income from welfare to earnings. Some have argued that income from welfare does not carry the same benefits as income from earnings. Our analyses of income sources show clear evidence that cash assistance was strongly associated with both material deprivation and psychological distress, especially following the full implementation of W-2 in 1997. The patterns following Q9 (1997 to 2000) are different from those preceding that period (1995 to 1997). In the earlier period, people who received no welfare (cash assistance or food stamps) or short-term assistance (who were a minority of the sample) did not differ appreciably from long-term recipients on material or financial health, but they had somewhat better psychological well-being and were more satisfied with their standard of living.

After 1997, however, the relatively small number of people who were long-term recipients had considerably greater levels of material hardship and lower levels of financial health and ability to sustain their families' needs by the year 2000 than did those who received no assistance or short-term assistance. Moreover, they reported an increase in material hardship over this 3-year period. Neither cash assistance nor food stamps served to counteract the material hardship that these parents experienced. Long-term recipients of cash assistance also had much lower levels of psychological well-being—more stress, financial worry, and poorer overall health as well as low levels of hope for the future.

Given that these patterns held with total income controlled and that they were much stronger for cash assistance than for food stamps, it seems that they are the result of changes in the population remaining in the cash assistance system by the year 2000. In our sample, the number of long-term recipients of cash assistance dropped from 58% in Q1–8 to 17% in Q9–20. During this period of strong policy pressures and economic incentives for employment, the people who remained in the cash assistance system were probably those who had multiple barriers to entering and sustaining employment. Some of these barriers may have been human capital problems—women receiving long-term cash assistance were less well educated and had less history of employment and earnings. And some barriers may also have been psychological. Although our measures of psychological well-being were taken at the end of the 5-year period, some of the characteristics we measured, such as depressive symptoms and poor health, tend to be stable over time. Hence, women who remained in the cash assistance system may have been experiencing high levels of psychological distress for several of the preceding years. Beyond such individual barriers, these women may also have experienced a higher level of family stress, including relationships with partners and children, which also impeded their ability to move from welfare to work. The overall pattern indicates that, although the changes in policy over the 5-year period served to move many parents into the work force, the group left behind by these changes were suffering a considerable amount of distress, both material and psychological, and their level of material hardship had actually increased over 3 years. They are the group that were not helped and may have been harmed by the policy changes they experienced.

Methodological Issues and Caveats

Our findings concerning relations of income dynamics to adult well-being are nonexperimental, so issues of causal direction arise in interpreting them. Initial income levels are undoubtedly influenced by pre-existing parent and family characteristics that may also affect well-being. Although all of the analyses included controls for several important baseline characteristics, unobserved differences among adults probably account for some of the relations of initial income to well-being. The same caveat applies to levels of income at the beginning of Q9, except that these levels represent in part the changes that occurred in the intervening 2 years.

Our analyses included several strategies for identifying effects of income dynamics that were independent of preexisting family characteristics. First, *changes* in income over time were evaluated as predictors of well-being at the end of the study period. These changes were independent of absolute levels of income. Although unobserved characteristics might enable some adults to improve earnings or lead some adults to enter or remain in the welfare system, most of these attributes are probably taken into account by controlling absolute level of income in analyses of change. Moreover, as noted earlier, the baseline characteristics that predicted levels of income did not, for the most part, have the same relations to change. Second, the analyses of income tested the effects with sources of income—cash assistance, food stamps, and earnings supplements controlled. Finally, we analyzed *changes* in some indicators of adult well-being from Year 2 to Year 5. These analyses control for stable characteristics of individuals, so the relations of income dynamics to improvement or decline in well-being can be interpreted as causal effects with some degree of confidence.

Effect Sizes

Although there were some consistent patterns of relations between the economic variables and the adult outcomes, the effect sizes were all in the small range, according to Cohen's (1988) criteria. For example, an increase of $1,000 per quarter in income over 5 years predicted an increase in material well-being of .085 (on a scale from 0 to 1.0). Or an increase of $2,000 per quarter predicted an increase in material well-being of .17, which is the equivalent of one less hardship (i.e., one less housing problem, unmet medical needs, etc.). Effects of small magnitude are typical in studies examining complex naturally occurring patterns, but they can still be socially significant.

CONCLUSION

Historical changes occur in the context of particular conditions that may determine their effects on adult lives. Welfare reform during the late 1990s came at a time when economic conditions and other public policies created a climate in which low-income parents could find employment and, at least in some cases, could improve their overall economic situation by doing so. It also coincided with large increases in the EITC and with decoupling of food stamps, medical care, and child care assistance from cash welfare. We see evidence of the results in our sample of low-income parents—a dramatic overall shift in patterns of employment and income sources. Relatively flat overall total income trajectories mask large changes in the sources of income over time toward more earnings (and earnings supplements) and less welfare, particularly cash assistance. Overall, income and improvements in income were associated with better material well-being for low-income single mothers, but changes in income were less clearly related to health and psychological well-being. Those whose incomes increased reported more stress and less adequate physical health, hinting at some strains of the employment that generated their income gains.

The small number of women who were not able to benefit from the positive economic situation (i.e., those who did not leave cash assistance) fared less well, both materially and psychologically. They reported considerable material hardship and financial insecurity as well as high levels of stress and worry.

After 2000, economic growth slowed, and unemployment increased, making it more difficult for single mothers to sustain their families with employment. From 1999 to 2002, the percent of the welfare caseload composed of recent entrants increased. Many of these people had no identifiable barriers to employment, but they are unable to find work. The effects of welfare policy can be understood only in the context of conditions that affect employment opportunities and of other related policies (e.g., the EITC, child care subsidies) that affect individuals' likelihood of improving financial well-being through employment.

REFERENCES

Belle, D. (1990). Poverty and women's health. *American Psychologist, 45,* 385–389.

Bos, J. M., Huston, A. C., Granger, R. C., Duncan, G. J., Brock, T., & McLoyd, V. C. (1999). *New hope for people with low incomes: Two-year results of a program to reduce poverty and reform welfare.* New York: Manpower Demonstration Research Corporation.

Cohen, J. (1988). Statistical Power Analysis for the Behavioral Sciences (2nd ed.). Hillsdale, NJ: Lawrence Erlbaum.

Conger, R. D., & Elder, G. H., Jr. (1994). *Families in troubled times: Adapting to change in rural America.* New York: Aldine de Gruyter.

Edin, K., & Lein, L. (1997). *Making ends meet: How single mothers survive welfare and low-wage work.* New York: Russell Sage Foundation.

Elder, G. H. (1974). *Children of the Great Depression.* Chicago: University of Chicago Press.

Elder, G. H., Jr. (1998). The life course as developmental theory. *Child Development, 69,* 1–12.

Elder, G. H., Jr. (1999). *Children of the Great Depression: Social Change in Life Experience.* (25th Anniversary Edition). Boulder, CO: Westview Press. (Originally published in 1974, University of Chicago Press.)

Greenberg, M., Levin-Epstein, J., Hutson, R., Ooms, T., Schumacher, R., Turetsky, V., et al.. (2002). The 1996 welfare law: Key elements and reauthorization issues affecting children. *Future of Children, 12*(1), 27–57.

Haskins, R., & Primus, W. (2002). Welfare reform and poverty. In I. Sawhill (Ed.), *Welfare reform and beyond* (pp. 59–70). Washington, DC: Brookings.

Henly, J. (2003). *Managing work and child care responsibilities in the retail sector: Informal relationships and their limits.* Paper presented at Northwestern University/University of Chicago Joint Center for Poverty Research 2002–2003 HHS-ASPE/Census Bureau Research Development Grants Conference, Washington, DC.

Mayer, S., & Jencks, C. (1989). Poverty and the distribution of material hardship. *Journal of Human Resources, 24,* 88–114.

McLoyd, V. C. (1998). Socioeconomic disadvantage and child development. *American Psychologist, 53,* 185–204.

Pawasarat, J. (2000). *Analysis of food stamp and medical assistance caseload reductions in Milwaukee County: 1995–1999.* Milwaukee: University of Wisconsin, Employment and Training Institute. Retrieved: http://www.uwm.edu/Dept/ETI/barriers/fsmasum.htm.

Presser, H. B. (2004). *Working in a 24/7 economy: Challenges for American families.* New York: Russell Sage Foundation.

Radloff, L. S. (1977). The CES-D Scale: A self-report depression scale for research in the general population. *Applied Psychological Measurement, 1,* 385–401.

Romich, J. L., & Weisner, T. S. (2002). How families view and use lump-sum payments from the Earned Income Tax Credit. In G. J. Duncan & P. L. Chase-Lansdale (Eds.), *For better or for worse: Welfare reform, families, and child well-being* (pp. 201–221). New York: Russell Sage Foundation.

Snyder, C. R., Sympson, S. C., Ybasco, F. C., Borders, T. F., Babyak, M. A., & Higgins, R. L. (1996). Development and validation of the state Hope scale. *Journal of Personality and Social Psychology, 70,* 321–335.

U.S. Department of Health and Human Services. (2003). *Indicators of welfare dependence.* Washington DC: Office of the Assistant Secretary for Planning and Evaluation. Retrieved December 4, 2004 from http://aspe.hhs.gov.hsp.

Commentary

Welfare Reform and Well-Being

Greg J. Duncan

The 1996 welfare reforms ushered in dramatic changes in the terms under which low-income families could receive cash assistance. Work requirements were imposed, as were five-year limits on the total amount of cash welfare receipt.

There is little doubt that these changes have had the potential for producing dramatic changes—for better and worse—in the lives of low-income, single-parent families. Consider the following two case studies, drawn from the qualitative interviews conducted as part of the Urban Change study directed by Kathryn Edin (Michalopoulos et al., 2003). (I am grateful to Susan Clampett-Lundquist for assisting me with these cases.) We use pseudonyms to preserve anonymity.

Lisa

Lisa is a Republican's dream of a welfare reform success story. On the eve of welfare reform in Philadelphia, she was a 31-year-old high school graduate. But she was addicted to crack, and none of her six children lived with her. Her two teenagers lived with Lisa's mother, while the four youngest (including an infant) were in foster care. Unbeknown to the welfare office, Lisa was (and still is) married to the father of her last five children, who is employed fairly steadily as a truck driver.

The confluence of welfare reform and the Adoption and Safe Families Act (ASFA) motivated Lisa to check herself into a drug rehabilitation program. She wished to take advantage of the training programs and work-support benefits under welfare reform, and she wished to reunite with her children back before they were adopted, since ASFA places a time limit on how long children can remain in foster care. Like almost all mothers interviewed as part of the study, Lisa was disgusted with the attitudes at the welfare office and was eager to be finished dealing with the people who worked there.

At the onset of welfare reform, Lisa had been volunteering at a church food pantry where she received bags of food in payment for her services. The support she received from the pastor of this church, as well as the support from her husband (who allowed her to move back in with him and cover household expenses), helped her get her life back on track. Lisa was also "paid" from the pantry with three to four bags of groceries a week, which helped her in her food purchases.

When first interviewed on the eve of the implementation of new welfare rules, Lisa did not know the specifics of the new rules, but she did know that there were time limits, and that the welfare recipient had to work. She signed an Agreement of Mutual Responsibility in which she promised to complete medical-technician schooling within 2 years. While going through drug rehab, she participated in the 8-week job search but tried very hard *not* to get hired so she would be eligible for more substantial training. She got her certified nursing assistant license through training. On her job applications, she lied about her experience in taking care of people and made up references. She soon got a job as a home health care aide with part-time hours and made a little over $6 per hour. Several months later, she landed a full-time union job at a nursing home where she still works. She has worked steadily since then and was making $10 an hour with health benefits when last interviewed.

In 1998, she and her husband bought a home on a small street in North Philadelphia using money from the enhanced Earned Income Tax Credit (EITC) program. In the summer of 1999, her two older daughters moved back in with her, and in 2000 she was able to have all of her children return from foster care.

As of the fall 2000 interview, Lisa had been off cash welfare for 11 months but was still receiving Medicaid medical insurance. Lisa had been offered coverage at her job, but she considered the co-payment to be prohibitively expensive. She worried about how she would deal with the loss of Medicaid in the face of some rather serious health problems. "I still get medical benefits but they trying to tell me they going to cut me off at the next month because I've been working [full-time] for [12 months], but I'm trying to fight it because I'm a diabetic and I'm Type II, which is uncontrolled. So I don't think that they should be able to cut me off. So I'm going to have to fight that." She was planning to go to school to become a registered nurse.

While one of her teenagers is struggling in school, the other was very successful throughout her high school years. She worked in the summers and after school, and was involved in a college-readiness program that took young people on tours of different campuses. Her after-school job was a paid apprenticeship program in which she tutored younger children and went to nursing homes to visit the residents. Lisa said, "She's gonna go places, that girl." She expressed a lot of pride in her oldest daughter's accomplishments and in her daughter's caring attitude toward her:

> and I'm proud of her 'cause all of this is enrichment, she learning but it's also, you get something in here from doing it. . . . She wants to be a nurse, but I was like, "No, child. Trust me. You can do more." I mean, I told her I'm proud of what I do for ME, this is good, for me. Because you know, I've been through the mill—I've been here, here and here. For me, this is very good and very well. But for you, you can do better.

Eileen

Welfare reform has not been as kind to Eileen, a White mother of six children living in the Kensington neighborhood of Philadelphia. On the eve of the implementation of welfare reform, she was 41 years old, living with her five youngest children, who ranged in age from 6 to 12 (her oldest child was living on his own) and not working. She had completed only ninth grade and found it difficult to understand many of the words used in her welfare training programs. Eileen had cycled through several different types of jobs, including housecleaning, delivering pizza, babysitting, and factory work. Five years prior to the baseline interview, she had escaped from an abusive relationship with the father of five of her children. Eileen expressed a desire to go through welfare's training programs but worried about how this might conflict with her children's needs. In her words:

> I want to go through programs but it takes so much time and I don't have time when it comes to raising my kids. . . . I'm caught in a mix like where it's very hard to balance two things at one time.

Soon after Eileen was first interviewed, she started to work full-time at a local laundromat for $5.15 an hour, and part-time at a nearby Dunkin' Donuts for $4.75 an hour. Eileen took on increasing management responsibilities at the Laundromat, but her pay stayed at minimum wage during the course of our study. Although she was once cut by a hypodermic needle as she was doing a customer's laundry, her boss (who was not there most of the time) refused to buy her rubber gloves.

When Eileen started working, her children would yell at her about never being home because of her work schedule, which Eileen felt powerless to change since she needed to earn money. Two of her children began to be abusive to her, particularly her 12-year-old daughter, Mary, who frequently punched her hard enough to cause bruises:

> My arms are like sore. She punches on me big time. I have marks all over me, I still got some on my legs. I'd never thought I'd see my kids beat me up. But, it's gettin' there. And it's not that I'm being mean with them, it's like, they have to understand my situation. They don't want to hear it.

Eileen believes that her daughter's problems stemmed from the abuse that she had witnessed and received from her father. She said that Mary had "a lot of anger built up over the years."

Eileen has serious health problems, including asthma. She lost her Medicaid because of problems related to the paperwork required for ongoing eligibility. When the management at the Dunkin' Donuts changed, the outgoing owners did not pay her for the final month she'd worked. Thus, she did not have a paycheck to submit to her caseworker that month. Her caseworker didn't believe her explanation and demanded the nonexistent paycheck. When she couldn't produce it, the caseworker cut off her food stamps and Medicaid. Eileen thought her caseworker had it in for her anyway; just before this incident, she had lost her child care subsidy because the caseworker claimed that her caregiver, an adult son, had filled out the provider forms incorrectly. Enraged, Eileen appealed to the supervisor, who reversed the caseworker's decision. Eileen was convinced that the most recent cut-off was her caseworker's retaliation for the prior complaint. Eileen lost her Medicaid benefits and did not get them back for the remainder of the study.

Daughter Mary was also engaging in delinquent activities. She and her mother were brought into court for truancy from school, and Eileen was given a $1,500 fine for this offense. Eileen felt that she was receiving little institutional support to help her to take care of a child involved in delinquency. She called on the local child welfare agency for assistance because she was afraid that she was "losing my family." Instead of getting assistance from them, however, she found her privacy invaded by a coterie of social workers, and she feared that they would take her other children as well. She perceived that they were criticizing her parenting too much and that they were making suggestions that were incompatible with the work requirements under welfare reform:

> I don't want youse coming in here telling me I don't prepare my food, or I'm never home, I, I'm working, I think more of my job, or telling me that I don't make my beds right. [They suggest that I] spread my time a little bit more. And I don't know how I can do that. I'm really stressed out.

Compelling case studies such as these force us to ponder the complexities of real peoples' lives and highlight the difficulty of quantifying the "effects" of social policy changes such as welfare reform. The seeming successes and failures of lives depicted in media accounts quickly blend into complicated mixtures of positives and negatives as we learn more and more about the details of those lives. How can we possibly draw conclusions about policy "effects" without attending to these complications?

But how can we fail to try to generalize enough to reach policy-relevant conclusions? Retreating to the position that the details preclude any attempted generalization is hardly an option, since the policy debate desperately needs generalizations based on a sophisticated understanding of the real-world lives of affected families.

THE HUSTON AND COLLEAGUES STUDY

The strategy adopted in the quantitative study conducted by Huston, Mistry, Bos, and Shim is to focus on a pair of manageable research questions, and then bring rich data and considerable analytic sophistication to the task of answering them. In brief, they seek to describe patterns of changing income packages in the wake of welfare reform and then estimate the impact of different patterns on families' material and psychological well-being. As Lisa's and Eileen's stories make clear, these are certainly not the only questions that need to be asked. But they are important questions, and much of the past work on family economic well-being has not done a good job of answering them.

Huston et al. find a remarkably diverse set of economic changes in the period following welfare reform for their Milwaukee-based families, particularly in earnings and income trajectories. Wisconsin was among the leaders in reducing its welfare rolls, which is clearly reflected in the reductions in welfare income seen in the Huston et al. data. Earnings often rose in response, sometimes enough to more than offset the losses in welfare income, and sometimes not. Some women like Lisa enjoyed positive trajectories with both earnings and household income increasing substantially over the 6-year study period. Like Eileen, others are in a holding pattern, while still others see declines in either earnings or household income, or both. On balance, there were about as many household income losers as there were gainers in the Huston et al. data.

How income trajectories relate to material and psychological well-being is a complicated question. Not surprisingly, families with higher levels of income and higher rates of income growth reported higher levels of material well-being, fewer financial worries and somewhat less stress than those with less income. But the type of income appears to matter as well. Consistent with both Lisa's and Eileen's stories of their dealings with welfare bureaucracies, parents continuing to receive welfare scored poorly in terms of both material and psychological health.

CRITIQUE

I focus my comments on three issues. First, to what extent are dramatic fluctuations in economic well-being unique to families directly affected by welfare reform? Second, what dimensions of the dynamics of family economic well-being are the most important determinants of psychological well-being? And finally, what policy lessons can be drawn?

The Dynamics of Family Economic Well-Being

Huston and colleagues show a striking diversity of earnings and family income trajectories in their low-income sample. As with Lisa and Eileen, the composition of household income changed dramatically over their 5-year observation period, with many families experiencing major drops in welfare income that were matched in varying degrees by gains in other sources of income. But while the trajectory of average household income was virtually flat (see figure 6.2), trajectories of household income for individual families were highly diverse. More than one quarter of their sample had either large gains ($500 or more per quarter, on average) or large reductions ($400 or more per quarter) in total household income.

It is tempting to attribute this remarkable turbulence in household income to the policy changes associated with Wisconsin's welfare reforms in particular and the financial instability of low-income families in general. But doing so risks making the common mistake of attributing surprising turbulence in family economic circumstances found in longitudinal data to conditions prevailing during the data's collection period (Duncan, 2002). In fact, virtually all longitudinal data on family income collected over the past 35 years show great diversity in income trajectories, for low-, middle- and high-income families. And even when we focus on low-income, single-parent families, changes in the composition of income are common, and driven by cycles of welfare and employment that long preceded welfare reform.

An idea of the scope of the household income fluctuations in the population can be gleaned from Table 6.7, which is taken from Duncan's (1988) analysis of household income trajectories using data from the Panel Study of Income Dynamics (PSID) over the 11-year period between 1969 and 1979. Since the longitudinal experiences of men and women are quite different, data are presented separately by gender. The first column shows the average level of family income over the 11-year period and displays typical life-cycle patterns. Household in-

TABLE 6.7   Level and Stability of Income, 1969–1979 by Age and Sex

Age in 1969/Sex	Mean Income Level, in Thousands of 1985	Percent with Income Rising Rapidly (%)	Percent with Income Falling Rapidly (%)	Percent with Big Drops in Income at Least Once (%)	Of Those with Drops Percent Expecting Income Loss
25–54 yrs					
Men	$43.1	35	6	18	9
Women	40.0	32	10	24	6
46–55 yrs					
Men	38.7	22	13	26	12
Women	32.3	21	20	33	24
56–65 yrs					
Men	29.5	7	38	38	34
Women	22.1	6	35	39	25

Note: Taken from Duncan (1988). "Rapid rise" in size-adjusted income is an increase greater than 5% per year. "Rapid fall" in size-adjusted income is a decrease greater than 5% per year. Over an eleven-year period, an annual real growth rate of 5% will increase a family's real income by over 70%; a negative 5% rate will nearly cut it in half.

comes are highest for individuals who spent the entire period in their prime earning years, and somewhat lower for those initially aged 46 to 55, some of whom will have retired during the 11-year period, and lower still for the next older cohort, who were between the ages of 56 and 65 when the 11-year period began. The gap between the family incomes of men and women increases substantially over the life cycle as a result of the increasing proportion of women who are not living with spouses or partners.

To what extent do these averages conceal diverse individual experiences? The second and third columns of table 6.7 show the fractions of the sample in various age and sex groups with either very rapid growth (more than 5% per year) or sharp declines (falling by at least 5% per year) in inflation-adjusted living standards over the period. (Over an 11-year period, an annual real growth rate of 5% will increase a family's real income by over 70%; a negative 5% rate will nearly cut it in half.) Several startling facts emerge, the foremost of which is the prevalence of either large positive or large negative trajectories. With the exception of 46 to 55-year-old men, at least 40% of all groups displayed either large positive or negative economic trajectories.

The direction of the trajectories varies predictably across the age groups. Rapid increases are concentrated in the early adult years, while most of the rapid decreases are experienced by the retirement cohort. But there are many exceptions to these age patterns.

Taken together, longitudinal PSID data show that it is a mistake to treat the "path" of average incomes as the typical income course of individuals as they age. Family incomes are quite volatile at nearly every point in the life cycle, making rapid growth or decline in living standards more the rule than the exception. We do not have to look with Huston et al. to welfare reform or with Elder (1974) to the Great Depression to find frequent instances of economic loss and hardship; the risk of sharp decreases in living standards is significant at virtually every stage of life, whatever the historical circumstances.

In light of economic turbulence in all segments of the U.S. population, a key question is whether trajectories have *changed* in fundamental ways with the advent of welfare reform, and, relatedly, whether observed trajectory changes can really be attributed to welfare reform rather than other conditions (e.g., a booming economy) or policies (e.g., the EITC) prevailing at the same time. Drawing data only within the post-welfare-reform period, the Huston and colleagues paper cannot do this.

Other evidence suggests that these comparisons would be fruitful. A comparison of pre- and post-welfare reform spells in the 1993 and 1996 panels of the Survey of Income and Program Participation shows fewer short spells and more longer spells of a number of forms of public assistance (AFDC/TANF, food stamps and Supplemental Security Income) in the panel beginning in 1993 compared with the panel beginning in 1996 (U.S. Department of Health and Human Services, 2003, Table IND 8b). For example, of spells of AFDC receipt begun during the pre-welfare-reform 1993 panel, 31% lasted less than 4 months. In the 1996 panel, this fraction had increased to 47%. And while 34% of spells in the early period lasted at least 20 months, only 13% of spells begun in the latter period lasted that long.

What Dynamic Components of Family Income Matter the Most?

Huston et al. test for whether indicators of psychological well-being—stress, depression, health, substance abuse, and hope—can be predicted by a combination of past levels and trends in income. They find considerable evidence of the explanatory power of income levels, but not trends. They caution that the associations between their outcomes and income levels may be the spurious result of omitted correlates of income. Worries over omitted variable bias are heightened by the failure of income trends to predict changes in psychological well-being, since, under certain conditions, relating income change to well-being change is equivalent to relating income level to level of well-being.

While few would question a role for the long-run level of economic well-being in reducing stress and increasing psychological well-being, the role of other aspects of income trajectories is more debatable. Huston and colleagues choose income trends, presuming that, everything else the same, positive income trajectories ought to increase psychological well-being. Although this is a sensible assumption, I would suggest that income *instability* is the most likely runner-up in the contest for economic dimensions that affect well-being.

Income instability—measured by, say, the variance of quarterly income or by a count of the number of income drops—can be quite independent of both the level and the trend in income. Table 6.7 presents Duncan's (1988) estimates of the incidence of adverse income "events," which he defined as instances in which family-size-adjusted income fell by 50% or more in consecutive years. This yardstick is similar to that employed by Elder (1974) and his colleagues in their studies of the effects of the Great Depression, which found long-lasting effects of income drops of one third or more.

The overall risk of large income drops is high: between 18% and 39% of the various groups in table 6.7 are estimated to have experienced such a drop at least once during the 11-year period. Most of these decreases left the individuals involved with, at best, modest incomes. Not shown in table 6.7 is the fact that 87% of the individuals experiencing these decreases saw their family incomes fall to less than $25,000.

Since the PSID questions respondents about their expectations of future changes in economic status, it is possible to calculate what fraction of the 50%+ income drops were preceded in either of the previous two annual interviews by a report that the respondent expected his or her family economic status to decline. The column 5 of table 6.7 shows that a majority of all income declines and the vast majority of pre-retirement income drops were unexpected.

Should these economic fluctuations be a concern? Elder's (1974) data from the Great Depression provide compelling but historical evidence of circumstances in which economic shocks can have devastating effects on both adults and children. In *Falling from Grace,* (1988) Katherine Newman draws data from the 1980s to document the psychological and other damage brought about by downsizing, divorce and other traumatic events. And Kathryn Edin and Laura Lein's *Making Ends Meet* (1997) documents some of the adverse consequences of unstable incomes among low-income families desperate to cobble together an income package large enough to provide basic necessities for their families.

McDonough, Duncan, Williams, and House (1997) use longitudinal data from the PSID to relate the level and stability of income to subsequent mortality. They treat PSID data as if they were a series of independent 6-year panels, the first spanning calendar years 1972 to 1978, the second spanning 1973 through 1979, and so forth, with the last one spanning the period from 1983 to 1989. Within each 6-year period they use the first 5 years to measure the level and stability of household income and the sixth and final year to measure possible mortality.

Key results are presented in Table 6.8. They are taken from a logistic regression in which the dependent variable is whether the individual died during the 6th and final year of the given period. Income level and stability over the 5-year period preceding the possible death are combined into a single classification of (a) low and unstable income

TABLE 6.8   Odds-Ratios of Mortality for Individuals Aged 45–64 Years, by Income Level and Stability, 1972 Through 1989

Five-Year Mean Income Level and Stability	Odds Ratio
Income <$20,000 and 1+ income drops	3.7*
Income <$20,000 and no income drops	3.4*
Income $20–$70,000 and 1+ drops	3.2*
Income $20–$70,000 and no drops	1.5*
Income >$70,000 and 1+ drops	1.4
Income >$70,000 and no drops	1.00 (reference group)

Note: Taken from McDonough et al. (1997), table 3. "Income drop" is defined as a situation in which size-adjusted family income fell by 50% or more in consecutive years. *indicates that the coefficient is at least twice its standard error. Odds ratios are adjusted for age, sex, race, family size, and period.

(i.e., mean income under $20,000 and at least one big income drop over the given 5-year period), (b) low but stable income, (c) middle-class (mean income between $20,000 and $70,000) and unstable), (d) middle-class and stable, and (e) affluent and unstable. Affluent individuals with stable incomes served as the reference group. Control variables include age of individual, calendar year, race, and the average size of the given person's household over the first 5 years of the window.

Consistent with numerous studies, mortality risks fall with income level. Individuals with low incomes have three to four times the mortality risk of the affluent individuals in the reference group. New in the analysis is the result that unstable incomes also contribute to mortality risk, but only among the middle class. When compared with the consistently affluent reference group, middle-income individuals with stable incomes had a marginally significant 1.5-times elevation of mortality risk. In contrast, an individual with middle-class but unstable income had a risk ratio more than three times that of individuals in the reference group, and almost as high as individuals in the two low-income groups. Instability did not matter at either the low or high end of the income distribution, perhaps because the disadvantages of low incomes and the advantages of affluence overwhelm the possible effects of instability. It would be very interesting to see in the Huston et al. data if psychological well-being and changes in it were more favorable for families with more stable incomes.

How Welfare Policies *Can* Affect Income and Well-Being

In fretting over some of the details of the Huston et al. analysis, we should not lose sight of the larger lessons emerging from the New Hope study itself. Some of them are discussed by Huston and colleagues, but they are important enough to reemphasize.

The New Hope program was started with the belief that a work-based approach to helping low-income families could improve their lives dramatically. The supports embedded in the program—an earnings supplement, child care assistance, medical insurance, a community service job if needed, all of which were delivered by supportive program staff—were designed to address key fundamental needs of families struggling to make it in a low-wage economy. The evaluation of 3 years of New Hope benefits used gold-standard random assignment, coupled with a serious qualitative component to understand how participants viewed the program and were affected by it. At nearly $5,000 per family per year, the program was expensive, but consider its documented benefits (Huston et al., 2003):

- Parents in the New Hope treatment group worked more and earned more than did parents in the control group. Although the effects diminished when the program ended after 3 years, they did persist for some parents. Poverty levels were lower for program families more than 2 years after the program ended.
- New Hope increased parents' instrumental and coping skills and improved their mental health. Program group members were more aware of "helping" resources in the community, such as where to find assistance with energy costs or housing problems. New Hope also increased children's time in formal center-based child care and after-school programs.
- Perhaps most notably, both 2 and 5 years into the evaluation, children in the New Hope group performed better than control group children on several measures of academic achievement, and their parents reported that the children got higher grades in reading and literacy skills. New Hope also improved children's positive social behavior. All these effects were more pronounced for boys than for girls.

Sadly, few states are using the occasion of welfare reform to support low-income working families in the way that the New Hope program has. But its evaluation, and that of a number of other experiments (Morris, Duncan, Huston, Crosby, & Bos, 2001), leave little doubt that historical changes in policies like welfare reform have the potential for producing large changes in families' lives.

REFERENCES

Duncan, G. (1988). The volatility of family income over the life course. In P. Baltes (Ed.), *Life-span development and behavior.* Hillsdale, NJ: Lawrence Erlbaum Associates.

Duncan, G. (2002). The PSID and me. In E. Phelps, F. F. Furstenberg, Jr., & A. Colby (Eds.), *Landmark studies of the 20th century in the US* (pp. 133–163). New York: Russell Sage,.

Edin, K., & Lein, L. (1997). *Making ends meet.* New York: Russell Sage.

Elder, G. H. (1974). *Children of the great depression.* Chicago: University of Chicago Press.

Huston, A., Miller, C., Richburg-Hayes, L., Duncan, G., Eldred, C., Weisner, T. S. et al. (2003). *New hope for families and children: Five-year results of a program to reduce poverty and reform welfare.* New York: MDRC.

McDonough, P., Duncan, G., Williams, D., & House, J. (1997). Income dynamics and adult mortality in the U.S., 1972–1989. *American Journal of Public Health 87*(9), 1476–1483.

Michalopoulos, C., Edin, K., Fink, B., Landriscina, M., Polit, D., Polyne, J., et al. (2003). *Welfare reform in Philadelphia implementation, effects, and experiences of poor families and neighborhoods.* New York: MDRC.

Morris, P., Duncan, G., Huston, A., Crosby, D., & Bos, J. (2001). *How welfare and work policies affect children: A synthesis of research.* New York: MDRC.

Newman, K. (1988). *Falling from grace: The experience of downward mobility in the American middle class.* New York: Free Press.

U.S. Department of Health and Human Services. (2003). *Indicators of welfare dependence: Annual Report to Congress.* Washington, DC: USDHH.

Author Index

Subject Index

Springer Publishing Company

Gerotechnology
Research and Practice in Technology and Aging

David C. Burdick, PhD
Sunkyo Kwon, PhD, Dipl-Psych, Editors

From the basics of gerotechnology—person-environment fit—to the core activity fields—computer and assistive devices and their applications—to prototypes for technical development and its application to everyday life, this volume explores the intersections of technology with aging and serves as both a primer and reference for educators, students, researchers, and practitioners.

Partial Contents:

Part I: Basic Aspects of Gerotechnology
- Technology in Everyday Life for Older Adults,
  W. Rogers, C. Mayhorn, and A. Fisk
- Perceptual Aspects of Gerotechnology, _C. Scialfa, G. Ho, and J. Laberge_
- Aging and Technology: Social Science Approaches, _H. Mollenkopf_

Part II: Computers, Older Adults and Caregivers
- Why Older Adults Use or Do Not Use the Internet,
  R. Morrell, C. Mayhorn, and K. Echt
- Educational Tools for Web Designers, Older Adults and Caregivers, _A. Benbow_
- Computer-Mediated Communication and Its Use in Support Groups for Family Caregivers, _K. Smyth and S. Kwon_

Part III: Assistive Technology, Home and Environment
- Monitoring Household Occupant Behaviors to Enhance Safety and Well-Being,
  D. Kutzik and A. Glascock
- Technologies to Facilitate Health and Independent Living in Elderly Populations,
  B. Tran

Part IV: Models, Prototypes, and Specific Applications of Gerotechnology
- Driving Simulation and Older Adults, _G. Rebok and P. Keyl_

Part V: Cautions, Integration and Synthesis
- Ethical Realities: The Old, the New, and the Virtual, _G. Lesnoff-Caravaglia_

2005   320pp   0-8261-2516-6   hardcover

11 West 42nd Street, New York, NY 10036-8002 • Fax: 212-941-7842
Order Toll-Free: 877-687-7476 • Order On-line: www.springerpub.com

Springer Publishing Company

Religious Influences on Health and Well-Being in the Elderly

K. Warner Schaie, PhD, Neal Krause, PhD
Alan Booth, PhD, Editors

This volume focuses on the ways in which religious institutions, religious practices, and religious organizations impact the health and well-being of older persons. Topics examined include the conceptualization and measurement of religion in late life; the relationship between religious coping and possible stress reduction; the role of forgiveness as an alternate mediator; and how social class, gender, and race can influence the specific effect of religion and religious institutions in a diverse aging society.

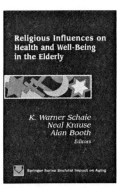

Partial Contents:

- Religious Observance and Health: Theory and Research, *E. L. Idler*
- Commentary: Religion and Health: A European Perspective, *C. J. Lalive d'Epinay* and *D. Spini*
- Commentary: Observing Religion and Health, *R. Finke*
- Prayer, Love, and Transcendence: An Epidemiologic Perspective, *J. Levin*
- Commentary: Next Steps in Understanding the Prayer/Health Connection, *K. F. Ferraro*
- Commentary: Prayer and the Elderly: Exploring a "Gerontological Mystery," *M. M. Poloma*
- Religion Forgiveness, and Adjustment in Older Adulthood, *M. E. McCullough* and *G. Bono*
- Commentary: Unforgiveness, Forgiveness, Religion and Health During Aging, *E. L. Worthington, Jr.*
- Commentary: Multiple Forms of Forgiveness and Their Relationships with Aging and Religion, *M. A. Musick*
- Race and Ethnicity in Religion and Health, *L. M. Chatters*
- Commentary: Race and SES Differences in the Relationship Between Religion and Health, *K. E. Whitfield* and *K. I. Jackson*

Societal Impact on Aging Series
2004   320pp   0-8261-2404-6   hardcover

11 West 42nd Street, New York, NY 10036-8002 • Fax: 212-941-7842
Order Toll-Free: 877-687-7476 • Order On-line: www.springerpub.com

Springer Publishing Company

Multidisciplinary Perspectives on Aging

Lynn M. Tepper, MA, MS, EDM, EdD
Thomas M. Cassidy, MA, Editors

"This is an exceptional book that examines the key social, health, financial, legal and ethical matters with which aging-services professionals, and older persons themselves, must contend. For the new and experienced aging-services professional alike, here, in one volume, is a detailed overview and ready reference on a multitude of issues facing an aging society."

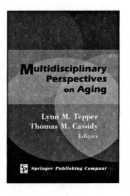

—**William L. Minnix**, Jr., D. Min.
President and CEO
American Association of Homes and Services
for the Aging

In this multidisciplinary text, noted leaders from a variety of fields provide students and professionals with a big picture approach to the best possible care for today's growing aging population.

Partial Contents:

Part I: Changing Relationships, Changing Care Needs
- Aging in America: Challenges and Opportunities, *L.M. Tepper, MA, MS, EdM, EdD*
- Family Relationships and Support Networks, *L.M. Tepper, MA, MS, EdM, EdD*
- The Nursing Home and the Continuum of Care, *W.T. Smith, MSW, PhD*

Part II: Health and Wellness in Later Life
- Medical Care of the Elderly, *R.H. Rubin, MD, FACP*
- Health Promotion in Later Life, *C. Kopes-Kerr, MD*
- Considerations for Oral Health in the Elderly, *B.M. Horrell, DDS, MS*

Part III: Financial, Ethical, and Legal Issues in Elder Care
- Financing Health Care, *T.C. Jackson, MPH, CEBS*
- Elder Law, *M.B. Kapp, JD, MPH, FCLM*
- Elder Ethics, *E.R. Chichin, PhD, RN*

2005   304pp   0-8261-2575-1   hardcover

11 West 42nd Street, New York, NY 10036-8002 • Fax: 212-941-7842
Order Toll-Free: 877-687-7476 • Order On-line: www.springerpub.com

⑤ *Springer Publishing Company*

Effective Health Behavior in Older Adults

K. Warner Schaie, PhD
Howard Leventhal, PhD
Sherry L. Willis, PhD, Editors

In what ways do health behaviors and societal mechanisms help or discourage individuals in assuming responsibility for their health? Highly-esteemed and diverse contributors examine the health behaviors of older adults and the ways in which these behaviors are affected by societal trends.

The volume begins with a discussion of the personal attributes affecting health behaviors and responsible health care choices in older adults. Additional topics explored include: psychosocial factors in the prevention of cardiovascular disease; behavioral interventions such as the role of exercise in preventing chronic illness; and how societal structures such as reimbursement patterns and changes in health insurance affect initiation, change, and maintenance of health behaviors.

Partial Contents:

- Biosocial Considerations in Chronic Illness Perceptions and Decisions, *T. Hickey*
- Linear and Dynamical Thinking about Psychosocial Factors and Cardiovascular Risk, *J. Suls* and *R. Martin*
- Commentary: Acute and Chronic Psychological Processes in Cardiovascular Disease, *D.W. Johnston*
- Psychosocial Factors in the Prevention of Cardiovascular Disease, *L.H. Powell*
- Ethnicity and Psychosocial Factors in Cardiovascular Disease Prevention, *K.E. Whitfield, T.A. Baker,* and *D.T. Brandon*
- Getting Help to Those Most Likely to Benefit: Patient Characteristics and Treatment Success, *J.C. Barefoot*
- Exercise Interventions and Aging, *J.A. Blumenthal* and *E.C.D. Gullete*
- Commentary: Challenges to using Exercise Interventions in Older Adults, *E.A. Burns*

Societal Impact on Aging Series
2002   344pp   0-8261-2401-1   hardcover

---

11 West 42nd Street, New York, NY 10036-8002 • Fax: 212-941-7842
Order Toll-Free: 877-687-7476 • Order On-line: www.springerpub.com